State Policy Making
for the
Public Schools

A Comparative Analysis of Policy Making
for the Public Schools in Twelve States
and a Treatment of State Governance Models

•

Roald F. Campbell
Ohio State University, Emeritus

Tim L. Mazzoni, Jr.
University of Minnesota

•

With chapters by

Edward R. Hines
JAlan Aufderheide
Peggy M. Siegel
Raphael O. Nystrand
David W. O'Shea

McCutchan Publishing Corporation
2526 Grove Street
Berkeley, California 94704

ISBN: 0-8211-0224-9
Library of Congress Catalog Card Number: 75-31311

Printed in the United States of America

Foreword

Two major trends convince us that state governments will, over the next decade, exercise an increasing role in the governance of the public schools. The first is the current effort of the federal government to push more of the responsibility for education back to the states. The second is the demand, particularly since *Serrano,* that the states provide an increasing portion, even to full assumption, of school support. These forces, along with ever-expanding budgets for both public education and higher education, require that governors and legislators scrutinize programs in education with greater care than ever before. Relatively little is known about how these newly energized participants will interact with more traditional forces, such as state board of education members, chief state school officers, and those involved with various education interest groups, in developing policy for the public schools. Even less is known about possible constraints and opportunities inherent in the structures or models of state government. This book, then, has two main purposes: to expand our knowledge of how states determine policies for the public schools and to develop alternative models of state educational governance for consideration by policy makers and others.

Part I is addressed to the first purpose; Part II, to the second. Since policy making and the governmental structures surrounding policy making are public concerns, a variety of persons should be interested. Formal actors in the state policy-making process—governors, legislators, state board members, and chief state school officers —and informal actors—representatives of teacher organizations, school board organizations, and administrators' organizations— should find the material informative. Other agencies at both local and federal levels should learn something about dealing with state governments. Citizens who wish to make government responsive to their wishes should find ways of thinking about the problem. And students of government will, we hope, find pertinent data and deductions that will stimulate further work having to do with the state governance of education.

The two parts of this book are based upon two major reports growing out of the Educational Governance Project conducted at Ohio State University from January 1972 through August 1974 under the direction of the two authors. That work was funded by the U.S. Office of Education under Title V (Section 505) of the Elementary and Secondary Education Act, Project #OEG-0-73-0499. While the reports, in their original form, were placed in the public domain, it seemed desirable to edit, revise, and publish them, thereby making them available to a much wider audience.

Many people who assisted in the Educational Governance Project have also aided in the preparation of this book. Martin W. Essex, Jack P. Nix, and Ewald B. Nyquist, chief state school officers in Ohio, Georgia, and New York, respectively, served as the Policy Board and provided useful guidance to the authors. The Department of Education for the state of Ohio also served effectively as the fiscal agent. A number of officials in the U.S. Office of Education served as liaison and provided continuing support. A contract for the major part of the work was let to Ohio State University, and university officers responded with interest and provided prompt assistance. A number of scholars across the nation thoughtfully criticized plans, proposed activities, and many segments of writing. Of particular help were the following: David J. Kirby, Memorial University of Newfoundland; Joseph M. Cronin, formerly Secretary of Educational Affairs in Massachusetts and now Superintendent of Education for Illinois; Kenneth H. Hansen, Superintendent of Public Instruction in

Nevada; Sam P. Harris, U.S. Office of Education; Lawrence D. Haskew, University of Texas; Gerald R. Sroufe, Nova University; and Michael D. Usdan, formerly of the City University of New York and now President of the Merrill-Palmer Institute. Some sixteen persons assisted at various times, and five of them contributed signed chapters:

Edward R. Hines, State University of New York, Albany;

JAlan Aufderheide, Superintendent, Northern Potter School District (Pennsylvania);

Peggy M. Siegel, Legislative Aid, Ohio Senate;

Raphael O. Nystrand, Ohio State University;

David W. O'Shea, University of California, Los Angeles.

To them, we express particular appreciation. Other staff members included: Gary Branson, Dudley Brown, Chase Crawford, Frank DePalma, Roger Farrar, Floyd Horton, Linda Moffatt, Joseph Prusan, William Smith, Don Steele, and Anthony Warren.

Grateful as we are for the suggestions and contributions of all of these persons, we take responsibility for what appears in the book.

R.F.C.
T.L.M.

Contents

PART ONE

COMPARATIVE ANALYSIS

I — Conceptual Framework and Research Methodology

As with many other institutions in the United States, those that govern the country's schools are being questioned and challenged. Despite an elaborate structure that involves thousands of public officials, there are indications of deficiencies in both process and performance. Deficiencies in process are most clearly revealed in demands from citizens, parents, teachers, and students for a larger voice in making decisions affecting education. And inadequate performance can be seen in everything from inequitable allocation of fiscal resources and erosion of taxpayer support to the popular demand that schools be held "accountable" for results. Issues arising from such discontent simultaneously confront existing political systems and test the viability of the systems.

States occupy a pivotal position in arrangements that have evolved for educational governance in the United States because they are constitutionally responsible for the establishment, support, and supervision of the public schools. Although much authority has been delegated to local districts, recent court decisions have demonstrated that this does not relieve the states of responsibility. Major education policies have always been set at the state level. This is true whether one looks at fiscal determinations or at areas such as teacher certification, curriculum standards, and school boundaries. And, even more

3

than national agencies or local boards, states can make federalism work. They can provide appropriate feedback to Congress and the executive branch; they can also respond to the problems of school districts. Both responsibility and opportunity dictate that the states must take the lead in meeting the challenges to educational governance.

Having accepted the validity of this assessment, the Educational Governance Project (EGP), from the outset, had as its primary objective the development and appraisal of alternative models of state educational governance. While there was a surfeit of proposals and recommendations, there had been little empirical research on the actual workings of different governance arrangements. Adequate descriptions in the literature were rare, and any examination of the causes and consequences of structural variations was even rarer. The chief task of the project was to describe and to analyze the process by which the states currently determine policy for their public schools in order to produce evidence relevant to a consideration of models and to extend knowledge of a crucial area of educational governance.

After it was widely discussed and substantially revised as a result of fieldtesting,[1] EGP research was organized to answer basic descriptive and analytic questions:

1. Who are the major participants in state education policy systems?
2. What policy-making resources are available to these participants?
3. How do participants seek to influence the policy-making process in education?
4. What are the significant relationships among participants in the determination of policy?
5. How much and what kind of a difference do features of governmental structure make for the operation of state education policy systems?
6. What factors other than governmental structures might explain the variations that exist among states with regard to policy making in education?

The scope of the inquiry was intentionally limited. The focus was on policy making for public elementary and secondary schools, and nonpublic schools and institutions of higher learning received attention only if they affected the public schools. Intergovernmental relationships were not ignored, but they were viewed from state capitols and not explored from local or federal vantage points. Neither environmental conditions nor policy consequences were examined in any detailed fashion. As to the first, data gathering was confined to general information on socioeconomic, political, and institutional characteristics. And, for the second, consequences of enactments were considered only as they emerged as feedback in the policy system.

CONCEPTUAL FRAMEWORK

The conceptual framework that guided the investigation was composed of related concepts, assumptions, and questions that appeared to be fruitful in attacking a research problem.[2] The purpose was not to generate hypotheses to be confirmed or denied by the marshaling of evidence; instead, in the words of Lasswell and Kaplan, it was "to serve the function of directing the search for significant data, not predicting what the data will be found to disclose."[3] The conceptual framework, then, offers a vantage point from which to view the subject, criteria for judging what information is relevant to its study, and a device for organizing the data that are gathered. The framework fashioned for this project was adapted from political systems theory and allocative theory.[4]

Political Systems Theory

The political systems approach, speaking generally, stresses the utility of viewing policy making as an interactive process through which inputs, including demands for change, are converted into outputs, including authoritative decisions. Though the full conceptual apparatus of this approach was not employed, three general notions —policy decisions, system actors, and functional relationships—did serve as a preliminary orientation.

Policy Decisions. These are system outputs. Policy decisions establish goals and priorities governing subsequent choices. Such parameter-setting decisions are not to be confused with either implementations of existing directives or goal-like pronouncements that fail to assign priorities. Policies, to borrow from Lasswell's classic definition, declare "who gets what, when, how."[5] Thus, it is education policy that gives direction to the allocation of such valued education goods as school funds, instructional personnel, curriculum innovations, bargaining authority, and the racial composition of student bodies.[6]

As a concept, "policy decision" refers to an event, not a process. Once a system has been engaged by a demand for change, this event can be said to happen either when a new policy has been promulgated or an existing policy has been upheld by the purposeful action of authorities capable of acting on the demands represented. The latter kind of decision can be manifested in an opposing vote or a veto. It can also be the outgrowth of informal action that prevents new policy from being made. Policy decisions, therefore, do not require that established goals be revised, nor that outputs always be the result of a formal enactment.[7]

Related to policy decisions are "outcomes." These can be regarded as the consequences of policy decisions. They represent the impact of choices on the environment. Easton offers an apt analogy: "In short," he writes, "an output [for example, a policy decision] is the stone tossed into the pond and its first splash; the outcomes are the widening and vanishing pattern of concentric ripples."[8] A treatment of policy outcomes was beyond the research resources made available to the EGP. The social effects of decisions are, however, linked to the flow of inputs by feedback mechanisms. Changes in the patterns of demands and their relationship to the modifications of public school policies were considered in this inquiry.

System actors. The application of a systems approach requires that the boundary which sets the system apart from its environment be specified. In doing this, Gross's distinction between the general environment and the immediate environment proved helpful.[9] By "general environment" is meant the physical, socioeconomic, and political milieu that forms the backdrop for policy making. As has been said, the design of the present study called for a limited investigation of this milieu, an investigation confined to readily accessible data on such phenomena as demographic trends, industrialization and urbanization, amount and distribution of wealth, and characteristic features of a state's political culture. The term "immediate environment" refers to the various individuals and groups with interests in state school policies, interests that on occasion come to be expressed as political demands.

Crossing the boundary from the immediate environment to the system itself, one finds a relatively stable group of actors who have a continuing concern with public school policy, who interact on a regular basis, and who together constitute the elements of the state education policy system. These actors, as identified by existing research, include the governor's office, the legislature, the state board of education, the chief state school officer and state department of education, the state courts, and the state-level educational interest groups.[10]

System actors were focal points in the inquiry, but they did not receive equal emphasis. Because the ultimate goal was the development of state governance models, most of the attention was devoted to the policy-making behavior of institutions—state board, chief state school officer, state department of education, and governor's office—seen as central to the consideration of models. Fewer resources were directed toward those institutions—the legislature, and, to an even lesser degree, the judiciary—that were to be treated largely as "givens."[11]

Functional relationships. Identifying the actors who make up a policy system is but the first step in using the systems approach. The second is to ascertain the relationships among actors that determine education policy. These relationships, not the internal attributes of the actors, are what receive emphasis when the policy process is viewed in system terms. To facilitate analysis, policy-making relationships were conceived of in relation to four functional stages:[12]

Issue definition—Process by which the preferences of individuals and groups become translated into political issues (that is, "a demand that members of the political system are prepared to deal with as a significant item").[13]

Proposal formulation—Process by which issues are developed as specific recommendations for policy changes or for maintaining the status quo.

Support mobilization—Process by which individuals and groups are activated to support or oppose alternative policy proposals.

Decision enactment—Process by which an authoritative (that is, governmental) policy choice is made among alternative proposals.

Distinguishing between functional stages is useful because it permits a more complete understanding of the relationships that lie behind a policy change. Specifically, there appear to be three advantages in using such a conceptualization.[14] First, it constitutes an appropriate frame of reference for investigating what actors actually do (as opposed to what they should do or are thought to do) in the deciding of policy. Second, it delineates clusters of activities that are likely to be found across policy systems, including the kind studied here. Finally, it stresses preenactment processes, processes that are crucial in establishing the agenda of policy options from which final choices typically are made.

Allocative Theory

Even if a political systems orientation is necessary (Spiro argues that "*anyone* who attempts to study politics scientifically must at least implicitly think of politics as though it were functioning as some sort of system"[15]), it is not sufficient to examine how state education policy is made. Indeed, what is striking is how little has been explained in other studies by the political systems construct.[16] No doubt there are a number of reasons for this. At best, the systems model is not an appropriate conceptual tool to deal with the phenomenon of influence when investigating the policy process, and, if influence is the dynamic in the pattern of actor relationships by which functions are performed, conflicts are overcome, and decisions are reached, then the research framework must be directed toward its study. The most fundamental concepts associated with the actor relationships are "power," "influence," and "resource." Since these terms have varied meanings, definitions are necessary:

power—actor's capacity or potential to select, modify, or achieve outputs of a system.[17]
influence—actual exercise of power by an actor.[18]
resource—anything controlled by one actor which can be brought to bear on another actor so as to alter the latter's subjective definition of the advantages and disadvantages in a decision situation.[19]

Assumptions. Before considering the requisites of policy-making influence in greater detail, some assumptions must be made explicit, for they shaped the data-gathering effort and affected attitudes toward the data. The following assumptions were made about policy-making influence:

1. Public policies are the results of an influence process in which competing actors seek to obtain decision benefits.[20]
2. Focal actors in the influence process are those seen as being entitled to render authoritative decisions.
3. Possession of policy-making influence is dependent on access to appropriate resources and their skillful use.[21]
4. The influence process involved in policy making is characterized by reciprocal relationships.[22]
5. Relationships among actors in the influence process are indirect as well as direct.
6. Informal as well as formal rules shape the application of influence in policy making.

Influence resources. In the third assumption given above, the power of a policy actor in the framework is seen as being based on command of resources. Many analysts have sought to explain how resources produce influence. While elaborate distinctions are possible, these ways of influencing can be thought of as falling into one of two categories proposed by Parsons:

Sanctioning influence is the addition of new advantages or disadvantages (conditional or not) to the situation of the decision-maker. Persuasion influence operates on the orientation of the decision-maker, changing the connection he sees between a decision outcome and his goals without the addition of any new advantages or disadvantages to the situation.[23]

Just as many things can alter an actor's perception of advantages and disadvantages, many kinds of resources can be converted into influence. Even Dahl's lengthy specification does not exhaust those resources:

A list of resources in the American political system might include an individual's own time; access to money, credit, and wealth; control over jobs; control over information; esteem or social standing; the possession of charisma, popularity, legitimacy, legality; and the rights pertaining to public office. The list might also include solidarity: the capacity of a member of one segment of society to evoke support from others who identify him as like themselves because of similarities in occupation, social standing, religion, ethnic origin, or racial stock. The list would include the right to vote, intelligence, education, perhaps even one's energy level.[24]

Enumerations like Dahl's do highlight the diversity of influence resources. Yet the productiveness of such a "grocery list" for research is limited by its diffuseness. Our approach to this problem was to be particularly sensitive to those resources that appeared to have the widest applicability in the policy system of interest; in this approach it is presumed that the command of such resources contributes most to the stable potential of a participant to exert influence.[25] Several empirical works, notably those dealing with legislative policy making, helped in identifying these sources of power[26] and suggested that special heed be paid to: legal authority, information and specialized expertise, social status, wealth, group cohesion, and electoral potency.

Willingness to mobilize resources. The possession of resources, regardless of type, is not the equivalent of actual influence. Resources are necessary for influence, but influence also depends on the intention of the actors to whom means are available. Even individuals who have powerful resources often exhibit no interest in employing them to affect public decisions. Wildavsky has generalized:

That resources exist does not mean that they will be used fully, skillfully, or at all. Most people use their resources sparingly, with varying degrees of effectiveness. The cost in time, energy, money, and ego damage usually seems too great in comparison to the benefits which appear remote and uncertain. As a result, there is a vast reservoir of resources lying untapped by people who prefer not to use them.[27]

If there is command of appropriate resources, why are actors so unlike in their disposition toward political involvement? Part of the answer has to do with the amount of resources possessed. The more of a resource that an individual possesses, the less are his opportunity costs for a unit outlay of that resource. A second explanation is to be found in the perceptions that people have of the benefits to be attained through political action.[28] In this connection, two variables —issue saliency and role expectations—might help explain the involvement of actors in state education policy systems.

The willingness to mobilize influence resources cannot be examined apart from situational factors. One such factor has to do with the content of issues, including differential saliency to individuals and groups. Not all issues arising within a policy system are equally vital to all participants. For a teachers' association, for example, school issues range from those that are of central concern (such as collective bargaining) to those that are of marginal interest (such as school desegregation). There are similar variations, with different placement of issues, for all actors in the state education policy system.[29]

Those who share in policy making do so from positions within the system, and they are subject to the expectations held for their positions. What incumbents of system positions, official or unofficial, expect of each other (and themselves) in making policies that affect state education influences their willingness to use resources.[30] In this regard, Sroufe looked at the self-role expectations of state board members and found that these officials, contrary to their impressive legal mandate to determine policy, rejected a "concept of the state board as a political actor within the system."[31]

Utilization of resources to exert influence. Just as actors differ greatly in their mobilization of resources, they differ, too, in their ability to practice the "art" of politics. Put most simply, this skill consists of the ability of an actor to gain a greater influence from the same resources than other actors can. Measuring the degree to which actors efficiently utilize their resources is always an imprecise undertaking. We attempted such an assessment by looking at the tactics resorted to by individuals and groups as they sought to gain access to policy-making structures and to exploit this access for the purpose of exercising influence.

Any discussion of the influence exerted by policy actors must begin with the concept of "access," for, notwithstanding goals, access is what they must immediately seek. "Access" means opening channels of communication between interest spokesmen and the policy system.[32] The extent of access can vary from just being heard at some stage in deliberations to having the agent of an interest group make the decision.

Though access is a *sine qua non* of policy-making influence, attaining it is just the beginning. Resources must be brought to bear at the points of access if policy making is to be influenced. Numerous classification schemes have been applied to political strategies (that is, the intentional use of resources to influence authoritative decisions), but most are not specifically directed at its exercise in systems where policy normally is accomplished through group decision making. In these systems, writes Riker, "policy making is invariably the same. It is a process of forming coalitions."[33] Hence, while access is the initial objective, the formation of coalitions is required for ultimate success.

The process of accommodation as practiced by policy makers in the forging of coalitions provides endless opportunities for nuance. Besides organized forms, such as the legislative committee structure, there are many techniques that serve as informal influences. Political scientists disagree, however, as to their relative importance. Some support the view that "the bargaining process is at the heart of the policy process."[34] The reference here is to a process in which competing actors seek agreement through the exchange of inducements. Yet, even given this broad meaning, bargaining is not the only way policy makers influence each other. Lindblom has argued that persuasion is as widely employed and that there are many times when a policy maker "achieves cooperation not by trying to manipulate others but by adapting himself to them."[35]

Systemic features. It is recognized, in considering policy influence, that such influence is exercised within a social system and that features of this system condition relationships among actors. Schoettle urges that investigators concentrate on "role structures and the rules of the game as the major determinants of the policy-making process,"[36] and other scholars stress such organizational variables as "established routines" and "standard operating procedures."[37]

The limited resources available for this study, coupled with the intention of studying at least a dozen states, precluded any in-depth investigation of systemic features. Concern for developing evidence relevant to models did, however, lead to careful scrutiny of formal governmental arrangements that, presumably, influence the expression of preferences and the flow of influence in policy making. This presumption was tested through an examination of whether (and how) governmental structure affected the number and type of actors who participated in state education policy making, the resources available to participants, the willingness of participants to mobilize these resources, the channels of communication and the degree of access open to different actors, and the influence exercised by these actors when a policy choice was being determined.

The Conceptual Framework Reviewed

A political systems orientation is, therefore, the point of departure here. This orientation emphasizes the relationships among the actors within education policy systems as demands are converted into authoritative decisions. Particular attention is directed toward actor relationships at each functional stage—issue definition, proposal formulation, support mobilization, and decision enactment—of the conversion process. Allocative theory was used to augment the political systems approach, and, consistent with its insights, education policy making was assumed to be a competitive process, the dynamic of which resides in the interplay of influence. The explanation for policy decisions, based on this perspective, comes from revealing patterns of accommodation among competing actors who differ greatly as to resources, intention, and skill. These patterns are organized through a governmental structure as well as being channeled and constrained by other systemic features. Figure I-1 depicts the general concepts employed in the framework.

RESEARCH METHODOLOGY

The research findings presented here are the product of a comparative case study methodology. Four facets warrant comment: selecting the states, conducting the fieldwork, assuring comparable data, and analyzing the findings.

Selecting the States

Inasmuch as governance models were intended to be a major product of the research, structural criteria took precedence in deciding upon the states to be investigated. There was, though, some question as to which of the innumerable variations in state government should be represented in the case studies and in what combination. Neither theory nor research provided much illumination, but another approach was suggested by Jacob and Lipsky. "Significant variables," they argued, "may be isolated by quantitative techniques, while the case method may be employed to approach greater understanding of the appearance of significant correlations."[38]

In this study statistical analysis was first applied to aggregate data to search for significant structure-policy relationships that could then be subjected to intensive case study. A number of measures were devised for each of four classes of variables: socioeconomic development, political culture, governmental structure, and education policy output. Data from readily available sources on these measures were

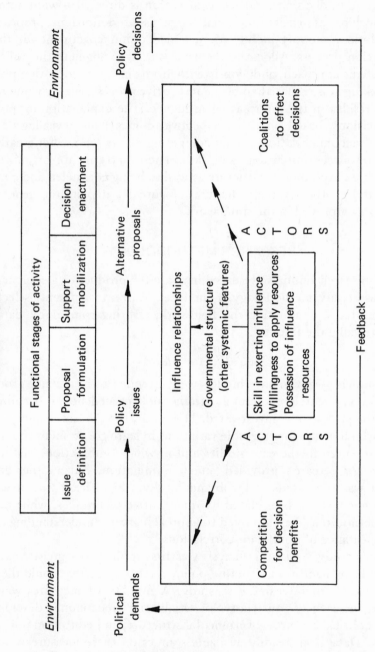

FIGURE I-1

EGP System and Influence Concepts

gathered from all of the fifty states, and partial correlation and multiple regression techniques were used to explore relationships between structural variables and policy output variables, while controlling statistically for socioeconomic and political culture differences. The results of this analysis were disappointing in terms of identifying governmental arrangements that appeared to have an independent effect on education policies,[39] so the twelve states to be studied were chosen in accord with the method used to select the state board and the chief state school officer (CSSO). It was assumed that these variables would be central to the governance models that would eventually be developed.[40] The twelve states and the selection methods for the state board and the CSSO are shown in Table I-1.

TABLE I-1 EGP States by SBE and CSSO Selection Methods

EGP states	SBE selection method	CSSO selection method
Colorado	Popular election	SBE appointment
Michigan	Popular election	SBE appointment
Nebraska	Popular election	SBE appointment
Texas	Popular election	SBE appointment
California	Governor appointment	Popular election
Georgia	Governor appointment	Popular election
Tennessee	Governor appointment	Governor appointment
Massachusetts	Governor appointment	SBE appointment
Minnesota	Governor appointment	SBE appointment
New York	Elected by legislature	SBE appointment
Florida	Ex-officio members	Popular election
Wisconsin	No state board	Popular election

Besides governmental structure, five other factors influenced the decision concerning the states to be studied. The desire to have states with large populations represented meant that six of the ten "megastates" were included. All major regions of the country were to be represented, and, when two regions, the Plains and the Rocky Mountain areas were not, Nebraska and Colorado replaced other states initially selected. In order to have several pairs of comparable cases in the study, it was important that the states in each pair be similar in, for example, political culture and socioeconomic development, but dissimilar in respect to such structural features as the separation of educational governance from general governance. States where there had been recent court intervention in education decision making were also included. Finally, for each of the states to be investigated, background data had to be available, as did access to both participants and informants.

Conducting the Fieldwork

Fieldwork had a twofold purpose. The primary one was to develop data for a comparative analysis of state education policy making. A secondary purpose was to ensure that accurate and reasonably complete accounts could be written about this process for each of the states.[41] While these purposes were not unrelated—some data pertain to both—they were different. In the case of comparative data, the intent was to generalize, with emphasis on abstraction and standardization. Producing adequate state reports, however, meant that some attention had to be given to the particular and the unanticipated.[42]

In fall 1972, EGP research teams collected background data on the twelve states where the case studies were to be done. One or more members of a team made a preliminary visit to each state to confer with informants about its education governance process and to prepare for a more extended visit to the state. From January to March 1973, teams composed of two or three research associates spent some three weeks in each of the states. This fieldwork, in addition to serving both purposes mentioned above, reflected a combination of two distinct research strategies: one based on an issue area approach; the other, on a policy systems (and reputational) approach.

Issue area approach. An issue area can be defined as a broad topical concern (for example, state aid for schools) in respect to which individuals and groups have disparate and often conflicting preferences that, when advanced as political demands, become grist for the decision process. Scholars in the pluralist tradition have long contended that each issue area tends to have its own power structure.[43] That is, each issue is held to have its own character and a salience that varies for each actor. The pattern of cleavage shifts with the controversy and allies in one are sometimes antagonists in another. Pluralists' findings are vulnerable to many criticisms. Still, it does appear that state education policy making is not likely to be the same for different issues. Various kinds of decisions must be investigated, consequently, to understand the participation of actors in the process. Comparative analysis of policy making is, however, facilitated by the standardization, so to speak, of issues across the states.[44]

It is obvious that all state education policy decisions could not be examined, but more needed to be done than simply looking at only one or two types of decisions. It was decided that resources would permit consideration of four issue areas in each state, to be determined, first, by perceived importance. Letters were sent to the chief state school officer, the governor (or his education aide), the executive secretaries of the state NEA and AFT affiliates, and a university professor specializing in the politics of education for each of the fifty states. Using a five-point scale, they were asked to rate eight issues as being critical to the policy system in their state. We received responses from 90 percent of the chief state school officers, 56 percent of the governors, 63 percent of the teacher organization heads, and 76 percent of the professors. The survey ratings, as aggregated for all respondents, appear in Table I-2.

TABLE I-2 Total Rating Values Given by Respondents to Eight Selected Policy Issues

Policy issue	Rating value
Financial support	237
Planning and evaluation	169
Curriculum reform	122
Teacher bargaining	108
District reorganization	93
Professional certification	90
School desegregation	54
Nonpublic school support	45

Perceived importance was not the only criterion in deciding upon the four issue areas to be studied. Selected issues also had to reveal the involvement of different actors and governmental institutions in education policy making. One area, therefore, had to be an issue demanding participation by both governor and legislature. School finance, clearly the most useful for this purpose, was viewed in the survey as the most critical issue to be examined. Another area focused on the state education agency as a policy-making arena. Even though teacher-administrator certification was not rated as critical by many respondents, decisions in this area were important and typified more routine policy enactments that must be made in every state. As for an issue where the courts were involved as policy makers, desegregation—though it ranked low in our survey, perhaps because the federal courts more than the state courts were the chief actors—appeared to be an obvious choice. Finally, the fourth issue was one in which the state education agency thought it had done its best job in exercising leadership. In gross terms this was called the program improvement area. In about half of the states participating in the study this involved attempts to establish evaluation, "accountability," or assessment programs.

EGP researchers collected data on a recent (1970 to 1973) policy decision in each of the four issue areas—school finance, professional certification, racial desegregation, and educational program improvement—for all twelve states. This required an examination of diverse sources including newspaper files, official documents and reports, interest group publications, and other written materials. The research team also conducted interviews with both issue participants and knowledgeable informants about the policy decisions. Issue-oriented interviews were not highly structured; nor was a single interview schedule used with all respondents. The purpose, for the most part, was to fill gaps in information and to probe questions about the decision process suggested by our conceptual framework. With regard to the latter, interviewers were to draw selectively, depending on their own knowledge as well as the information believed to be possessed by the respondent, from these basic questions:

1. Who initiated the demand for a policy change or was most responsible for making it an issue? What was the position taken by that individual or group? Whom did this individual or group speak for or represent?

2. Why do you think this individual or group took that position? What background factors were particularly important?

3. Were other individuals or groups important participants? Which ones and what positions did they take on the matter?

4. Did this issue become associated with other state issues? What

issues, and how did this occur? What positions did the various participants take on this other issue?

5. When did all this take place? Did the early alignments and positions undergo major shifts over time? How did they change? Why?

6. What did the participants do to win support or neutralize opponents? Which participants seemed to be particularly effective? Why?
What were their sources of influence and points of access?

7. When did the matter come up for formal consideration by the
state legislature or the state board of education? While it was being
considered by the legislature or the state board, what policy proposals were the main focus of attention?

a. What, in summary, was the content of each proposal?
b. Who presented them? Who actually formulated them?
c. Which of the contending individuals and groups supported each
one? How did they attempt to mobilize supporters or neutralize
opponents?

8. Basically, how did the final decision get made? Who persuaded
(or bargained or directed) whom, and how did they do it?

9. Which individual or group was most responsible for the decision
that was finally enacted? Which individual or group might be said to
have "won" by this decision? Who might have "lost"?

One section of each individual state report deals with education
policy making as reflected in the selected issue areas. Many of these
treatments, especially those on school finance, are reasonably comprehensive and provide research-based answers to most of the questions set forth above.[45] Unfortunately, some of the issue descriptions
turned out to be short on detail, spotty in coverage, and deficient in
process analysis. Two things, above all, limited use of the issue area
approach. First, in-depth study of a decision process is costly, attempting to examine four such processes, coupled with other research tasks, stretched resources thin in some states. Second, policy
decisions that do not become public issues—that is, those that receive
little or no media attention—are hard to study. Even participants
often can recall only the most sketchy outline of events, and contemporary written accounts that might be used to structure, supplement,
and verify these recollections do not exist. In this sense, if in no
other, school finance was an easy area to investigate; teacher certification and school desegregation, as state-level issues, proved to be

quite difficult. Partly for these reasons, the issue area approach did
not yield as much data as had originally been expected for the comparative analysis contained in this report, though school finance
reform in four states is the subject of one chapter, and some use is
made of the issue-oriented data in several of the other chapters.

Policy system approach. Besides issue-specific information, data
also were sought on the perceptions that the major actors had of the
way the education policy system typically worked in their state in
terms of role performance and policy-making relationships. Included
in this approach were questions in which respondents were asked
about how much "influence" (or "importance" or "leadership")
they attributed to the various system participants. Structured interview schedules were employed to obtain the perceptual data, and ten
different schedules, one for each class of actors, were constructed.
The classes of actors were as follows:

State board member
Chief state school officer
SDE administrator-legislative liaison
SDE administrator-state board liaison
Governor
Governor's education staff
Director of finance or administration
Legislative committee (Education or "Money") leader
Legislative house or senate leader
Educational interest group leader

The individual respondents within these classes were preselected
with an eye toward their being comparable across the states. An
effort was made, for instance, to interview the state board president,
the chief state school officer, the governor's key education aide, the
chairmen of the education committees, and the lobbyists for the
state-level education organizations in each of the twelve states. There
was also a procedure for substituting respondents when first choices
were unavailable in an attempt to obtain substitutes whose general
viewpoints resembled those of the initially selected respondents.

As can be seen from Table I-3, over four hundred structured interviews were held with policy actors. The interviews averaged about
one hour in length, though some, notably those with chief state
school officers, were much longer. Political leaders, in general, posed

TABLE I-3 Number of Interviews (Structured) with State Policy Makers[a]

State	CSSO	SDE administrators[b]	SBE	Governor	Governor's staff	Finance-administration	Legislative leaders[c]	Legislative staff[d]	Educational organizations	TOTALS
California	1	3	10	0	1	2	15	3	7	42
Colorado	2	2	4	1	2	1	14	2	6	34
Florida	1	3	7[e]	1	1	1	9	1	6	30
Georgia	1	3	7	1	1	1	13	0	5	32
Massachusetts	2	2	7	0	7[f]	2	12	4	8	44
Michigan	1	3	6	1	2	1	15	0	10	39
Minnesota	1	3	6	0	1	1	15	0	5	32
Nebraska	1	3	5	1	1	1	7	0	5	24
New York	1	5	9	0	3	1	13	9	8	49
Tennessee	2	2	8	1	2	1	11	0	6	33
Texas	1	2	11	1	2	1	10	0	6	34
Wisconsin	1	1	—	0	2	1	15	2	7	29
TOTALS	15	32	80	7	25	14	149	21	79	422

[a]In addition to these structured interviews, some two hundred unstructured interviews were held with informants (e.g., newspaper reporters, university professors, legislative staff members, and SDE administrators) in the twelve states regarding specific policy decisions.

[b]Includes both legislative relations expert and state board expert.

[c]Includes both legislative committee leader and House-Senate leader.

[d]Interviewed using the legislator schedules.

[e]Five of these are cabinet aides.

[f]Includes the Secretary of Education and his staff.

the most severe problems in interviewing. We were not successful with five governors. Legislative leaders in New York, California, Florida, and Texas were especially difficult to interview and required considerable deviation through substitution from the original list of respondents. Nonetheless, a representative cross section of influential state education policy actors was obtained, and the data gathered from interviewing these actors are relied upon heavily in this analysis. The different respondents were also encouraged to complete a short questionnaire—the "Education Policy Maker Inventory"—and some of their replies are presented in the chapters on the state board and the chief state school officer.

The structured interview schedules, collectively, contained hundreds of specific questions, many of which were addressed to only a single class of respondents. Underlying these questions, however, were several general concerns that were based on the conceptual framework used in this study:

1. What were the policy-making capabilities of the different system actors? That is, what access did each have to influence resources, and how willing was each to mobilize these resources?

2. What were the policy-making relationships among the different system actors? That is, what were the channels of communication and points of access that connected the actors to one another and to the various decision arenas? What patterns of conflict and cooperation existed? Who sought to influence whom, how, and with what success?

Assuring Comparative Data

From the beginning it was determined that data obtained from fieldwork would be suitable for comparative analysis. Specific steps, several of which have already been mentioned, were taken in attempting to assure this. First, the focus was on a common set of issue areas. Second, data-gathering instruments were the same in each state, except for language changes to make them appropriate to a particular setting. Third, a common panel made up of incumbents in homologous positions was included in each state study. Finally, there was an eight-week summer session devoted to familiarizing research associates (ten persons organized into four teams) with the conceptual framework and to having them work on the various interview schedules. Toward the end of the summer (August 1972), the entire group participated in a pilot study so that the research procedures and interview schedules could be tested and modified as necessary. The state education policy system in Ohio was the subject for the pilot.

The typical procedure in constructing the interview schedules was for team members, working individually or in small groups, to formulate questions they considered most relevant to both the research purpose and the class of actor who was the intended respondent. The questions were then analyzed in group meetings, and new drafts were written and rewritten to eliminate ambiguity and enhance the content validity of the instruments. Next, the interview schedules were pilot tested in Ohio with some thirty respondents, which led to extensive revision. During this period the interview schedule drafts were shared with various outside consultants—persons with recognized expertise in state education politics, instrument construction, and "elite" interviewing. As the final step, the schedules were organized, through the adaptation of a format developed by the National Opinion Research Center, so as to facilitate the interviewing process, the recording of responses, and the eventual coding of the data.[46]

Analyzing the Findings

Some of the data collected by the EGP are amenable only to qualitative treatment. The chapter on school finance reform offers a good illustration of a systematic examination of such data. But many data are quantifiable; hence, considerable use is made of tables to display frequency distributions. Beyond engaging in a comparative description of state education policy systems, however, this study also investigates the relationships among variables, especially those that might provide evidence as to the structural effects of different governmental arrangements.

To accomplish this, some measures of the phenomena of interest had to be constructed. Each state was assigned a score on each variable, a score based usually on the structured interview responses, but occasionally on information from case study analyses, or on both. Often the replies of different classes of actors were incorporated when measuring a variable, to serve as a corrective for respondent bias.

The strengths and weaknesses of such a measurement approach have been well assessed by Gurr and McClelland:

The quantification of historical [and other qualitative] materials makes it possible to index and compare concepts which have been previously operationalized poorly or not at all, but the use of judgmental scales raises questions about the validity of the indicators and the reliability of coders that we can only begin to answer. The use of multiple measures of each variable helps allay the criticism that single measures of complex conditions are useless because they ignore too much important variation, but our combination of these multiple measures into summary ones raises the same criticism transformed by one turn of the screw: the conditions whose measures are being combined may seem incommensurable. Finally, the treatment of judgmental data as though they were . . . susceptible to . . . statistical manipulations will offend methodological purists in spite of the now-conventional argument that many important comparisons cannot otherwise be made.[47]

In this case the advantages of these judgmental procedures appeared to outweigh their disadvantages. And it was the only way to create measures necessary for a quantitative assessment of some of the "why" questions about state education politics. In any event, scoring procedures for the variables are discussed in either the chapters or the technical appendixes.

Working with crude measures and a small N, we limited ourselves for the most part to the Spearman rank-order correlation (rho) in investigating our data. It should be emphasized that the twelve EGP states do not constitute a probability sample. No statistical inferences applicable to all the American states can be derived from the findings of this study, and the generalizations made pertain, strictly speaking, only to the states studied.

*   *   *

The findings, whether the result of quantitative or of qualitative inquiry, do not speak for themselves. They are selected, arranged, and given meaning through interpretation. Thus, the conceptual framework not only performs the function of giving initial direction to research (by indicating where to look and what to look for), but it also serves to organize the presentation of findings. Even within the constraints of this framework, however, many interpretations are possible and can be supported by data from this study. Whether the findings and interpretations presented are persuasive in terms of logic and evidence is a matter for the reader to decide.

NOTES—CHAPTER I

1. An early statement of the conceptual framework and research methodology used by the EGP appears in Roald F. Campbell and Tim L. Mazzoni, Jr., "Investigating State Education Policy Systems: Methodological Approach and Research Framework," unpublished draft, May 5, 1972, pp. 1-83 (mimeo).

2. For a brilliant treatment of the use of conceptual models, see Graham Allison, *Essence of Decision* (Boston: Little, Brown, 1971).

3. Harold Lasswell and Abraham Kaplan, *Power and Society* (New Haven, Conn.: Yale University Press, 1950), p. xxiii.

4. The political systems approach has been given many distinct formulations. See, for example, William C. Mitchell, *The American Polity* (New York: Free Press, 1962); Karl W. Deutsch, *The Nerves of Government* (Glencoe, Ill.: Free Press, 1963); David Easton, *A Framework for Political Analysis* (Englewood Cliffs, N.J.: Prentice-Hall, 1965). The classic statement of allocative theory is in Harold Lasswell, *Politics: Who Gets What, When, How* (New York: McGraw-Hill, 1936).

5. Lasswell, *Politics.*

6. This definition corresponds to that found in Gerald R. Sroufe, "State School Board Members and the State Education Policy System," *Planning and Changing*, 2 (April 1971), pp. 16-17.

7. See Robert E. Agger, Daniel Goldrich, and Bert E. Swanson, *The Rulers and the Ruled* (New York: John Wiley, 1964), pp. 43-47.

8. David Easton, *A Systems Analysis of Political Life* (New York: John Wiley, 1965), p. 353.

9. Bertram H. Gross, *The Managing of Organizations* (New York: Free Press, 1964), chs. 17, 18.

10. The major studies of state education policy making include the following: Stephen K. Bailey et al., *Schoolmen and Politics* (Syracuse, N.Y.: Syracuse University Press, 1962); Nicholas A. Masters et al., *State Politics and the Public Schools* (New York: Knopf, 1964); Michael D. Usdan, David W. Minar, and Emanuel Hurwitz, Jr., *Education and State Politics* (New York: Teachers College, Columbia University, 1969); Laurence Iannaccone, *Politics in Education* (New York: Center for Applied Research in Education, 1967); Joel S. Berke and Michael Kirst, *Federal Aid to Education* (Lexington, Mass.: D. C. Heath, 1972); and Mike M. Milstein and Robert Jennings, *Educational Policy Making and the State Legislature* (New York: Praeger, 1973).

11. See Part Two in this volume.

12. These categories are adapted from those developed by Schneier. See Edward Schneier (ed.), *Policy Making in American Government* (New York: Basic Books, 1969), pp. xi-xii.

13. David Easton, "An Approach to the Analysis of Political Systems," *World Politics*, 9 (April 1957), p. 389.

14. Many criticisms have, of course, been directed at the theoretical and explanatory usages of functionalism. See the review article by William Flanagan and Edwin Fogelman, "Functional Analysis," in James C. Charlesworth (ed.), *Contemporary Political Analysis* (New York: Free Press, 1967), pp. 72-85.

15. Herbert J. Spiro, "An Evaluation of Systems Theory," in Charlesworth (ed.), *Contemporary Political Analysis*, p. 164.

16. See Gerald Sroufe, "Political Systems Analysis in Educational Administration: Can the Emperor Be Clothed?" unpublished paper presented at the American Educational Research Association, February 1969.

17. The definition is Terry Clark's. See the discussion in Terry N. Clark (ed.), *Community Structure and Decision Making: Comparative Analyses* (San Francisco: Chandler, 1968), ch. 3.

18. This distinction between "influence" (the actual exercise) and "power" (the potential) is made by several authors. For example, see Daniel Katz and Robert Kahn, *The Social Psychology of Organizations* (New York: John Wiley, 1966), pp. 218-222.

19. The definition is adapted from Ronald L. Nuttall, Erwin K. Scheuch, and Chad Gordon, "On the Structure of Influence," in Clark (ed.), *Community Structure and Decision Making*, pp. 352-353.

20. Charles E. Lindblom, *The Policy-Making Process* (Englewood Cliffs, N.J.: Prentice-Hall, 1968), p. 30.

21. For a brief discussion of the potency of resources in respect to policy-making stages, see Clark (ed.), *Community Structure and Decision Making*, ch. 4.

22. Lindblom, *Policy-Making Process*, pp. 102-105.

23. William A. Gamson, "Reputation and Resources in Community Politics," in Clark (ed.), *Community Structure and Decision Making*. His distinction is based on those of Talcott Parsons. See Talcott Parsons, "On the Concept of Influence," *Public Opinion Quarterly*, 37 (Spring 1963), pp. 37-62.

24. Robert A. Dahl, *Who Governs?* (New Haven, Conn.: Yale University Press, 1961), p. 226.

25. While the idea of "generality" is used often, one of the few theoretical discussion is in Parsons, "On the Concept of Influence."

26. These included John C. Wahlke *et al.*, *The Legislative System* (New York: John Wiley, 1962); and Herbert Jacob and Kenneth N. Vines (eds.), *Politics in the American States* (Boston: Little, Brown, 1971).

27. Aaron Wildavsky, "Why American Cities are Pluralist," in Thomas R. Dye and Bret W. Hawkins (eds.), *Politics in the Metropolis* (Columbus, Ohio: Charles Merrill, 1967), p. 351.

28. Robert A. Dahl, *Modern Political Analysis* (Englewood Cliffs, N.J.: Prentice-Hall, 1963), pp. 55-71.

29. On issue saliency, see particularly Ernest A. T. Barth and Stuart D. Johnson, "Community Power and a Typology of Social Issues," in Willis D. Hawley and Frederick M. Wirt (eds.), *The Search for Community Power* (Englewood Cliffs, N.J.: Prentice-Hall, 1968), p. 265.

30. Heinz Eulau, *Journey in Politics* (New York: Bobbs-Merrill, 1964), p. 256.

31. Sroufe, "State School Board Members and the State Education Policy System," p. 22.

32. The best theoretical treatment of access is still David Truman, *The Governmental Process*, 2nd ed. (New York: Knopf, 1964).

33. William H. Riker, *The Theory of Political Coalitions* (New Haven, Conn.: Yale University Press, 1962).

34. Raymond A. Bauer, "The Study of Policy Formation," in Raymond A. Bauer and Kenneth Gergen (eds.), *The Study of Policy Formation* (New York: Free Press, 1971), p. 13.

35. Lindblom, *The Policy-Making Process*, pp. 93-99.

36. Enid Curtis Bok Schoettle, "The State of the Art in Policy Studies," Bauer and Gergen (eds.), *Study of Policy Formation*, p. 171.

37. See Kirst's conclusions in Michael W. Kirst, "Six States and Federal Aid: Key Conclusions and Methodological Considerations," unpublished paper presented to the annual meeting of American Educational Research Association, Chicago, April 5, 1972.

38. Herbert Jacob and Michael Lipsky, "Outputs, Structure, and Power: An Assessment of Changes in the Study of State and Local Politics," Richard Hofferbert and Ira Sharkansky (eds.), *State and Urban Politics* (Boston: Little, Brown, 1971), p. 33.

39. Our findings are reported in Tim L. Mazzoni, Jr., and Roald F. Campbell, "State Governmental Structure and Education Policy Decisions: A Statistical Exploration," unpublished American Educational Research Association paper, March 1, 1973.

40. Again, see Part Two in this volume.

41. Case studies were published in 1974 on each of the twelve states.

42. Combining the comparative method with the case study is, of course, much more easily said than done. Too much standardization in advance means that important factors are likely to be overlooked; too little standardization often results in little more than a juxtaposition of case studies.

43. "Pluralist" assumptions are set forth in Nelson W. Polsby, *Community Power and Political Theory* (New Haven, Conn.: Yale University Press, 1963).

44. A good recent example of such issue standardization is found in David J. Kirby *et al.*, *Political Strategies in Northern School Desegregation* (Lexington, Mass.: Lexington Books, 1973).

45. See, for example, the treatment of the school finance issue by Peggy Siegel, in Edward R. Hines *et al.*, *State Policy Making for the Public Schools of Michigan* (Columbus: Ohio State University, Educational Governance Project, June 1974).

46. We looked, especially, at the interview schedule format used by Robert Crain and David Kirby in their work on the politics of school desegregation.

47. Ted Robert Gurr and Muriel McClelland, *Political Performance: A Twelve-Nation Study* (Beverly Hills, Calif.: Sage, 1971), p. 8. A particularly imaginative example of the use of this approach is Robert Crain, *The Politics of School Desegregation* (Garden City, N.Y.: Doubleday-Anchor, 1969).

II — The Policy-Making Influence of State Boards of Education

The activities and influence of state boards of education is a dark continent in view of the paucity of research.

Frederick M. Wirt and Michael W. Kirst, 1975

While the "dark continent" of state board behavior has by no means been explored fully here, some care has been taken to examine the policy-making role of these institutions. In particular, research-based answers were sought to two general questions:

1. How influential are state boards of education in the process by which state-level policy decisions are determined for the public schools?
2. What factors account for the variations in policy-making influence among state boards of education?

To answer these questions, this chapter has been divided into five sections. The first section contains reports on the perceptions that a cross section of policy participants and knowledgeable observers had of the influence exerted by each of ten state boards of education in the two arenas where most public school policies are enacted—the legislature and the state education agency. In the second section there is a description of access to policy-making resources possessed by state boards. The willingness of board members to utilize their resources is treated in section three, and a statistical analysis undertaken in section four provides evidence on the correlates of state board policy-making influence. The chapter concludes with general observations about state boards of education as actors in education policy systems.

The intent is not to examine state board performance across a range of governmental functions, much less to evaluate this performance. The research focus of the Educational Governance Project (EGP), as stated in Chapter I, is on state education policy making —setting the goals and fixing the priorities that give direction to subsequent choices—and, particularly, on the relationships among the actors who participate in this process. Policy formation, not policy implementation or adjudication, is our concern. In this chapter we present what essentially is a "snapshot," dated late 1972 to early 1973, of the policy-making role of ten selected state boards as that role was assessed by various policy participants and by EGP researchers. Wisconsin and Florida were not included in the analysis; the first, because it has no state board; the second, because its board consists entirely of ex officio members.

Lay boards have long been an integral part of school governance arrangements in the United States. State boards of education (SBE's), though they have not existed for as many years as their local counterparts, go back to the early 1800's in several states. (The New York Board of Regents is even older, but it did not have authority over elementary-secondary education until 1904.)[1] By the beginning of the twentieth century, this governmental institution had been established by either constitutional or statutory provision in more than one-half of the states.[2] And, by 1972, the number of state boards of education stood at forty-eight. Wisconsin and Illinois were the only exceptions, and a state board began functioning in Illinois in 1974.

In the late 1800's most state boards of education were ex officio in composition—that is, they were comprised of various elected state officials, one of whom customarily was the chief state school officer (CSSO).[3] During the twentieth century there has been a steady movement away from ex officio boards toward ones appointed by the governor, and, more recently, ones elected directly by the people or their representatives. This trend, along with selection methods for the state boards in the EGP sample, is indicated by figures reported in Table II-1. As is evident from this table, only two selection procedures—gubernatorial appointment and popular election—have become prevalent, and these procedures are used in nine of the twelve EGP states.

TABLE II-1 SBE Selection Methods, 1940 and 1972

Selection method	Used in the 48 states in 1940	Used in the 50 states in 1972	Used in the 12 EGP states in 1972
Election by popular vote	4	12	4
Appointment by governor	27	31	5
Election by peoples' representatives	0	3	1
Ex-officio members	8	2	1
No state board	9	2	1

Source: Dewey Wahl, "State-Level Governing Structures for Education—Alternatives and Implications for Change," Indiana State Department of Public Instruction, 1973.

Although twenty-six state boards of education, as of 1972, appointed the CSSO, the other twenty-four boards did not have this legal power. Of the ten state boards considered in this chapter, there are four—in Colorado, Michigan, Nebraska, and Texas—whose members are elected, and they all appoint their CSSO. So do two of the appointed state boards—in Massachusetts and Minnesota. The other three appointed boards—in California, Georgia, and Tennessee—lack this authority. The CSSO is popularly elected in California and Georgia; in Tennessee the official is appointed, as is the state board, by the governor. The New York Board of Regents, whose members are elected by the legislature, appoints its Commissioner of Education (Table II-2 contains additional structural information on these state boards). An analysis of the importance of these different selection methods appears in the fourth section of this chapter.

TABLE II-2 Structural Features of SBE's Studied by EGP (Late 1972)

State	Size[a]	Term[b]	Compensation	Method of selection	Special qualifications[c]	Appoints CSSO	Authority over— Vocational education	Vocational rehabilitation
California	10	4	Expenses	Appointment by governor, with approval of Senate		No	Yes	Yes
Colorado	5	6	Expenses	Election by partisan ballot, four from each congressional district; one at-large		Yes	No	No
Georgia	10	7	$20 per day, plus expenses	Appointed by governor, with approval of Senate, one from each congressional district		No	Yes	Yes
Massachusetts	11	5	Expenses	Appointed by governor from nominees supplied by advisory council	One labor representative, two women, one student	Yes	Yes	No
Michigan	8	8	$60 per day, plus expenses	Elected at-large by partisan ballot		Yes	Yes	Yes
Minnesota	9	6	$25 per day, plus expenses	Appointed by governor, with approval of Senate, from separate congressional districts	Three members must have local school board experience	Yes	Yes	Yes

TABLE II-2 (continued)

State	Size[a]	Term[b]	Compensation	Method of selection	Special qualifications[c]	Appoints CSSO	Authority over— Vocational education	Vocational rehabilitation
Nebraska	8	4	Expenses	Elected by nonpartisan ballot, one member from each of eight districts		Yes	Yes	Yes
New York	15	15	Expenses	Elected by legislature, one from each of eleven judicial districts, four at-large		Yes	Yes	Yes
Tennessee	12	9	$15 per day, plus expenses	Appointed by governor, four from each of the three "grand divisions"	Each political party must have three members	No	Yes	Yes
Texas	24	6	Expenses	Elected by partisan ballot, one from each congressional district		Yes	Yes	Yes

[a]Ex-officio members not included.
[b]All terms are overlapping.
[c]A number of states prohibit professional educators, and state-local government officials, from being state board members.
Source: Sam P. Harris, *State Departments of Education, State Boards of Education, and Chief State School Officers,* Department of Health, Education and Welfare Publication (Office of Education) 73-074000 (Washington, D. C.: U.S. Government Printing Office, 1973).

State boards of education vary not only as to method of selection and control of the CSSO, but also as to membership size, term of office, scope of authority, and performance of governmental functions. The largest such body, having twenty-four members in 1972, is in Texas; the smallest, with just three members, is in Mississippi. It is more common that boards contain either seven or nine members. Terms of office range from fifteen years on the New York Board of Regents (reduced in 1974 to seven years for newly elected members) to three years on the Delaware State Board of Education. Terms that last from four to six years occur most frequently.[4]

Although four states have a governance structure that places all levels of education under a single agency, in most states decisions concerning higher education are separate from those affecting elementary and secondary schools. Most state boards of education have authority over vocational education, as well as vocational rehabilitation,[5] and over a number of K-12 areas of substantive jurisdiction, categorized by Schweickhard in the mid-1960's as: foundation aid programs, certification of professional personnel, school standards and curriculum, district organization and reorganization, buildings and sites, federal assistance programs, and transportation of pupils.[6]

Even with respect to such common areas of jurisdiction, however, state boards do not have parallel authority or duties. Legally, they are administrative boards. Yet most are authorized to undertake judicial and quasi-legislative functions as well. Harris concluded, after studying the formal powers of state boards, that:

most State boards of education have the authority to formulate or determine administrative-level policies and adopt such rules and regulations as are necessary to carry out the responsibilities assigned to them by the constitution and statutes of the State. In many instances State boards can formulate and approve policies needed to supplement those already prescribed by the legislature for the guidance of the chief State school officer and the staff of the State department of education and of local school districts.[7]

Besides exercising general supervision over K-12 schools and, in most cases, over vocational education and rehabilitation, state boards often approve top-level appointments to the state department of education, upon the recommendation of the CSSO. They generally are charged, along with the chief, to submit recommendations to both the governor and the legislature regarding the financial needs of both the education agency and the schools of the state. All in all, then, the legal powers delegated to state boards of education are such that we, with Sroufe, "would expect them to be effective instruments for the formation and implementation of state education policy."[8]

POLICY-MAKING INFLUENCE OF STATE BOARDS

Under the most ideal circumstances one is seldom certain that he has correctly attributed or weighed policy-making influence. Attempting to assess empirically that exercised by state boards of education, particularly in their interaction with CSSO's, posed special problems. Board members and state department administrators alike were prone to make such legalistic responses as: "the state board determines policy; the chief state school officer carries it out." Most policy matters that appeared before state boards aroused little or no controversy. Media coverage was skimpy, and even participants were hard pressed to recall any but the most sketchy outline of the events that led to a given decision. Apart from state department staff, there were few knowledgeable observers of board activities. Educational interest group leaders came closest to filling this function in most states. In a couple of states, however, an official from the League of Women Voters proved to be a discerning "board watcher." Finally, while they are legally distinct, the state board of education and the state department of education were sometimes looked upon as one entity by the people being interviewed, a perspective that made it difficult to examine the respective roles. For all of these reasons, the decision analysis approach proved to have serious limitations. Most of the comparative assessments presented in this section are, therefore, based on the attribution of influence, or noninfluence, to state boards by legislators, governors' staffs, and educational interest group spokesmen, as well as by board officials themselves.[9]

The Legislative Arena

The legal powers of state boards of education, unlike those of most local school boards, do not include independent access to monetary resources. Fiscal power in all states belongs with the legislature and the governor. And since "issues of educational finance," to quote Wirt and Kirst, "inevitably involve judgments on educational programs and priorities, so the constitutional separation of education from general state government can never extend to many important educational issues."[10] Moreover, legislatures can, and often do, enact laws on a wide spectrum of nonfiscal education policies, which has unmistakeable implications for the policy-making influence of state boards. Either its officials wield influence with key lawmakers, or the boards have no influence on basic allocative decisions or on many other policies set for the schools of the state.

Legislator relationships. Legislative leaders interviewed were asked to evaluate their state board "in actually formulating and working for education legislation." The responses of the lawmakers are shown in the first column of Table II-3. Only about one-fourth (28 percent) said their state board was "important" in determining education legislation; the remainder assessed board significance as being either "minor" (50 percent) or "not important at all" (22 percent). In just one state, Texas, did a majority of respondents (60 percent) rate the state board as being an important actor in legislative policy making for education, though in two states, Georgia and New York, the percentages (46 and 45, respectively) constituted a near majority. At the other extreme, the Nebraska State Board of Education was not viewed as being important in education legislation by a single member of the state legislature who responded. Four of the six leaders interviewed dismissed the board as being of no consequence in the process.

Legislators also assessed the strengths and weaknesses of their state boards as actors in the legislative arena, and these assessments were coded into some broad categories. Those strengths and weaknesses indicated at least five times are listed below by frequency of mention (in parentheses):

Perceived strengths

Prestige of the state board (23)
Legal authority of the state board (9)
Board member specialization in education (8)
State board access to state department data (5)
Personal involvement (for example, lobbying) of board members (5)
Board member standing with the governor (5)

Perceived weaknesses

Traditional apolitical posture of state board (15)
"Invisibility" of state board to the legislature (13)

TABLE II-3 Assessment of SBE Influence in the Legislative Arena

SBE's by state, according to means of selection	Legislative leaders who said board is "important"		Education lobbyists who said board "took lead"		Governor's office staff who said board is "important source of ideas and advice"	
	Number[a]	Percent	Number[b]	Percent	Number	Percent
Elected by people						
Colorado	13	38	4	25	3	67
Michigan	14	36	4	50	4	25
Nebraska	6	0	3	0	3	33
Texas	10	60	3	67	3	67
Appointed by governor						
Massachusetts	9	11	4	25	5	20
Minnesota	14	7	4	50	2	100
California	14	14	4	0	1	0
Georgia	13	46	3	0	3	0
Tennessee	8	13	4	0	3	67
Elected by legislature						
New York	11	45	3	100	2	0
ALL STATES	112	28	36	31	29	38

[a]Number of legislative leaders who responded to the question. In Massachusetts this includes two staff members.

[b]Respondents were sought in four state education interest groups (EIG's): teachers—National Education Association (NEA) and American Federation of Teachers (AFT) affiliates, administrators, and school boards. Where an interest group had two or more respondents, we chose for this rating the one who seemed most knowledgeable about the legislature. In Nebraska, Texas, and Georgia there was no state affiliate of AFT. In New York NEA and AFT affiliates have merged.

[c]Respondents include the governor in Colorado, Michigan, Nebraska, Texas, Georgia, and Tennessee. In Massachusetts the offices of lieutenant governor and secretary of education are included.

Dependence of state board on the CSSO (10)
State board lack of political "clout" (9)
Board member lack of expertise (9)
No direct channels between board and legislature (9)
State board factionalism (6)
"Unrealistic" state board pronouncements (5)
Board member lack of time (5)

Of the perceived strengths, the resource we have termed prestige—
the respect accorded board members because of presumed personal
or positional attributes—was cited more often by legislative leaders
than any other. The weaknesses most often identified by legislators
were the state boards' not having a tradition of political involvement
or any "clout" (apparently meaning an inability to mobilize constituents of importance to politicians); their lack of visibility to many
legislators (a number said that they did not know what state boards
did or recognize a single board member); and the dependence of the
boards on CSSO's (a "real Charley McCarthy-Edgar Bergen act," one
respondent tartly phrased it).

Both board members and legislators interviewed were asked to
describe the channels by which the state board "usually" communicated its positions and recommendations to the legislature. The discrepancy in perceptions between the two groups was quite marked.
State board members were more likely to see definite channels of
communication than the legislative leaders were. Indeed, almost one-
third of the latter did not recognize that the state board communicated with the legislature at all. Despite the fact that they typically
reported contacts with the CSSO or other department staff, these
legislator respondents evidently did not see such administrators as
acting for the state board. Perceptions also differed in respect to
board member testimony before legislative committees. Approximately one-half of the board officials indicated that this was a customary means of communication. Yet, of the legislators who recalled
board members testifying (only 19 percent), most stated their recollections with a qualification like "rarely" or "only occasionally."

There was an even greater disparity in perceptions concerning the
extent and impact of individual board member contacts with legislators. State board officials tended to identify such contacts as the
principal way to influence legislators. Of the forty-four board

members (61 percent of the total) who claimed to have "any means" of legislative influence, exactly half suggested "personal persuasion" as being among those means. (No other influence technique was named more than eight times, and the one receiving eight mentions was for the state board to work through the CSSO.) On the other hand, when asked specifically if "board members on a personal basis ever attempted to persuade you regarding their legislative concerns and recommendations," 57 percent of the legislative leaders replied "no," implying that they had never been so contacted. Of those that answered "yes," nearly all (some 90 percent) singled out only one or at most two board members as having done this, rather than specifying most members or the state board as a body. Legislative respondents also intimated that board member efforts at persuasion did not take place often, language such as "seldom" or "rarely" being used to characterize such efforts.

Because we expected state board officials to have more person-to-person communications with education committee chairmen and the ranking minority members of these committees than with other legislative leaders, we calculated a separate frequency distribution for this group of respondents. But, while we found some differences by state between all legislators interviewed and just those serving on the education committees, the overall percentage totals were quite similar. More exactly, 54 percent of the legislators serving on education committees reported no board member contact on a personal basis, as against 57 percent of all legislators responding.

Besides this attempt to question participants about channels of communication and means of influence between state boards and legislative leaders, there was also some effort to examine the perceptions of policy actors external to this relationship by approaching the leaders of the four major state-level educational interest groups—the state teachers' association (NEA affiliate), the state teachers' union (AFT affiliate), the state school boards association, and the state administrators' association. While they are hardly disinterested observers, these persons are probably less involved than, say, state department officials or members of the governors' staffs, and they understand the workings of the legislature. Spokesmen for the educational interest groups were asked whether "the state board ever takes the lead in promoting education legislation." Their responses are summarized in the second column of Table II-3.

Of the thirty-six interest group assessments reflected in Table II-3, twenty-five (69 percent) are negative regarding the legislative influence of state boards. There is considerable similarity between these perceptions and those of the legislative leaders. The state boards in New York, Texas, and Michigan are near the top in both, and those in Nebraska, Tennessee, and California are at the bottom. Marked discrepancies occur only in Minnesota and Georgia.

Relationships with the governor. There are, of course, other ways to influence state legislatures besides establishing direct relationships with the members. Indeed, in most states the crucial access point to the legislative process is probably the governor's office, a fact that has become increasingly true when deciding educational policies in recent years. But the state boards in our sample were no more likely to sit on the "inner councils of the mighty" in the office of the governor than they were in the legislature.

Only 51 percent of the board members interviewed believed that their state board had any sort of "direct working relationship with the governor or his staff." And many of these even made it clear, in elaborating on this relationship, that governor-state board contacts were infrequent and largely formal. The CSSO and his staff undertook most of the communications. In only four states—Colorado, Michigan, Texas, and Georgia—did a majority of the board members mention personal contacts with the governor or his staff.

Persons in the governor's office, including the governor himself in six states, were asked to compare state board members with other individuals as "a source of ideas and advice for the governor's office" (again, see Table II-3, the third column). Just 38 percent considered board officials to be an "important source," while 62 percent considered them either a "minor source" (48 percent) or "not at all important as a source" (14 percent). In only four states—Colorado, Texas, Minnesota, and Tennessee—did a majority of the respondents say that the state board was important for its ideas and advice.

Although more than one-third of those we interviewed in the governor's office attributed significance to state board proposals, none singled out a board official as being among the governor's confidants in determining education policy. And, with few exceptions, neither did board member respondents. Some 38 percent did think that they had some influence with the governor—personal contacts and party standing being referred to most frequently. Yet only 13 percent (nine of sixty-nine respondents) saw either themselves or any of their colleagues as having a close advisory relationship with the chief executive. There was some congruence between these perceptions and those held by the governor or his staff. In particular, the state boards in Colorado, Minnesota, and Tennessee were judged by both groups of respondents as having influence in the governor's office.

School finance policy. Of the education issues resolved in the legislative arena, the most fundamental involves raising and allocating revenue for the public schools. In each of the EGP states the process of determining school finance policy was investigated.[11] The major concern was not the substance of the decision; it was to identify influential participants. One important finding from this analysis was that state boards of education were on the periphery of school finance decisions.

Typically, the state board did adopt a position on the school finance issue confronting the legislature, a position communicated by such means as formal resolutions or budget requests. Beyond taking a position, however, most boards did little. Neither policy-making participants nor informed observers gave any weight to board activity in the process through which school finance decisions were enacted. And investigators could find little evidence that most state boards even sought to exert influence by, for example, trying to mobilize supporters or arousing the public.

There were some notable exceptions to the description presented above. The Nebraska State Board of Education was so factionalized that its members found it impossible even to arrive at a common position on the school finance dispute that erupted in 1972 between the legislature and the governor. Conversely, the New York Board of Regents not only made fiscal "pronouncements," but they also gave them wide public visibility and legislative impetus through SDE-developed proposals. Although a number of legislative respondents from New York denounced these pronouncements as "unrealistic," they did take them seriously. Another illustration of a state board's attempt to exert influence on the school finance issue can be found in Texas. The Texas State Board of Education, responding to the Federal District Court's decision in the *Rodriguez* case, declared that it accepted full responsibility for developing an acceptable school finance proposal. The board established a Committee on School Finance that eventually did formulate a long-range plan. While legislative enactment of school finance reform was not forthcoming in 1973, the board had taken an active and visible role.

State Education Agency Arena

Not all state education policy is decided in the legislature or in the governor's office. Broad discretionary authority is normally delegated to the state education agency. Within this agency, it is the state board of education that is legally authorized to set public school policy in such areas as teacher certification, curriculum standards, district organization, educational planning, and federal assistance programs. But whether state boards undertake functions other than formal enactment—whether they participate in initiating new policies, in formulating alternative proposals, or in seeking to activate supporters—is a question that must be answered in assessing their policy-making role. In considering this question, one relationship above all must be examined: that between the state board and the CSSO.

State board-CSSO relationship. The importance of the CSSO in the world of state board members is obvious from responses to many different questions asked in interviews. For example, board member respondents were handed a list of nine categories of persons and asked to indicate whether each was "very important," "important," or "unimportant" in helping them attain "a perspective on state education policy issues." Although board officials were prone to assign some significance to nearly all possible influences (except party leaders and noneducator organizations), the distribution of "very important" ratings is revealing. Individuals and groups ranked by percentage of board members (shown in parenthesis) who gave each this rating follows:

Chief state school officer	(74)	Teacher organization	(17)
Other state board members	(50)	Administrator organization	(14)
Local school people	(32)	Political party leaders	(4)
Governor	(28)	Noneducator groups	(2)
Legislator	(25)		

As can be seen, approximately three-quarters of the state board respondents indicated that the CSSO was "very important" in their forming a view on policy issues. It should be added that there was not a single state where this figure was less than 50 percent, and every board member, with one exception, gave the CSSO at least an "important" rating.

Many personal and positional factors contribute to the preeminent status of the chief among board members. Two that are especially germane to policy making are the CSSO's control over both the issues that appear before the state board and the information systematically developed on those issues. In neither case is there total control, but in both it is clearly dominant and probably decisive for state board action on most policy matters.

State boards rely on the chief and other state department personnel to establish meeting agendas. According to board member respondents, their agendas normally are "checked" or approved by the state board chairman, and individual members can add items if they wish. The first appears, however, to be essentially pro forma; the second, infrequent. Three of the state boards studied had instituted procedures or were assigned state department personnel in a way that seemed to give board officials a greater voice in setting the agenda. In New York, in addition to a well-developed committee structure, there was a Secretary of the Board of Regents, a department employee who served as an assistant to the Commissioner for Regents' Affairs. The California State Board of Education had a Special Assistant, also a department employee. And in Michigan each meeting agenda was previewed for the state board at the conclusion of the preceding meeting.

When we asked our board member respondents to identify their "main sources of information" on agenda items, these officials nearly always pointed to the CSSO or another administrator from the department of education. Interviewers were instructed to probe this matter further by asking if respondents had other sources of information that were "sometimes" relied upon or sought out. Nearly half of the board officials (47 percent) indicated that they had no such sources, implying that they were dependent on the chief and his staff for information on agenda items. Of those who did mention an external source, most named either one of the educational interest groups —most frequently the teachers' association—or local school superintendents and school board officials.

In a national survey of local school boards, Zeigler and his associates took as a behavioral indicator of board members' involvement in decision making their willingness on occasion to muster significant opposition to the superintendent about the content of his programs. The scholars reasoned that it would be the superintendent who was likely to advance the policy proposals and that the main function of the school board would be to react (much as Congress reacts to the President's legislative initiatives). They discovered that only about one-quarter of the boards surveyed ever manifested opposition to the superintendent in their reactions to his proposals.[12]

The board members who participated in the present study were questioned about whether there were members of their board who "frequently" opposed the CSSO on major policy issues. Few education officials (19 percent) perceived such opposition on their boards. Only in Michigan and California did most board member respondents identify the presence of an opposition bloc, two or three persons in each case, to the CSSO's policy thrust. Two state board officials in Massachusetts and the same number in Tennessee also said that there was frequent opposition by at least one board member to the chief, but neither their colleagues nor observers corroborated this assessment.

The interview data obtained for this study suggest that most CSSO's were not often challenged by their boards in their approach to major policy issues. The chiefs certainly did not face, with the possible exceptions of the state boards in Michigan and California, anything like the "loyal opposition" that a President or governor could expect to encounter from a legislative body. Still, there was somewhat more state board-CSSO conflict in the ten states than is indicated by these data. For example, in Nebraska, a few years prior to the time of the EGP study, the State Board of Education and the Commissioner of Education engaged in a bitter public dispute that resulted in the Commissioner being dismissed.

While CSSO's and their staffs formulate board meeting agendas, supply nearly all information on agenda items, and encounter little overt resistance from board members, it still is an exaggeration to portray all state boards of education as simply legitimating decisions made elsewhere. Some board members, and some boards, do have a say about the agenda, consult diverse sources of information, and react critically to the policy recommendations of administrators. And, what Friedrich has called the "rule of anticipated reactions"[13] certainly operates in state board-CSSO relationships. That is, what the chief state school officer does in preparing the agenda or developing information is based to some degree on his anticipation of what board members want or need. Such premises of action, since they usually are not articulated, are exceedingly difficult to study. State board respondents were, however, asked to estimate the frequency with which their CSSO took "ideas or suggestions" from board members and formulated them into policy proposals. Less than one-third (29 percent) checked "often," whereas 59 percent replied "sometimes" and 12 percent indicated "rarely" or "never."

A final point that needs to be mentioned here is that some state boards do set definite limits on the policy positions a chief can advocate without jeopardizing his job. Former Commissioner Floyd Miller evidently exceeded these limits in taking positive stands, notably on school district consolidation, in Nebraska, as did former Superintendent Ira Polley in publicly opposing aid to parochial schools in Michigan. Both of these men, partly because of their stands on these issues, found it impossible to remain in office. Yet setting policy constraints of this sort is not the same as giving the chief positive and sustained direction. It has been possible, furthermore, for some CSSO's—for example, California's Max Rafferty in the 1960's—to defy the state board openly and successfully.

Does the state board of education, then, give real direction to the chief state school officer, or does it just formalize his policy recommendations? We directed this very question to the spokesmen for each of the major state-level educational interest groups. Of the thirty-six respondents, twenty-six (72 percent) said they detected no "real direction" on policy issues being given the CSSO by the state board. A majority of the educational interest group respondents in only four states—Texas, New York, Minnesota, and Nebraska— thought that the state board ever offered such direction. Even the two boards with opposition blocs—California and Michigan—were not considered to have much influence over the CSSO. The responses given by the interest group leaders, along with the board members' assessment of the CSSO's taking their ideas and suggestions, are shown in Table II-4.

The last evidence we have that pertains to policy-making relationships between the state board and CSSO comes from the case study investigation of three issue areas: certification, desegregation, and educational program improvement.[14] For reasons discussed at the beginning of this section, the use of decision analysis did not prove

TABLE II-4 Assessments of SBE Influence in the SEA Arena

SBE's by state, according to means of selection	SBE members who said CSSO "often took their ideas or suggestions"		Education lobbyists who said that their SBE "gave real direction" to the CSSO	
	Number[a]	Percent	Number[b]	Percent
Elected by people				
Colorado	4	25	4	25
Michigan	6	50	4	0
Nebraska	5	60	3	67
Texas	11	18	3	100
Appointed by governor				
Massachusetts	7	14	4	0
Minnesota	6	50	4	50
California	7	14	4	0
Georgia	7	29	3	0
Tennessee	8	13	4	0
Elected by legislature				
New York	7	43	3	67
ALL STATES	68	29	36	28

[a]Number of SBE members who responded to the question.

[b]Where a state EIG had two or more respondents, we chose for this rating the one who appeared to be most knowledgeable about the SEA. No state affiliates of the AFT were found in Nebraska, Texas, and Georgia; in New York the NEA and AFT affiliates had merged.

very helpful in illuminating the respective policy roles of the board and chief. As far as could be determined, though state board members often sat on policy-oriented committees or task forces and gave formal approval to the enactment of a major decision, the basic policy-making functions of initiation, formulation, and support mobilization were largely exercised by the CSSO's and their staffs.

It was, in fact, hard to identify, in the ten states and three issue areas, many clear-cut examples of state boards *actively* involved in the performance of policy-making functions other than formal legitimation. Some such involvement might well have been overlooked by EGP researchers, especially when investigating a lengthy and complex decision process. And we do not doubt that "in some cases," in the words of one observer, "the policy recommendation attributed to the CSSO really started as the result of individual board members' personal inputs, research, and digging for alternatives and then working with the CSSO and SDE staff." Also, CSSO's might have taken cues from anticipated, rather than actual, behavior of state boards, and, in this sense, these bodies might have influenced, perhaps significantly, the policy-making activities of their chief administrative officers. Decision analysis, unfortunately, does not easily lend itself to the detection of this sort of influence. The most that can be said here is that a review of the case studies done on each state and discussions with their primary authors did not reveal many decision processes in which the state board's overt actions marked it as the central policy actor or even as sharing that role with the CSSO.

Board leadership, however, was not absent in all of the states. While educational program issues provide some examples, the most significant ones involve school desegregation. The New York Board of Regents has been a pacesetter in this area, its actions dating back to 1962. The Massachusetts State Board of Education, though responding to legislative action (the Racial Imbalance Act of 1965), strongly supported CSSO's favoring desegregation. And the Minnesota State Board of Education assumed a leadership role in developing an effective state-level desegregation policy in the early 1970's.

Review of Findings

This section relies primarily on the perceptions of different actors, augmented by evidence from the examination of specific decisions, to assess the policy-making influence of state boards of education. Findings are restated in terms of state boards in general and board-by-board comparisons.

State boards in general. The ten state boards we studied were not widely viewed as significant actors in the legislative arena:

1. Most legislative leader respondents evaluated their state board as either of minor importance (50 percent) or of no importance at all (22 percent) in "actually formulating and working for education legislation." Only about one-quarter (28 percent) said the board was important in this process. These respondents most frequently identified the legislative weakness of state boards as resulting from their apolitical traditions, lack of visibility to lawmakers, absence of political "clout," and dependence on the CSSO.

2. Nearly 70 percent of the spokesmen for the four major state-level educational interest groups did not perceive the state board of education in their state as "ever taking the lead" in promoting education legislation.

3. Less than two-thirds (61 percent) of the board member interviewees, themselves, believed that they had "any means of influence" with the legislature, with half of the respondents indicating personal contacts ("persuasion") as these means. But 57 percent of the legislative leaders could recall no such contact with board members. Those legislators who did give an affirmative reply usually indicated only one or two members doing this, and on only a few occasions.

4. Just half (51 percent) of the board members we interviewed saw their state board as having any sort of "direct working relationship with the governor or his staff." And only nine of the sixty-nine interviewees (13 percent) considered either themselves or any of their colleagues as having a close advisory relationship with the chief executive.

5. None of the persons interviewed from the governor's office felt that board members were on the inner council of gubernatorial advisers. While 38 percent of these respondents perceived their state board, compared to other individuals and groups, as being an "important source of ideas and advice for the governor's office," 62 percent assessed this body as being either a "minor source" (48 percent) or "not at all important as a source" (14 percent).

6. Our investigation of school finance policy making in each state revealed that state boards typically were marginal participants. They usually took a position on the issue and communicated it by some formal means to the legislature. Beyond these actions, state boards did little. In only a few cases did we find any evidence of the state board working with the governor or legislative leaders in this area.

Because of their constitutional or statutory authority, or both, the state boards we studied were clearly more influential regarding school policies established by the state education agency than those determined in the legislative arena. Nonetheless, the dominant influence in the process by which the state education agency decided policy for the public schools appeared to be the CSSO:

1. Three out of four board member respondents (74 percent) indicated that the CSSO was "very important" in their developing "a perspective on state education policy issues."

2. Agenda-setting for state board meetings was a function per-

formed almost entirely by the CSSO and his staff. Virtually all board members pointed to these administrators as their primary source of information on agenda items; indeed, some 47 percent suggested by their replies that they had no other source which they "sometimes" turned to or relied upon.

3. Most board member respondents (81 percent) did not perceive any frequent opposition to the CSSO on their boards. In only two states did a majority indicate the presence of a continuing opposition bloc.

4. While the policy-making behavior of CSSO's no doubt reflected to some extent their anticipation of the wants and needs of state boards, less than one-third (29 percent) of the board member respondents checked the category "often" when asked how frequently the CSSO took "ideas and suggestions" from board officials. Some 59 percent replied "sometimes" and 12 percent indicated "rarely" or "never."

5. Just over 70 percent of the spokesmen for the major state-level educational interest groups said that they perceived no "real direction" on policy issues being given the CSSO by the state board.

6. Our investigation of policies made by state education agencies in the areas of certification, desegregation, and educational program improvement did not reveal many decision processes in which the overt action of the state board marked it as the central policy actor or even as sharing that role with the CSSO. Though board members often sat on policy-oriented committees and special task forces—and were required to give their approval at various stages in the enactment process, including legitimation of the final decision—the policy-making functions of initiation, formulation, and support mobilization were largely performed by the CSSO and state department administrators.

Board-by-board comparison. To summarize board-by-board variation in policy-making influence, as well as to prepare for the analysis section of this chapter, subjective procedures were used to quantify and combine a number of state board characteristics that have been described into an index of legislative influence, and an index of state education agency influence.[15] Then, by adding their scores, a composite index of policy-making influence was developed. (Scoring procedures are described in Appendix A.)

Rank orders of the ten state boards on each index and on the composite measure are contained in Table II-5. Based on our data and

TABLE II-5 Rank Orders of SBE's on the Dimensions of
Legislative Influence, SEA Influence, and
Overall Policy-Making Influence

Influence in the legislative arena		Influence in the SEA arena		Overall policy-making influence	
State	Rank	State	Rank	State	Rank
Texas	1	Minnesota	1	Texas	1
New York	2	New York	2[a]	New York	2
Colorado	3	Texas	2[a]	Minnesota	3
Michigan	4[a]	Nebraska	4	Colorado	4
Minnesota	4[a]	Colorado	5	Michigan	5
Georgia	4[a]	Michigan	6	Nebraska	6
Tennessee	7	California	7	Georgia	7
Massachusetts	8	Tennessee	8[a]	Tennessee	8
California	9	Massachusetts	8[a]	Massachusetts	9
Nebraska	10	Georgia	10	California	10

[a]A tie in the rankings.

scoring procedures, we would judge that Texas, New York, and Minnesota had, overall, the most influential state boards in their respective policy systems at the time of our study. Though our case study of education policy making in New York did indicate that the power of the Board of Regents has probably diminished somewhat in recent years, it still was near the top of the ten states. As for Texas and Minnesota, their state boards had come to be seen as influential only in the early 1970's, with the former seizing the opportunity (and responsibility) afforded by the *Rodriguez* decision and the latter exhibiting leadership in trying to desegregate the schools of the state. Somewhat below these three came the state boards in Colorado and Michigan, both of which received above average scores on our measures. Then came the Nebraska State Board of Education, a body that was widely, albeit not always positively, seen as being directive in its relationships with the CSSO, but as having no impact at all in the legislature. The remaining four state boards—Georgia, Tennessee, Massachusetts, and California—received many negative assessments on their policy-making influence in both arenas, though the Georgia board was viewed rather positively by legislative leaders.

The policy-making influence of a state board is, of course, a relative matter. Its scope and strength depend largely on the power, interests, and skill of the other actors in state education policy systems. In California and Massachusetts, for example, it is quite clear that the presence of a powerful and assertive legislature narrowly constrains the role that the state board can play. Even so, the policy-making resources accessible to a state board, along with the willingness of its members to apply these resources, are factors that affect state board influence.

POLICY-MAKING RESOURCES

Potential for policy influence is contingent on access to resources, resources that can be drawn upon to command, persuade, or bargain in the decision process. This section examines the access of state boards to six kinds of resources: authority, time, information, cohesion, prestige, and votes.

Authority

Constitutional and statutory language setting forth the powers of state boards of education is extensive and specific in some states, brief and general in others. Yet the fact that these institutions are intended to be education policy makers can be concluded from the language in nearly all ten states being studied. In Texas, for example, the state board is authorized to be the "policy-forming and planning body for the public school system of the state." The broad charge to this body in Michigan is that it provide "leadership and general supervision over all public education . . . except . . . institutions of higher education," while in Nebraska the Board of Education is called upon to be the "policy forming, planning and evaluative body for the state school program."[16] It must be pointed out, however, that the policy-making authority of a state board, no matter how extensive it appears, always exists in the legal shadow cast by the state legislature.

Despite the fact that seven of the ten state boards studied here— Massachusetts, Minnesota, and Tennessee are the exceptions—were constitutionally established, most of their formal power, as well as the policy areas actually open to them, depends on legislative action. (Even the powerful Board of Regents is not independent of legislative authority since the constitution of New York stipulates that it "shall be governed and its corporate powers may be increased, modified, or diminished by the legislature. . . .")[17] Legislatures and the governors make all the tax decisions, establish the level of school appropriations, decide the essential features of the state aid distribution formula, and enact countless other laws pertaining to the public schools.

While the authority of state boards is constrained, sometimes narrowly, by constitutional and statutory provisions, these bodies are charged with exercising general supervision over elementary-secondary education, and they are usually delegated broad discretionary powers to undertake this basic responsibility. These powers are such that state boards of education can appropriately be seen as setting, as well as implementing, public school policy in such areas as professional certification, district organization, pupil assignments, education standards, school sites and buildings, and federal assistance programs.

Comparing the legal powers vested in state boards with those assigned to CSSO's makes it clear that it is the boards that have the principal authority for state governance of elementary and secondary education. An examination of constitutional and statutory language by an EGP researcher indicated that only in California is there any marked deviation from the prevailing legal pattern whereby the chief is largely dependent on state board authorization for his power to govern the schools.[18]

In seven of the ten EGP states, the CSSO attains his position as a result of state board appointment and serves either for a fixed term or at the pleasure of this body. But in three states—California, Georgia, and Tennessee—the selection of the chief occurs independently of the state board, which gives the board no formal control over this administrator. In some states, moreover, the appointment of upper-echelon personnel in the department of education, apart from the CSSO, does not require the approval of the state board. In six of the ten EGP states the state board approves the appointment of all persons to positions on the deputy or assistant commissioner level, but this is not so for some positions at this level in the other four states.

A final component of state board authority that merits discussion has to do with its institutional scope. Only one of the ten boards—the New York Board of Regents—is comprehensive in scope and has overall supervision of education in that state from prekindergarten to postgraduate programs.[19] Nine of the other state boards are responsible for vocational education as well as elementary-secondary education. Only Colorado's state board does not have authority over vocational education. And the state boards in Minnesota and California must share some of their authority in the teacher certification area with semi-independent commissions.

Time

Of the resources available to a public official, time is among the most crucial. Investing time, coupled with some skill, can often extend a policy makers' influence over an issue. State board member respondents were asked about the time they gave "to the work of being a board member." A majority on the state boards in Nebraska, Massachusetts, and Tennessee indicated they spent only two or three days per month. Four to six days per month was the modal response from officials in Texas and Minnesota. Most of the respondents from Colorado, Michigan, California, Georgia, and New York answered that they gave the equivalent of at least one week each month to state board duties.

Inspection of state board agendas indicated that a substantial portion of each involves the formal approval of routine matters. To quantify this, the board members interviewed were asked to estimate the amount of meeting time their boards devoted to the "legal approval of routine items." Of those questioned, 46 percent said that such action consumed about one-quarter of their board's meeting time; 26 percent estimated the time expenditure at one-half; 8 percent thought it to be as high as three-quarters. Nearly 20 percent, on the other hand, checked "almost none" in reply to this question.

The state board spending the least time on routine matters, according to board member estimates, is the New York Board of Regents. Seven of the nine persons interviewed from this body said that the Regents spent almost no time in their regular meetings on such matters, and the remaining persons perceived about one-quarter of the meetings being used in this fashion. At the other extreme, five of the California board member respondents checked the one-quarter category in answering this question: three said one-half; and two claimed that the figure was closer to three-quarters.

Information

That information is central to policy-making influence is obvious. Many analysts would support Iannaccone's contention that:

the control of information and its quantity at points of access to the legislative process are extremely important sources of influence in the modern legislature. By having data on this dimension alone, a researcher who had no other might pinpoint more accurately the sources of influence over the sources of legislation than he would with any other data.[20]

Since state boards of education, like legislatures, need information, it becomes important to identify individuals or groups to whom board members frequently turn for information and to assess the quality of the information they receive.

The board members interviewed were first asked to name their "main sources of information" for agenda items. In virtually all cases, as was noted earlier, the first person named was either the CSSO or another department administrator. If the respondent stopped at this point, interviewers were instructed to probe to see if the board member would identify "other sources of information that you sometimes rely upon or seek out." The replies that state board members made to these questions are shown in Table II-6.

Two points bear emphasis from the data presented in this table. The first is that nearly half (47 percent) of the board members indicated no source of information on agenda items other than the chief or the department. The second is that, when outside sources were cited, they usually were educators or persons, like local school board members, who were closely identified with education. The types of groups most frequently named were:

Type of group	SBE respondents who named groups	
	(number)	(percent)
Local school people (superintendent/board members)	20	27
State-level educational interest groups (unspecified)	8	11
State teachers' association	8	11
University spokesmen	5	7
School boards' (local) association	4	5
Local citizens	3	4
Media	3	4
Legislators or governor's office	3	4
Noneducator groups	3	4

TABLE II-6 SBE Members' Identification of Groups, Other Than SDE, on Which They Relied for Information on Agenda Items (N = number of SBE members responding)

SBE's by state, according to means of selection	Teachers' association	Teachers' union	Administrators' association	School boards' association	Educational groups (unspecified)	Local school people	University spokesmen	SBE advisory committee	Other SBE members	Noneducator interest groups	Legislators or governor's office	Media	Nonpartisan research group	Local citizens	No source other than CSSO–SDE Number	Percent
Elected by people																
Colorado (N = 4)	1			1		2		1			1			1	1	25
Michigan (N = 6)					2										3	50
Nebraska (N = 5)					1	2					1				3	60
Texas (N = 11)	2					4	1		1	1					6	55
Appointed by governor																
Massachusetts (N = 7)						4	2			1	1		1	1	1	14
Minnesota (N = 6)	2		1	2	1										3	50
California (N = 10)					2	1	1		1	1		1			5	50
Georgia (N = 7)						5	1							1	1	14
Tennessee (N = 8)	2			1		2									5	63
Elected by legislature																
New York (N = 9)	1				2							2			6	67
ALL STATES (N = 73)	8	0	1	4	8	20	5	1	2	3	3	3	1	3	34	47

The heavy reliance by state board members on information supplied by the CSSO and the state department was not matched by a uniformly high assessment of its quality by board member respondents. Only one-third of those interviewed saw state department information as "almost always" meeting their needs. Slightly less than half (46 percent) felt that this information "usually" met their needs. More critical were the board members (19 percent) who checked the response "sometimes meets your needs" in answering the information-assessment question. Still, only one board member interviewed maintained that state department information was "almost never" satisfactory. There was considerable state-by-state variation ranging from New York, where 56 percent of the Regents interviewed checked the highest category of satisfaction, to Nebraska, where 60 percent of the respondents assessed state department information as being only sometimes responsive to their needs.

Cohesion

The board members interviewed were questioned about the extent of agreement on their state board when it confronted a major policy issue. Specifically, these officials were asked to indicate which of the following statements best characterized their board's decision behavior:

Board is harmonious, little serious disagreement.

Board is usually in agreement, but there are board members who sometimes dissent.

Board often is divided, but the lines of division depend on the issue that is confronting the board.

Board tends to divide into rival factions, but there is a clear working majority on the board.

Board tends to divide into rival factions of nearly equal strength.

Nearly 60 percent checked one of the first two alternatives, suggesting that their boards were basically consensual in dealing with policy issues. A pluralist pattern—issue-by-issue division—was perceived by one-third of the board members interviewed, and just six (8 percent) characterized their boards as being factional in policy-making behavior.

Many factors combine to encourage agreement among state board members: they are quite homogeneous in social background; they do not typically have political constituencies; they pay great heed to expertise; and they operate largely from a common information base. In addition, many, perhaps most, of the items on the meeting agendas of state boards of education are routine in nature and not apt to spark controversy. Lastly, there are informal norms on most boards that discourage "special interest" representation and favor acting collectively for "the entire state."[21]

A consensual decision-making style does enable a state board to move expeditiously through crowded agendas in a manner that reduces controversy and vulnerability to external groups. It also permits a state board to act in a unified manner in advancing a policy proposal in the legislature. The state boards in the EGP sample that were most divided—Nebraska, California, and Michigan—were perceived by several lawmakers as being hampered by disunity in effectively advocating a board position on education legislation. While in some ways it is an influence resource, stress on internal cohesion and on consensual decision-making style is not without shortcomings. Such a style, because it seeks to avoid or suppress conflict, does not encourage the generation or searching examination of different policy alternatives, at least at the board level. It is not, therefore, as conducive to board member control as it is to bureaucratic control of policy making.[22]

Prestige

A number of the factors that have been discussed—the historic origins of state boards, the legal authority delegated to these bodies, and the ability of state boards to pursue goals in a cohesive fashion— are relevant to a more generalized influence resource, a resource that might be termed "prestige." This concept is hard to pin down with any great precision, and it refers here to the capacity to evoke respect. Those who possess this resource are believed to have certain stable personal or institutional qualities—for example, impartiality, wisdom, tradition, or social distinction—that transcend specific issues and influence the opinions of many people.[23]

Of the ten state boards studied, the New York Board of Regents, albeit "cracks are appearing in the pedestal," was undoubtedly the most prestigious. Nearly two centuries old (founded in 1784), it was constitutionally established as an independent body with a comprehensive sweep of authority, and some of the most distinguished citizens in New York have served on it. Even state lawmakers sharply critical of the Regents for their school finance pronouncements and their controversial efforts in school desegregation acknowledged that the institution had a stature, as well as legal powers, that made it a force to be reckoned with. In the words of one legislator, the Regents "are important for who they are rather than what they do."

Most of the other state boards studied were also perceived by policy actors in their states as "having status" though not usually as having power. The social background of the board members probably contributed to this image. Board officials among our respondents were typically white (94 percent), male (75 percent), and middle aged (84 percent were forty-one years of age or older). Most were to be found in business or the professions (70 percent). They were affluent (51 percent earned more than $30,000 annually) and well educated (92 percent were college graduates; 58 percent held an advanced degree). In this connection, it might also be pointed out that 47 percent had had experience as professional educators.[24]

Turning back to the prestige of the state boards, four—Texas, Georgia, Minnesota, and Massachusetts—were almost uniformly seen by different respondents as possessing that resource. Four other state boards—California, Michigan, Colorado, and Tennessee—were widely perceived as being prestigious institutions, but there was an undercurrent of negative comment. The well-publicized forays of the California State Board of Education into "creation" politics were ridiculed by more than a few respondents, and several in Michigan condemned the board recruitment process in that state for partisanship. The appellation "rubber stamp" was applied with some frequency to the policy-making function of state boards in both Colorado and Tennessee, even though respondents in each state argued that changes in the early 1970's presaged a more assertive role for the state board. As for the Nebraska State Board of Education, many of those interviewed saw it as being the victim of, among other things, a debilitating factionalism.

Votes

Whether interest groups can effectively bring electoral sanctions to bear on lawmakers is doubted by some analysts, who cite various reasons why such groups find it difficult to convert their resources into votes. Yet interviews with political leaders showed that the

electoral strength ascribed to a group was viewed as a critical factor
in terms of having "clout" with the legislature. State education policy making has, furthermore, become highly politicized as a result of
the growing assertiveness of governors and legislatures, the emergence
of "teacher power," and the widening controversy over school
finance. Such politicization can only make the capacity to mobilize
constituents an increasingly potent resource in arenas like the state
legislature.

How much political muscle of the sort described above is commanded by state boards of education as a means of influencing legislative policy making for the public schools? The answer to this question is "almost none." Any state board in the sample studied here,
whether elected or appointed, would have been hard pressed, on the
basis of its "low profile" recruitment process, to claim that it spoke
for some broad constituency, let alone that it had powerful sources
of external support. Outside, perhaps, of the New York Board of
Regents, there was little effort to focus or to heighten public expectations for legislative performance regarding the schools, expectations that might have translated into votes when legislators had to
stand for election.

Review of Findings

The overall situation of state boards with respect to policy-making
resources is a curious mixture of strengths and weaknesses, with the
latter being clearly the more pronounced for most of these bodies.
True, state boards have been delegated considerable legal authority
to set education policy for elementary-secondary schools. But it is
the legislature—the "big school board"—that enacts the laws and
determines all basic fiscal policy. State boards of education do not
have the financial independence (that is, the taxing authority) of
most of their local counterparts. As a result, state boards do not have
direct access to monetary resources. To obtain these resources for
their agency and its programs, or for the public schools of the state,
board officials must have the capacity to influence state lawmakers.[25] For the ten state boards examined here, this capacity as measured by such resources as time, information, cohesion, prestige, and
votes was not impressive, though significant variation by both resource and state did exist.

The board members studied were part-time officeholders (most
devoted less than the equivalent of a week per month), and much of

their time in board service was spent on functions other than policy making. They were heavily dependent on state department administrators for data on agenda items. To the limited degree that they relied upon other sources (only 53 percent indicated any such a reliance, however meager), board members were most likely to turn to educators, or their allies, for information and advice. Some state boards of education were seen as cohesive and prestigious bodies; others as deficient in both of these resources. None of the state boards had developed much capacity to arouse or mobilize voter sentiment regarding legislative policy making for the public schools, which meant they were without "clout," a resource reported to be much respected by constituency-oriented legislators.

The rankings ascribed to the ten state boards of education on the influence resources where substantial differences among these bodies could be discerned are presented in Table II-7. It must be reiterated that our indexes are always relative and, for the most part, judgmental. Certainly they do not measure the resource capability of a state board on any absolute scale. (Scoring procedures are described in Appendix A.)

POLICY-MAKING EXPECTATIONS

The possession of resources, irrespective of type, is not the same as actual influence in policy making. Resources are always necessary for such influence, but, in themselves, they are not sufficient. Much depends on the intention of the actors to whom the means of influence are available. How willing are state boards of education to use their resources to play an active part in the determination of education policy? In order that data relevant to this question could be gathered, board members were asked to indicate their agreement or disagreement with statements measuring their sense of policy-making efficacy and their expectations for the policy-making role of both state boards and CSSO's.

Sense of Policy-Making Efficacy

"Sense of policy-making efficacy" is a gross index of motivation.[26] The assumption is that a public official who believes he can both understand the issues confronting him and act effectively upon them is more likely to seek an active policy-making role than one who has reservations about such matters. The three questionnaire items we

TABLE II-7 Rankings of SBE's on Six Influence Resource Dimensions

| SBE's by state, according to means of selection | Legal authority | Time | | Information utility | Cohesion | Prestige |
		Given by SBE members	Policy emphasis			
Elected by people						
Colorado	4	4	7.5	3	2.5	7.5
Michigan	4	1	4.5	5	8	7.5
Nebraska	2	9	9	10	10	10
Texas	4	6	2	4	5	3.5
Appointed by governor						
Massachusetts	6	8	6	8	1	3.5
Minnesota	7	7	4.5	6	2.5	3.5
California	9.5	5	10	7	9	7.5
Georgia	8	2.5	3	2	6	3.5
Tennessee	9.5	10	7.5	9	4	7.5
Elected by legislature						
New York	1	2.5	1	1	7	1

employed, the replies indicating a sense of efficacy, and the percentage of board members who replied—all are reported in Table II-8. For comparative purposes, the responses of legislative leaders who completed the questionnaire are also shown.

TABLE II-8 SBE Respondents Compared with Legislative Leader Respondents on Their Sense of Policy-Making Efficacy (N = number responding)

Attitude statement	Item response indicating sense of efficacy	Percentages indicating sense of efficacy	
		State board members (N = 64)	Legislative leaders (N = 74)
"Many educational issues are so complicated that a policy maker cannot really make wise decisions."	Disagree	73	72
"There is much that a public official in my position can do to initiate new policy ideas for education."	Agree	83	81
"A public official in my position really does not have the time to study the consequences of policy decisions he made, say, four or five years ago."	Disagree	77	76

Almost equal proportions of both groups (board officials, 73 percent; legislators, 72 percent) eschewed the notion that educational issues were too complicated for them to understand. And 83 percent and 81 percent, respectively, expressed the belief that a person in their position could take a major initiating role in education policy making. Variation between the two groups on whether a public official lacked the time to study the consequences of his decisions was equally nonexistent (77 percent of the board members and 76 percent of the legislative leaders rejected this contention).

Role Expectations

A sense of efficacy in policy making may motivate a public official to seek involvement in that process, but the behavioral content of this involvement will also be shaped by the official's expectations for relationships with other policy actors, as well as by their expectations for his role.[27] Such policy role expectations were examined through several different sets of items, some contained in our questionnaire and others completed during an interview. Five of the questionnaire items, the replies indicating a state board policy role, and the percentages of both board member and legislator respondents who replied are contained in Table II-9.

It is understandable that legislator respondents did not take quite as positive a view of the state board's policy role as board member respondents. Yet, on each item most lawmakers did concur with such a role and on one—the state board's developing proposals for the legislature—a slightly higher percentage of legislative leaders (76 percent) agreed with this prescription than did board members (70 percent). Legislator respondents, however, indicated less agreement than board member respondents on the legislature "limiting itself to broad goals" (62, as against 95, percent), on state board views being "taken into account by the governor" (95, as against 100, percent), on the CSSO being supervised by the state board (78, as against 90, percent); and on rejecting, as its "major function," the state board's granting approval to CSSO-developed proposals (55, as against 69, percent).

The major difference between these two groups of respondents was over the distribution of education policy-making authority between legislature and state board. Even though a majority of both favored having the legislature establish "broad goals for the public schools," the gap between the two groups was a substantial 33 percentage points. And on a state-by-state basis, not shown in Table II-9, the difference was particularly wide in Michigan (86 percentage points), Colorado (50 percentage points), Nebraska (50 percentage points), and California (40 percentage points). At least half of the legislative leader respondents from each of these states indicated that the legislature should retain the authority to act as the "big school board" for elementary-secondary education and not confine itself to setting general goals.

If the role conceptions that state board members hold for themselves help shape their policy-making activities, the expectations of these officials for the role of the CSSO are probably more crucial in determining the actual policy involvement of both boards and chiefs. This is so because the potentially dominant figure in the state board

TABLE II-9 SBE Respondents Compared with Legislative Leader
Respondents on Their Policy Role Expectations for
SBE's (N = number responding)

	Item response indicating SBE policy role	Percentage indicating SBE policy role	
		State board members (N = 64)	Legislative leaders (N = 74)
Attitude statement			
"The Legislature should limit itself to determining broad goals for the public schools and leave most policy-making authority to the state board or state superintendent (commissioner)."	Agree	95	62
"The views of the state board of education should be taken into account by the governor in his major proposals for education legislation."	Agree	100	95
"The responsibility of the state board of education should include supervision over the activities of the state superintendent (commissioner)."	Agree	90	78
"The most important task for the state board of education should be to develop major policy proposals for the legislature to consider."	Agree	70	76
"The major function of the state board of education should be to approve programs developed by the state superintendent (commissioner) and his staff."	Disagree	69	55

arena is the CSSO. Notwithstanding his formal subordination to the
state board in most states, the CSSO's full-time commitment to his
position, acknowledged status as an educational expert, access to the
resources of a large state agency, and control of policy-relevant data

give him a powerful position vis-à-vis the state board. If the board concedes policy initiation, formulation, and leadership to the chief, retaining for itself only advisory and approval functions, then that administrator has the resources and sometimes the interest to relegate the state board to little more than a symbolic entity.

To examine the policy role expectations held by state boards and CSSO's for the latter's position, a number of agree-disagree items were included in the interviews. Eight of these items and the replies indicating a policy role for the chief are listed below:

Attitude statement	*Response indicating CSSO policy role*
"A state superintendent (commissioner) should assume leadership in shaping the policies enacted by the state board of education."	Agree
"A state superintendent (commissioner) should maintain a neutral stand on education policy issues that are very controversial among the citizens of his state."	Disagree
"A state superintendent (commissioner) should actively seek to influence legislative leaders with regard to education policies."	Agree
"A state superintendent (commissioner) should work to have people he respects become members of the state board of education."	Agree
"A state superintendent (commissioner) should administer the state department of education and leave education policy matters to other state officials."	Disagree
"A state superintendent (commissioner) should actively work with party leaders in order to attain education policy goals."	Agree
"A state superintendent (commissioner) should take a policy position in which he believes even when most professional educators may be hostile."	Agree

"A state superintendent (commissioner)   Agree
should be the principal advocate of major
changes in state education policy."

Data on the policy role expectations for CSSO's are presented in
Table II-10. It is obvious from the data that state board members
emphatically rejected the policy-administration dichotomy and
wanted their chief to be a central policy participant. An overwhelming majority of respondents indicated that this administrator should
take policy positions even in the face of educator hostility (93 percent), actively seek to influence legislative leaders (89 percent),
assume leadership in shaping state board policies (87 percent), voice
positive policy stands on highly controversial issues (83 percent), and
be "the principal advocate" of major education policy changes (80
percent). Some two-thirds of the board members interviewed (67
percent) rejected the contention that the CSSO should manage the
state department and leave education policy matters to other officials. Well more than half (61 percent) believed that the chiefs' policy-making participation should extend to working with party leaders. Only with respect to board member recruitment itself did most
of our respondents prescribe a narrow role for the chief state school
officer. And, even on this item, a surprising 27 percent expressed a
preference for CSSO involvement.

Review of Findings

Whatever the factors that constrain the policy-making involvement
of state boards of education, a feeling of futility about this involvement does not seem to be among them. Our state board respondents
were every bit as likely as the legislative leaders who were interviewed to exhibit a strong "sense of policy-making efficacy," at least
as we operationalized the concept. The great majority of both groups
(more than 70 percent for each item making up the index) said, in
effect, that educational issues are understandable, that time is available to study the consequences of prior decisions, and that public
officials in their positions can do much to initiate new policies.

Most board member respondents also held policy role expectations
for the state board. Specifically, they replied it should exercise quasi-
legislative authority (95 percent), give advice to the governor (100

TABLE II-10 SBE Member Expectations for the Policy Role of CSSO's, in percentages (N = number of SBE members responding)

SBE's by state, according to means of selection		Leadership for SBE (Agreed)	"Neutral" on educational matters (Disagreed)	Influence legislators (Agreed)	Work to recruit SBE members (Agreed)	Leave policy matters to other officials (Disagreed)	Work with party leaders (Agreed)	Position in opposition to educators (Agreed)	Advocate of major changes (Agreed)
Elected by people									
Colorado	(N = 4)	100	100	75	0	75	25	78	50
Michigan	(N = 6)	83	100	100	50	67	67	100	100
Nebraska	(N = 5)	100	60	80	40	80	80	100	100
Texas	(N = 10)	80	50	50	10	50	10	90	90
Appointed by governor									
Massachusetts	(N = 7)	100	86	100	14	86	71	100	100
Minnesota	(N = 6)	83	83	100	50	83	17	100	67
California	(N = 9)	78	100	100	25	78	78	89	44
Georgia	(N = 7)	71	86	86	14	57	71	71	71
Tennessee	(N = 8)	100	87	100	63	75	100	100	100
Elected by legislature									
New York	(N = 9)	89	89	100	11	37	78	100	78
ALL STATES	(N = 71)	87	83	89	27	67	61	93	80

percent), supervise the CSSO (90 percent), formulate legislative proposals (70 percent), and reject as "the major board function" the legitimating of CSSO-developed programs (69 percent). A majority of legislators interviewed also subscribed to these role prescriptions, albeit they generally did not agree with them as strongly, notably when the authority of the legislature to set education policy was in question.

But while most board officials in our study said they wanted to be policy makers and indicated they felt efficacious in that role, their conception of the policy functions of the CSSO was so expansive as to raise doubt about just what functions, other than advice and approval, state boards themselves were willing to undertake. State board members advanced a set of expectations for the CSSO which cast that administrator as the key innovator, formulator, advocate, and influential in education policy making. One wonders whether other governmental bodies envisage such a sweeping policy role for their administrative officers.[28]

Just as with influence resources, the ten state boards can be ranked according to the attitude and expectations measures described in this section, and the rankings appear in Table II-11. There

TABLE II-11 Rank Orders of SBE's on "Sense of Policy-Making Efficacy" and on Policy Role Expectations for the SBE and CSSO[a]

Sense of policy-making efficacy		SBE's policy role		CSSO's policy role	
Colorado	1[b]	Colorado	1	Tennessee	1
Michigan	1[b]	New York	2	Michigan	2
Tennessee	3	Texas	3[b]	Massachusetts	3
Minnesota	4	Nebraska	3[b]	Nebraska	4
Massachusetts	5	California	5	California	5
New York	6	Massachusetts	6	Minnesota	6[b]
Nebraska	7	Minnesota	7	New York	6[b]
California	8	Tennessee	8	Georgia	8
Texas	9	Michigan	9	Colorado	9
Georgia	10	Georgia	10	Texas	10

[a]Scoring procedures are described in Appendix A.
[b]A tie in the rankings.

is little correlation between the rank orders shown in the first two columns—one based on sense of policy-making efficacy, and the other based on an index of state board members' self-role expectations. Significantly, perhaps, there is a moderate inverse relationship between the rank order based on the state board members' self-role expectations and that based on state board members' expectations for the policy role of the CSSO.

CORRELATES OF POLICY-MAKING INFLUENCE

Up to this point, the effort has been largely to describe how the ten state boards of education differed in the influence they were perceived as having in their respective legislative and education agency arenas. There has also been a description of how the state boards differed in their policy-making resources and expectations for role performance. But describing such variations is a far simpler task than explaining them. In the next section there is an attempt to identify some of the major correlates of state board policy-making influence.

Selection Method

Much of the normative literature on state board selection methods assumes that they make an important difference for the kind of member who is recruited and what this person does once in office. Yet the few empirical studies that exist cast doubt upon this assumption.[29] Is selection method related to policy-making influence for our state boards? As a first step toward answering this question, the ten state boards were divided into two ordered categories in terms of their perceived influence: medium and low. (The evidence did not support the label "high influence" being applied to any of the boards.) The state boards in each category are listed below:

Medium influence	Low influence
Texas	Nebraska
New York	Georgia
Minnesota	Tennessee
Colorado	Massachusetts
Michigan	California

Figure II-1 indicates the association between selection method and policy-making influence for the state boards in the sample studied.

	Medium influence	Low influence
Popular election	Texas Colorado Michigan	Nebraska
Gubernatorial appointment	Minnesota	Georgia Tennessee Massachusetts California

FIGURE II-1

Relationship for State Boards between Selection Method and
Policy-Making Influence (New York is not included.)

As can be seen, a disproportionate number of the elected boards are
in the medium category, whereas most of the low-influence boards
are appointed. The statistical association between the two variables,
using the index phi (ϕ), is .55. This means that, relative to the maximum relationship possible between the two variables, the set of data
shown in Figure II-1 represents an association of about 30 percent
(the percentage value of phi squared).[30] But, as our next figure will
show, it is questionable whether this difference between elected and
appointed boards is attributable to formal selection method.

Figure II-2 depicts the association between state boards' formal
control over the CSSO and their policy-making influence. The most
striking thing about this distribution is that all three of the boards
which do not appoint their chiefs are in the low-influence category.
The phi value is .65, which means that some 43 percent of a perfect
relationship between the two variables are represented by the data in
Figure II-2.

Is a state board's legal authority over the CSSO a more critical factor in its policy-making influence than how board members are selected? The data support such an inference. First, the index of association (phi squared) is somewhat higher, 43 percent compared with
30 percent, for the distribution shown in Figure II-2 than for that in
Figure II-1. Second, and more important, the perceived influence of
the appointed state boards that select their CSSO is considerably
higher than the appointed state boards where the CSSO is selected

	Medium influence	Low influence
SBE appoints CSSO	Texas New York Minnesota Colorado Michigan	Nebraska Massachusetts
SBE does not appoint CSSO	(None)	Georgia Tennessee California

FIGURE II-2

Relationship for State Boards between SBE Appointment of the CSSO and Policy-Making Influence

either by the people or by the governor. Indeed, the influence scores subjectively assigned to the former are nearly equal to those of the elected state boards, though there is still a gap in the legislative arena (see Table II-12).

Policy-Making Resources

Access to such resources as authority, time, information, cohesion, and prestige affect the policy-making influence exerted by a state board. Table II-13 shows the relationships between the measures of these resources used in this study and state board influence.

The index of association is rho (r_s). To obtain this for each resource-influence relationship we correlated the variables as sets of rank orders. The value of rho represents the extent of agreement between two sets. A rho of, say, .25 indicates only a slight tendency for the same state boards to have similar rankings on both variables; a rho of .5 indicates a moderate relationship, and a rho of .7 indicates strong agreement between the two rank orders.[31]

Inspection of the rho coefficients in Table II-13 reveals, first, that the legal authority of state boards has a fairly strong association (.66) with policy-making influence. While several of the individual

TABLE II-12 Relationship for SBE's between Three Selection
Models and Policy-Making Influence Scores[a]

Selection model for SBE and CSSO	State	Legislative influence	SEA influence	Overall policy-making influence
SBE is popularly	Colorado	2.7	2.6	5.3
elected; it	Michigan	2.6	2.4	5.0
appoints CSSO	Nebraska	1.1	3.4	4.5
	Texas	4.6	3.6	8.2
	AVERAGE	2.75	3.00	5.75
SBE is appointed;	Massachusetts	2.0	2.0	4.0
it appoints CSSO	Minnesota	2.6	4.0	6.6
	AVERAGE	2.30	3.00	5.30
SBE is appointed;	California	1.7	2.2	3.9
it does not	Georgia	2.6	1.8	4.4
appoint CSSO	Tennessee	2.1	2.0	4.1
	AVERAGE	2.13	2.00	4.13

[a]New York is not included in the analysis.

components of the legal authority index contribute to this relationship, one, the legal control over the state department of education
exercised by its state board, stands out, and the key element appears
to be whether or not the state board appoints the CSSO.

If board member perceptions of their resources are close to reality,
the magnitudes of the rho coefficients in Table II-13 indicate that
the policy-making influence of a state board is strongly related to the
time emphasis given in its meetings to nonroutine matters (rho of
.69) and is moderately related (rho of .56) to the utility of state
department information for board members. Neither the time devoted to board service by individual members, the internal cohesion
of state boards, nor the prestige accorded to these bodies appears to
be a major contributor to state board policy-making influence.

The relative weakness of prestige (rho of .44) as an influence resource is puzzling, especially since so many of those interviewed

TABLE II-13 Relationship for SBE's between Resources,
Expectations, Background Characteristics, and
Policy-Making Influence

Measures	Relationship (rho) with policy-making influence
Resources	
Legal authority	.66
Time devoted by SBE members	.29
Emphasis in SBE meetings on nonroutine matters	.69
SDE information utility to SBE	.56
SBE cohesion	.09
SBE prestige	.44
Expectations	
Sense of policy-making efficacy	.06
SBE expectations for a board policy role	.42
SBE expectations for a CSSO policy role	−.59
Background characteristics	
Population size, 1970	−.03
Rate of population growth, 1960-70	−.07
Per capita income, 1972	−.03
Population with four or more years of school, 1970	−.28
Urbanism (people in towns of 2,500 or less, 1970)	.05
Party competition, Ranney Index, 1956-70	.08
Voter turnout, 1970 House elections	−.33
Political culture, Elazar-Sharkansky Scale, 1969	.26
Legislative "effectiveness," Citizens Conference Index, 1970	−.09
Formal powers of the governors, Schlesinger's Index, 1970	.01
Localism (percent revenue to K-12 schools from local sources)	−.26

pointed to it as the primary one in their evaluation of state boards.
Since the measure of this resource was particularly subjective, some
"hard" indicators constructed from social background data obtained
from board member responses to a questionnaire were tried. Nor did
this produce correlations of any consequence. Thus, while we think,
based upon intuition as well as information from many respondents,

that prestige is an important board resource, the quantitative data offer little to sustain this belief.

Policy-Making Expectations

Are the policy role expectations that board members hold for themselves and for their CSSO related to the perceived influence of state boards? The rank order correlations among these measures also are reported in Table II-13. Again, all the relationships are in the expected direction. Influential boards tend to rank higher on a sense of policy-making efficacy and in their expectations for a state board policy role, and to rank lower in their conception of a policy role for the CSSO. But, except for the last, these relationships are not very strong. The negative association (rho of −.59) for state boards between their members' expectations for an expansive CSSO policy role and their own policy-making influence is worth noting, however.

Background Characteristics

A few sizable correlates are apparent by now, but such associations in the data could merely reflect more fundamental socioeconomic and political forces at work in the ten states. To explore this possibility, an array of indexes of socioeconomic development and political culture were correlated with the influence variable. (The socioeconomic and political variables are discussed in Appendix B.) The coefficients in Table II-13 show that the values of rho for all these associations are miniscule for the most part, and none exceeds −.33. Certainly they are not so great as to suggest that background characteristics, and not other attributes more immediately related to state boards, account for much of the variation in the policy-making influence of these bodies.

Relative Importance of Policy-Making Correlates

The EGP analysis of quantitative data about ten state boards of education has identified only four moderate to strong correlates of their policy-making influence. These are legal authority (rho = .66), time devoted to nonroutine matters (rho = .69), member expectations for an expansive CSSO policy role (rho = −.59), and perceived utility of SDE information (rho = .56). While all the other correlations involving either policy resources or role expectations are in the predicted direction, they are of rather small magnitude. And none of the socioeconomic and political indicators employed as background measures has a value of rho exceeding —.33 with state board policy-making influence. As for selection methods, there is a positive association between elected board members and their perceived influence. This could, however, be largely, perhaps entirely, attributable to the fact that all four of our elected state boards appoint their CSSO, a power that is lacking for three of the five appointed state boards.

Because the number of states involved was only ten, little could be done to sort out the relative importance of the four variables that correlate most strongly with policy-making influence. Still, some statistical assessment was possible. In the first place, the absence of sizable socioeconomic or political correlates permitted an examination of the relationships for the ten state boards among resources, expectations, and influence with some confidence that environmental characteristics of the states were not confounding the results. Second, inspection of a correlation matrix involving just the four variables of interest disclosed that legal authority was only weakly related to the other three measures, measures that in turn tended to be strongly associated with each other. This suggests that legal authority and at least one of the remaining variables are additive in their effects on policy-making influence. Indeed, by using as the base variable whether or not the state board appoints the CSSO and by adding in each state board's score on one or more of the other variables, rho values in the neighborhood of .80 could be obtained.

*   *   *

The findings pertaining to the policy-making influence, resources, and expectations of the ten state boards studied that are reviewed at the end of each of the preceding sections will not be restated here. Instead, the conclusions are organized in relation to three general observations about state boards:

1. They tend to be minor participants in establishing state education policy.
2. Many of their members, at least in a few states, are concerned about and striving to enhance board influence.
3. Strengthening the state board relative to other actors seems to be possible, but the constraints on these institutions are many and serious.

Based on questionnaire data on the self-role expectations of board members, data gathered in the late 1960's, Sroufe inferred that "state boards of education, rhetoric to the contrary, have little capability as actors in the education policy system of the state."[32] Judging from the perceptions of our respondents in state legislatures, governors' offices, and educational interest groups, as well as the evidence contained in individual case studies, this assessment applies to most state boards examined here. Their policy-making role in the legislative arena was marginal, and they were so overshadowed by the CSSO in the agency arena as to raise doubt about what policy-making functions, if any, they performed beyond the one (that is, formal enactment) that was legally required.

To be sure, there were some exceptions—for instance, the involvement of Texas' State Board of Education in the school finance issue and Minnesota's State Board of Education in an attempt to effect a desegregation policy. Furthermore, the perceptions of board member respondents toward their policy-making role were generally more positive than the perceptions of other actors. Board officials were more likely to see channels of communication and influence with the legislature, as well as with the governor's office, and they were likely to consider the CSSO and the state department as being basically implementers of state board directives. Such perceptions are not to be discounted. Still, the data, on balance, point unmistakably to the weakness, rather than the strength, of state boards of education as policy-making participants.

While board members are unlikely to agree with the EGP assessment, some officials in the states studied did indicate that "in the past" their board had been too passive and that they wanted it to take a more anticipatory and aggressive posture. These attitudes appeared to be most prevalent in Texas, Minnesota, and Colorado, but they were voiced in other states as well. In Texas the push for a more vigorous role coincided with the reapportionment of the State Board election districts in 1972 and the opportunity for involvement afforded by the *Rodriguez* decision. In Minnesota the efforts of the State Board, especially in the desegregation area, caused one observer to remark: "In 1967 people were talking about abolishing the State Board because it didn't do anything; by the 1970s the talk was about abolishing the State Board because it was doing too much." Several of our respondents from the State Board of Education in Colorado said that they were seeking a more active role, including individual lobbying, in the legislative arena, and by 1973 the State Board presented its platform to the General Assembly for the first time.

What does the EGP research have to say to board members who are concerned about and seeking to enhance the policy-making influence of these institutions? Our analysis of state-by-state variations in this influence suggests several steps that might be taken. One that appears to be necessary, though hardly sufficient, is for the state board to have the power to select and to remove the CSSO. The three state boards in our sample that lack this authority are all near the bottom on the different rankings of policy-making influence.

A second step is for the state board to organize its time so that policy concerns, not routine financial and procedural items, receive emphasis. The experience of the state boards in New York and Texas, both large boards, it might be noted, indicates that a well-developed committee system may contribute toward this end, as well as providing some subject matter specialization and expertise. A third step is for the state board to insist that useful information on policy issues and alternatives be furnished by the state department of education. The question here is whether this can be done effectively through existing authority relationships (for example, by the board requesting such information from the CSSO and, if met by repeated inadequate performance, by replacement of the chief), or whether it requires that a board have a small staff of independent assistants. Fourth, the members of the state board should examine their policy role expectations both for themselves and for the CSSO. If the pendulum of power, as EGP research suggests, has swung a long way toward the CSSO, then board members need to consider how an appropriate balance can be achieved between professional expertise and public control.

Finally, the plenary authority lodged with legislatures and governors to set education policy means that a state board has to be able to influence lawmakers if it is to have an impact on "who gets what, when, and how" with regard to valued school services. To accomplish this, board members cannot just rely, as did most in the EGP sample, on a few formal channels to the legislature and the governor's office, or on the CSSO to carry *their* program into the legislative arena. Effective points of personal access to legislative leaders and governors need to be forged, and board members need to consider how they can convincingly act as the public's spokesmen in these endeavors.

Although the steps outlined above would probably strengthen the state boards, there are still genuine constraints on these bodies. State board members, like others who sit on lay governing boards, serve on a part-time basis, lack expertise, and have limited data sources. In this connection, students of business management have repeatedly pointed to the weakness of corporate boards of directors, and a recent comprehensive survey of local educational decision making bluntly concludes that school board members, legal authority notwithstanding, are "virtually without power" in that process.[33] Unlike most of their local counterparts, moreover, state boards of education have no independent access to monetary resources through taxing authority, and their policy-making capacity is contingent on the influence and interest of other governmental actors. In California and Massachusetts, for example, the extensive involvement of the legislature in determining public school policy narrowly constricts the role the state board can play. In Texas and New York, on the other hand, the legislature has traditionally delegated much school policy making to education agencies. But even in states such as these, if New York is any test, the rapid politicization of education is working to curtail the scope of agency prerogatives.[34]

Perhaps, when all is said and done, state boards of education should not seek a highly active policy-making role, particularly in the legislative arena, devoting their energies more to the performance of other governmental functions. This study did not examine the participation by state boards in other functional areas; another study might find the boards to be effective in such areas. If, however, the rationale for a state board is predicated on its policy-making involvement, then this study shows cause for concern.

NOTES–CHAPTER II

1. E. Dean Coon, "Judicial Functions of State Boards of Education," unpublished dissertation, University of Denver, December 1973, p. 27.

2. Robert F. Will, *State Education, Structure and Organization* (Washington, D. C.: U.S. Government Printing Office, 1964), p. 12.

3. Lerue W. Winget *et al.*, "State Departments of Education within State Governments," Edgar Fuller and Jim B. Pearson (eds.), *Education in the States* (Washington, D. C.: National Education Association, 1969), II, pp. 77-78.

4. Sam P. Harris, *State Departments of Education, State Boards of Education, and Chief State School Officers*, Department of Health, Education, and Welfare Publication (Office of Education) 73-074000 (Washington, D. C.: U.S. Government Printing Office, 1973), pp. 69-74.

5. *Ibid.*, pp. 60-61.

6. Dean M. Schweickhard (ed.), "The Role and Policymaking Activities of State Boards of Education," A Special Study Project Report to the U.S. Office of Education, St. Paul, Minnesota, September 1967), pp. 47-66.

7. Harris, *State Departments of Education*, p. 57.

8. Gerald Sroufe, "State School Board Members and Educational Policy," *Administrator's Notebook*, 19 (October 1970), p. 1.

9. The relative merits of the decision and the reputational methods are discussed in Terry N. Clark (ed.), *Community Structure and Decision-Making: Comparative Analyses* (San Francisco: Chandler, 1968), pp. 72-81.

10. Frederick M. Wirt and Michael W. Kirst, *Political and Social Foundations of Education* (Berkeley, Calif.: McCutchan, 1975), pp. 114-115.

11. An analysis of a school finance decision process is contained in the issues section of each of the 12 case study reports produced by the EGP.

12. Harmon Zeigler, "Creating Responsive Schools," *The Urban Review*, 6 (No. 4, 1973), p. 41.

13. Carl J. Friedrich, *Constitutional Government and Democracy* (Boston: Little, Brown, 1941), pp. 589-591. Also see on "cuing," Harry L. Summerfield, "Cuing and the Open System of Educational Politics," *Education and Urban Society*, 3 (August 1971), pp. 425-439.

14. Again, analyses of these decision processes are found in the issues section of each of our 12 case study reports.

15. The utility of such highly judgmental measures in the investigation of social phenomena is demonstrated by such diverse studies as Robert L. Crain, *The Politics of School Desegregation* (Garden City, N. Y.: Anchor Books), 1969, and Ted Robert Gurr and Muriel McClelland, *Political Performance: A Twelve-Nation Study* (Beverly Hills, Calif.: Sage, 1971).

16. *Texas Education Code*, 11.24; *Constitution of the State of Michigan*, Art. 8, Sec. 3; *Nebraska School Laws*, 79-321 (amended 1971).

17. Article II of the Constitution for the state of New York provides for the Board of Regents.

18. Gary Branson, "Constitutional and Statutory Provisions for State Boards of Education and Chief State School Officers," unpublished EGP paper, 1973, p. 2.

19. Stephen K. Bailey *et al.*, *Schoolmen and Politics* (Syracuse, N. Y.: Syracuse University Press, 1962), p. 27.

20. Laurence Iannaccone, *Politics in Education* (New York: Center for Applied Research, 1967), p. 61.

21. Sroufe, "State School Board Members and Educational Policy," pp. 2-3.

22. On the relationship between conflict and policy control, see, particularly, Herbert Simon *et al.*, "Dividing the Work: Specialization among Organization Units," in Edward V. Schneier (ed.), *Policy-Making in American Government* (New York: Basic Books, 1969), pp. 218-221.

23. See the discussion of "reputation as a resource" in William A. Gamson, "Reputation and Resources in Community Politics," in Clark (ed.), *Community Structure and Decision-Making*, pp. 336-337.

24. Data on the representativeness of state boards of education are presented in the second section of this volume.

25. This point is particularly stressed by Gerald Sroufe. See his article on "State School Board Members and the State Education Policy System," *Planning and Changing*, 2 (April 1971), pp. 16-17.

26. "Sense of political efficacy" was originally conceptualized in 1952 by the Survey Research Center. See the discussion in Heinz Eulau, *Micro-Macro Political Analysis* (Chicago: Aldine, 1969), pp. 170-172.

27. Self-role expectations are central to Sroufe's analysis in his "State School Board Members and the State Education Policy System," pp. 15-23.

28. The questions we employed were largely adapted from a set used in the mid-1960's with city councilmen in the San Francisco Bay Region. It might be noted that the city councilmen, generally speaking, tended to restrict the appropriate policy activities of the manager to those of adviser and rejected his claim to broader community leadership. See Ronald O. Loveridge, "The City Manager in Legislative Politics: A Collision of Role Conceptions," unpublished paper delivered at the 1967 annual meeting of the Western Political Science Association, March 16-18, 1967.

29. Sroufe, "State School Board Members and the State Education Policy System." Also see Edwin M. Bridges, "Elected versus Appointed Boards: The Arguments and Evidence," unpublished paper, University of Chicago, n.d.

30. The interpretation of ϕ (phi) is from William L. Hays, *Basic Statistics* (Belmont, Calif.: Brooks/Cole, 1967), p. 95. The formula used is

$$\text{phi} = \frac{ac - bd}{\sqrt{(a+b)(c+d)(b+c)(a+d)}} \text{, for the four-cell table}$$

b	a
c	d

See Jum C. Nunnally, *Psychometric Theory* (New York: McGraw-Hill, 1967), p. 119.

31. The formula for the Spearman rank correlation coefficient is

$$r_s = 1 - \frac{6\Sigma d^2}{N(N^2 - 1)} \ .$$

Nunnally, *Psychometric Theory*, p. 121. All the correlations are computed using the Spearman rho formula under the assumption that only an ordinal level of measurement can be claimed for most of our variables.

32. Sroufe, "State School Board Members and the State Education Policy System," p. 23.

33. Summary statement by Max Abott introducing a symposium on local educational decision making, Annual Meeting of AERA, March 1, 1973. Some of the findings of the national survey are reported in Harmon Zeigler, "Creating Responsive Schools," *The Urban Review*, 6 (No. 4, 1973), pp. 38-44. On corporate boards of directors, see "Needed: An Effective Board" in Peter F. Drucker, *Management* (New York: Harper and Row, 1973), ch. 52.

34. Edward R. Hines, *State Policy Making for the Public School of New York* (Columbus, Ohio: Ohio State University, Educational Governance Project, January 1974), pp. 89-119.

III — The Chief State School Officer as a Policy Actor

In every state the position of chief state school officer (CSSO) has been established by law. Such officials are called superintendents of public instruction, commissioners of education, or some similar title. New York (in 1812) was the first state to provide for such a position. Some years later the office was abolished, but it was reestablished in 1854 and has survived, with some modification, since that date. Michigan provided for a state superintendent in 1836; Kentucky and Massachusetts, in 1837.[1] In all three cases the position lasted, with some modification of duties and titles. Other states followed the example set by these leaders and established comparable offices. At present the position is authorized by constitutional provision in thirty-five states and by statutory enactment in the remaining fifteen.[2]

The CSSO serves in most states as executive officer of the state board of education, as head of the state department of education, and as chief administrative officer of the state for executing the laws and regulations of the state pertaining to education. While many of his functions are administrative, the CSSO also becomes an actor in the process by which policies for education are made, and that role is the one of interest here. The decision to concentrate on the policy-making role of the CSSO should in no way be interpreted as denigrating the importance of the implementation or management functions of the office. It simply means that, in a study of state governance for education, it seemed most useful to begin with policy decisions and to determine who the major actors were and how they influenced those decisions.

Some attention was given to CSSO's in all fifty states. Most of the data, however, were collected on CSSO's in twelve states, and this analysis focuses on those states. There is no way of saying that these twelve states are a true sample of the fifty states, but the variables found in the fifty states are also largely found in the twelve. Methods of selecting CSSO's are shown in Table III-1. In the United States,

TABLE III-1 Methods of Selecting Chief State School Officers
in the U.S., 1972

Method	All states	States in study
Elected	19[a]	4[b]
Appointed by state board	26	7
Appointed by governor	5	1

[a]13 partisan, 6 nonpartisan
[b]2 partisan, 2 nonpartisan
Source: Sam P. Harris, *State Departments of Education, State Boards of Education, and Chief State School Officers,* Department of Health, Education, and Welfare Publication (Office of Education) 73-074000 (Washington, D. C.: U.S. Government Printing Office, 1973).

nineteen CSSO's are elected; this study includes four such officers. A total of twenty-six CSSO's are appointed by state boards of education; this study includes seven. And five CSSO's are appointed by the governor; this study includes one.

The two major questions considered in this chapter are: What is the policy-making influence of the CSSO? What factors or conditions help explain that influence? In approaching these two questions it is necessary to determine, first, who the CSSO's are, which is followed by a look at the policy-making resources available to them and a report on the policy-making influence they are perceived as exercising. After weighing factors that help explain the differential influence among CSSO's, it is finally possible to draw whatever conclusions the analyses seem to warrant. It is, again, important to recognize that this study was done in selected states and that it covers the time period from 1972 to early 1973.

WHO ARE THE CSSO'S?

Describing CSSO's requires that a number of their personal and professional characteristics be examined. Identification in each case is by state, not by the person who held office in 1972-73. In a number of states the incumbent has changed since the data were collected.

Personal Characteristics

The age, sex, and race of CSSO's are shown in Table III-2. All twelve incumbents at the time of this study were male; ten were white, and two were black; the youngest was forty-one years old, and the oldest was sixty-eight. The average age for the entire group was 56.8 years old, and there was no appreciable difference in age between elected and appointed officials. One black was in the elected group, and one was in the appointed group—the only blacks among all fifty CSSO's. When this study began, only Montana had a female CSSO. More recently, Wisconsin and Arizona elected women to that office. Thus, of fifty CSSO's, three are now female.

Officials of many kinds have frequently been examined in terms of their local or cosmopolitan orientations,[3] so this appeared to be a useful dimension upon which to examine CSSO's. In this case, however, in-state data were used to establish the dimension. Six of the twelve CSSO's were born in the state where they later served. Seven received their K-12 schooling in the same state, eight finished their undergraduate programs in the same state, six completed graduate programs in the same state, five maintained their only permanent address in the same state, and eleven of the twelve studied had held a prior position in the same state immediately before becoming the CSSO.

By counting one point for each in-state identification across these six characteristics, a total in-state score was developed for each CSSO. Scores of 4, 5, and 6 designated in-state orientation, scores of 1, 2, and 3, out-of-state orientation. It is clear that most, seven out

TABLE III-2 Personal and Professional Characteristics of Twelve CSSO's, 1972-73

CSSO's by state, according to means of selection	Age	Sex	Race	In-state orientation	Rural orientation	Prior experience			Salary[a]
						Public school teacher	District school superintendent	State department of education	
Elected									
California	55	M	B	no	part	yes	no	yes	$35,000
Florida	57	M	W	yes	part	no	yes	no	36,000
Georgia	51	M	W	yes	yes	yes	yes	yes	28,000
Wisconsin	64	M	W	yes	yes	yes	yes	yes	21,000
AVERAGE	56.8								30,000
Appointed									
Colorado	54	M	W	no	no	yes	yes	no	35,000
Massachusetts	61	M	W	yes	part	yes	yes	yes	30,000
Michigan	41	M	B	no	no	yes	no	yes	39,550
Minnesota	46	M	W	yes	yes	yes	yes	no	29,400
Nebraska	63	M	W	yes	no	no	no	yes	21,900
New York	58	M	W	no	no	no	no	yes	51,275
Tennessee	64	M	W	no	yes	yes	yes	no	25,000
Texas	68	M	W	yes	yes	yes	yes	no	31,500
AVERAGE	56.9								32,953
TOTAL AVERAGE	56.8								31,969

[a]The source for this information is Harris, *State Departments of Education*.

of twelve, CSSO's are local or in-state products, as noted in Table III-2. In the case of elected CSSO's, three out of four are local; in the appointed group, four out of eight are local. Thus, in the matter of in-state identification there appears to be a real difference between elected and appointed CSSO's, a finding that should come as no surprise.

The literature on state education agencies frequently alludes to the rural identification of personnel in these agencies.[4] This identification of CSSO's was determined by the location of their K-12 schooling and their prior job experience. Half received their K-12 schooling in rural communities, and seven out of twelve had prior job experience in rural schools. By combining these factors, a rural score was established for each CSSO.

The scores were divided into three categories: 2 for rural, 1 for part rural, and 0 for nonrural or urban, as shown in Table III-2. As a group, CSSO's do appear to represent a rural background, perhaps more so than might be expected in an urban society. Here, again, there appears to be a real difference between elected and appointed CSSO's, with all elected CSSO's being rural or part rural and only half of the appointed CSSO's being rural or part rural.

Recruitment and Salary

In any study of an occupational group, recruitment routes to the occupation are matters of interest. Such routes for CSSO's are reflected in Table III-2. Nine of the twelve incumbents had been public school teachers, and eight had been public school superintendents. Some of the incumbents had also served as public school principals and as subordinate administrators in a school district office, often in several such positions prior to becoming members of state departments of education. Two had served in nonpublic school positions: one, in a civil rights agency; the other in a business firm. Both had, however, also been teachers and principals in the public schools as part of their early experience. Recent attempts to recruit administrative talent from such fields as business, law, and public administration to serve in top administrative posts in education were not reflected in the recruitment patterns of the twelve CSSO's involved in this study.

Positions held by CSSO's immediately prior to their selection as chiefs were also considered. In seven cases (California, Georgia,

Wisconsin, Massachusetts, Michigan, Nebraska, and New York) the officer was recruited from the staff of the state department of education, also noted in Table III-2. In five cases the chief was recruited from outside that staff. In Florida the governor reportedly encouraged the candidate to run for the office. In Colorado, Minnesota, and Texas state boards of education sought persons outside the state department of education. In Colorado a businessman who had formerly served as a district school superintendent outside the state was selected; in Minnesota and Texas district superintendents from within the state were selected. In Tennessee the governor made the selection, and he, too, chose a district superintendent from the state. Practices followed in all twelve states suggest two main routes to the office of the CSSO: public school superintendency or service in the state department of education, or a combination of both.

These patterns of recruitment deserve additional examination. When Carlson did a study of district superintendents, he was able to categorize them as place-bound (insiders) and career-bound (outsiders).[5] Insiders, says Carlson, are usually selected when a board is relatively satisfied with the operation of the district, and under such conditions insiders have difficulty in persuading the board to make changes. Conversely, outsiders are usually selected when a board is not satisfied with the status of things, and outsiders thus have more opportunity to effect changes in the school system. At the time the twelve CSSO's considered here were selected, seven were true insiders and four were insiders in the sense of holding a district superintendency in the same state. In only one case was the new CSSO secured from beyond the state boundaries. Following Carlson, it appears that, even in states where the selection was made by boards and governors, those officials were so satisfied with the operation of the state education agencies that they felt no need to look beyond state boundaries.

As to constraints, CSSO's reported a number of factors that affected recruitment to their positions. One was that a CSSO be a resident of the state, and it pertained in five cases. Educational experience of some nature was stipulated in six cases. Educational preparation was demanded in eight cases. Endorsement of a political party was required in three cases. In some instances these requirements were established by the constitution of the state; in other cases, by state statute; in still other cases, by state board regulation. Constraints of any kind do, it must be recognized, limit the pool of potential candidates for any office.

There are other differences between elected and appointed CSSO's. Four of the five states with a residency requirement have elected CSSO's. Stipulation of a particular type of educational experience is much more prevalent among the states with appointed CSSO's. Educational preparation required does not seem to differ much for the two groups; the stipulation was made in the case of three of the four elected CSSO's and five of the eight appointed ones. Only Florida and Georgia in the elected group and Tennessee in the appointed group require endorsement or support of a political party. In Tennessee it is well to note again that the appointment is by the governor, which may help explain the party affiliation.

Salary levels also appear to be a factor in recruiting persons for a position. In Table III-2 the salaries of CSSO's are shown. In 1972, salaries ranged from $21,000 to over $51,000 per year, a wide range, indeed. The average for the elected CSSO's was about $3,000 below the average for the appointed CSSO's, a difference almost entirely owing to the high salary paid in New York.

There is no way of knowing just how much CSSO's should be paid, but one useful comparison can be made. In a comprehensive study of district school superintendents, Knezevich[6] collected salary data for 1969-70. Those data for school districts with large pupil enrollments are summarized in Table III-3. Since the data on district superintendents were collected two years earlier than the data on

TABLE III-3 Median Salaries Paid District School Superintendents by Pupil Enrollment Categories in 1969-70 with Estimated Increases for 1971-72

Enrollments	Number of districts	Median salaries for 1969-70	Adjusted salaries for 1971-72
100,000 and above	19	$35,000	$38,500
50,000 to 99,999	26	30,250	33,275
25,000 to 49,999	67	29,465	32,411
TOTAL	112	30,000	33,000

Source: Adapted from Stephen J. Knezevich (ed.), The American School Superintendent (Arlington, Va.: American Association of School Administrators, 1971), p. 38.

CSSO's, estimated median salaries for district superintendents for 1971-72 have been adjusted by increasing them 10 percent over those of 1969-70. If the average salary for CSSO's ought to be at least comparable to that of district superintendents in the 112 larger districts of the country, $33,000 can be used as a yardstick.[7] By applying such a yardstick, five CSSO's, two elected and three appointed, are paid salaries equal to or above that figure. On the other hand, seven CSSO's, two elected and five appointed, are paid salaries below that figure. Salaries in Wisconsin and Nebraska seem to be much out of line. Although the Wisconsin legislature has recently approved a salary of $25,000 for the CSSO, that figure still seems very modest.

Summary

These are, then, some of the personal and professional characteristics of CSSO's found in the twelve states included in this study. As for personal characteristics, all were male, ten were white, and two were black. In terms of personal characteristics, there were no appreciable differences between elected and appointed chiefs.

In terms of professional characteristics the CSSO's most frequently had in-state and rural orientations. But appointed CSSO's were not as often in-state or rural as elected CSSO's. By way of recruitment, the route to office was clearly through teaching and administration in the public schools and frequently through an appointment in the state department of education. Eight of the twelve CSSO's had at one time been district superintendents and seven of the twelve held a position in the state department of education immediately prior to being selected as CSSO. There were a few constraints to holding the office. Elected CSSO's were required in every case to be residents of the state. Appointed CSSO's were frequently confronted with a legal stipulation regarding prior experience in public school work. Salaries on the whole were below those paid superintendents in populous school districts in the United States.

RESOURCES OF THE CSSO

One aspect of the influence of CSSO's to be considered is the resources at their command, including formal power of office, capacity to attract staff, freedom to select and discharge members of his team, and perceptions about the information generated by the office.

Formal Power of Office

Table III-4 shows a number of characteristics that, taken together, would seem to represent the formal power of the office. If the office has constitutional status, it is potentially more powerful than if it does not. Also, if the CSSO is a member of the state board of education, his potential influence is increased, and, if he is the chairman or the executive officer of the board, his potential influence is further enhanced. If he is required to report to the governor or the legislature, his formal powers are even greater. Only in New York has the Commissioner of Education been given quasi-judicial powers, which seem to represent an addition to formal power. The CSSO who serves under a term contract or can be reelected seems to be more powerful than one who simply serves at the pleasure of the board. Formal power of office is, however, only one side of the picture. Actually, as is well recognized in administrative literature,[8] the full power of any official leader is some kind of combination of vested and entrusted authority. Vested authority springs from the nature of the office, and entrusted authority springs from the esteem and respect subordinates in an organization have for the official leader. The fact remains that the office does represent some potential for power.

The weight assigned to each of the items enumerated in Table III-4 makes possible a formal power score for each chief. Elected chiefs have, on the average, more formal power than their appointed counterparts. The two exceptions to this seem to be found in Michigan and New York, where, in one case, the increase in formal powers is primarily due to the fact that the chief is, by law, not only a member of the state board of education, but also its chairman, and, in the other case, that the chief exercises quasi-judicial power. In the case of Wisconsin, the power of board chairman is ascribed to the CSSO since he is obviously the top education official in the state and there is no state board of education.

Attract Personnel

Another potential resource of CSSO's is their capacity to attract and hold personnel. Two indexes, level of training and level of salary, serve as evidence of this capacity, but neither index is a perfect

TABLE III-4 Formal Powers of the Office of the CSSO (N = 12)

CSSO's by state, according to means of selection	Constitutional officer Yes = 1; No = 0	Ex-officio member of board Yes = 1; No = 0	Administrative officer of board Chairman = 2 Executive Officer = 1 Secretary = 0	Required to report to governor or legislature Yes = 1; No = 0	Quasi-judicial power Yes = 2; No = 0	Tenure indefinite = 1 At pleasure = 0	Formal power score
Elected							
California	1	0	1	1	0	1	4
Florida	1	1	1	0	0	1	4
Georgia	1	0	1	1	0	1	4
Wisconsin	1	0[a]	2[b]	0	0	1	4
AVERAGE							4
Appointed							
Colorado	1	0	0	0	0	0	1
Massachusetts	0	0	1	0	0	0	1
Michigan	1	1	2	1	0	0	5
Minnesota	0	0	1	0	0	1	2
Nebraska	1	0	1	0	0	0	2
New York	1	0	1	0	2	0	4
Tennessee	0	1	2	0	0	0	3
Texas	0	0	1	1	0	1	3
AVERAGE							2.6

[a]No state board.
[b]Power of chairman.

Source: Harris, State Departments of Education.

measure. Persons with advanced degrees are not always competent to perform specialized tasks; nor are relatively high salaries a guarantee that more expertise is being purchased. Yet, if one turns the matter around, it seems that CSSO's would indeed be handicapped if they were unable to attract persons with advanced training and unable to pay attractive salaries.

In Table III-5 we have shown the number of responses and percent of top staff (CSSO, associate or assistant CSSO's, and directors) in

TABLE III-5 Percent of Top Staff of CSSO's with the Doctorate and with Salaries of $25,000 or More (N = 12)

CSSO's by state, according to means of selection	Number of responses from top staff[a]	With doctorate	With salary of $25,000 or more	Staff attraction score
Elected				
California	22	41	50	91
Florida	16	25	75	100
Georgia	14	43	22	65
Wisconsin	18	33	17	50
AVERAGE		35	41	76
Appointed				
Colorado	14	21	7	28
Massachusetts	19	42	37	79
Michigan	14	57	86	143
Minnesota	13	23	31	54
Nebraska	16	19	0	19
New York	33	70	88	158
Tennessee	18	22	0	22
Texas	15	33	7	40
AVERAGE		36	32	68

[a]Top staff included the CSSO, the associate and assistant CSSO's, and directors of major programs. In states with large SDE's, a 30 percent sampling of directors was used.

state departments of education with doctoral degrees. We have also shown the percent of top personnel in each department with salaries of $25,000 or more per year. The two percentage columns have been combined to represent a staff attraction score. In these terms the states of New York, Michigan, Florida, and California rank high, while the states of Nebraska, Tennessee, and Colorado rank low. Differences between elected and appointed CSSO's are not great.

Form Own Team

Another aspect of resources available to the CSSO has to do with freedom to employ and discharge members of the top staff, thereby establishing his own team. There are two answers to this question. One has to do with formal arrangements for the appointment of top staff, and the other has to do with informal practices that pertain. A part of the *Interview Schedule* for CSSO's contained the question: "How free are you with regard to civil service provisions to appoint and remove top administrators?" Whatever the answer regarding formal provisions, there was still an attempt to obtain the best picture possible of actual practice. Responses to the question have been summarized in Table III-6. Six of the twelve CSSO's had great freedom

TABLE III-6 Freedom of CSSO to Appoint and Remove Top Administrative Staff (N = 12)

CSSO's by state, according to means of selection (N = 12)	Great 3	Some 2	Little 0	Staff freedom score
Elected				
California		1		2
Florida	1			3
Georgia		1		2
Wisconsin			1	0
AVERAGE				1.7
Appointed				
Colorado	1			3
Massachusetts	1			3
Michigan		1		2
Minnesota			1	0
Nebraska	1			3
New York	1			3
Tennessee			1	0
Texas	1			3
AVERAGE				2.1

to form their own administrative teams, three had some freedom, and three had little freedom.

Some additional insight into this situation is provided from selected excerpts from the interview protocols. In Michigan, where freedom was somewhat limited, the CSSO commented, perhaps wryly, "not very free, but there's no difficulty. I kill them off by expecting much hard work." In Wisconsin, where civil service regulations were very strict, we got the following comment, "He (CSSO) has two positions he can appoint, period." From Minnesota came a similar remark: "Not free at all, everyone in the Department is in civil service." The EGP interviewer for Tennessee recorded what may be an extreme comment: "Since all are patronage appointees they are really very well protected, negating any CSSO power." Except for Wisconsin, Minnesota, and Tennessee, each CSSO appeared to have considerable freedom to set up his own administrative team.

Related to this matter is another response from CSSO's. The question was: "Have there been occasions when you could not get the full support of State Department administrators . . . ?" In this instance ten of the twelve CSSO's responded "no," and the "yes" response from Michigan was qualified by the remark, "We thresh things out and come to agreement." While two CSSO's appear to have been constrained in terms of employment of staff and staff support after employment, such constraints seemed to be more severe in Wisconsin than in Michigan. Appointed chiefs appeared to have more freedom to set up their administrative teams than elected chiefs did.

Information Resources

As heads of their respective state departments of education, CSSO's have established within their organizations a unit of some kind to generate information about the schools of the state. Information generated by the office of the CSSO is made available to the state board of education and frequently to legislators and to the governor, and it may be used as the data base for policy decisions. The extent to which legislative leaders, governors, and state board members perceived that the information met their needs seemed to be another way of assessing the resources of the CSSO. Thus, on the *Interview Schedule,* legislative leaders were asked: "In terms of meeting your needs in deciding upon education and school finance bills, how would you rate the information coming to your office from the

State Department of Education?" Responses were keyed to the four-point scale shown below:

Almost always meets our needs   1
Usually meets our needs   2
Sometimes meets our needs   3
Almost never meets our needs   4

Responses of legislative leaders to items 1 and 2 and to items 3 and 4 were collapsed, and the first collapsed set, "almost always" and "usually" responses, are shown, by percentage, in Table III-7. These percentages provide a kind of legislative information score. In the case of Georgia this was 100 percent so Georgia received a score of 100. Wisconsin, Minnesota, and Texas also ranked high. States given low information ratings by legislators included California, Massachusetts, New York, and Colorado. The data suggest that in three of the four states with low ratings legislatures have strong staff arrangements and rely on their own people, in large measure, to generate information. In terms of elected and appointed CSSO's, the average information score for elected chiefs is 74.5, as contrasted with 61 for the appointed chiefs.

We also asked governors' personal staff members to indicate the extent to which information generated by the departments met their needs. Their "almost always" and "usually" responses are also shown in Table III-7. In this case high information scores are ascribed to California, Georgia, Colorado, Nebraska, and Texas. Low scores are ascribed to Florida, Minnesota, Massachusetts, Michigan, and New York. A governor's personal staff agreed with legislators in terms of high scores only in the case of Georgia. In terms of low scores, there was agreement in the cases of Massachusetts and New York. There is, therefore, more discrepancy than agreement in the judgments of the two sets of respondents regarding how well SDE information met their needs. It may be that the information needs of governors' offices are different than the needs of legislators and that SDE efforts are more adequate for one than for the other. Or it may be that the limited number of respondents in some governors' offices provided biased perceptions of the situation. In this case the difference between elected and appointed CSSO's was not great, but it favored the elected chiefs.

TABLE III-7 Perceptions of Legislative Leaders, Governor's Staffs, and SBE Members Regarding the Extent to Which SDE Information Met Their Needs (responses in percentages)

CSSO's by state, according to means of selection	Legislative leaders		Governor's staff		SBE members	
	Number of respondents	Almost always and usually	Number of respondents	Almost always and usually	Number of respondents	Almost always and usually
Elected						
California	15	47	1	100	9	55
Florida	8	63	1	0	6	83
Georgia	13	100	1	100	7	100
Wisconsin	17	88	2	50	(no state board)	
AVERAGE		74.5		62		79
Appointed						
Colorado	11	54	1	100	4	100
Massachusetts	12	50	4	25	8	75
Michigan	16	56	3	33	6	83
Minnesota	14	72	1	0	6	83
Nebraska	6	67	1	100	5	40
New York	17	53	3	33	9	100
Tennessee	11	63	2	50	8	63
Texas	14	71	3	100	11	91
AVERAGE		61		55		79
TOTAL AVERAGE		65.3		57		79

We also asked SBE members to assess the extent to which the information provided by the chiefs, and generated by the state departments, was useful to them as board members. Responses obtained from this inquiry are also shown in Table III-7. In contrast to responses from legislators and governors, there was strong affirmation by most board members that the information "almost always" or "usually" meets their needs. In three states, Georgia, Colorado, and New York, information scores were 100. In six other states the scores ran from 75 to 91. Only in Nebraska, with a score of 40, and California, with a score of 55, could it be sensed that SBE members have appreciable reservation about the information they have been receiving. Average scores for elected chiefs and appointed chiefs are identical. Clearly, the information generated by state departments was thought to be more useful by board members than it was by legislative leaders and governors and their staffs.

Summary

In terms of a number of rather discrete elements having to do with resources available to CSSO's, there is appreciable variation within each state. For instance, Michigan ranks relatively high in terms of formal power of office, capacity to attract staff, freedom of the chief to form his own team, staff support enjoyed by the chief, and how well SDE information is seen as meeting the needs of state board members. But the same state ranks low in the extent to which SDE information meets the needs of the governor's staff, and it is in the middle range regarding the extent to which SDE information is seen as meeting the needs of legislative leaders. There is even more variation in Colorado, where relatively high ranks were assigned to the freedom of the chief to form his own team, to staff support enjoyed by the chief, and to how well SDE information met the needs of state board members. Colorado stands about in the middle with respect to SDE information meeting the needs of legislative leaders and the governor's office. Colorado ranks low on the formal power of office and the capacity to attract staff. Relationships between a number of these variables and the influence of the CSSO will be analyzed later.

THE POLICY-MAKING INFLUENCE OF THE CSSO

The policy-making influence of the CSSO will be examined largely through the perceptions that various actors in the policy-making process had of the influence of the CSSO. These perceptions are supplemented by case study data. First, there are the self-perceptions of the chiefs; then, their perceived influence in the legislative arena; and, last, their perceived influence in the state education agency arena.

Self-Perceptions of CSSO

The *Interview Schedule* used with CSSO's contained a section in which ten statements regarding the desirable leadership role of the CSSO in the policy-making process were listed, and chiefs were asked to indicate, for each statement, one of four possible responses: strongly agree, tend to agree, tend to disagree, or strongly disagree. Six of those ten statements seemed to be particularly appropriate by way of revealing the self-perceptions of the chiefs concerning the desirable leadership role of the office of CSSO. Those six statements are shown below:

1. A state superintendent (commissioner) should assume leadership in shaping the policies enacted by the state board of education.
2. A state superintendent (commissioner) should maintain a neutral stand on education policy issues that are very controversial among the citizens of his state.
3. A state superintendent (commissioner) should actively seek to influence legislative leaders with regard to education policies.
5. A state superintendent (commissioner) should administer the state department of education and leave policy matters to other state officials.
7. A state superintendent (commissioner) should take a policy position in which he believes, even when most professional educators may be hostile.
8. A state superintendent (commissioner) should be the principal advocate of major changes in state education policy.

Table III-8 shows the responses of the twelve CSSO's to these statements. The two agreement categories were collapsed into one, and the two disagreement categories were treated in the same way. Each chief was also given a self-perceived leadership score. If the chief agreed with items 1, 3, 7, and 8, we gave him a point for each one. If he disagreed with items 2 and 5, we gave him a point for each. This required, as noted in Table III-8, a reversal in scoring the self-

TABLE III-8 Self-Perceptions of CSSO's Regarding Their Leadership Role in Policy Making (N = 12; A = agree, D = disagree)

CSSO's by state, according to means of selection	Assume policy leadership with SBE		Remain neutral on controversial issues (reverse to score)		Actively seek to influence legislative leaders		Administer department and leave policy to others (reverse to score)		Take policy positions even if educators hostile		Be principal advocate of policy changes		Self-perceived leadership role score
	A	D	A	D	A	D	A	D	A	D	A	D	
Elected													
California	1			1	1			1	1		1		6
Florida	1			1	1		0		1		1		5
Georgia	1			1	1			1	1		1		6
Wisconsin	1			1	1			1	1		1		6
AVERAGE													5.8
Appointed													
Colorado	1			1	1		0		1		1		5
Massachusetts	1			1	1			1	1		1		6
Michigan	1			1	1			1	1		1		6
Minnesota	1			1	1			1	1		1		6
Nebraska	1			1	1		0		1		1		5
New York	1			1	1			1	1		1		6
Tennessee	1			1	1			1	1		1		6
Texas	1		0		1		0		1		1		4
AVERAGE							0						5.5

perceived leadership role of the chief. The most notable finding was the almost unanimous self-perception of the CSSO's that they should be leading participants in the policy-making process. All chiefs believed that they should be assuming leadership in shaping the policy positions of the state board of education. All chiefs believed that they should actively seek to influence legislative leaders with respect to educational policy. All chiefs believed that they should be the *principal advocate* of change in state policy for education. It was clear that CSSO's held for themselves a very significant role in the policy-making process, a generalization that applied equally to elected and appointed chiefs.

Besides noting responses of the chiefs to general role statements, their responses to a number of specific items on the *Interview Schedule* also proved interesting. In item 19 they were asked: "Are there board members who frequently oppose you on major policy issues?" Three chiefs, as noted in Table III-9, answered "yes," eight answered "no," and in Wisconsin, where there was no state board of education, the question was not applicable. Item 22 raised the following question: "Have there been occasions when you could not get the full support of state department administrators for implementing a major policy of yours or the board's?" Two chiefs responded "yes," and ten responded "no," which has also been noted in Table III-9. In terms of arriving at a self-perceived influence score for the chiefs, responses to items 19 and 22 were scored in reverse, and a point was given for a "no" response.

Item 23b read in part as follows: "Compared to other sources of advice and ideas available to the governor, how important is the office of the state superintendent (commissioner)?" Chiefs were requested to respond on a four-point scale as follows:

Most important single source	1
Among his most important sources	2
A relatively minor source	3
Not at all an important source	4

All responses were either 1 or 2, so only two categories are shown in Table III-9. Five of the twelve chiefs saw their advice and ideas as the *most important* source to the governor; the other seven felt their advice and ideas were among the governor's most important sources. In item 24 we asked chiefs to rate their communication with legislative leaders and with committee chairmen in the legislature. In most

TABLE III-9 Self-Perceptions of CSSO's Regarding Their Influence with Other Policy Actors (N = 12)

CSSO's by state, according to means of selection	Board members who frequently oppose you (19) (reverse scoring)		Sometimes lacks support of department administration (22) (reverse scoring)		Importance of advice to governor (23b)		Rate communication with legislative leaders (24c)		Success with legislative program (24e)		Cooperation of EIG (28)		Self-perceived influence score
	Yes	No	Yes	No	Most	Some	Excellent	Good	Half or more	Less than half	Much	Little	
Elected													
California	0					0	1		1		1		4
Florida	0				1		1		1		1		5
Georgia		1			1		1		1		1		6
Wisconsin[a]			0			0		0		0		0	0
AVERAGE													3.8
Appointed													
Colorado		1				0		0	1		1		4
Massachusetts		1	0		1			0	1		1		5
Michigan		1			1			0	1		1		3
Minnesota		1			1		1			0	1		6
Nebraska	0					0	1		1		1		1
New York		1				0		0	1		1		5
Tennessee		1				0		0	1			0	4
Texas		1				0		0	1		1		4
AVERAGE													4

[a] No board.

instances there were eight such persons, and we sought a rating of excellent, good, fair, or poor for each one. The rating shown in Table III-9 is the composite of these ratings. Again, there were few "fair" and "poor" ratings; hence, only the two categories "excellent" and "good" were required to portray the responses. Overall, five chiefs thought they had "excellent" communication with legislative leaders, while seven thought their communication was "good." Going beyond communication, however, in item 24 each chief was asked to indicate how successful his legislative program had been with the legislature. Responses were sought on the five-point scale shown below:

Almost always successful	1
Successful most of the time	2
Successful about half of the time	3
Successful less than half the time	4
Almost always unsuccessful	5

Nine of the chiefs' responses could be interpreted as success about half of the time or more, and two chiefs indicated success less than half of the time. For Nebraska this question proved difficult since the CSSO noted that, by law, neither he nor the Department of Education could formally sponsor a legislative program. In arriving at a self-perceived influence score for the chiefs, they received a point for "most" under item 23b, a point for "excellent" under item 24c, and a point for "half or more" for item 24e.

In item 28 of the *Interview Schedule* the chiefs were asked to respond to the question: "When you are seeking support in the legislature for an important proposal, do you usually work closely with the major educational organizations?" In addition to the simple yes-no responses, there was an attempt to determine the degree of success the chiefs thought they had with these organizations. Their comments established the "much" and "little" categories shown in Table III-9. Ten chiefs thought they had received much cooperation from the interest groups, and only two felt that cooperation had been limited. We attached a score of one to those responses that indicated much cooperation.

By combining the six measures shown in Table III-9, a self-perceived influence score for each of the CSSO's could be established. These scores have a wide range, from zero in Wisconsin to the maximum of six in Georgia and Minnesota. Wisconsin is at some disadvantage in the scoring since they have no state board of education. Even so, the range of scores is of interest and deserves further comment. The range in Table III-9 contrasts markedly with the lack of range in Table III-8. This contrast may derive from the fact that the role statements in Table III-8 deal with what the responsibilities of CSSO's should be, and they are phrased in general terms. The items in Table III-9 are not only more specific, but they require an assessment of what did happen as contrasted to what should happen. Again, there appears to be little difference between elected and appointed chiefs. The next consideration is what other actors thought the influence of the chief to be.

The Legislative Arena

The policy-making influence of CSSO's in legislative and state education agency arenas, and particularly the attempt to place the chiefs in order, are potentially sensitive subjects. Thus, it is necessary to be very clear about what the study did and did not do. It was the policy-making role of the chief, not his managerial or implementing role that was examined. Data were derived largely from the perceptions of other actors in the policy system, not from direct observation or some measurement of performance. Moreover, the reference point for the influence of each chief was his own situation, and the situations varied greatly. There is no way to determine how influential chiefs would be in a common situation. Finally, influence was not equated with good; it was recognized that persons in government can have too much as well as too little influence.

Many of the policy decisions for public education are made in the legislative arena. This is particularly true regarding decisions having to do with the financing of education. Because the governor frequently recommends policy positions to the legislature, he and his staff, as well as members of the legislature, are important participants in the legislative arena. If the CSSO is to affect policy decisions in the legislative arena, he must influence the governor, the legislature, or both. Interviews conducted in the twelve states provided judgments from official actors in the legislature and in the governor's office about the influence of the CSSO. Leaders of education interest groups, as informed observers, also judged the influence of CSSO's in the legislative arena.

Table III-10 shows the responses of legislative leaders and, in some cases, of legislative staff members to the question of how successful

TABLE III-10 Perceptions of Legislative Leaders and Interest Group Leaders of Success of Legislative Programs Sponsored by the CSSO (responses in percentages)

CSSO's by state, according to means of selection	Legislative leaders		Interest group leaders	
	Number of respondents	Almost always and most of the time	Number of respondents	Almost always and most of the time
Elected				
California	17	77	8	88
Florida	8	62	4	75
Georgia	13	100	6	83
Wisconsin	14	50	7	29
AVERAGE		72		69
Appointed				
Colorado	10	20	7	14
Massachusetts	14	7	8	0
Michigan	15	33	10	60
Minnesota	13	62	4	75
Nebraska	7	43	5	40
New York	20	25	7	0
Tennessee	11	100	6	83
Texas	16	94	6	100
AVERAGE		48		46.5
TOTAL AVERAGE		56		54

CSSO's have been in getting their legislative programs adopted by the legislature. Responses were recorded on a five-point scale similar to the one reported earlier. For example, the responses from Georgia suggest that the CSSO was very successful in getting his legislative program adopted. Thirteen legislative leaders responded to this question, one person or 8 percent of the respondents indicated "almost always" and twelve persons or 92 percent of the respondents agreed with "most of the time." In order to arrive at a kind of legislative success score for the chiefs, the percentages of responses in the "almost always" and "usually" categories were combined, giving Georgia 100 percent. In Massachusetts the results were very different. Of fourteen legislative leaders, none said "almost always," 7 percent said

"most of the time," 21 percent said "about half the time," 29 percent said "less than half the time," and 43 percent said "almost
never." Based on these responses the legislative success score in Massachusetts is 7 as compared to 100 in Georgia.

Other CSSO's with high legislative success scores included Tennessee, Texas, and California. We should note, however, that the score
for Tennessee may be spurious since the CSSO is appointed by the
governor, and, in a sense, the chief's legislative program is the governor's program. Other CSSO's with low legislative success scores
include Colorado, New York, and Michigan. It should be made clear
what these legislative success scores represent. Each score is built on
the perceptions of the legislators. In some cases, Texas and California, for instance, perceptions tend to cluster. In other cases, New
York and Nebraska, for example, there is much more spread in the
perceptions. In cases where the spread is considerable, different
respondents may be looking at different aspects of the chief's legislative program. It should also be noted that in one state a chief may
have an ambitious program and get relatively little of it through the
legislature, while in another state the chief may have a less extensive
program and get much of it through the legislature. Some respondents, in Nebraska, for instance, made note of the latter situation by
such remarks as "for what little they propose."

There seems to be a significant difference between the legislative
success of elected and appointed CSSO's. The average legislative success score for elected CSSO's is 72, in contrast to an average score of
48 for those appointed. It may be that legislators, who are themselves elected, feel a closer kinship to elected than to appointed
chiefs. Or, elected chiefs may have a stronger power base with the
voters. Or, it may be that elected chiefs are indeed more skillful in
the legislative arena than their appointed counterparts.

But legislators are not the only observers of how successful CSSO's
are in getting their legislative programs enacted. Table III-10 shows
the responses of education interest group leaders to the same question. In this instance high legislative success scores were recorded for
Texas, California, Georgia, and Tennessee. Again, we suspect the
result in Tennessee has to be interpreted somewhat differently than
results in the other states. Scores were low for Massachusetts, New
York, Colorado, and Wisconsin. It seems significant that the interest
group leaders ascribed high legislative success scores to the same four

states receiving high scores from the legislative leaders. At the other end of the scale, interest group leaders agreed with legislative leaders in ascribing low legislative success scores to three out of four states ranked low by legislators.

Agreement between these two sets of observers also holds with respect to the difference between elected and appointed CSSO's. With the interest group leaders the average legislative success score for the elected chiefs is 69, and for the appointed chiefs it is 46.5, a difference that seems to have considerable significance.

This scheme for scoring legislative success may make some CSSO's look like failures. Even zero scores for Massachusetts and New York cannot be so construed. It is entirely possible that when 71 percent of the interest group leaders in New York indicate that the CSSO's legislative program is successful "about half the time" that the achievement is as high as one could possibly expect. This does seem to be the case when one recalls the demographic, economic, and governmental characteristics of the state. Perhaps, even more important, the governor's office and the legislature have established competent and sophisticated staffs to help them with data collection and analysis. These agencies are clearly in a position to be quite independent of the CSSO and his office, if that is their wish.

As for the perceptions of governors and their staffs about the influence of CSSO's, these data are reported in Table III-11. One item in the *Interview Schedule* was: "Compared to the other sources of advice and ideas, how important is the state superintendent (commissioner)?" Responses were recorded on a four-point scale similar to the one used above. All responses fell within the 1, 2, 3 range; hence, in Table III-11 only those three categories are shown. Another item in the *Interview Schedule* was: "If the state superintendent (commissioner) is strongly opposed to an education bill in the legislature, are its chances of passage greatly diminished?" Responses, listed as "yes" or "no," are reported in Table III-11. There was a single respondent in three of the states, and the respondent in each instance was a member of the governor's personal staff. In other states more personal staff members were interviewed, and in six of the states the governor himself was among the respondents. There was an effort to have at least three or four respondents, including the governor, from each state, but the research teams were only partially successful in that effort.

TABLE III-11 Perceptions of Governors and Their Personal Staffs Regarding Influence of CSSO (responses in percentages)

CSSO's by state, according to means of selection	Number of respondents	Importance of CSSO ideas and advice			Power of CSSO to stop legislation		Influence score (percentage × weight ÷ 100)
		Most	Among most	Minor	Yes	No	
		3	2	1	3	0	
Elected							
California	1		100		100		5.0
Florida	1	100			100		6.0
Georgia	2[a]		100		100		5.0
Wisconsin	2		50	50	100		4.5
AVERAGE							5.1
Appointed							
Colorado	2[a]		100		50	50	3.50
Massachusetts	4	25		75	75	25	3.75
Michigan	4[a]		100		75	25	4.25
Minnesota	1			100		100	1.00
Nebraska	2[a]		100		50	50	3.50
New York	3		100		67	33	4.00
Tennessee	3[a]	100			67	33	5.00
Texas	4[a]		100		75	25	4.25
AVERAGE							3.66

[a] Included the governor.

In order to provide for comparisons among states, responses were converted to percentages. Thus, in Wisconsin, where there were two respondents, one respondent, or 50 percent, indicated the CSSO's ideas and advice were "among the most important single source," and one respondent, or 50 percent, indicated that such ideas and advice were "a relatively minor source." As shown in Table III-11, weights were assigned to these responses and also to the responses having to do with the power of the CSSO to stop legislation. An influence score was developed by multiplying the percentages by the weights and dividing by one hundred. While the spread between high and low influence scores is not as dramatic as in the preceding tables, it still seems worth noting. High influence scores are assigned to CSSO's in Florida, California, Georgia, and Tennessee. Again, the Tennessee situation is atypical. Low influence scores are ascribed to CSSO's in Minnesota, Colorado, Nebraska, and Massachusetts.

In terms of averages, the four elected CSSO's are once again seen by governors' offices as having more influence than the appointed CSSO's as represented by scores of 5.1 and 3.66, respectively. Since this difference is supported by three independent sets of observers, it must be taken with some seriousness. Perhaps the chief in Colorado had a point when he said: "As an appointed official, I am not really a policy maker; I am a manager." We should note, however, that this remark runs counter to the very strong policy roles all of the chiefs set for themselves as reported earlier.

On the basis of appraisals made by legislators, interest group leaders, and members of the governor's staff, we can deduce something about the overall influence of chiefs in the legislative arena. Table III-12 shows the rankings provided by these sets of actors for each of the chiefs. In the attempt to aggregate these rankings, it became necessary to take account of some descriptive and analytical statements found in the case studies. Thus a brief characterization of that material is also shown in Table III-12. As has already been noted in other contexts, the Tennessee situation is atypical since the governor appoints the CSSO and the chief has no legislative program separate from that of the governor. There seemed to be no way of compensating for this condition; thus, Tennessee was removed from cross-state comparison.

The overall influence rank ascribed to each of the eleven CSSO's in the legislative arena, shown in Table III-12, reflects the best judg-

TABLE III-12 Overall Influence of the CSSO in the Legislative Arena

CSSO's by state, according to means of selection	Rank, legis-lators	Rank, EIG	Rank, governor's office	From case study	Ascribed overall rank
Elected					
California	3	2	2.5	Strong with governor and legislature	3
Florida	4.5	4.5	1	Has lost some influence with legislature	5
Georgia	1	3	2.5	Great influence with legislature; often successful in challenging governor	2
Wisconsin	6	8	4	Strong deputy CSSO; effective with governor and legislature	7
Appointed					
Colorado	10	9	9.5	Growing in stature but too soon to be sure	9
Massachusetts	11	10.5	8	CSSO and SDE weak in total state context	11
Michigan	8	6	5.5	A strong advocate in a complex state	4
Minnesota	4.5	4.5	11	Moderately effective with legislature and governor	6
Nebraska	7	7	9.5	Holds line, meager program	10
New York	9	10.5	7	Effective in highly competitive situation	8
Texas	2	1	5.5	Low profile, but trusted in legislature	1

ment of those who conducted the study as they assessed the perceptions of actors near the scene (recorded on the *Interview Schedule*)
and as they considered the interactions of the chief with other actors
(reflected in the case studies). In Texas, Georgia, and California the
CSSO is perceived to be very influential by all three sets of actors,
and there is abundant confirmation in the case studies. For Michigan,
Florida, Minnesota, Wisconsin, and New York the influence of the
chiefs in the legislative arena appears to be moderate, sometimes less
with one set of actors than with another. In Colorado, Nebraska, and
Massachusetts the chiefs have relatively little policy influence in the
legislative arena. But there is another arena in which the CSSO is a
policy actor, and that arena will be considered now.

The State Education Agency Arena

While the legislature in all states studied is the plenary body for
the enactment of policy, in certain education areas policy functions
are delegated to the state education agency. Usually these functions
are assigned specifically to the state board of education, but sometimes they are lodged with the CSSO and sometimes with the department of education. The term "state education agency," as it is used
here, includes all three of these components. It is well to note again
that this study looks only at the policy-making functions that obviously command much of the state agency's time and energy. Specifically, the concern here is with the influence of the CSSO in policy
enactments stemming from the agency of which he is a part. In most
cases these policy expressions will be formalized by the state board
of education. Only Wisconsin, of the twelve states studied, does not
have a state board of education. While the ex officio nature of the
Florida board makes it somewhat atypical, it is included in some of
the discussion.

To test the role that state board members believe the CSSO should
play, the members were asked to respond to the same role questions
posed for the chiefs. The responses of SBE members are shown in
Table III-13. State board members in every state hold very strong
leadership expectations for the CSSO. In four states, Colorado, Massachusetts, Nebraska, and Tennessee, 100 percent of the board members "strongly agree" or "tend to agree" that the CSSO should
assume the leadership role in shaping policy proposals coming to the
boards. In no state were these leadership expectations expressed by

TABLE III-13 SBE Members Who Contend That the CSSO Should Assume Leadership in Shaping Policies Enacted by the SBE (board responses in percentages)

CSSO's by state, according to means of selection	Number of respondents	Strongly agree	Tend to agree	Tend to disagree	Strongly disagree	Leadership expectation score (percent strongly agree and tend to agree)
Elected						
California	8	50	25	25	0	75
Florida	5	80	20	0	0	100
Georgia	7	57	14	14	14	71
Wisconsin[a]	—	—	—	—	—	—
AVERAGE						82
Appointed						
Colorado	4	75	25	0	0	100
Massachusetts	8	87	13	0	0	100
Michigan	6	67	17	17	0	84
Minnesota	6	50	33	17	0	83
Nebraska	5	100	0	0	0	100
New York	9	67	22	0	11	89
Tennessee	8	75	25	0	0	100
Texas	10	60	20	20	0	80
AVERAGE						92

[a]No state board.

less than 71 percent of the board members. Indeed, expectations of SBE members for strong leadership on the part of the CSSO's were almost as high as the expectations the chiefs set for themselves. Interestingly, the expectations of board members for appointed chiefs, on the average, were even higher than for elected chiefs, average scores of 92 and 82, respectively, but the most notable finding is the high expectations held for all chiefs.

The next attempt was to get some appraisal of the leadership style of the CSSO. We asked SBE members, CSSO's, and a state board expert, a person in each state department whose major assignment was to work directly with the state board of education, to describe the approach used by CSSO's in the development of policy proposals for board consideration. Table III-14 reports responses of board members, chiefs, and board experts to the question of how often chiefs developed a detailed proposal for the entire board to consider. These responses were reported on a four-point scale: often, sometimes, rarely, and never. A directive score for each chief was reached by simply taking the percentage of board responses under the "often" column. In this sense, chiefs in Colorado, Michigan, and Georgia were seen as most directive. Not only do most board members in these states ascribe such behavior to the chiefs, but the chiefs themselves and the board experts concur with the descriptions. Using the same criteria, chiefs in Tennessee, California, and Florida were found to be least directive. In these three states there was less agreement among board members and no agreement between chiefs and board experts. In the case of Florida the chief responded "often" and the expert "never," a difference that is difficult to explain. Chiefs in the other five states appeared to have rather high directive scores, clustered between 67 and 50. In three of these five states both chiefs and board experts concurred with a majority of the board members, while in the other two states there was some dispersion between the responses of the chief and the board expert.

In Chapter II, board members responded to another part of the question having to do with the approach used by the CSSO's in preparing a major policy proposal. The board members indicated the extent to which chiefs took ideas or suggestions from the members and developed them into a policy proposal. Table II-4 showed that on the average only 29 percent of the board members saw chiefs responding "often" in this manner. It seemed useful to compare the

TABLE III-14 Perceptions of SBE Members, the CSSO, and the SBE Expert Regarding Extent to Which CSSO Develops Detailed Proposals for Entire Board (board responses in percentages; C = CSSO, E = Expert)

CSSO by state, according to means of selection	Number of respondents	Often	Some-times	Rarely	Never	Directive score (percent often)
Elected						
California	8	25E	25C	37	13	25
Florida	3[b]	33C	0	67	0E	33
Georgia	7	71CE	14	14	0	71
Wisconsin[a]	—	—	—	—	—	—
AVERAGE						43
Appointed						
Colorado	4	100CE	0	0	0	100
Massachusetts	8	50CE	37	13	0	50
Michigan	6	83CE	17	0	0	83
Minnesota	6	67	16	0C	16E	67
Nebraska	5	60CE	0	20	20	60
New York	8	62CE	25	0	13	62
Tennessee	8	13E	37C	13	0	13
Texas	11	55C	9E	18	18	47
AVERAGE						60

[a]No state board.
[b]Three of the cabinet members did not respond.

responses of chiefs and board experts to the same question, and this is done in Table III-15. The percentage of board members who indicated "often" was again used as a basis for establishing a score for each of the chiefs, in this case a receptive score.

Whereas chiefs as a group rank high by way of "directive" scores, they rank relatively low by way of "receptive" scores. This seems reasonable since in some ways directive and receptive approaches to the development of policy proposals are at opposite ends of a continuum. The highest receptive scores were ascribed to Nebraska, Minnesota, Michigan, and New York. In the case of Nebraska and Michigan both the chief and the board expert tended to agree with board members. In the case of New York board members divided between "often" and "sometimes." The chief agreed with a majority of the board and the expert, with the minority. The receptive scores for Nebraska and New York seemed rather logical when compared to the directive scores, which were in the middle range. That kind of agreement did not hold as well for Michigan and Minnesota, which had both high receptive scores and high directive scores.

The lowest receptive scores were noted for California, Massachusetts, Texas, and Tennessee, and three of these states were also at the very bottom on the directive dimension. This strange finding obviously requires an explanation. It could be that the two concepts of direction and reception have not been adequately operationalized; in one case bringing a fully developed proposal for board consideration, and in the other case beginning with a consideration of ideas generated by board members themselves. Or, it could be that the two notions are not incompatible; a chief might begin with board-generated ideas and then develop a detailed proposal. Or, it could be that respondents were providing, particularly in the receptive part of the question, "good" answers, those that made their chiefs, whom they respected, look good. All three conditions probably pertain to some degree.

The difference between the average score for elected chiefs, 23, and the average for appointed, 34, seems to suggest that appointed chiefs begin with board ideas more frequently than their elected counterparts. In comparing Tables III-14 and III-15, it also seems clear that CSSO's, on the whole, are much more prone to bring in policy proposals than to solicit them.

TABLE III-15 Responses of SBE Members, CSSO's, and SBE Experts to the Extent to Which Chiefs Take Ideas and Suggestions from Board Members and Develop These into Policy Proposals (board responses in percentages; C = CSSO, E = Board Expert)

CSSO's by state, according to means of selection	Number of respondents	Often	Some-times	Rarely	Never	Receptive score (percent often)
Elected						
California	7	14	29CE	43	14	14
Florida	4	25	50E	25C	0	25
Georgia	7	29	43CE	29	0	29
Wisconsin[a]	—	—	—	—	—	—
AVERAGE						23
Appointed						
Colorado	4	25	75CE	0	0	25
Massachusetts	7	14	86CE	0	0	14
Michigan	6	50CE	50	0	0	50
Minnesota[b]	6	50	50C	0	0	50
Nebraska	5	60CE	40	0	0	60
New York	7	43E	57C	0	0	43
Tennessee	8	13	87CE	0	0	13
Texas	11	18CE	64	0	0	18
AVERAGE						34

[a] No state board.
[b] No response from board expert.

To this point, chiefs appear to be lords in their own manors. SBE members expect them to exert strong leadership on policy issues; information generated by the state departments at the behest of the chiefs is highly valued by board members; most chiefs formulate their policy proposals in detail and bring them to their boards for legitimation most of the time. While this provides some feel for the milieu in which the chief works, there is still no firm indication of his influence in that milieu. In another part of the *Interview Schedule,* state board members were asked to rank the importance of a number of actors in providing perspective on state education policy issues. As noted in Chapter II, CSSO's were most frequently cited as important actors. Table III-16 shows the importance ascribed to CSSO's by state board members in each state. In spite of the fact that chiefs are relatively important in providing understanding to SBE members in

TABLE III-16 Importance Ascribed to CSSO's by SBE Members to Their Understanding Education Policy Issues (board responses in percentages)

CSSO's by state, according to means of selection	Number of respondents	Very important	Impor- tant	Unimpor- tant	Impor- tance score
Elected					
California	9	44	44	11	44
Florida	6	67	33	0	67
Georgia	7	71	29	0	71
Wisconsin[a]	—	—	—	—	—
AVERAGE					61
Appointed					
Colorado	4	50	50	0	50
Massachusetts	8	100	0	0	100
Michigan	6	67	33	0	67
Minnesota	6	83	17	0	83
Nebraska	5	80	20	0	80
New York	9	89	11	0	89
Tennessee	8	75	25	0	75
Texas	11	82	18	0	82
AVERAGE					78

[a]No state board.

all states, there is some differentiation among the states. Examination of the "very important" column suggests that greatest importance is ascribed to chiefs in Massachusetts, New York, Texas, and Minnesota. Moderate importance is indicated for chiefs in Nebraska, Tennessee, Georgia, Florida, and Michigan. Somewhat less importance is indicated for Colorado and California, while Wisconsin, it will be recalled, has no state board of education. Boards with appointed chiefs rate their importance appreciably higher than boards with elected chiefs.

Another indication of the influence of CSSO's in the state agency arena was dealt with in Chapter II. This had to do with whether or not board members opposed the chief on major policy issues. Board members did not often oppose the CSSO. Only in California and Michigan did a majority of board member respondents acknowledge that some board members frequently opposed the chief. We raised this same question with the CSSO's, and, in the cases of California and Florida, they confirmed the responses of the board members. The chiefs in the cases of Massachusetts, Michigan, and Tennessee did not agree with board respondents that board members frequently opposed them on major policy issues. In the case of Nebraska the CSSO indicated that board members frequently opposed him, while no board members acknowledged such behavior on the part of their colleagues. In the cases of Georgia, Colorado, Minnesota, New York, and Texas, both sides of the partnership agreed that board members did not oppose the CSSO. Only in the case of Michigan where 67 percent of the board members indicated opposition to the chief and the chief did not acknowledge opposition did we find the responses difficult to understand. Perhaps, in Michigan, board members and the chief have different interpretations of what is meant either by opposition or by major policy questions. Or, the Michigan chief may be more of an optimist than some of his board members. Despite the emergence of some disagreement between boards and chiefs and some differences in perceptions about these disagreements, the central tendency is one of harmony between boards and their chiefs, as can be seen in Table III-17.

In Chapter II, Table II-4, interest group leaders, who may be impartial observers of boards and chiefs, responded to the question of whether or not state boards ever gave real direction to the CSSO. For the state of Texas, three observers said "yes"; for the states of

TABLE III-17 Overall Influence of CSSO in the SEA Arena

CSSO's by state, according to means of selection	Ranked importance of CSSO to SBE on issues	Extent of opposition from SBE	Extent of direction from SBE	From case studies analyses	Ascribed overall rank
Elected					
California	11	Some	None	Still some opposition in the board	9
Florida	8.5	Little	None	Many see SDE as stronger than the CSSO	8
Georgia	7	None	None	Strong with board and staff	5
Appointed					
Colorado	10	None	Little	Coping well with independent board	7
Massachusetts	1	Little	None	Board loyal to CSSO	2
Michigan	8.5	Some	None	CSSO moves with majority of board	6
Minnesota	3	None	Some	Supportive and collegial	4
Nebraska	5	None	Some	Holds line, little leadership	11
New York	2	None	Some	SDE seen as better than U.S. Office of Education	1
Tennessee	6	Little	None	Board is not sure who is the captain	10
Texas	4	None	Some	Low profile, long tenure, respected	3

New York, Minnesota, and Nebraska, two said "yes"; for the state of Colorado, one EIG spokesman said "yes." In the other five states, no EIG spokesmen saw the state boards as giving real direction to the CSSO's. In other words, the chiefs in Michigan, Massachusetts, California, Georgia, and Tennessee follow a course that has few constraints or guidelines established by state boards. This is not to say that there are no constraints. In Tennessee, for instance, the chief serves at the pleasure of the governor, and, when he does not follow the bidding of the governor, he is replaced. In California and Georgia, where chiefs are elected, constraints may well be set by the electorate. The significant point, however, is that in at least half of the states, in the view of EIG leaders (as noted in Table III-17), boards do not give real direction to the chiefs. Even in the other states where EIG spokesmen say boards sometimes establish guidelines, such direction is probably gentle and infrequent.

Another source of data about the influence of chiefs in the state education agency is contained in the case studies. Even though these data cannot be quantified, there has been an attempt to characterize each of the case studies briefly, as shown in Table III-17.

The basic concern is how much influence CSSO's have in the state education arena. Again, it was necessary to drop one state, Wisconsin, which has no state board of education. In Table III-17 ranks are established for the importance question. The only categories shown are for extent of opposition and extent of direction to the chief. We have already noted that the attempt to provide evidence from case studies on this point relies on brief characterizations. After taking these four lines of evidence into account, the states appear to fall in the overall order shown in Table III-17.

New York appears at the top because the importance score was very high, there was no reported opposition to the CSSO by board members on major issues, the board gave direction to the chief but did not dominate him, and board members and state department members clearly revealed respect, confidence, and support for the CSSO in interviews. Nebraska appears in last place because the importance score was in the middle range, and, while now there was no reported opposition on the part of the board, there was still some direction given by the board. Even more significant, board members, when interviewed, did not see the CSSO as guiding their own deliberations. For each of the other states, a similar process was employed to establish comparative rank. CSSO's in New York, Massachusetts, and Texas seemed to have great influence in their respective state agencies; chiefs in Minnesota, Georgia, Michigan, Colorado, and Florida, somewhat less influence; and chiefs in California, Tennessee, and Nebraska, while still influential in their respective state agencies, ranked below those already named by comparison. Comparisons were not easy to establish. In California there was reason to believe that data were influenced by a former CSSO who was often in open conflict with board members. In Nebraska lack of leadership, often ascribed to the CSSO, may have resulted, at least in part, from his early frustration in dealing with a divided board; any recommendation was certain to meet opposition from one faction or the other. In both cases the situational factors were peculiar to the state in question.

It is intriguing to compare the influence of CSSO's in the state agency arena with their influence in the legislative arena. Only in Texas was influence high for both arenas, and only in Nebraska was influence low for both arenas. In California influence was high for the legislative arena and low for the state agency arena. Massachusetts, on the other hand, occupied a reverse position: influence was high in the state agency arena and low in the legislative arena. The possible implications of these relationships are examined later.

A CORRELATIONAL ANALYSIS

At several points in this chapter it has been suggested that there are possible relationships between certain variables and the policy-making influence of CSSO's. Some of those relationships can now be tested statistically. Since the numbers are small and some measures are ordinal, the best method for the purpose appears to be the Spearman rank-difference correlation or rho.[9]

Influence of CSSO's in Two Arenas

Initially, it was expected that this study would arrive at some indication of the overall influence of the CSSO in the policy-making system, including both the legislative arena and the state education agency arena. As has already been noted, however, there appears to be relatively little congruence between CSSO influence in the two arenas. Because a chief could have much influence in one arena and little in another, it seems best to examine the influence of CSSO's in each arena and not try to combine them. To test that proposition further, the first correlation has to do with the relationship of CSSO influence in the legislative arena to CSSO influence in the state agency arena. As has already been noted, Tennessee was eliminated from consideration in the legislative arena; Wisconsin, in the state agency arena. This left ten states to be tested. We found that rho = −.02.

A correlation of this order means there is no relationship at all. In other words, a chief may have influence in both arenas, in neither arena, some influence in both, or great influence in one and little in the other. This finding confirms what was said above and makes it clear that the two arenas are quite distinct. To attempt a combined overall measure of influence would only confuse the matter.

Aside from methodological considerations, this may also be one of the important findings of the study. If many assume, as we did, that a chief with great influence would be so perceived by all or most of the other policy actors, it now seems quite clear that a chief may have great influence with the state board and with members of the department of education and be relatively weak in dealing with the governor and legislators. Or, a chief may exert great influence with the governor and legislators and not be as highly regarded by state board members and members of his own department. It does not follow systematically, however, that chiefs are high in one arena and low in the other. Many combinations of influence patterns may exist. The important point the study demonstrates is the need to look at influence patterns in both arenas; it is hazardous to assume that degree of influence in one arena indicates degree of influence in the other.

Relation of Selected Variables to CSSO Influence

Having established the point that selected variables must be related to two measures of CSSO influence, it is time to turn to that task. Table III-18 shows the correlations derived from these calculations. For these computations, except for one case (Tennessee), eleven states were included in the legislative arena, and, except for one case (Wisconsin), eleven states were included in the state agency arena. The one exception had to do with the policy influence of the SBE, a rank order derived in Chapter II, where ten states made up the population.

TABLE III-18 Rank-order Correlations of Two Measures of CSSO Influence with Selected Variables

	Influence of CSSO in legislative arena	Influence of CSSO in SEA arena
Structural variables		
Method of selection (elected or appointed)	.45	−.15
Size of SDE staff	.50	.45
Political variables		
Interparty competition (Ranney index)	−.42	−.19
Voting turnout	−.44	−.07
Political culture (Elazar-Sharkansky index)	−.29	.15
Socioeconomic variables		
Personal income per capita	−.43	.36
Population size	.52	.38
Percent of urban population	−.04	.39
Industrialization index (Hofferbert-Sharkansky index)	−.06	.52
Other selected variables		
Formal power of office	.56	−.09
Percent of doctorates in top staff	.28	.65
Percent of salaries over $25,000 in top staff	.12	.46
Staff attraction capability	.19	.48
Freedom to select and discharge staff	.27	.27
SDE information usefulness	.15	.37
Self-perceived influence	.17	.58
CSSO directive style	−.18	.22
Policy influence of SBE	.20	.45

As a rough guide for interpreting the correlations, we can say that a rho of .3 to .4 indicates a trend only, a rho of .5 to .6 indicates a moderate relationship, and a rho of .7 and above indicates a strong relationship. We should point out that these relationships are statistical associations, that is, one variable tends to go with the other.

Such relationships may or may not have anything to do with cause and effect.

A few general observations can be made about the relationships. Many are not high enough to have any significance. Eleven correlations are in the .3 to .4 range, which suggests a trend or slight relationship. Only six correlations are in the .5 to .6 range where moderate relationships are indicated. No correlations are as high as .7 or above. Each set of relationships is discussed briefly since it may be as important to note what is not related as to note what is.

The first consideration is the relationship between the method of selecting the CSSO and his influence in the two arenas. In this instance, since there were only two categories of selection, a two-by-two table and a chi-square formula were used to compute the relationship.[10] A phi (ϕ) of .45 indicates a tendency for elected chiefs to have more influence in the legislative arena. Method of selection apparently has no relationship to CSSO influence in the state agency arena. Clearly, these results do not support method of selection as having a strong relationship to the influence of the CSSO.

Size of SDE staff apparently has a moderate association with the influence of the CSSO in both arenas. The positive correlations of .50 and .45 go in the logical direction, but, again, size of staff alone does not seem to represent an overriding influence.

When looking at the political variables as a group, interparty competition, an index developed by Ranney,[11] has a slight negative relationship to the influence of chiefs in the legislative arena and no relationship in the state agency arena. This may mean that less interparty competition permits the chief to be slightly more influential in the legislative arena. The political culture index developed by Sharkansky out of work done by Elazar[12] was designed to portray a reform as opposed to a traditional approach to government. Either the index is too crude to be useful, or there is no relationship between such a dimension and the influence of chiefs in either arena.

From the outset of this study there was some question as to how socioeconomic variables would be related to the influence of chiefs. A look at the eight correlations under this category in Table III-18 suggests that most such relationships are very modest. For income, the tendencies are negative in the legislative arena and positive in the agency arena. There is no reasonable explanation for this difference. There may be some logic in the cluster of negative income, negative voter turnout, and negative party competition and their relationship to legislative influence of the CSSO, but all correlations are too modest to press the point. Population size appears to have a moderate relationship to the influence of the chief in the legislative arena, but it is merely a trend in the agency arena. Percent of urban population is not related to the influence of the chief in the legislative arena, but it is slightly related to his influence in the agency arena. Industrialization, using an index developed by Hofferbert and Sharkansky,[13] follows the same pattern as urbanization: no relationship to the influence of the CSSO in the legislative arena and a somewhat stronger relationship in the agency arena.

A number of variables discussed earlier in this chapter, particularly those having to do with the resources of the CSSO, are now discussed. The first is the formal power of the office of the CSSO. The correlation of .56 suggests a moderate relationship between the power of the office and the influence of the chief in the legislative arena. The strength of this relationship may be somewhat inflated since, in ranking the states on formal powers of office, there were a number of ties. The correlation of −.09 suggests there is no relationship between power of office and the policy influence of the chief in the agency arena.

The next six correlations are related. The first and second pairs, having to do with doctorates and salaries, are used to make up the third pair, designated staff attraction capability. All three pairs of correlations run in the same direction: no relationship to the influence of the CSSO in the legislative arena and moderate relationship in the agency arena. It may be that legislators and governors are somewhat unaware or unconcerned about the capability of the CSSO to attract and hold staff members. Or, it may be that the actors in the legislative arena ascribe more importance to political skills than they do to expertise usually thought to be associated with highly trained and well-paid staff members. Another aspect of staffing has to do with the freedom of the chief to select and discharge his top assistants. There was considerable variation among the states on this matter, but such a measure does not appear to represent a relationship of any significance for the CSSO in either the legislative or the agency arena.

After the usefulness of SDE information to legislators, governors' staffs, and state board members was acknowledged, the responses from these actors were combined into a total SDE information score. As suggested by the earlier analysis, SDE information does not seem to be related to the influence of the chief in the legislative arena, but there is a tendency for it to be related to his influence in the agency arena. With such low correlations, it seems clear that many variables other than information affect the influence of the CSSO.

There is a relationship between the self-perceived influence of the chiefs and the influence ascribed by others to the chiefs in the two arenas. For the legislative arena, the correlation was .17, which must be interpreted as no relationship. Apparently chiefs see themselves as being much more influential in the legislative arena than other policy actors in that arena do. On the other hand, with a correlation of .58 between the self-perceptions of the chiefs and the perceptions of the other actors in the agency arena, there is considerable agreement. Put otherwise, the CSSO's appear to make a more realistic appraisal of their influence in the agency arena than in the legislative arena.

There has already been some consideration of what has been called the directive style of the chiefs. We were able to array the chiefs on this dimension and then relate such rankings to their influence in the two arenas. In both cases the correlations were too low to have any significance. Either a chief's directiveness has no effect on his influence in either arena, or the operationalizing of the term was inadequate.

The final relationship to be considered was between the policy influence of the state board of education, as developed in Chapter II, and the influence of the CSSO in both arenas. A rho of .20 for the legislative arena suggests there is no relationship. In other words, whether boards have much or little influence is not systematically related to the influence of the chief. In the agency arena, with a rho of .45, there is a moderate positive relationship between the influence of the board and the chief.* This suggests that both the board and the chief can have influence; it does not sustain the notion that a strong board will have a weak chief or a strong chief will have a weak board. While there are examples of both such cases, the relationship precludes making any such generalization. This may suggest that influence is not a zero-sum game where one actor gains at the ex-

---

*It might be noted that one item is common to both indexes.

pense of another; rather, many actors in the policy system may exert influence.

Summary

There is no systematic relationship between the chief's influence in the legislative arena and his influence in the agency arena. The old question of elected versus appointed chiefs produced only one moderate relationship, and that favored elected chiefs in the legislative arena. Relationships to all political variables were too modest to be of much significance. For the most part, the same was true for all socioeconomic variables. The formal power of the office of the chief was positively related to his influence in the legislative arena only. The capacity of the chief to attract staff was modestly related to his influence in the agency arena only. CSSO's appear to make rather realistic assessments of their influence in the agency arena but their perceptions of influence in the legislative arena are less reliable. There is some evidence to suggest that both boards and chiefs may exert influence and that one does not have to dominate the other.

*   *   *

These findings suggest a few implications for the future role of the CSSO as a policy maker. CSSO's are generally male; they frequently have rural and in-state orientations; they most often reach their office through service as a district superintendent of schools and as a member of a state department of education. As to resources, chiefs vary with respect to formal powers of office, their ability to attract and hold staff, and their freedom to select their top administrative team members. Elected chiefs appear to have more formal power, and appointed chiefs seem to have more freedom in establishing their own administrative teams. The perceived usefulness of SDE information to governors' offices and legislators varies greatly among the states with information from elected chiefs held in somewhat higher regard than information from appointed chiefs. On the other hand, SDE information tends to be seen as very useful by state board members, whether it is provided by elected or appointed chiefs.

As to how influential CSSO's are as policy makers, almost without exception they exert great influence in the state education agency arena. SBE members expect the chief to provide leadership; board members ascribe great importance to the chief in providing understanding on policy issues; board members seldom oppose the chief on major issues; and most boards give the chief little or no general direction. Even though the general picture is one of great influence, using data such as that noted above and additional insight from the case studies enables one to ascribe an influence rank for chiefs in the state agency arena, as shown in Table III-17. It is interesting to note that the four chiefs with most influence in the state agency arena were appointed, but the two with least influence were also appointed.

The influence of the chief as a policy maker in the legislative arena is quite another picture. Legislators, interest group leaders, and governors and their offices ascribe influence to the chiefs, but it is clearly not so overwhelming as that ascribed to chiefs by state education agency actors. Using the perceptions of actors close to the legislative process along with insights from the case studies, one can ascribe an influence rank for chiefs in the legislative arena as shown in Table III-12. In this case, it should be noted that, of the four chiefs with most influence, two were appointed and two were elected. Those at or near the lower end of influence were all appointed, a finding that may reflect the fact that eight of the twelve chiefs in the EGP study were appointed.

Examination of the influence ranks ascribed to chiefs in the two arenas are most revealing. Only Texas is found in the high influence group in both arenas. Only Nebraska is found in the low influence group in both arenas. California is high in the legislative arena and low in the agency arena, while in Massachusetts the positions are reversed. Inspection suggests that these are, indeed, two quite different arenas of operation. A correlation between the two sets of influence ranks showed a result of rho = $-.02$, or no systematic relationship. This means that a chief can have much influence in both arenas, much in one and little in the other, or little in both, a finding of considerable import.

Again, the rankings in the two arenas have to do only with the policy-making roles of the chiefs. The implementation or management roles of chiefs were not part of the study and, hence, are not taken into account. These rankings suggest the policy influence of each CSSO in his own situation, and the situations vary appreciably. In some states governors and legislatures are strong; in others they are weak. In some states the education agency enjoys high status; in others it does not. In some states the political culture encourages responsive public officials; in others it does not. In some states financial resources are abundant; in others they are not. In those states where governors' offices, legislatures, or state boards are powerful, a CSSO may find it very difficult to influence the situation. Perhaps in those states where governors' offices, legislatures, or state boards of education are less powerful, the opportunity for the CSSO to exert influence is somewhat greater. This is to say that there is no way of arraying the twelve CSSO's on some abstract scale of influence. All the data suggest is the policy-making influence of each chief in his own state. Finally, influence cannot be equated with what is best. In any systems approach to government it seems reasonable to assume that influence should be spread among the major actors and not concentrated in the hands of one.

Differentiating among major actors in terms of their influence is at times difficult. A colleague who read an early draft of this chapter reminded us of this problem:

when the CSSO is operating in the legislative arena it is awfully difficult to disentangle the CSSO influence (even in the minds of perceivers) from that of other actors. Legislation proposed and lobbied for by EIGs, for example, may bear CSSO input unbeknownst to observers. Observers may be unaware of telephone calls to the chief from individual legislators, or of the fact that a given piece of legislation was "cleaned up" by the chief before it went into the hopper. On the other side, it may be friendly legislative stalwarts who actually "wrote" and then carried through some components of the chief's legislative program.

Tempting as it may be to despair of the complexities involved and thus do nothing about ascribing influence to particular actors, the other course was chosen here even though the findings may be incomplete and at times even appear naive. This line of study must be begun.

Through a correlational analysis the relationships were ascertained between a number of variables and the influence of chiefs in both arenas, as shown in Table III-18. Formal structure, specifically election as opposed to appointment of the CSSO, was modestly related to the degree of influence of the chief in the legislative arena; there was no relationship to the influence of the chief in the agency arena. This confirms some other findings. For instance, SDE information from elected chiefs was perceived as more useful by legislators and governors' offices than SDE information from appointed chiefs. It may be that elected officials tend to look with more favor upon chiefs who are also elected. In a sense, they have come through the war together. But the relationship is not high enough to become too persuasive, particularly in view of the fact that some appointed chiefs, notably those in Texas and Michigan, have achieved considerable influence with the legislature.

Most of the relationships between political and socioeconomic variables and the influence of chiefs were too low to be significant. One pattern of moderate strength did emerge. Apparently, in states with little interparty competition, low voter turnout, and low personal income, the chief has somewhat more influence in the legislative arena. It may be that, in states with these characteristics, other agencies of government are less developed and the chief can more easily emerge as a leader in the situation. The rho of .52 between industrialization and the influence of the chief in the agency arena may be something of a reverse picture. If it can be assumed that industrialization may also mean more interparty competition, higher voter turnout, and higher income, it is interesting to note that the greater influence of the chief is in the agency, not the legislative, arena.

There is a moderate relationship between the formal power of office and the influence of the chief in the legislative arena. Formal power of office, as shown in Table III-4, is an aggregate of six variables: the legal status of the office of CSSO, the membership status of chief on the board, the board role prescribed for the chief, the reporting relationships to governor and legislature, the quasi-judicial power of the chief, and the tenure status of the office. Taken alone, few of these variables provide much differentiation among the chiefs. Taken together, the formal power scores run from 1 to 5. Elected chiefs have an average score of 4; appointed chiefs, 2.6. Because elected chiefs enjoy greater power of office and they are also seen as having greater influence in the legislative arena, power of office and the elected status of the chief have a relationship. Or, to put it differently, formal power of office, as defined here, seems to be more visible and more significant to legislators and governors than to members of the state boards and state departments.

Only three other variables suggest relationships strong enough to merit comment, and these all pertain to the influence of the chief in the agency arena. The power of chiefs to attract staff is related to the influence of chiefs in the agency but not in the legislative arena. Of particular interest is the rho of .58 for the relationship of the self-perceived influence of chiefs to their state agency influence as perceived by other actors in that arena. In this instance, the chiefs apparently have a rather good sense of reality, in contrast to the legislative arena where the chiefs do not have the same sense of reality. Finally, the rho of .45 between the policy influence of state boards and the policy influence of CSSO's in the agency arena suggests that chiefs and boards may share power and that one actor need not achieve influence at the expense of the other.

For those concerned that CSSO's have significant but not necessarily dominant influence in making policy for education, these findings may suggest some implications.

1. *While the formal structure of the office does not come through as the overriding variable related to the influence of the chief, it does seem to have some significance.* In some states the office should be given more legal status, its relationship to the governor and legislature should be stipulated, and the leadership and administrative roles of the chief vis-à-vis the board should be made explicit. It also seems clear that the board should have the right to appoint and hold responsible their own chief executive officer. This can be argued from the standpoint of administrative principle; it can also be argued from some of the data shown above. For instance, appointive chiefs more frequently solicit ideas from board members. This fact alone suggests that one way to make both the board and the chief important policy actors is to let the board select its own chief. Also, the data show that appointed chiefs can more frequently select and discharge their own top staff members, a condition essential to an effective organization. Apparently, boards are more disposed to give the chief such freedom when they choose him. Finally, a term appointment gives the office more status than an "at the pleasure of the board" arrangement.

2. *People also make a difference.* In California, for instance, the formal structure for educational governance has not changed much in recent years. Yet, the present state superintendent and his immediate predecessor are quite different people, as many respondents in the California case study[14] kept insisting. Superintendent Max Rafferty was elected to two four-year terms, and he apparently looked to the electors as his constituency. From all reports he was less concerned about relationships with the state board of education, the legislature, or even the governor. In a sense, he was an ideologist, and his basic

message was a return to the fundamentals. He pressed his point eloquently from the platform and through the public press. In time, the message, or the ensuing controversy which the exponent of the message provoked, apparently lost its appeal. In any case, in the election of 1970 the people rejected Rafferty and chose Wilson Riles who came over as sincere, warm, approachable, and concerned about youngsters. Since his election, Riles has been characterized by many as "the great peacemaker." He took the position that he would not submit a legislative program independent of the state board of education, he has worked closely with the legislature, and he and the governor apparently agreed not to "shoot at each other." Despite his peacemaking efforts, Riles got only part of what he was seeking for early childhood education in the first round, but he apparently sees other rounds coming. In any case, Rafferty and Riles, while in the same formal structure, have responded quite differently to it.

Much the same point can be observed in three other case studies where respondents kept drawing contrasts between the incumbent CSSO and his immediate predecessor. In Colorado[15] the former commissioner was often characterized as aggressive; the incumbent, as diplomatic. In Massachusetts[16] the former commissioner frequently was seen by legislators as chastizing them; the incumbent (1973), as being more inclined to mollify them. In Tennessee[17] the former commissioner seemed to employ a directive style in dealing with the state board, the legislature, and the governor; the incumbent, a nondirective approach. To note that people respond differently to formal structures does not suggest that one kind of behavior on the part of the CSSO is more effective than another. Much depends on other factors in the situation.

3. *In many states the balance of influence between chiefs and boards should be redressed.* As noted in Chapter II, most boards do little more to influence policy than legitimate the recommendations of the chief. One way for appointed chiefs to exercise more influence in the legislative arena, a place where many of them are now relatively weak, might well be through the active participation of their board members. It is obvious that this often requires more of a team relationship between the chief and his board members than exists now. The EGP data suggest that more influence on the part of board members does not necessarily mean less influence on the part of the chief. Such a team effort might actually enhance the influence of both actors in the policy process.

4. *To exercise influence in policy making for education, many CSSO's must find ways of operating more effectively in the legislative arena.* Policy, by its very nature, is most frequently enacted in that arena. It will be difficult to increase CSSO influence in the legislative arena since most chiefs now think, often mistakenly, that they are already influential with governors and legislatures. Apparently, the accurate perception of great influence at home confounds the perception CSSO's have of their influence abroad. In addition to helping chiefs recognize their limited influence in the legislative arena, ways might be found of making SDE information more useful to governors and legislators. It may be, too, that chiefs and board members need to give consideration to the kinds of behavior required when they work with elected officials as contrasted to professional educators.

5. *The personal characteristics and operating styles of CSSO's are important to other policy actors.* Some evidence for this position is present in each of the twelve case studies, but the point is made more dramatically in the four case studies referred to above where respondents kept contrasting the incumbent CSSO with his immediate predecessor. For many, sincerity was preferred to arrogance, compromise to obduracy, listening to pronouncing, and direction to nondirection. Perhaps the best example of what legislators respect was found in Texas. The chief there, whose advice was seen as sound, had worked at his job for twenty-five years, had not sought the limelight for himself, and had in time come to be trusted implicitly.

It should be recognized that the operating style of any CSSO is a product of both the person and the situation. This brings us to the consideration of congruence between the person and the situation. While one chief was seen as bringing little leadership to the state board of education, the fractionated nature of that board almost forced the chief to reduce his leadership to the lowest common denominator. In another case, the directive style of one chief apparently established the expectations of other policy actors in the system for the office of CSSO and a new chief with a nondirective style could not meet those expectations. These examples suggest that any style may be effective if it is congruent with the expectations held by other actors in the system.

6. *When a CSSO is to be selected, whether by the board or by the electorate, every effort should be made to find a person who gives promise of exercising appropriate influence in both the state agency*

and the legislative arena. For the state agency, professional expertise and some political skill is required. For legislators and governors, the requirements must be posed in reverse order: political skill and professional expertise. These criteria are far more important than age, sex, pattern of experience, or place of residence. It is obvious, in the selection of a CSSO, that boards have more direct control over such a process than the voters of the state have. In states where chiefs are elected, however, more attention should be given to nomination procedures to the end that candidates with both political skills and professional expertise are placed in nomination. In keeping with what was noted above, those who select chiefs should also consider to what extent the leadership style of the candidate will be congruent with the expectations of other actors in the policy system.

NOTES—CHAPTER III

1. See Ellwood P. Cubberley and Edward C. Elliott, *State and County School Administration* (New York: Macmillan, 1915), II, pp. 213-286.

2. Sam P. Harris, *State Departments of Education, State Boards of Education, and Chief State School Officers*, Department of Health, Education, and Welfare Publication (Office of Education) 73-074000 (Washington, D. C.: U.S. Government Printing Office, 1973), ch. 3.

3. Alvin W. Gouldner, "Cosmopolitans and Locals: Toward an Analysis of Latent Social Roles," *Administration Science Quarterly*, 1 (No. 2, 1957), pp. 281-306; 2 (No. 2, 1958), pp. 444-480.

4. David J. Kirby and Thomas A. Tollman, "Background and Career Patterns of State Department Personnel," in Roald F. Campbell *et al.*, *Strengthening State Departments of Education* (Chicago: University of Chicago, Midwest Administration Center, 1967), ch. 4.

5. Richard O. Carlson, *Executive Succession and Organizational Change* (Chicago: University of Chicago, Midwest Administration Center, 1962).

6. Stephen J. Knezevich (ed.), *The American School Superintendency* (Arlington, Va.: American Association of School Administrators, 1971).

7. One reader of an early draft of this chapter thinks $33,000 is too low. He notes that 1973-74 Educational Research Service data reported average salaries of superintendents in 562 large school systems as $36,983.

8. J. W. Getzels, J. M. Lipham, and R. F. Campbell, *Educational Administration as a Social Process* (New York: Harper and Row, 1968), pp. 133-150.

9. See Chapter II, n. 30.

10. See Chapter II, n. 31.

11. Austin Ranney, "Parties and State Politics," in Herbert Jacob and Kenneth Vines (eds.), *Politics in the American States: A Comparative Analysis* (Boston: Little, Brown, 1971), p. 87.

12. Ira Sharkansky, "The Utility of Elazar's Political Culture: A Research Note," *Polity*, 2 (January 1969), p. 67.

13. Richard I. Hofferbert and Ira Sharkansky (eds.), *State and Urban Politics* (Boston: Little, Brown, 1971), p. 456.

14. JAlan Aufderheide, *State Policy Making for the Public Schools of California* (Columbus: Ohio State University, Educational Governance Project, February 1974).

15. Linda Clare Moffatt, *State Policy Making for the Public Schools of Colorado* (Columbus: Ohio State University, Educational Governance Project, February 1974).

16. Peggy M. Siegel, *State Policy Making for the Public Schools of Massachusetts* (Columbus: Ohio State University, Educational Governance Project, February 1974).

17. Gary V. Branson and Donald J. Steele, Jr., *State Policy Making for the Public Schools of Tennessee* (Columbus: Ohio State University, Educational Governance Project, June 1974), p. 55.

IV — Governors and Educational Policy Making

— Edward R. Hines

The governors' roles in policy making for public schools are examined, first, by describing the governors' involvement in each stage of the policy process. An index of gubernatorial involvement in educational policy making can then be constructed by analyzing the extent of involvement in each stage of the process. By comparing governors' rankings on this index of educational involvement with other background and policy-making variables, gubernatorial involvement in state policy making for public schools can be explained more fully.

As was indicated in Chapter I, the policy-making process occurs in four functional stages: issue definition, proposal formulation, support mobilization, and decision enactment. Examination of governors' educational involvement in each functional stage has to be somewhat arbitrary for, in reality, the four stages are highly interrelated. The primary data for the description and analysis contained in this chapter were 422 formal interviews conducted by Educational Governance Project (EGP) researchers. Material from secondary sources, as well as detailed case studies describing state policy-making systems for public schools in each state, provided additional data on the governors. Table IV-1 contains some background characteristics of governors in the twelve states being studied as part of the EGP.

TABLE IV-1 Governors in Office at the Time of the EGP, 1972-73
(N = 12)

States	Political party	Length of term in years	Present term began	Number of previous terms	Interviewed by EGP
California	R	4	1971	1	No
Colorado	R	4	1971	2	Yes
Florida	D	4	1971	0	Yes
Georgia	D	4	1971	0	Yes
Massachusetts	R	4	1971	0[a]	Yes
Michigan	R	4	1971	0[a]	Yes
Minnesota	DFL[b]	4	1971	0	No
Nebraska	D	4	1971	0	Yes
New York	R	4	1971	3	No
Tennessee	R	4	1971	0	Yes
Texas[c]	D	2	1971	1	Yes
Wisconsin	D	4	1971	0	No

[a]The Massachusetts and Michigan governors took office in January 1969 to fill the unexpired terms of former governors.

[b]Democratic-Farmer-Labor.

[c]Preston Smith, Governor of Texas from 1969 through 1972, was defeated in the 1972 primary by Dolph Briscoe, who became Governor and began his term of office in 1973.

Source: The Book of the States, 1972-1973 (Lexington, Ky.: Council of State Governments, 1972), p. 151.

ISSUE DEFINITION

In this initial stage of the policy-making process the preferences of individuals and groups become translated into political issues. As chief executive, the governor can define state issues. The visibility of the governor and the resources available to him enable him to select, define, and emphasize those policy issues deemed important. Gubernatorial involvement in the issue definition stage of the policy process was considered from two perspectives: the emphasis given to educational issues in 1970 campaigns, and the extent to which public school issues were a top priority in subsequent legislative programs.

Education and Gubernatorial Campaigns

The views of governors, members of their staffs, and other executive officials were used to determine the extent to which governors were involved with educational matters during their 1970 campaigns. Four of the governors, despite repeated efforts, could not be interviewed, but of the eight who were, six believed that there were educational issues in the 1970 campaigns. Governors in Massachusetts and Nebraska did not believe education was a campaign issue that year.

In the eight states where both governors and their staffs were interviewed, there was disagreement only in Colorado, where staff members did not believe that education had been a campaign issue. Careful examination of the EGP interview schedules revealed that the governor and the lieutenant governor were hesitant about whether education had been used as a campaign issue. It seems that, although citizen concerns about taxes were beginning to surface in Colorado by 1970, education was evidently not regarded as a major state policy concern until late 1972. Education was not, therefore, seen as a 1970 gubernatorial campaign issue in Colorado, Massachusetts, or Nebraska.

Governors and Educational Legislation

Three groups of individuals—persons from state departments of education (SDE) working on legislative matters herein designated legislative experts, legislators, and educational interest group (EIG) leaders—were interviewed regarding the extent to which governors emphasized public school issues in their legislative programs. The responses of these three groups are summarized in Table IV-2. SDE legislative experts in Colorado, Massachusetts, and Nebraska, in agreement with responses from governors' staffs, said that the governors had not emphasized public school issues in their legislative programs. On the other hand, 63 percent of the Colorado legislators interviewed and two-thirds of the EIG leaders believed that the governor had emphasized educational legislation. These differences can be explained. Colorado legislators who said that the governor had given emphasis to educational legislation were confronted, at the time of the field interviews (early 1973), by a school finance issue, and their responses were probably affected by that pending concern.

TABLE IV-2 Views of SDE Legislative Experts, Legislators, and EIG Leaders Regarding the Extent to Which the Public Schools, Including School Finance, Were Emphasized by Governors in Their Legislative Programs (N = 246 respondents)

States	SDE legislative experts			Legislators			EIG leaders		
	N	Educational issues Emphasized	Not emphasized	N	Educational issues Emphasized	Not emphasized	N	Educational issues Emphasized	Not emphasized
California	1	0	1	15	4	11	7	0	7
Colorado	1	0	1	16	10	6	6	4	2
Florida	2	2	0	6	3	3	6	4	2
Georgia	2	2	0	13	12	1	5	5	0
Massachusetts	1	0	1	16	4	12	7	3	4
Michigan	1	1	0	15	13	2	9	7	2
Minnesota	2	2	0	15	15	0	3	3	0
Nebraska	1	0	1	7	1	6	3	2	1
New York	4[a]	4	0	18	12	6	5	3	2
Tennessee	1	1	0	11	11	0	5	5	0
Texas	1	1	0	10	8	2	6	6	0
Wisconsin	1	1	0	17	16	1	7	6	1
TOTAL	18	14	4	159	109	50	69	48	21

[a]In New York the number of "legislative experts" in the State Education Department exceeded those found in other states because in New York individuals were located who worked on both the legal and the fiscal aspects of educational legislative matters.

Further, examination of the Colorado interview schedules for legislators and EIG leaders showed that the governor was not considered to
be a strong voice for or against education. Rather, he seemed to have
been considered as supportive of education because he had not
opposed educational measures such as increasing state school aid.
The governor of Colorado had no apparent record of involvement in
educational policy making. The governor of Massachusetts, according
to a majority of legislators and EIG leaders, had not emphasized educational legislation and had assigned educational matters to the lieutenant governor. It appeared that elementary and secondary education in Massachusetts was regulated primarily by statutory guidelines,
leaving little room for executive initiative in education. Six of seven
legislators from Nebraska viewed the governor as not being active in
education, but only one-third of the EIG leaders saw him as not
being active in educational legislation. EIG leaders who viewed him
as active in educational legislation did so because he had recently
vetoed a major school finance bill (1972). One EIG leader in Nebraska, a former legislator, said that, although the governor may have
been disposed to sign the bill for increased school aid, he was under
pressure from conservatives to hold to his campaign pledge that there
would be no new taxes. It was his determination to reduce state
spending that led him to veto the major school finance bill.

According to members of his personal staff, the governor of California emphasized education. But in subsequent educational legislation, as one aide saw it, school finance was emphasized only "in the
sense that it was part and parcel of the overall tax reform problem."
The California SDE legislative expert and all EIG leaders believed
that the governor had not emphasized educational legislation. Of the
California legislators interviewed, 73 percent agreed that the governor had not emphasized public school issues in his legislative proposals.

Turning to those governors who emphasized public school issues in
their legislation, SDE legislative experts and at least half of the legislators and EIG leaders believed that governors had emphasized public
school issues in Florida, Georgia, Michigan, Minnesota, New York,
Tennessee, Texas, and Wisconsin. Table IV-2 reports a nearly unanimous response regarding governors actively supporting educational
legislation, except in Florida and New York. A small number of legislators were interviewed in Florida, and the group may not have been

entirely representative. In early 1973 there were feelings of uncertainty about the governor because the issue of school finance was far from resolved when the legislative session opened. A major school finance bill was finally passed late in the 1973 session, apparently influenced by the work of scholars in school finance who were brought to Florida to work with legislators and a citizens' committee appointed by the governor. In the process, however, the governor gained a reputation as an education advocate because he supported reform in school finance. In New York, the governor's primary legislative thrust in 1972 was to hold the line in fiscal matters. EIG leaders there expressed concern about the governor's recent critical position toward education. Unlike the governor of Nebraska, however, the governor of New York had a long-standing record of support for education. His shift toward a more conservative posture, in the opinion of some observers, was made for other political reasons.

Legislators were asked which educational issues had surfaced as top priority in governors' legislative programs. There can be no doubt that school finance was the primary concern. It was mentioned more than twice as often (see Table IV-3) as the next most frequently mentioned issue, tax reform, which is related. In Minnesota, Wisconsin, Michigan, and Florida, school finance and tax reform were viewed essentially as a single issue.

Comparative Summary

According to the perceptions of those interviewed, governors in nine of the twelve EGP states were involved in education either because it was a campaign issue or because it received emphasis in legislative programs. In this initial policy-making stage of issue definition, governors should be viewed not only according to the extent of their educational involvement but also according to the nature of this involvement. Four governors appeared to be oriented toward fiscal reform in the areas of school finance and taxation. By fiscal reform is meant an attempt to increase the overall funding for education, raise the state's share of aid to education, or alter the allocation formula to achieve greater interdistrict equalization and to relieve the property tax burden. Governors in Minnesota, Michigan, Wisconsin, and Florida were actively involved in defining educational issues so as to stress the need for reform in school finance and taxation.

While governors in Georgia, Tennessee, and Texas were involved in

TABLE IV-3 Legislators' Responses to the Open-ended Question about Which Educational Issues Were Given Top Priority in Governors' Legislative Programs (N = 159)

State	N	School finance[a]	Tax reform	Early childhood education	Hold the line on spending	Higher education	Reorganization[b]	Vocational education	Special education	Teacher salaries	Education rhetoric with no follow-up	Accountability[c]	Pupil-teacher ratio	Remedial instruction	Total[d]
California	15	2	7		7	1									17
Colorado	16	14	4				3				1	1			23
Florida	6	2	2		1										5
Georgia	13	4		11				4	6	4			2	2	33
Massachusetts	16	3			1	3	5				3				15
Michigan	15	12	3				2				2	1			20
Minnesota	15	12	11									1			24
Nebraska	7		6		5										11
New York	18	13				5		1	2		1	3			25
Tennessee	11			12	1	1	2		2	3	1				22
Texas	10	3		1		1		7		2					14
Wisconsin	17	16	6		2	5	2					1			32
TOTAL	159	81	39	24	17	16	14	12	10	9	8	7	2	2	241

[a] School finance includes increasing state aid to education and improving equalization.

[b] Accountability refers to efforts in Colorado, Michigan, and Wisconsin to define educational output in quantifiable terms. Accountability in New York appeared to refer to the press by state lawmakers for greater fiscal efficiency in education.

[c] Reorganization refers to district consolidation of schools in Colorado. In the other four states, reorganization refers to new arrangement in education structure at the state level.

[d] Total responses are for each state. The total exceeds the aggregate of those interviewed because of multiple responses.

education, school finance and tax reform had not emerged as major state-level issues. The definition of educational issues for these three governors appeared to be more in the traditional sense of focusing upon programs and their possible expansion. In Georgia, a major issue was early childhood education; in Tennessee, it was kindergarten education; in Texas, the issues were vocational and technical education.

In this initial stage of issue definition, the governors of Colorado, Massachusetts, and Nebraska were not particularly involved in education. Although school finance and tax reform emerged as major issues in Colorado during the 1973 legislative session, the governor apparently had not been involved in education prior to that date. In like manner, the governor of Massachusetts could not be pictured as an "education governor."

Another way in which governors became involved in making educational policy was to exercise fiscal restraint in state spending practices. Holding the line on state spending and levying no new taxes, campaign promises made by the governor of Nebraska in 1970, led him to veto a major school finance bill in 1972, even though he had no record of educational policy involvement. That same year California enacted legislation in school finance and tax reform. The impetus for school finance reform came from the legislature; the initiative for tax reform came from the governor.

In New York, the legislature did not enact major legislation in school finance reform until 1974. In 1972, except for a few areas, including education, in which some allowance for growth was mandated by previous legislation, New York held to the governor's insistence on slowing the state's spending pattern. The governor proposed an "Office of Education Inspector General in the executive department to review performance in relation to expenditures under present programs and to recommend means of improving their effectiveness and efficiency," a clear manifestation of his frustration with the autonomy of the state education agency and his perception that efficiency in fiscal management had to be restored to education.[1]

PROPOSAL FORMULATION

Proposal formulation can be thought of as the process by which issues are specified as recommendations for a policy change or for maintaining the status quo. In this stage of policy making, governors drew upon available resources for information and advice in order to formulate issues into policy proposals. A consideration of those resources helps to determine the potential of governors for involvement in proposal formulation, and EGP case studies provided data for examining the actual involvement of governors in this process.

Governor's Staff and Other Resources

The governor's personal staff, that group of aides and advisers who assist him in his many duties, provides such basic services as "information control and presentation," according to Sprengel.[2] His staff facilitates the generating of information, filters external input into the governor's office, organizes agenda, and presents information to the chief executive. Although any intensive examination of gubernatorial staffing was beyond the purview of this study, education aides to governors were interviewed in all twelve states.

Table IV-4 presents a cross-sectional view, as of late 1972 and early 1973, of those members of governors' personal staffs who worked on educational matters. Some findings are noteworthy. The mean number of years of service, through 1972, was 3.8, indicating frequent staff turnover in governors' offices. Yet, with eight of the twelve governors serving their first terms, it is not surprising that brief tenure of staff was a result. Of those on the staff, 75 percent had completed postgraduate work, a percentage considerably higher than the 47 percent reported in the Sprengel study.[3] Of twenty-four staff members interviewed, 46 percent had served in state government in the legislature, or in student campaigns for the office of governor. This figure was higher than that reported in Sprengel's study, where 38 percent of the respondents in a forty-state survey had held some type of political position prior to serving on governors' staffs. Of the education aides interviewed, 21 percent had held positions as professors, administrators in higher education, or officials in state education departments. These findings are of particular interest. Over one-half of the aides had participated in politics or in state government, but only one-fifth had worked in education. Of those who had worked in education, their most recent professional positions had been, *without exception*, in higher education, as either teachers or administrators.

TABLE IV-4 General Characteristics of Members of Governors' Personal Staffs Whose Responsibilities Included Education (N = 24)

State	N	Year employment began on governor's staff	Previous occupation	Highest degree	Full-time equivalent staff working on educational affairs	
					Policy-program development	Finance
California	1	1968	Professor and university administrator	Ph.D.	3	2
Colorado	1	1965	Lawyer, office of Attorney General	J.D.	Less than 1[a]	1
Florida	1	1969	University administrator	Ph.D.	2	2
Georgia	1	1971	University administrator	Ph.D.	2	1
Massachusetts	6[b]	1965 (2) 1970 (1) 1971 (2) 1973 (1)	Lawyers (2) Legislators (1) Students (3)	J.D. (2) M.A. (2) B.A. (2)	1½[c]	1/2
Michigan	2	1969 1971	Professor State budget director	Ph.D. J.D.	1	1
Minnesota	1	1968	Researcher in state government	M.A.	1	1/2
Nebraska	1	1961	State senator	B.A.	Less than 1	1/5

TABLE IV-4 (continued)

State	N	Year employment began on governor's staff	Previous occupation	Highest degree	Full-time equivalent staff working on educational affairs	
					Policy-program development	Finance
New York	4	1969 (1) 1970 (1) 1971 (2)	Military (2) Banker (1) Student (1)	J.D. (1) M.P.A. (1) M.S. (2)	3+[d]	3+
Tennessee	2	1970 1970	Newspaper editor Legislative assistant in Congress	B.A.	1/2	1/5
Texas	2	1969 1969	Staff in state government	M.P.A. B.A.	1/10	1/2
Wisconsin	2	1972 1972	Professor State government	Ph.D. B.A.	Less than 1	1

[a]In the three states designated by "less than 1," and in Tennessee and Texas, there were no staff members working full-time in education. Rather, these small staffs had responsibilities in many areas including education.

[b]There were many respondents in Massachusetts because of staff turnover, and there were staff working for both the governor and the lieutenant governor who had educational responsibilities. These respondents did not include the personnel in the newly created Office of the Secretary for Educational Affairs.

[c]This number included both the offices of the governor and the lieutenant governor.

[d]The New York staffing pattern was large and diffuse. A total of three staff members in each area is an approximation. There were two tiers of top policy staff, in addition, whose responsibilities may have included education on a part-time basis.

An attempt to determine how heavily governors relied upon their own staffs for information and advice about public schools showed that governors solicited information from as many sources as possible, yet input from outside organizations seemed to be offset by reliance upon staff advisers. A possible exception to this may be found in Texas, where the governor had a strong personal relationship with the head of the teachers' association and relied heavily on the association for information. In general, governors did not depend on any one informational source outside their own staffs.

It should be noted, however, that, although governors relied on their own staffs for policy advice in education, there were those outside the executive branch who were useful sources of information. Twenty-two members of governors' personal staffs were asked which individuals provided them with useful information about public schools. Table IV-5 indicates that state departments of education in nine states and other state government sources in seven states were mentioned by staff members as being the single most useful source of information on education.

In Massachusetts the new Secretary of Educational Affairs was seen as more useful to the governor than the chief state school officer. The secretary, a gubernatorial appointee, was to serve the entire educational system in the state "as a means of better coordinating the operation of the state educational systems, of increasing citizen participation in decision making, and of rationally balancing the growth of public higher education in Massachusetts with the private sector."[4] Recognizing the secretary's potential impact in higher education, one university president warned that the new structure was "a serious threat to the quality of public higher education in Massachusetts."[5]

The governors' personal staff members were asked how important the chief state school officer (CSSO) was to the governor as a source of advice on public schools. CSSO's were considered to be the most important single sources of advice in Florida and Tennessee. They were seen as tending toward being of minor importance in Minnesota and Nebraska, while they were considered to be of minor importance or not at all important in Massachusetts and Wisconsin. In the other six states they were considered to be among the most important sources of advice to governors regarding education.

Another resource available to a governor in formulating proposals for legislative consideration are recommendations of commissions,

State	N	Administrative, finance, budget units in state government[a]	SDE	SBE	Education interest groups[b]	Local educators	"A Variety"	Single most useful source
California	1	1	1					Department of Finance and SDE
Colorado	1		1		1	1		SDE
Florida	1		1		1	1		SDE
Georgia	1		1		1	1		SDE
Massachusetts	4[c]		2	1			3[d]	Secretary of Educational Affairs
Michigan	2	1	1		1			SDE
Minnesota	1	1	1					State Planning Agency
Nebraska	1	1	1					Department of Administrative Services
New York	4	1	3		1	1	2	"The Public" SDE
Tennessee	2	1	2	1	1			Commissioner and SDE, and Department of Finance

	1	2	3	4	5	
Texas	2	1	1		1	SDE, SBE, and Department of Finance
Wisconsin	2	1			1	SDE and Department of Finance
TOTAL	22	8	16	3	8	

[a]This category is inclusive of those individuals working within state government in departments, offices, or bureaus of administration, finance, or budget.

[b]The educational interest group category was an aggregate of all educational interest groups; the most frequently mentioned group was the state educational association (teachers).

[c]In Massachusetts, four responses were included rather than the six responses found in Table IV-4 because two responses were unusable in this area.

[d]In Massachusetts, two of the three responses of "A Variety" included mention of the new Office of Educational Affairs, established in January 1972.

citizen groups, and task forces. Such groups were active in six of the twelve states studied. Four of the states were the same states where governors' educational involvement in issue definition was oriented toward reform in school finance and taxation: Minnesota, Michigan, Wisconsin, and Florida. In Nebraska, where there was a tax study committee, and in New York, where the distinguished Fleischmann Commission was appointed by the governor in 1969, governors were perceived to have exercised fiscal restraint in state spending. The fact that broad-based citizen groups existed in the same states where governors were active in educational reform may be a finding of note. Visible citizen organizations, by using the public forum, may prove to be a valuable resource for governors.

It is apparent, then, that governors have a variety of internal as well as external resources to utilize in formulating policy proposals, and it has been established that virtually all twelve governors studied had the information capability to formulate policy proposals. Their actual involvement in initiating policy proposals in education is, therefore, the next consideration.

Governors as Proposal Formulators

The office of governor is the locus for the generation of policy proposals in education. Still, governors vary in the extent to which they initiate policy proposals in education. Four governors in this study appeared to be key initiators, four tended to share initiation with others (primarily the legislature), and four were reactive in proposal formulation. Even though some governors only attempted policy initiation and some governors reacted to policy proposals initiated by others, gubernatorial activity in policy initiation in all twelve states suggests that Ransone's observation that the governors' preeminent role is to formulate and initiate state-wide policies,[6] made twenty years ago, is still accurate.

An outstanding example of a governor's office serving as a key initiator in proposal formulation can be found in Minnesota, where the governor initiated a proposal for education and tax reform and followed it through to final resolution by a legislative conference committee late in 1971.[7] In Michigan, the "Thomas Report," a study of national significance, drew attention to the increasing problem of school funding.[8] The governor, an experienced state legislator, encountered a long series of entanglements with such issues as aid to parochial schools, fiscal austerity, and a state-wide referendum on property taxes. Following a State Supreme Court ruling on the unconstitutionality of Michigan's school finance system in December 1972, legislation based on an equal-yield formula was enacted in 1973, raising the state contribution and providing some interdistrict equalization. The initiative in the effort was provided by a Republican state senator, head of the Senate Education Committee, but the long-term goal of educational reform was the governor's. The key role in initiating educational reform in Wisconsin was unmistakably carried out by the governor. He formed a task force to study the problem in 1972, drew on his political support in the Assembly to obtain passage of a district power equalization bill in 1973, came to a political standoff in the Republican Senate, and was able to achieve success through a legislative conference committee that passed the bill late in the session.[9] The governor of Florida also served as the major source of initiation in passing major school finance legislation in 1973. Using the recommendations of a citizen's committee, the governor persisted in enlisting public support. Final enactment came after extended deliberation by a Joint Conference Committee.[10]

Four other governors, as mentioned earlier, tended to share in the initiating of policy proposals, particularly with the legislature. In Tennessee, the major school finance issue in 1972 was the financing of a state-wide kindergarten program. The governor used this issue in his 1970 campaign. When it was submitted to the legislature after the election, however, only 20 percent of the governor's original proposal was funded.[11] The governor saw his proposal diluted by lack of legislative support when the proposal was confronted by opposition that included the powerful teachers' association. In California, the governor clearly shared the role of policy initiator with the legislature in 1972, when major school finance legislation reflected the governor's initiative in tax reform and the legislature's initiative in school finance.[12]

The governors of New York and Colorado generally could be thought of as sharing policy initiation. In both 1972 and 1973 the governor of New York waited to react to the school finance proposals of the Fleischmann Commission, the Assembly Ways and Means Committee, the Board of Regents and the State Education Department, and the Educational Conference Board. Apparently, not knowing which of these proposals was politically feasible, the

governor and the legislature delayed any major school finance decisions until the next legislative session. Democrats charged that the
governor wanted no action so as to use "hidden surpluses" in the
state budget for a tax cut in an election year.[13] The governor of
Colorado, inactive in education through 1972, emerged as a major
actor in 1973. He proposed a "percent equalization" formula for the
legislature's consideration. If the formula had been implemented, it
would nearly have doubled state support for schools.[14] Several proposals for school finance reform were put before the Colorado legislature in 1973. Although the legislation in school finance finally
enacted resembled a proposal submitted by the Council on Education Development in Colorado (COED is a coalition comprised of
educational and noneducational groups; see Chapter V), portions of
the governor's bill were also included. In a sense, the governor and
COED shared in the legislative enactment.

The third and final category of governors serving as policy initiators was to be found in Massachusetts, Georgia, Texas, and Nebraska,
where governors generally reacted to policy proposals initiated by
others. The governor of Massachusetts, who was inactive in education, "broke with his political party [Republican] to support the
graduated income tax as a means of relieving reliance on the property
tax" in 1972. He was, thus, active as a formulator of policy proposals
affecting education.[15] Although the graduated income tax proposal
was defeated at the polls, the governor must be credited with attempting tax reform in Massachusetts. The nature of the political
process in Massachusetts tends to curb the governor's initiative in
proposal formulation because school aid is distributed administra-
tively according to a formula established by the legislature. With the
governor being of the opposite political party in a state dominated
by a strong legislature motivated by the ethic of localism, the governor's potential as a policy formulator was limited. He generally
functioned as a reactor to policy proposals formulated and enacted
by the legislature. As for Georgia, the governor took a reactive stance
to a move by the teachers' association in the legislature, in 1972, to
obtain a thousand dollar salary increase for teachers. In an election
year, with considerable public support for the increase, the governor
acquiesced with passive support, and the legislature enacted legislation just ninety dollars short of the teachers' goal.[16] That same year

the governor of Texas reacted to that State Board of Education, which took the responsibility for a study on school finance in an attempt to meet the mandate of the Federal District Court in the *Rodriguez* decision. Following proposals submitted to the Texas legislature by committees from the Senate, the Texas State Teachers' Association, and the State Board of Education, a new governor took a "no new taxes" position that produced a stalemate in the legislature in 1973.[17] And, a major school finance bill was vetoed by the governor of Nebraska in 1972. It had been developed in the legislature with the assistance of several educational interest groups, and it would have changed the distribution formula and increased state support to schools.[18]

Comparative Summary

Governors tend to draw upon a diverse set of resources to formulate policy proposals. Most governors maximize the number of contacts with external groups, and few limit these contacts to a minimal number of groups. In all twelve states, state departments of education were considered to be useful sources of information for governors; in fact, SDE's were *the* most useful sources of information in nine of the twelve states. By the same token, CSSO's were considered as being at least among the governors' most important sources in seven of the twelve states. Yet, were not educators' roles more to generate raw data than to serve as trusted policy advisers? Each governor maintains a staff that is located within the inner circle of policy advisers. Its size appears to vary according to the size of the state population, and, in the twelve states studied, the staff apparently can carry on necessary research and analysis for the governor so that he need not rely upon the education agency.

MOBILIZATION OF SUPPORT

After issues have been defined and formulated into proposals, but before they can be enacted, a vital stage of the policy process occurs when support for alternative proposals is generated from available resources and mobilized in the legislative arena. Mobilization of support can take several forms, including obtaining legislative votes, marshaling public support, and citing the professional opinions of recognized experts. Support mobilization is the process by which individuals and groups are activated to favor or oppose alternative policy proposals.

Governors and the State Education Agency

One resource that governors can use in mobilizing support for their legislative proposals is the state education agency (SEA). The structural relationship between the agency and the governor may enhance or diminish the governor's ability to rely upon its support for or against a policy proposal. As indicated in Chapter I, there are many different ways by which members of state boards of education (SBE's) and chief state school officers can be selected. The twelve states studied in the EGP included seven different combinations of state board and CSSO selection methods.

This structural variability, set in the context of what has already been learned about governors and educational policy making, may reveal little about governors' actual involvement in education. Yet, states falling into extreme categories can be easily identified. Perhaps the governor of Tennessee is involved in education simply because he appoints state board members and, as already noted, he appoints and can dismiss the commissioner and serves as an ex officio member of the State Board of Education. The CSSO, in turn, serves as a member of the governor's cabinet.

There was, however, no state board in Wisconsin, and the CSSO was a popularly elected constitutional officer. This insulation from state government was further enhanced by the apolitical style of the past CSSO, as seen in this observation by an aide close to the governor:

Potentially, the importance of this office (CSSO) is great. The State Superintendent had no great policy thrusts in any area. Communications have been minimal and by some kind of Memorandum. Informally, the Superintendent is not effective. Through practical politics, this influence could be effected, however, much as WEA [the Wisconsin Education Association] has done.

The elimination of educational requirements for the CSSO position by the legislature in 1971, along with the governor's activity in educational reform and policy initiation, may indicate that, in Wisconsin, education moved closer to the broader state legislative policy arena, apparently without initiative by state educators.

Of the twelve states studied, the SEA in New York was by far the most removed from the governor's office. Not only were members of the SBE elected by the legislature, but the CSSO was no longer part of the governor's cabinet. Elected to long terms of office, the Board of Regents had the primary responsibility for formulating educational policy, for the most part according to CSSO and SDE priorities and in closed sessions. Although most of the fifteen years during which Nelson Rockefeller was governor were years in which educational expansion was fiscally supported by a willing governor and legislature, the early 1970's marked the beginning of a new era. Fiscal austerity in state spending, increased public criticism of education, the autonomy of the SEA, and the governor's unprecedented proposal for an Education Inspector General brought the SEA to the brink of open conflict with him.

Gubernatorial control over the SEA varied in the other nine states. It was evident that structure was only one of several important factors in the governor-SEA relationship. With the exception of Georgia, where the governor-CSSO relationship was openly contested, the states were evenly divided between those having a positive, working governor-SEA relationship and those without much of a relationship. Even in the four states where governor-SEA relationships were harmonious at the time of the study, previous relationships did show conflict. In California, Colorado, and Michigan, such conflict involved previous CSSO's; in Florida, it involved the previous governor. CSSO's or governors in the four states were, during 1972, evidently more disposed toward establishing better working relationships. Indeed, the CSSO in California was viewed as having made peace with the governor. The CSSO in Colorado worked hard to reestablish communications with the governor's office, and, in Florida, both the CSSO and the SDE were viewed as the single most useful source of information for the governor's staff. In Michigan, the governor believed that the CSSO was a "committed, honest educator," and the state superintendent won the respect of the governor by taking a forceful stand on the issue of accountability in the schools.

In the four states where education was viewed by the SEA as being apart from politics, two of the states (Massachusetts and Minnesota) had governor-appointed state boards and SBE-appointed chiefs. In addition to the fact that the governor's educational activities were indirect and reactive, the governor-SEA relationship in Massachusetts

was further diminished by a traditionally weak SDE. With three commissioners of education during the period 1969 through 1973, the
Massachusetts SEA was hampered by CSSO's with widely varying
leadership styles and legislative effectiveness. In Minnesota, contacts
between the governor and the SEA were limited and lacked rapport
for several reasons: the governor's staff did not believe that SDE data
were highly usable; the commissioner and the governor, although of
the same political party, did not work together closely; the CSSO
allegedly took policy positions that were sometimes politically embarrassing to the governor; and the SBE was insulated from both
executive and legislative branches. In Nebraska, where the governor
was minimally active in education, the state board was split along
conservative and liberal lines, and a commissioner was hired to replace a CSSO fired because he favored school district reorganization.
The Texas situation, with little overt SEA involvement in the legislative arena, a structurally weak governor, and a long-term commissioner who commanded widespread respect in the state, was somewhat different.

Governors and Educational Interest Groups

As far as governors working closely with EIG's, they seemed to do
so only in Texas and Wisconsin and, in those states, primarily with
teachers' associations. While they did not work closely with EIG's,
governors did solicit information and policy viewpoints from interest
group leaders in Georgia, Massachusetts, Michigan, Nebraska, Minnesota, New York, and Tennessee, a tactic that seemed to be a means
of keeping communications open and should not be confused with
"working closely" together. In Colorado the governor paid some
attention to the recommendations of the formal coalition comprised
of educational and noneducational groups, whereas in Florida the
governor was concerned more with the work of his appointed Citizen's Commission on Education than directly with EIG's, although
interest groups did have input into the commission. Finally, the governor of California appeared to have a minimal relationship with
EIG's.

Another aspect of the EIG-governor relationship is conflict that
may have been evident. In the opinions of members of governors'
personal and administration or finance staffs, there was no EIG-

governor conflict in California or Texas. In California, an absence of conflict was related to an absence in any relationship with the governor; in Texas, the governor and the head of the teachers' association were personal friends. There was also an absence of contention in Colorado, but the governor was somewhat concerned that the teachers' association was oriented so completely toward teacher benefit issues. Some conflict between EIG's and governors was observed in Florida, Massachusetts, Michigan, Minnesota, Nebraska, New York, Tennessee, and Wisconsin, and there was a "very strained relationship," in one respondent's words, between the teachers' association and the governor in Georgia because the governor became increasingly suspicious of the teachers' apparent desire to ensure that increased aid to education go into teacher salaries and benefits. It must be noted, in describing governor-EIG relationships in the states, that some organizations, primarily for teachers, were singled out for discussion. It may well be that in some states where either harmony or conflict has been evident between a governor and the teachers' association, relationships might well be different with other educator organizations.[19]

Governors and the Legislature

In mobilizing support for governors' policy proposals in the legislature, it might be assumed that more powerful governors would exert greater influence. Governors' powers do vary among states. Schlesinger studied the formal powers of governors and categorized them according to potential for tenure, appointment, budget, and veto. Table IV-6 indicates how each state ranked on a five-point scale for each of four elements of formal power. An overall ranking of the twelve states is shown, using Schlesinger's scheme, with New York being most powerful and Texas least powerful.

Two areas of governors' formal powers, as described by Schlesinger, are related particularly to governors' legislative powers. In one area, control over the budget, eight of the twelve governors in this study were ranked highest where governors had responsibilities for budget formulation and shared this responsibility only with appointees. In the second area, veto power, seven of the twelve governors were ranked at the top because they had item veto power requiring at least a 60 percent vote of the legislature to override a veto.

TABLE IV-6 Governors' Formal Powers

State	Category and assigned score[a]				Combined index of formal powers	
	Tenure	Appoint-ment	Budget	Veto	Schlesinger score[b]	Twelve-state rank[c]
California	1	2	1	1	19	3
Colorado	1	5	2	1	15	8.5
Florida	3	4	5	3	9	11
Georgia	3	5	1	1	14	10
Massachusetts	1	1	1	3	18	5
Michigan	1	2	1	1	19	3
Minnesota	1	2	1	1	19	3
Nebraska	2	3	2	1	16	7
New York	1	1	1	1	20	1
Tennessee	3	1	1	2	17	6
Texas	4	5	5	3	7	12
Wisconsin	1	4	1	3	15	8.5

[a]There were five possible scores ranging from 1 (strongest) to 5 (weakest).

[b]The Schlesinger score included fourteen categories ranging from twenty (strongest) to seven (weakest).

[c]The twelve-state rank ranges from New York ranked first (strongest gubernatorial formal powers) to Texas ranked twelfth (weakest formal powers).

Source: Joseph A. Schlesinger, "The Politics of the Executive," in Herbert Jacob and Kenneth N. Vines (eds.), *Politics in the American States* (Boston: Little, Brown, 1971), pp. 210-237.

Summary

This study of governors' means of mobilizing support as they attempted to advance policy proposals in the legislature showed that relationships with state education agencies varied, as did the degree of structural control over SEA's. Relationships between governors and EIG's also varied appreciably. Governors were seen to differ in their formal powers with some having strong formal powers (New York, California, Michigan, Minnesota) and some having weak ones (Georgia, Florida, Texas). Before interpreting these data by ranking governors' overall policy-making involvement in education, governors' roles in legislative decision enactment, the fourth policy-making stage, will be considered.

DECISION ENACTMENT

This final stage of the policy-making process deals with ways by which an authoritative policy decision emerges from among alternative proposals. This is the stage at which hard choices may have to be made—the point of reckoning for those who attempt to influence policy making by defining issues, formulating proposals, and mobilizing support. As chief executives, governors make important decisions and set executive policy. As an example, when the state legislature in New York did not enact the necessary legislation to implement the governor's Education Inspector General proposal, the governor made an administrative appointment within the executive branch. This research does not focus on executive decision enactment, but, rather, on governors' involvement in the legislative enactment of decisions affecting public elementary and secondary schools.

Governors and Legislative Support

The influence of the state education agency and outside organizations such as educational interest groups can be helpful in mobilizing support for governors' policy proposals. The recommendations of so-called experts, the testimony of educators, and the policy demands of interest groups, while they are factors to be considered, are subordinate to the support a governor receives from the state legislature, support that, in turn, is dependent upon party strength. Table IV-7 indicates the political party lineup in state legislatures and reflects changes as a result of the general elections held in 1972.

Governors belonged to the party that was in the majority in both houses of the legislature (1971 and 1973) in Colorado, Florida, Georgia, New York, and Texas, while those in California, Massachusetts, and Tennessee belonged to the party that was in the minority in both houses. In Minnesota the governor's party was in the minority in both houses in 1971 and in the majority by 1973. The parties were split in their control of the legislatures in Michigan and Wisconsin.

Further understanding of governors and their political strength in legislatures must include the extent of interparty competition. In traditionally one-party states, a governor may be weaker politically because of party factionalism than he would be if he had legislative control in a two-party state. Ranney[20] classified Texas and Georgia as one-party Democratic states, and the Democratic governors had

TABLE IV-7 Political Party Lineup in State Legislatures

State	Year	Senate			House of representatives			Election of governor and lieutenant governor on same ticket	Political party of governor
		Democrat	Republican	Other	Democrat	Republican	Other		
California	1971	21	19		42	37	1	No	R
	1973	20	19	1	49	31			
Colorado	1971	14	21		27	38		Yes	R
	1973	13	22		28	37			
Florida	1971	33	15		81	38		Yes	D
	1973	25	14	1	78	42			
Georgia	1971	50	6		173	22	1	No	D
	1973	48	8		150	29	1		
Massachusetts	1971	27	13		177	62	1	Yes	R
	1973	32	8		184	51	3		
Michigan	1971	19	19		58	52		Yes	R
	1973	19	19		60	50			
Minnesota[a]	1971	33	34		65	70		No	DFL[c]
	1973	38	28	1	78	56			
Nebraska	Nonpartisan election				Unicameral legislature			No[b]	D

State	Year								
New York	1971	25	32		71	79		Yes	R
	1973	21	37	2	69	79	2		
Tennessee	1971	19	13	1	56	43		No	R
	1973	19	13	1	51	48			
Texas	1971	29	2		140	10		No	D
	1973	28	3		132	17			
Wisconsin	1971	13	20		65	34	1	Yes	D
	1973	15	18		62	37			

[a] In Minnesota the Democrat-Farmer-Labor Party statistics appear under the Democratic label and the Conservative Party statistics appear under the Republican label.

[b] Beginning November 1974, the governor and the lieutenant governor in Nebraska will be elected jointly.

[c] Democrat-Farmer-Labor Party.

Source: The Book of the States, 1972-1973 and 1974-1975 (Lexington, Ky.: Council of State Governments, 1972, 1974).

majorities in both houses. Florida was considered to be a modified one-party Democratic state, and the governor had a majority in both houses in 1971 and 1973. Colorado and New York were considered two-party states, and Republican governors had majorities in both houses during 1971 and 1973. Minnesota, Michigan, and Wisconsin were two-party states, and Tennessee was a modified-one party Democratic state. Massachusetts and California were two-party states, but tended toward being one-party Democratic ones. Thus, Republican governors in Tennessee, Massachusetts, and California probably faced formidable political party opposition in the legislatures.

Governors and Legislative Party Influence

In the legislative enactment of educational policies, a key factor in a governor's being able to influence legislative decisions is the extent to which he can activate his political strength in legislatures (see Table IV-8). Having party majorities in both houses of the legislature

TABLE IV-8 Governors, Legislative Political Party Lineup, and Interparty Competition

Interparty competition	Legislative political party lineup, 1971 to 1973				
	Remained majority	Remained minority	Majority to minority	Minority to majority	Split
One-party Demo- cratic	Georgia Texas				
Modified one-party Demo- cratic	Florida	Tennessee			
Two-party	Colorado New York	California Massachusetts		Minnesota	Michigan Wisconsin
Modified one-party Repub- lican					

Sources: *The Book of the States, 1972-73*; Austin Ranney, "Parties in State Politics," in Jacob and Vines (eds.), *Politics in the American States,* pp. 82-121.

may be a deceptive measure of a governor's influence since studies have shown that gubernatorial influence may be stronger in more competitive two-party states than in states where the governor has overwhelming political majorities in both houses of the legislature.[21]

In order to determine a governor's legislative party influence, the views of members of his personal and administration or finance staffs and those of SDE legislative experts were obtained through open-ended questions. Respondents indicated that, in Minnesota, the governor was in a strong legislative party position. One of the reasons for the Democratic-Farmer-Labor (DFL) success at the polls in 1972 had to do with the governor, who, in addition to his considerable formal powers, commanded significant additional resources: position and personality, high standing among key members of his political party, and his own personal staff resources.

The governors in Michigan and Wisconsin, based upon interview data, appeared to be in strong legislative positions, although perhaps not quite as strong as that of Minnesota's governor. One aide in Michigan said that the governor realized his political situation early in his tenure and began making bipartisan appeals. A fiscal analyst in Michigan believed that the governor was more successful at getting Democratic support than that of his own political party. A staff aide from Wisconsin noted that Democratic party support was relied upon in the Assembly but that a variety of approaches had to be used in the Senate, including the influence of outside groups, the weight of the recommendations of task forces, and compromise with the Senate leadership.

Qualitative assessment of interview data would indicate that the governors in Colorado and New York, in having legislative party majorities in 1971 and 1973, were in positions of strength with the legislatures. Other than "working with legislative leadership," neither the governor nor the lieutenant governor of Colorado cited any particular strategies or approaches used in mobilizing legislative support. One personal staff aide noted that the governor was successful 80 percent of the time in the legislature and that recently issues seemed to be considered more on their merit than on a partisan basis. While a fair degree of political maneuvering seemed to be characteristic of New York politicians, the prime strategy of the governor was to arrive at an early agreement with the legislative leaders, namely the Assembly Speaker and Senate Majority Leader, and to maintain close relations with these key figures as the legislative session drew to a close and bills were being rushed through based on political party backing.

Governors in Tennessee, California, and Massachusetts were faced with majority party opposition in their legislatures in both 1971 and 1973. All three governors were faced with an uphill climb in getting legislative support for their educational proposals. The governor's political position was far from favorable with the Tennessee legislature. In California the governor appeared to rely upon caucus support while at the same time entering into compromises with the legislative leadership. In Massachusetts the Republican governor appealed to a strong liberal Democratic faction when possible, in addition to arguing issues on a merit basis and compromising with legislative leadership, especially in the House.

Governors in Florida, Georgia, and Texas had political legislative majorities in 1971 and 1973, but in each state the governor was faced with constraints that resulted in a legislative support base characterized as being somewhat weak. One aide noted that the governor of Florida, a former legislator, worked in a "low-key" fashion to try to convince individual legislators of his points of view. There were some very real constraints on him. The executive cabinet included six other elected officials, and any agency head could lobby directly in the legislature if more funds were desired. The legislature had grown so strong that a national study in 1971 ranked Florida fourth among all states in legislative performance.[22]

The governor of Georgia was more independent, somewhat aloof, certainly more liberal than his predecessor, and faced with a liberal-conservative legislative split based not on party but on the politics of geography and values. The governor of Texas was ranked last in formal powers. But, as in Georgia, state politics did not follow along traditional party lines since the Democrats were in overwhelming control. Rather, politics were intensely divided along conservative-liberal lines. Conservatives tended to represent wealthier suburban and rural areas, and liberals spoke for the cities and a coalition of blacks and Mexican-Americans. Other factors that contributed to a weak governorship included: the dispersal of executive authority among six other elected executive officials; separate elections for governor and lieutenant governor; and a situation where the lieutenant governor was chairman of the powerful Legislative Budget

Board, an agency that developed the budget jointly with the governor but made independent recommendations to the legislature. Although the Texas governor had line item veto powers, his veto powers, which required that more than a majority of legislators be present to override, were not as great as the veto powers of twenty-nine other governors.

Nebraska was not included in Table IV-8 because the state has a unicameral legislature and nonpartisan elections. The governor was not particularly active in education. A major concern in Nebraska, according to gubernatorial aides, was the fact that the governor was viewed as representing state-wide interests in a state where the ethic of local control has been strongly advocated by individual legislators and even by state-level groups representing local interests.

In looking at the ways governors mobilize support for educational legislation, legislators were interviewed about ways in which governors work to get educational legislation passed by the education and fiscal committees. Table IV-9 summarizes legislators' responses. The most frequent response was that governors used their own staffs as means of influence when working for educational legislation. Thus, an expanded role can be seen for members of governors' personal staffs. Not only are staff members relied on for policy and program development, but they are used by governors in working directly in the legislature. Legislators believed that governors had diverse ways in which to mobilize support in legislatures. At least one legislator in every state except Colorado mentioned that the governor used the media and other means to make issues public. While top education officials are contacted for useful information and advice on educational matters, Table IV-9 demonstrates that, when it comes to the critical use of influence in the legislature, education officials are used in only a few states and to a lesser extent than other resources. It appears that the governors generally have emerged as skilled politicians who, when entering the legislative arena, draw upon diverse support to influence the outcome of legislation in education.

Comparative Summary

In obtaining political party support in legislatures to get their policy preferences enacted, governors pay heed to those legislators most able to affect desired outcomes. Thus, political party lineup, interparty competition, the extent of party factionalism—combined with

TABLE IV-9 Legislators' Views about Governors' Means of Influence in Working for Educational Legislation (N = 157)

State	N	Through his own staff	Through public visibility including the media and citizen groups	Through legislative leadership	The governor is not active in promoting educational legislation	Through political party caucuses	The governor has virtually no influence in promoting educational legislation	By means of political trade-offs and pressure tactics	Through state agencies such as administrative, budget, and finance	Giving state of the state budget messages and introducing bills	Through issue-oriented merits and persuasion	Through the CSSO, SDE, or SBE	Through outside groups including educational interest groups	The governor gives us educational rhetoric but does not follow through with legislation
California	16	5	1	1	8	3	3	2	4					
Colorado	16	4		6	8	5		2	1	3				1
Florida	3[a]	1	2						2		1			
Georgia	13	5	7	1	1	1	1	1	1		4			
Massachusetts	14	2	4	4	9		7							
Michigan	15	8	11	4		2	3			3	1	1	3	
Minnesota	15	11	4	2	2	1	1	8						1
Nebraska	7	4	2					1	1					1
New York	20		4	14		7		1		2		2	1	
Tennessee	11	5	6	1				1				2		1
Texas	10		1		1	2	6				3	1	1	
Wisconsin	17	5	1	4		3		6	4	2				
TOTAL	157	50	43	37	29	24	21	20	13	10	9	6	5	5

[a]More than three legislators were interviewed in Florida, but only three responses dealt with this question.

an adroit sense of timing to gauge the political climate—are elements that must be weighed by governors who wish to have policy proposals enacted by legislatures.

Governors varied in the degree to which they were able to activate their political party strengths in the legislatures. Governors in Minnesota, Wisconsin, and Michigan appeared to be more involved than other governors in mobilizing political party strengths when legislation was being enacted. The governors of Georgia and Texas, in contrast, were only slightly involved in mobilizing political support in legislatures when decisions were being enacted.

CORRELATIONAL ANALYSIS

Governors' involvement in each functional stage of the policy process in education has been described. In seeking to explain gubernatorial involvement in legislative policy making for the public schools, an index was developed to show the extent of governors' overall educational policy-making involvement. If this involvement can be related to other socioeconomic and political background variables, school finance and tax variables, and policy-making variables, it might explain more fully the conditions related to governors' involvement in educational policy making.

The index of gubernatorial involvement in educational policy making was constructed by assigning numerical values to the extent of governors' educational policy-making involvement in each functional stage of the policy process, as shown in Table IV-10. By combining the score for each governor in each policy-making stage, a total score was obtained and a ranking was derived.

As a dependent variable, this index of gubernatorial involvement in educational policy making was correlated with other selected variables using the Spearman rank-order correlation coefficient (rho), an appropriate correlational statistic for ranked data when the number of cases is small.[23] As a guideline for the interpretation of rho, a correlation of .3 to .4 indicates only a trend, .5 to .6 indicates a moderate association, and .7 or higher indicates a strong degree of association. These associations, which indicate the direction and the degree of the relationship between the variables, cannot be extended to cause and effect.

TABLE IV-10   Index of Gubernatorial Involvement in Educational Policy Making

State	Issue defi-nition	Proposal formu-lation	Support mobili-zation	Decision enact-ment	Total score	Ranking
California	2	4	4	4	14	6
Colorado	2	2	2	1	7	10
Florida	4	4	3	4	15	5
Georgia	5	1	1	1	8	9
Massachusetts	1	2	2	1	6	11
Michigan	5	4	4	4	17	3
Minnesota	5	5	4	5	19	2
Nebraska	1	1	2	1	5	12
New York	3	5	3	5	16	4
Tennessee	5	4	2	2	13	7
Texas	5	1	4	1	11	8
Wisconsin	5	5	5	5	20	1

Scoring procedure: For each of the first four columns scores vary from 5 points for great involvement to 1 point for no involvement. See Appendix C for more information.

The degree of gubernatorial involvement in educational policy making was correlated with selected variables of socioeconomic and political background, as shown in Table IV-11. Of the socioeconomic variables there was only a slight association (.38) between industrialization (Hofferbert-Sharkansky) and involvement. Two political variables were, however, moderately associated with governors' involvement.[24] The technical effectiveness of state legislatures, as determined by the Citizens' Conference on State Legislatures, was correlated (.55) with governors' educational involvement. And, there was an association of .44 between political culture (Elazar-Sharkansky) and governors' involvement. (The Elazar-Sharkansky index is a measure of the extent to which states are moralistic in their political culture, rather than individualistic or traditionalistic.) States having some history of reform-orientation in state government, such as Wisconsin, Minnesota, and Michigan, were ranked high in having moralistic political cultures, and these states also had legislatures with greater technical effectiveness. It was in these same states that

TABLE IV-11 Relationships between Governors' Educational Policy-Making Involvement, and Socioeconomic and Political Variables

Variables	Governors' educational policy-making involvement
Socioeconomic	
State population size, 1970	.29
Educational attainment, 1970[a]	−.06
Per capita personal income, 1972	.08
Industrialization (Hofferbert-Sharkansky Index)	.38
Percent Urban Population, 1970	.06
Political	
Interparty competition (Ranney Index)[b]	.27
State legislatures' technical effectiveness (Citizen's Conference Index)	.55
Political culture (Elazar-Sharkansky Index)	.44
Voter turnout	.15

[a]Percent of the state population twenty-five years or older who completed four years of high school.

[b]See n. 24 for an explanation of the Ranney Index.

governors were found to have been most involved in educational policy making.

There were even stronger relationships between the governors' educational policy-making involvement and some of the school finance and tax variables. Table IV-12 indicates that there was a correlation of .87 between state tax burden and governors' involvement and a correlation of .75 between educational effort and governors' involvement. It was not surprising that governors' involvement was strongly associated with both of these fiscal variables since educational effort was, itself, associated with tax burden (.67). Data also focused upon school finance and tax reform as major educational issues. But the magnitude of these correlations indicates that, in states where greater state tax efforts were made to create revenue and where efforts were made to support education, there was greater likelihood of gubernatorial involvement in educational policy making.

Not only was gubernatorial involvement in creating educational

TABLE IV-12 Relationships between Governors' Educational
Policy-Making Involvement, and Measures of
School Finance and Taxation

School finance and tax variables	Governors' educational policy-making involvement
Need	
School-age population as percent of total resident population, 1972	.28
Percent of change in public school enrollment, 1962 to 1972	.30
Ability	
Personal income per child of school age, 1972	.06
Educational effort	
Public school revenue receipts as a percent of personal income, 1971	.75
Educational expenditures	
Per capita state expenditures for all education, 1971	.64
General tax effort	
State and local tax collections as a percent of personal income, 1971	.50
State tax burden	
State tax revenue as percent of personal income, 1971	.87

policy greater in states making greater tax and educational effort, but
the actual state expenditures for education were also found to be
greater in those states. There was a correlation of .64 between governors' educational involvement and the measure of educational expenditures. It is interesting that no relationship could be found
between a state's fiscal ability and the governor's involvement.

Relationships between governors' involvement in educational policy making and selected resource and policy-making influence variables were analyzed. As shown in Table IV-13, there was a tendency
(.33) for governors to be more involved in educational policy making
in states where they had greater formal powers, as measured by the
Schlesinger Index. And there was a slightly higher degree of associa-

TABLE IV-13 Relationships between Governors' Educational
Policy-Making Involvement, and Selected Resource
and Policy-Making Influence Variables

Variables	Governors' educational policy-making involvement
Resource	
Governors' formal powers (Schlesinger Index)	.33
Size of governors' personal staffs	.29
Access to legislative party resources[a]	.40
Policy-making influence	
CSSO influence in the SEA arena[b]	.18
CSSO influence in the legislative arena[b]	.18
SBE overall policy-making influence[c]	.06
Legislators' perceptions of EIG influence[d]	.13

[a]An index of governors' access to political party legislative resources, as determined by the extent of political party competitiveness in legislatures, and the governors' political party lineups in legislatures. See Appendix C for scoring procedure.

[b]See Chapter III.

[c]See Chapter II.

[d]See Chapter V.

tion (.40) between governors' access to legislative party resources and governors' involvement. Where governors had access to political party resources, they were somewhat more involved in educational policy making. There were no correlations of any size between governors' involvement and selected policy-making influence variables involving CSSO's, SBE's, and EIG's.

*   *   *

Based upon the preceding description and analysis of governors' roles in state policy making for the public schools, some concluding observations can be made.

1. *Governors have become involved in educational policy making.* In this population of twelve states, 75 percent of the governors included education as a campaign issue in 1970. Yet, it would appear that education might provide governors with an issue that is more attractive for campaigning than for sustained legislative programs.

Legislators interviewed in Colorado, Massachusetts, Michigan, New York, and Tennessee mentioned that governors sometimes gave pro-education speeches, but did not carry through with legislative programs and fiscal appropriations. Governors in Georgia and Texas were heavily involved in defining educational issues but much less involved in formulating policy proposals in education. On the other hand, governors in Wisconsin and Minnesota were quite involved in all four stages of the policy process in education. Governors in California and New York, although not as involved in defining educational issues as part of their legislative programs, were deeply involved in the legislature enactment of decisions affecting education.

2. *Governors varied in the extent of their involvement in educational policy making.* Governors in Wisconsin and Minnesota were found to be seriously involved in educational policy making. Governors in Michigan, New York, and Florida had considerable involvement, and governors in California and Tennessee, moderate involvement in educational policy making. The governor of Texas was only slightly involved in educational policy making, and governors in Georgia, Colorado, Massachusetts, and Nebraska were hardly involved at all.

3. *Governors differed in the nature of their involvement in educational policy making.* It was evident that some governors (Minnesota, Michigan, Florida, Wisconsin) were oriented toward achieving fiscal reform in school finance and taxation. Other governors (California, New York) appeared to have fiscal concerns, also, but were more oriented toward holding the line on state spending and restraining increases for areas such as education. Although inactive in educational policy making, the Nebraska governor moved to curb spending and held to his campaign pledge of no new taxes. There were governors oriented toward expanding specific educational programs (Tennessee, Texas). The Georgia governor actively defined early childhood education as an area of policy interest, but he did not follow through with specific legislative action. Two other governors (Colorado, Massachusetts) were not involved in educational policy making.

4. *Governors have resource capacities for independent involvement in educational policy making.* There were gubernatorial aides in all twelve states who either worked full time on educational matters or had part-time responsibilities in education. These personal staffs tended to be employed by governors currently in office, and nearly one-half of the educational staff had had previous experience in state

government or in higher education. None came from the public schools. While outside sources were utilized widely by governors in generating information and policy viewpoints about education, it appeared that policy formulation was accomplished by aides and advisers close to the governor.

Not only did all twelve governors have the resource capacity for educational policy-making involvement; they also became involved in education. This involvement was independent of the influence of CSSO's, SBE's, and EIG's.

An outside resource that governors may be using more frequently is the citizen commission or task force. These organizations were found in six of the twelve states, but all four governors categorized as being oriented toward fiscal reform in school finance and taxation made use of this resource. Particularly where major fiscal decisions must be made by governors, the legitimacy of the citizen committee may provide the governor with an important tactical resource in planning strategy.

5. *Governors were crucial in the formulation and initiation of fiscal legislation affecting school finance and tax reform.* Although governors differed in the nature of their educational policy-making involvement, virtually all twelve governors were involved in either the initiation or attempted initiation of policy. Even in the three states where governors had not been particularly active in education, one governor (Colorado) attempted to initiate a policy proposal in school finance in 1973; another (Massachusetts) attempted to initiate a policy proposal for a graduated state income tax, and the third (Nebraska) vetoed a major school finance bill.

In describing and analyzing governors' involvement in educational policy making, the view in this study was cross-sectional as of 1972 and 1973. In the three states where governors were viewed as having the greatest educational policy-making involvement (Wisconsin, Minnesota, Michigan), school finance and tax reform were major state-level issues at that particular time. In other states, such as California, New York, and Massachusetts, where characteristically one finds a high level of educational attainment,[25] governors were found to be somewhat less involved in educational policy making. This is not to question the overall importance or probable influence of these governors. On the Schlesinger Index of governors' formal powers, New York ranked first; California, third; and Massachusetts, fifth.

6. *The structure for education and state government is only one*

among several important policy-making elements. The Tennessee structure for state government may cause the governor to be more involved in education if only because he can appoint and dismiss the commissioner. In New York and Wisconsin, on the other hand, the structure for education tended to insulate education from state government. In spite of structure, however, these governors became more involved in education. The governor of New York moved to appoint an Inspector General as a "watchdog" over education, and the governor of Wisconsin drew upon the recommendations of a task force and carried his proposal for more equalization in school finance to successful legislative enactment. In the other nine states, governors' control over state education agencies varied. No causal relationships could be identified between governors' structural control over the SEA and policy-making relationships between governors and agencies.

7. *Of the variables used in the correlational analysis, the measures of state tax burden, educational effort, and educational expenditures were associated most strongly with gubernatorial involvement in educational policy making.* Correlational analysis of school finance and tax variables provided the key to explaining gubernatorial involvement in educational policy making. One possible reason for this was the very strong relationships between governors involved with education and states making greater tax efforts generally, showing greater fiscal effort for education, and spending greater amounts on the public schools. Because they were concerned with the allocation of state resources, governors appeared to be drawn into educational policy making, and this happened more often as school finance became more visible as a state issue.

A second possible reason was because, in states where governors were more involved in education, their concern for education as a fiscal issue of major significance was unmistakable. Thus, the catalyst for governors' educational involvement was chiefly fiscal, and education has been propelled into state-wide prominence because of its demands on state revenue.

A third consideration is that, as chief executives who react to state-wide constituencies in formulating policy, governors found themselves in the limelight. Public expectation of a solution to this fiscal dilemma forced governors to make policy choices among alternative solutions. Yet governors differed in their responses. In Texas, the governor encouraged others to propose solutions. In Georgia and Tennessee, there were no major issues in school finance and taxation. In Nebraska the governor reacted to a legislative proposal for increasing school aid. Governors in Colorado and Massachusetts attempted policy initiation. In the other six states, the issues of school finance and taxation were highly visible in 1972. The governor's prime interest in California was tax reform. The governor delayed acting on the recommendations of the Fleischmann Commission and others until a future legislative session in New York. Four other governors (Wisconsin, Minnesota, Michigan, Florida) approached the issues directly and worked toward their solution in the legislature.

The correlational analysis indicated that governors who were more involved in educational policy making were from states characterized by legislatures having greater technical effectiveness and in states characterized as having a moralistic political culture. The correlational analysis further indicated that neither a governor's formal powers nor the size of his education staff was strongly associated with educational policy-making involvement. It should be noted, however, that all twelve governors had at least some independent staff capability.

Whether governors succeed in getting their policy preferences enacted by legislatures is dependent upon many elements. It would appear that capacity for defining salient legislative issues, capability in formulating policy proposals, and access to political party and legislative resources are among the critical ones. Governors have the potential for involvement, and, based upon this analysis, they are involved in state policy making for the public schools.

NOTES—CHAPTER IV

1. Edward R. Hines, *State Policy Making for the Public Schools of New York* (Columbus: Ohio State University, Educational Governance Project, January 1974), p. 101.

2. Donald P. Sprengel, *Gubernatorial Staff: Functional and Political Profiles* (Iowa City: University of Iowa, Institute of Public Affairs, 1969), p. 3.

3. *Ibid.*, pp. 15-17.

4. Peggy M. Siegel, *State Policy Making for the Public Schools of Massachusetts* (Columbus: Ohio State University, Educational Governance Project, February 1974), p. 80.

5. *Ibid.*, p. 82.

6. Coleman B. Ransone, Jr., *The Office of Governor in the United States* (Freeport, N. Y.: Books for Libraries Press, 1970), p. 157.

7. Tim L. Mazzoni, Jr., *State Policy Making for the Public Schools of Minnesota* (Columbus: Ohio State University, Educational Governance Project, June 1974), pp. 52-76.

8. Edward R. Hines, JAlan Aufderheide, Peggy M. Siegel, Linda C. Moffatt, and William E. Smith, *State Policy Making for the Public Schools of Michigan* (Columbus: Ohio State University, Educational Governance Project, June 1974), pp. 58-87.

9. Dudley E. Brown, *State Policy Making for the Public Schools of Wisconsin* (Columbus: Ohio State University, Educational Governance Project, February 1974), pp. 38-43.

10. Frank DePalma, *State Policy Making for the Public Schools of Florida* (Columbus: Ohio State University, Educational Governance Project, January 1974), pp. 70-75.

11. Gary Branson and Donald Steele, *State Policy Making for the Public Schools of Tennessee* (Columbus: Ohio State University, Educational Governance Project, June 1974), pp. 37-42.

12. JAlan Aufderheide, *State Policy Making for the Public Schools of California* (Columbus: Ohio State University, Educational Governance Project, February 1974), pp. 47-52.

13. Hines, *State Policy Making for the Public Schools of New York*, pp. 51-54.

14. Linda C. Moffatt, *State Policy Making for the Public Schools of Colorado* (Columbus: Ohio State University, Educational Governance Project, February 1974), p. 27.

15. Siegel, *State Policy Making for the Public Schools of Massachusetts*, p. 98.

16. Gary Branson and Donald Steele, *State Policy Making for the Public Schools of Georgia* (Columbus: Ohio State University, Educational Governance Project, January 1974), pp. 37-40.

17. Gary Branson, *State Policy Making for the Public Schools of Texas* (Columbus: Ohio State University, Educational Governance Project, January 1974), pp. 35-44.

18. Roger Farrar, *State Policy Making for the Public Schools of Nebraska* (Columbus: Ohio State University, Educational Governance Project, July 1974), pp. 68-70.

19. See J Alan Aufderheide, "The Place of Educational Interest Groups in State Educational Policy Systems," unpublished dissertation, Ohio State University, 1973.

20. Austin Ranney, "Parties in State Politics," in Herbert Jacob and Kenneth Vines (eds.), *Politics in the American States*, 2nd ed. (Boston: Little, Brown, 1971), pp. 85-89.

21. See Thomas R. Dye, "State Legislative Politics," in Jacob and Vines, *Politics in the American States*, pp. 163-209, and Sara P. McCally, "The Governor and His Legislative Party," *American Political Science Review*, 60 (December 1966), pp. 923-942.

22. John Burns, *The Sometime Governments* (New York: Bantam Books, 1971), p. 52.

23. In this analysis, simple correlations were calculated because of the small number of cases (12) and the ordinal nature of the data. It is recognized that in a more extensive correlation analysis, where the interactive effect of more than one independent variable is considered in correlations with the gubernatorial involvement index and where partial correlations are used to control for specified variables, different results may be obtained.

24. The categorization of interparty competition, as measured by the Ranney Index (See Tables IV-8 and IV-11), is more accurately a measure of the extent to which states were Democratic in their interparty competition. Using the Ranney Index in its original form, it correlated −.48 with the involvement index. Arranging the Ranney Index around the midpoint of the extent to which states were two party in interparty competition (assuming the midpoint of two-party competition is the greatest extent of two-party competition) the Ranney Index than correlated .27 with the involvement index.

25. *Rankings of the States, 1973* (Washington, D. C.: NEA Research Division, 1973), p. 31. On the measure of "Per Cent of Population Age 25 and Older with 4 Years of College or More, 1970," California ranked 7th; New York, 14th; Massachusetts, 11th; Minnesota, 20th; Wisconsin, 29th; Michigan, 31st.

V — Educational Interest Groups and the State Legislature

—J Alan Aufderheide

Interest groups have long been recognized as playing a basic role in public policy making, particularly in democratic governments. Group structures, relationships, and influence have received the careful attention of many scholars. But the politics of education, including the activities of educational interest groups, is a relatively new area of study.[1] Much systematic investigation is needed if this area is to be better understood. This chapter presents some of the EGP findings on the role of educational groups in legislative policy making for the public schools. More specifically, the chapter is organized to answer five questions:

1. What basic resources are available to the educational interest groups?
2. How do these groups convert their basic resources into a working capacity (that is, power) to exert legislative influence?
3. How much unity exists among educational interest groups on legislative issues, and what is the current status of educational coalitions?
4. How influential, collectively and individually, are the educational interest groups in the state legislature?

5. How might the differences in legislative influence among the groups and across the states be explained?

First, however, there should be some understanding of the focus of the chapter and the data used. Research attention was limited to four major state-level educational interest groups in each state studied. The four groups were the teacher association (TA), the state affiliate of the National Education Association; the teacher federation (TF), the state affiliate of the American Federation of Teachers; the administrator association (AA), the state affiliate of the American Association of School Administrators; and the school boards association (SBA), the state affiliate of the National School Boards Association. The focus was further restricted to the legislative arena. Since the legislature sets all fiscal policy for the schools and enacts countless other laws that affect these institutions in fundamental ways, that is "where the action is" for most educational interest groups. This chapter examines legislator-educational interest group relationships, but not relationships between these groups and other state policy actors.[2]

The data reported here are drawn primarily from interview schedules completed by EGP interviewers with educational interest group leaders and legislative leaders. (See Table I-3 for the number of respondents.) The researchers who actually conducted the fieldwork were also interviewed to obtain intuitive impressions and a better perspective on the situation in each state. Several follow-up procedures employed to fill in data gaps included:

1. contacting the national offices of the groups (National Education Association, American Federation of Teachers, National Schools Boards Association, American Association of School Administrators) by mail and telephone;
2. contacting representatives of the various interest groups in a number of states to gain specific data or to conduct full interviews by telephone;
3. reviewing the individual case studies written by EGP staff to determine whether data other than those from interview schedules had been used relative to educational interest group activity.

These and other follow-up procedures, albeit not without difficulties, were fairly effective in filling gaps. Though some gaps remained, there did not appear to be enough to challenge the preponderance of the evidence.

BASIC RESOURCES

Basic resources, in effect, represent "raw materials" that can be utilized by educational interest groups to "manufacture" power and influence at the state level. The number of members, the amount of money available, and the prestige of some or all of the members are the basic resources to be considered here.

Number of Members

Perhaps the most fundamental resource available to any group, and the easiest to compare, is size of membership. Table V-1 reports state figures for the four major educational interest groups—TA, AA, SBA, and TF—in terms of active members. Active members are the most comparable data since many organizations enroll corporate, student, retired, and other members who do not fully participate. The data are for the 1972-73 membership year, except for SBA's; the most current data available for them covered 1971-72.

A greater problem with the SBA membership data is that the first SBA column shown in Table V-1 reflects the number of school boards, not persons, affiliated because these organizations have institutional memberships. These data had to be transformed. This was done (see second SBA column in Table V-1) by multiplying the number of boards by five. The most common size for local school boards appears to be five members, and the new figures for the SBA's closely approximate the number of individuals represented by these organizations. Such weighting efforts, however, can be inaccurate because some boards may have six or more members. For purposes of generalizing here, however, this margin of error is tolerable. From Table V-1, then, it is possible to cite four general findings:

1. The teacher associations enroll by far the largest membership, anywhere from roughly twice to hundreds of times as large as the other organizations.
2. The teacher federation's membership ranks it second in a number of states, but the federation is virtually nonexistent in three states as a state-level group.
3. The school boards associations generally are smallest in size if

TABLE V-1 Educational Interest Group Membership
(Number of Active Members)

State	TA[a]	AA[b]	SBA[c]	TF[d]
California	150,980	3,229	1,142(5,710)	27,000
Colorado	19,628	1,174	129(645)	2,000
Florida	33,000	67	67(335)	5,000
Georgia	36,762	143	170(850)	NSO
Massachusetts	44,458	375	341(1,705)	DNA
Michigan	78,805	783	560(2,800)	18,000
Minnesota	34,376	502	436(2,180)	14,000
Nebraska	18,505	839	266(1,330)	NSO
New York	101,250[e]	555	754(3,770)	M
Tennessee	39,149	500	141(705)	DNA
Texas	139,911	1,217	525(2,625)	NSO
Wisconsin	45,331	397	422(2,110)	DNA

Key:

NSO = No state organization as reported by the American Federation of Teachers.

DNA = Data not available.

M   = Data for TF portion of merged TA-TF not available.

[a]Teacher association, data 1972-73, from National Council of State Educational Associations.

[b]Administrator association, data 1972-73, from American Association of School Administrators.

[c]School boards association, data 1971-72, from National School Boards Association. First number = member boards; number in parentheses = member board X 5.

[d]Teacher federation, data 1972-73, from interview schedules.

[e]Data are for association portion of merged TA-TF.

only institution members are counted, but they rank ahead of the administrator groups when numbers of persons represented are the figures used.

4. The administrator groups represent the fewest individuals, ranging from 67 in Florida to 3,229 in California.

Money

The enrollment of members in educational interest groups (EIG) is an important consideration for various reasons, not the least of which is money. Attention is given here to resources obtained in the form of dues. Table V-2 contains data on the dues levels of the interest groups in the twelve states. Insofar as possible, these data are presented in dollar amounts.

TABLE V-2 Educational Interest Group State Dues in Flat Amount, Average, or Range

State	TA[a]	AA[b]	SBA[c]	TF[d]
California	$ 72[e]	$ 95[f]	$ 60	$21
Colorado	50	64[f]	358-7,051[g]	34.80
Florida	40	INC[h]	250-2,000	17
Georgia	25	10	158-4,177	NSO
Massachusetts	76	125	75-500	30
Michigan	100	100	69-1,500	24
Minnesota	48	100[f]	236-2,833	42
Nebraska	30	INC[h]	100	NSO
New York	55	83[f]	225-1,700	M
Tennessee	25	DNA	30-2,100	DNA
Texas	18	35	110-575	NSO
Wisconsin	46	DNA	180-1,876	DNA

Key:

INC = Inconclusive data
DNA = Data not available
NSO = No state organization
M   = Separate TF data not available; TF merged with TA

[a]From National Council of State Education Association's, "Profiles of State Education Associations, 1972-73."

[b]From American Association of School Administrators' "Profile '73: State Associations of School Administrators."

[c]From National School Boards Association, by telephone.

[d]From respective teacher federation state offices, by telephone.

[e]All state teacher associations report flat dues, usually as percentage of average salary in state.

[f]Four state administrator associations report the "average" of a flexible dues schedule.

[g]All but two state school board groups report flexible dues; the range is given here.

[h]Inconclusive data (e.g., Florida AA reported ½ of one percent of individuals' salary. Nebraska reported dues at .004 percent. These data are inconclusive in that they do not compare with other data in Table V-2 given in dollars).

Both teacher groups in all of the states reported their dues as a flat dollar amount. The school board and administrator groups, however, were another story. While four administrator groups reported flat dues, at least six others had a flexible dues structure that allows for reporting only an average, and in two groups dues represented a percentage of the members' salaries. In the case of school boards, only two states reported flat amounts; the other ten states reported the range of institutional dues. It is important to remember that school board groups enroll institutions, not individuals, and that these dues almost universally come from public tax monies (that is, from school board budgets). Further, dues structures are flexible, based upon number of students, teachers, or annual budgets of the school districts.

To generalize, Table V-2 shows that school board groups, by and large, have the highest dues, running as much as $7,051 in Colorado (but as little as $30 in Tennessee). Administrator groups seem to have the next largest dues, although data are inconclusive or unavailable in four states. Teacher association dues, while generally substantial, still rank third on an outlay per member basis. Teacher federation dues were reported at levels below the other organizations.

A more meaningful comparison of the financial resources of these groups comes from a consideration of the income they derive from dues. Annual income figures are presented in Table V-3. In the case of the administrator and school board groups, the American Association of School Administrators and the National School Board Association had compiled data that reported such income. For both teacher groups, however, it was necessary to multiply members (Table V-1) times dues (Table V-2) to estimate annual income. These data are not precise if for no other reason than the fact that in at least one column (SBA) the data were for 1971-72, rather than for 1972-73, as they were for the other groups. Still, for purposes of generalization, the data imperfections are relatively minor.

Table V-3, reporting approximate annual income from dues, demonstrates the effect of the number of members as a significant variable. Whereas the teacher associations have generally lower dues than either administrators or school boards, the large number of members generates a great deal of revenue. These data reveal that the teacher association income from dues, in some instances, runs a hundred times that of administrator organizations and easily ten times that of school board groups. The teacher federations also rank ahead

TABLE V-3 Educational Interest Group Estimated Annual Income from State Dues (in Thousands of Dollars)

State	TA[a]	AA[b]	SBA[c]	TF[a]
California	10,870	120	444	567
Colorado	981	65	175	70
Florida	1,320	13	63	85
Georgia	919	1	90	NSO
Massachusetts	3,379	37	101	DNA
Michigan	7,880	77	277	432
Minnesota	1,650	58	296	588
Nebraska	555	49	97	NSO
New York	5,569	54	571	M
Tennessee	979	DNA	33	DNA
Texas	2,518	38	74	NSO
Wisconsin	2,085	28	199	DNA

Key:

NSO = No state organization

DNA = Data not available

M   = Separate TF data not available; TF merged with TA

[a]Income from dues estimated as members (Table V-1) times dues (Table V-2).
[b]Income from dues as reported to and by American Association of School Administrators.
[c]Income from dues as reported to and by National School Boards Association.

of administrators and school boards where the federation exists at the state level. School board groups rank well ahead of administrators in all cases, and ahead of the federation in one case, Colorado. Administrators uniformly rank fourth out of four groups in all twelve states.

Miscellaneous Monetary Resources

While income from dues constitutes by far the largest portion of educational interest group income, income generated from other sources is also worth mentioning. Various groups reported income from conferences and conventions sponsored wholly or in part by the organizations. Among the administrator groups, one striking example was the Association of California School Administrators which, while reporting $1.2 million from dues, also reported $148,000 in income from conference fees.

Such income clearly reflects activities beyond what might be considered normal ongoing programs. Several interest group respondents were asked about this category of income, and the consensus was that such income usually was balanced, or in some cases exceeded, by conference or convention expenses. It would be relatively safe and accurate, therefore, to consider these special sources of income as "rotary" accounts. They do not produce any substantial "after expenses" income for the groups.

There is another "fringe" category of income that is difficult to pin down but nevertheless is highly significant. It seems that a number of interest groups—almost exclusively teachers—have engaged in fund-raising efforts to elect public officials "friendly" to education. (Or, perhaps more accurately, "friendly" to that particular group's point of view.) All of the teacher groups except for one affiliate of the American Federation of Teachers reported the existence of a "political action arm." But only a few administrator groups and no school board groups had such "arms." Educational interest group leaders explained that, due to legal constraints of state and federal statutes and Internal Revenue codes, corporations may not directly engage in political campaigns. As a result, semiautonomous political action arms serve to provide legal vehicles for the parent corporations to collect and disburse political funds.

Because these political contributions are generally on a voluntary basis and typically in unspecified amounts, it is extremely difficult to discover the total dollars involved. Such political campaign income and expenses are usually reported somewhere by someone, but there appears to be ample opportunity to disguise the actual figures. As one group leader said: "Our local groups report the amount they spend, and, if you really want to know, you could go to each county board of elections office." Similarly, the Governmental Relations Office of the National Education Association, which has helped organize and coordinate such activity, "respectfully declines" to give out such information.

In at least two cases—Michigan and California—enough is known about the political action arms to speculate on the dollar levels involved. In both states a political action contribution of $5.00 is attached to the state dues as a "negative checkoff." ("Negative checkoff," like many record and book clubs, means that the individual has to take action to prevent participation, rather than the converse.) As one group leader explained: "We run a small box in the back of one of our publications telling people how they can get their money back if they want to." The consensus is that, with this technique, a negative dues checkoff typically means 95 percent participation or better. Informed observers claimed that the California Teachers Association, for example, has "a $600,000 political war chest."

Status of Members

In addition to the resources just described, there is another kind of basic resource that is available in varying degrees to EIG's. This resource, which might be termed "status of members," is particularly hard to study. An abstract definition can be offered, but an operational definition widely shared among respondents is difficult to extract. As a concept, "status of members" refers to the degree to which individual members of the respective groups command respect and credibility because of the positions they hold. For example, some respondents claimed that superintendents, because of their positions as administrative heads of school systems, had a valuable source of influence, while others claimed that board members, because they were elected by the people and had no "vested interest" other than to represent and protect the people, should be considered the most credible educational spokesmen at the state level.

The "status of members" concept is also difficult to deal with because of such questions as "status with whom and on what matters?" It is, moreover, impossible to measure "status" in as objective a manner as numbers of members or amounts of money. In any event, "status of members" as a resource is mentioned here because sufficient evidence does exist that interest group leaders, to varying degrees, claim status as a reason for group influence. A number of legislator respondents also recognize and perhaps give legitimacy to such claims.

Review of Findings

EIG's had access to two basic types of resources: members and dollars. Besides these, the interest groups sought other monetary resources. Both the teacher association and teacher federation leaders, in every case but one, said that they maintained a political action arm which, among its functions, collected and disbursed campaign monies. Administrator and school board groups indicated some cash flow outside of dues, especially from conferences, clinics, and workshops. Administrator and school board groups apparently also enjoyed another more nebulous type of resource—"status of members"—having to do with the credibility or prestige of local members as a reason for group strength.

In terms of sheer numbers of members, teacher associations had an overwhelming margin compared with other groups. The ratio of teacher association members to administrator association members was typically ten to one, running as high as one hundred to one in several states. When school board groups were compared with teacher associations, the ratio was only slightly lower. The teacher federations were nonexistent or otherwise noncompetitive in nearly half the states. The notable exceptions were in New York, Minnesota, Michigan, and California, which were all northern states with strong union movements. In New York, the United Federation of Teachers membership was large enough to force merger with the New York State Teacher Association on an equal basis.

As for state dues, the school board groups typically reported the highest dues, followed by administrators, teacher associations, and, finally, teacher federations. Educational interest group income from dues was substantial. Across the twelve states, the teacher associations, for example, reported nearly forty million dollars yearly income from dues. In comparison, the administrator groups reported less than one million and school board groups reported a little over two million. Where teacher federations existed and were willing to report, it appeared they were able to exceed administrator and school board group income somewhat.

Teacher associations characteristically had extremely large memberships and moderately high dues. The combination of the two gave the associations a much larger income than the other groups. Teacher associations also uniformly reported having political action arms. School board groups typically reported having the largest dues of any group, though they had only a small number of members compared with teacher associations. Hence, school board groups received but a fraction of the income reported by teacher associations. School board associations did report a greater number of members and higher dues than administrator groups. Administrator associations were usually third and sometimes fourth among the state educational interest groups on the basis of members, dues, and income. The teacher federation profile was considerably less clear, partly because there were no state-level organizations in Georgia, Nebraska, and Texas and partly because of the lack of cooperation in several other states. It can be said that federation memberships were related to urbanization and that this might be considered a characteristic. Over-all, however, federations were weak at the state level.

POWER

Basic resources left in raw form, as, for example, money, are not in themselves capable of anything. Such resources generate power only when they are transformed, as into a professional staff or a lobbying establishment. The power section of this chapter is based on the belief that resources are manipulated, or are at least capable of being manipulated, by interest groups to produce the most prom-ising kinds of power. Thus, the notion of power is used here to refer to the capacity of the interest group to affect policy enactments.

Professional Staff

The most logical starting point in presenting the findings on power is to report data on staff capabilities. These data (see Table V-4) dis-close that teacher associations in all twelve states employ by far the largest professional staffs and that only in the smaller states are other groups able to come close numerically (Nebraska has a gap of only seven persons between the TA and the SBA). On a percentage basis, none of the groups employs a staff half as large as that of the teacher association. The Colorado Association of School Boards comes closest with a staff not quite half the size of the Colorado Education Association.

Generally speaking, school board associations run a distant second to teacher associations in terms of size of professional staffs. The administrator associations and teacher federations rank either third or fourth in terms of size of staff, depending on the state. In Colo-rado, Florida, Massachusetts, Minnesota, and Michigan the teacher federation had the larger staff. In the balance of the states—including three by default because no state teacher federations were organized —the administrator associations were larger in terms of staff size. In looking at individual states, California stands out as having the great-est number (257) of professional staff people employed by the four groups. In contrast, Nebraska reported only fourteen staff persons employed by three groups.

TABLE V-4 Numbers of Professional Staff Employed by
Educational Interest Groups

State	TA	AA	SBA	TF
California	216	12	19	10
Colorado	15	3	7	4
Florida	32	1 PT	3	1[a]
Georgia	16	1 PT	6	NSO
Massachusetts	45	2	9	6
Michigan	127	2	8	5
Minnesota	42	1	10	7
Nebraska	10	1	3	NSO
New York	150	2	29	M
Tennessee	27	0	2	DNA
Texas	31	1	5	NSO
Wisconsin	34	1 PT	12	DNA

Key:

NSO = No state organization
DNA = Data not available
M   = TF merged with TA; data not available for TF only
PT   = Part-time staff

[a]Florida Federation's one staff position was vacant at the time of this study.

Lobbying Staff

Along with total staff capabilities, EIG respondents were also asked to identify the number of part- and full-time lobbyists employed by their organization. The data contained in Table V-5 show the numbers of lobbyists so employed. Again, these data demonstrate the substantial edge of the teacher associations. Yet when one considers the vast differences in income among the groups, the relative differences in lobbying staffs do not loom large. In Nebraska, for example, the School Boards Association reported a lobbying corps (two full-time) larger than that of the Teacher Association (one full-time, one part-time). In Minnesota, the School Boards Association also reported the largest lobbying corps. At the other extreme, the TA in California reported an edge of roughly five to one over the other groups.

It should be pointed out that the data in Table V-5 are reliable for gross comparisons only. No effort was made to report part-time

TABLE V-5 Number of Lobbyists Employed by Educational
            Interest Groups

State	TA	AA	SBA	TF
California	5 FT[a]	1 FT, 5 PT	1 FT	1 FT
Colorado	2 FT, 3 PT	2 PT	1 FT	3 FT
Florida	1 FT[b]	0	1 FT, 1 PT	1 FT[c]
Georgia	1 FT, 4 PT	0	1 FT, 2 PT	NSO
Massachusetts	3 FT	1 PT[d]	1 PT	2 PT
Michigan	2 FT, 3 PT	1 FT	1 FT	1 FT, 1 PT
Minnesota	2 FT[e]	1 FT	3 FT, 6 PT	2 FT
Nebraska	1 FT, 1 PT	1 FT	2 FT	NSO
New York	4 FT	1 PT	3 PT	M
Tennessee	2 FT, 4 PT	0[f]	2 PT	DNA
Texas	4 FT, 10 PT	0[f]	2 PT	NSO
Wisconsin	1 FT, 4 PT	1 PT	2 PT	DNA

Key:

  FT = full-time
  PT = part-time
  NSO = No state organization
  DNA = data not available
  M   = TF merged with TA; separate if data not available

[a]Also reported an FT "PR" man attached to lobbying corps.
[b]Also reported one more FT lobbyist about to be employed.
[c]At the time of this study, this position was vacant.
[d]Massachusetts AA and SBA share same lobbyist.
[e]Also reported an FT intern.
[f]Relies on TA for lobbying.

lobbyists on a percentage of full-time equivalent basis. In some cases, where interest groups reported "other" staff as lobbyists, the full-time equivalency percentage could be as much as half-time. In still other cases, members holding full-time public school employment (for example, a president of an administrator group who served as a local superintendent) could not be devoting more than a small fraction of time to lobbying activities. In any event, Table V-5 does indicate rough approximations of educational interest group lobbying power.

Research Capabilities

EIG's have another kind of power in the form of research capabilities. Interest group respondents were asked whether they had a research department or division and, if they did, how many staff members were assigned to that function. These data (see Table V-6) show

TABLE V-6 Educational Interest Groups Having Own Research
Department or Division

State	TA[a]	AA	SBA	TF
California	Yes (3)	No	No	No
Colorado	Yes (2)	No	Yes (1.5)	No
Florida	Yes (3)	No	No	No
Georgia	Yes (1)	No	Yes (1)	NSO
Massachusetts	Yes (3)	No	No	No
Michigan	Yes (2)	No	Yes (1)	No
Minnesota	Yes (1.5)	No	Yes (3)	No
Nebraska	Yes (1)	No	No	NSO
New York	Yes (4)	No	Yes (3)	M
Tennessee	Yes (3)	No	No	DNA
Texas	Yes (3)	Yes[b]	No	NSO
Wisconsin	Yes (1)	No	Yes (.25)	DNA

Key:

NSO = No state organization

M   = TF merged with TA; separate TF data not available

DNA = Data not available

[a]The number in parentheses following a "Yes" gives reported number of staff assigned.

[b]Texas AA is affiliated with Texas TA, which provides research.

that in all twelve states the teacher associations reported the existence of such research capabilities. Staff so assigned by the teacher associations ranged from a high of four in New York to a low of one in Georgia, Nebraska, and Wisconsin.

In contrast, only one of the state administrator groups, Texas, reported research capabilities and, in this instance, such capability was due to direct affiliation with the Texas State Teachers

Association. In looking at the respective school board groups, Table V-6 data indicate that half of the groups had research capabilities, although one might question the value of the Wisconsin school board group's reported quarter-time staff so assigned. The teacher federations reported no research capabilities, but a number of respondents indicated that they could rely on the American Federation of Teachers or the AFL-CIO for such needs.

To review, Table V-6 shows that in at least six of the twelve states the teacher association was the only group to have research capabilities. In the other six states, the teacher associations were joined in this capability by the school board groups. Neither administrators nor teacher federations were able to compete in this regard.

Political Action Arms

Early in this chapter the EIG's that had established political action arms were identified. The data included in that section show that some interest groups had access to fiscal resources outside of the normal dues structure. But such political activities must also be included here as an indicator of the power such arms represent. The ideal situation would be to report in detail the amount of support given to each candidate in such areas as dollars, man-hours, and supplies. Unfortunately, EIG's make a point of not releasing much of these data, though expenditure information must be reported to governmental agencies.

The best that can be done is to report the types of campaigns in which the groups having political arms were involved. Data included in Table V-7 depict this participation in legislative, state board of education (SBE), and chief state school officer (CSSO) elections. Opportunities in the latter two cases were, of course, limited to those states where these officials were elected as opposed to being appointed.

The data in Table V-7 demonstrate that the teacher groups were far more inclined to become active in political campaigns than either administrators or school board groups. Yet even among teacher groups an important distinction must be noted. In no case did any teacher federation report having its own political action arm. Rather, these federations stated that their political activities were coordinated through and by state AFL-CIO political arms. Teacher association political arms, on the other hand, were reported to be independent except for their link to the national teacher association.

TABLE V-7 Participation in Types of Campaigns by Those
Educational Groups Having Political Action Arms

State	TA	AA	SBA	TF
California	L			L
Colorado	L,SBE			L,SBE
Florida	L,SBE,CSSO[a]			L
Georgia	L			NSO
Massachusetts	L			—
Michigan	L,SBE	L		L,SBE
Minnesota	L			L
Nebraska	L,SBE	L,SBE[b]		NSO
New York	L			L[c]
Tennessee	L			DNA
Texas	L,SBE[d]			NSO
Wisconsin	L,CSSO			DNA

Key:

L   = Campaigns for legislative seats
SBE   = Campaigns for state board of education seats
CSSO = Campaigns of elected chief state school officers
NSO   = No state organization
DNA   = Data not available

[a]Florida TA political activity is highly decentralized.
[b]Nebraska AA does not have a formal arm; indirect activity.
[c]TF merged with TA; separate TF data not available.
[d]Texas TA does not campaign as such, but does "interview and rate," a form
of campaign activity.

Data in Table V-7 reveal that in only two states, Michigan and
Nebraska, were administrator groups involved in any way in political
activity. In the case of Nebraska, there may be some question as to
whether the administrator group is committed to political action.
The group's executive secretary was reported to have "taken some
time off" to get politically involved "as an individual," presumably
thus protecting the group from charges of partisanship.

In essence, the data in Table V-7 provide evidence as to the large
degree to which teacher associations dominate the field of educational interest group political involvement. In all twelve states association political arms were active in legislative races, with a few also

participating in state board and CSSO races. The activity of the teacher federations is perhaps suspect to the extent that their activity might be either overshadowed or precluded by the AFL-CIO. Only two administrator groups became politically involved. One of them compensated for such temerity by saying "we prayed a lot." Finally, not surprising given their membership, no school board group found it practical or desirable to engage in direct political action.

Sources of Lobbying Strength

A final way to ascertain the kinds of power available to and used by educational interest groups is to examine the means employed in lobbying activities. In this connection, EIG leaders were asked: "Speaking generally, what means of influence or persuasion can your organization draw upon in its lobbying efforts in the legislature?" In other words, the group leaders were asked to offer their perceptions of the sources of power used in lobbying. Their responses are summarized in Table V-8.

Examination of the data in Table V-8 discloses certain patterns of power, at least in the eyes of the interest group leaders. In terms of money for political campaigns, for instance, only teacher association or federation spokesmen identified this as a source of power in lobbying activity. Six of the teacher association leaders and one federation leader mentioned money as a source of power. No administrators or school board members referred to campaign money, which is consistent with their limited resources and absence of political action arms.

Staff contacts were mentioned as a source of power more frequently than money. It is surprising, given their large staffs, that just half of the teacher association leaders cited staff contacts as a source of power. Three administrator leaders, one school board leader, and one federation leader also identified staff contacts. Teacher associations, then, apparently rely more heavily on the power of their staffs than other groups.

The source of power most frequently mentioned by interest group leaders was local member contacts with legislative leaders. Eight administrator leaders, seven teacher association leaders, seven school board leaders, and two federation leaders named this factor as a source of power. This is not an unexpected finding, especially in light of one group leader's comment that "we try to emphasize that legis-

TABLE V-8 Sources of Power Utilized by Educational Interest Groups in Lobbying

State	TA	AA	SBA	TF
California	$,SC,RE,LO	TBS,INF	INF,LO	LO
Colorado	$,INF,RE	LO	INF,LO	SC
Florida	INF,LO,CO[a]	LO	CR	DNA
Georgia	SC,LO	LO	LO	NSO
Massachusetts	$,INF	LO,SC	LO	INF,TBS
Michigan	INF,LO	INF,LO	INF,SM	PP
Minnesota	$,LO	INF,LO	INF	$,LO
Nebraska	SC	SC,LO	SC	NSO
New York	SC,PC,$	SC,INF	INF,LO	M
Tennessee	INF,LO,SC	_[b]	INF,LO	DNA
Texas	INF,LO	_[b]	INF	NSO
Wisconsin	$,SC,INF	SM,LO	LO	DNA

Key:

$	= Campaign money	CR	= Credibility and respect of organization
SC	= Staff contact	DNA	= Data not available
RE	= Research	NSO	= No state organization
LO	= Local members	SM	= Status of members
TBS	= Telling both sides	PP	= Political power
INF	= Information	PC	= Personal contacts
CO	= Coalition activity	M	= Merged with TA

[a]Coalition involves only local TA's, state organization weakness.
[b]Indicates AA used power of TA.

lative influence is most effectively applied where legislators live, not where they vote."

Another important source of power as perceived by the interest group leaders had to do with providing information. Seven school board leaders, seven teacher association leaders, four administrator leaders, and one federation leader cited information and their capability to provide it as a principal source of power. Given the substantial edge in research capability possessed by teacher associations, it is interesting that only two association respondents mentioned it as a source of power; nor did the leaders of any of the other educational groups mention research. It is likely, however, that when our interviewees pointed to information they also meant the kinds of data that might be generated out of a research capability. Status of members, while specifically cited by only two group leaders, probably also was included in the context of another factor—local member contacts.

Besides the factors that have been discussed, there were several less important and less descriptive sources of power cited by respondents. One group leader mentioned "credibility of the organization." Similarly, two other leaders suggested that "telling both sides" was a source of power. These less descriptive and infrequently mentioned factors might reflect a communications gap between the interviewer and the respondent.

To summarize, the data in Table V-8 indicate that teacher associations seemed to value information, local member contacts, campaign money, and professional staffs, in that order, as means of power. Administrator groups relied heavily on local member contacts, with information and staff activity being much less important. School board groups cited local member contacts and information equally, with staff being of little significance. Teacher federation responses reveal no pattern of emphasis. In part this is because between "data not available" and "no state organization" nearly half the states in our sample show no information for the federations.

Review of Findings

EIG's sought to transform resources into power primarily through the employment and use of professional staff. The numbers of staff employed by the groups generally paralleled the amount of interest group income from dues. There was, apparently, high priority given to the employment of legislative advocates, since only four groups in all twelve states reported no lobbyists employed. This was particularly significant to groups with small staffs; for some of these groups the legislative arena was important enough to draw half or more of their staff time.

Teacher associations, and to a lesser extent school board groups, allocated resources in such a way as to secure employment of research staff on a regular basis. Administrator groups and teacher federations probably found their resources spread too thin to permit acquisition of research capabilities. Political action arms were also in evidence as an expression of group power, but they were limited almost exclusively to the two teacher groups. Such political power was directed predominantly toward legislative campaigns.

As for sources of lobbying power, teacher associations valued and made the most of campaign money, sizable memberships, and large professional staffs. Administrator and school board groups tended to emphasize information giving and local member contacts to obtain power in the legislative arena. Teacher federation data were too fragmented to draw any picture of their power sources, except perhaps for the matter of political power (that is, the ability to participate meaningfully in legislative campaigns). Federations, like teacher associations, stressed political activism, whereas administrator and school board groups did not.

RELATIONSHIPS AMONG THE EDUCATIONAL INTEREST GROUPS

Commentators in the 1960's often spoke of an "establishment," at the core of which were alliances of EIG's.[3] There is abundant evidence that this "establishment" is no longer as united as it supposedly was a decade ago. Historic forces have shattered many, perhaps most, such coalitions. The aftermath, as interpreted by several scholars, has been a "breakdown of political order" in respect to public education at the state level.[4] The extent of this "breakdown," its causes, and the current status of the educational coalitions were of great interest during this study.

Extent of Educator Unity

To test perceptions of educator unity, a number of different groups of respondents were asked: "To what extent do the major educational interest groups act in unison and speak with one voice? Do they do so on: nearly all, most, some, or almost no legislative issues?" Governors' personal staff members, state department legislative experts, educational group leaders, and, perhaps most important, legislators—all responded to this question, and their answers formed the basis for Tables V-9 and V-10.

The data in Tables V-9 and V-10 suggest that Georgia, Tennessee, and Texas most closely approximated a high degree of unity among EIG's. These data also show Massachusetts, Michigan, Minnesota, New York, and perhaps California at the other extreme, manifesting much disunity. The remaining states fell in the middle ground. With few exceptions, the different respondents were rather consistent in their assessments, indicating a substantial degree of accuracy in these rankings.

TABLE V-9 Perceptions of Unity among Educational Interest
Groups on Legislative Issues

State	Extent of unity as perceived by:					
	GPS[a]	SDE-LE[b]	TA	AA	SBA	TF
California	3	3	3	3	3	3
Colorado	DNA	2	2	2	2	3
Florida	3	2	2.6[c]	3	2	2
Georgia	2	2	2	1	1	NSO
Massachusetts	3.5[c]	4	3.5[c]	1.5[c]	4	3
Michigan	3.6[c]	4	3.6[c]	3	4	4
Minnesota	4	3	1	3	3	3
Nebraska	3	1.5[c]	2	1	4	NSO
New York	3	3.5[c]	3.5[c]	4	2	M
Tennessee	1	2	1	2	1	DNA
Texas	2	2	1.6[c]	1	1	NSO
Wisconsin	3	2	3	1.6[c]	2	DNA

Key:
1 = "nearly all legislative issues"
2 = "most"
3 = "some"
4 = "almost no issues"
DNA = Data not available
NSO = No state organization
M = TF merged with TA; separate TF data not available

[a]Governor's personal staff responses.
[b]State department legislative expert responses.
[c]Other than whole numbers indicate mean of several responses.

Aside from determining the extent of unity among the educational groups constituting the "education lobby," there was an attempt to discover which issues were seen as producing division among the groups. Accordingly, state department legislative experts, legislators, and governor's personal staff members were all asked: "What issues tend to divide the major educational organizations the most?" The replies of all respondents are summarized in Table V-11. These replies identify five issues—collective bargaining, tenure, salaries, school finance, and certification, probably in that order—as being most divisive in educational organizations. The fact that these issues

TABLE V-10 Legislator Perceptions of Unity among the Educational Interest Groups on Legislative Issues

State	Number of legislators describing unity on issues as:				
	Nearly all	Most	Some	Almost no	(N)
California	1	3	8	4	16
Colorado	0	5	6	3	14
Florida	0	0	1	2	3
Georgia	6	4	3	0	13
Massachusetts	0	2	3	8	13
Michigan	0	2	11	2	15
Minnesota	0	1	6	7	14
Nebraska	0	2	3	0	5
New York	0	1	5	2	8
Tennessee	5	5	1	0	11
Texas	1	5	4	0	10
Wisconsin	2	5	8	2	17

are far from mutually exclusive suggests that an even more tightly knit set of factors produces conflict.

Status of Educational Coalitions

The literature on state school policy making has ascribed great significance to educational coalitions.[5] The first question asked related to this concern aimed at determining which states had coalitions. To provide a common frame of reference, the initial question was preceded by a definition of "coalition" as "a number of different organizations that have consciously worked together over a period of years to achieve some common purpose." With this definition in mind, EIG leaders were asked: "Are there any such enduring coalitions among the major state-level education organizations in this state?" The responses indicate that, in all of the states except Florida, Nebraska, and Wisconsin, EIG leaders believed that an enduring coalition existed. And it might be noted that Florida did report two coalitions of sorts.

Following the question on the existence of coalitions, the respondents giving "yes" answers were asked to indicate if these coalitions were formal or informal. Formality was determined by the presence or absence of a constitution or bylaws, officers, and regular meetings.

TABLE V-11 Perceptions of Selected Respondents as to the Issues
Most Dividing the Educational Interest Groups

State	SDE-LE[a]	Legislators	GPS[b]
California	Cb,Crt,Ten	Cb,Ten	Crt,Ten,Cb
Colorado	INC	Ten,Cb	DNA
Florida	Cb,Sal	Fin,Cb	Cb
Georgia	Ten	Sal,Fin	Sal
Massachusetts	INC	Fin,Crt,Sal	Sal
Michigan	INC	Ten,Sal,Cb	Most
Minnesota	Sal,Cb	Cb,Ten,Sal	Cb,Ten
Nebraska	Cb	Cb,Ten	Fin,Ten,Sal
New York	Cb,Sal	Sal,Fin,Cb	DNA
Tennessee	Fin	Ten,Cb,Sal	None
Texas	Ten,Cb	Cb,Ten	Cb
Wisconsin	Ten	Sal,Ten,Cb	Sal,Fin

Key:

Cb   = Collective bargaining
Crt = Certification
Ten = Tenure
INC = Inconclusive response
DNA = Data not available
Sal   = Salaries
Fin   = School finance, including the state aid formula

[a]State department of education legislative expert.
[b]Governor's personal staff.

Nine states reported coalitions; seven also reported that these coalitions were formal in their establishment.

Beyond determining where coalitions existed and whether they were formal or informal, there was an attempt in the study to identify the coalition memberships and which organizations or persons, if any, were perceived as providing leadership. In this regard, EIG leaders were questioned about member groups in the coalitions. The typical coalition, as can be seen from Table V-12, included the major educational organizations and perhaps one or two closely related school groups like PTA's particularly and, less frequently, AAUW chapters. In only two states, Tennessee and Colorado, did the coalition include a broad range of noneducational organizations. In

TABLE V-12 Educational Interest Group Description of Coalition
Membership

State	Coalitions include:									
	TA	AA	SBA	TF	RSG	C/U	B/I	F	L	LWV
California	Yes	Yes	Yes	Yes	Yes	No	No	No	No	Yes
Colorado	Yes	Yes	Yes	Yes	Yes	No	Yes	Yes	Yes	Yes
Florida				(No Coalition)						
Georgia	Yes	Yes	Yes	NSO	No	No	No	No	No	No
Massachusetts	Yes	Yes	Yes	No	Yes	Yes	No	No	No	No
Michigan	Yes	Yes	Yes	Yes	No	No	No	No	No	No
Minnesota	Yes	Yes	Yes	Yes	Yes	No	No	No	No	No
Nebraska				(No Coalition)						
New York	Yes	Yes	Yes	Yes	Yes	No	No	No	No	No
Tennessee	Yes	Yes	Yes	—	Yes	No	Yes	No	No	Yes
Texas	Yes	Yes	Yes	NSO	Yes	No	No	No	No	No
Wisconsin				(No Coalition)						

Key:

C/U = College/university representatives
B/I = Business/industry representatives
F   = Farm groups
L   = Labor groups
RSG = Related school groups such as PTA, AAUW, Delta Kappa Gamma
LWV = League of Women Voters
NSO = No state organization

Tennessee the coalition included such diverse groups as the American
Legion, the AAUW, the Junior Chamber of Commerce (Jaycees), the
Citizens Committee for Better Schools, and the Federation of Business and Professional Women. In Colorado, coalition membership
was perhaps even more diverse, reaching to the Colorado Association
of Commerce and Industry, cattlemen, mining interests, sheepmen,
and other farm representatives.

EIG leaders were asked to identify the organizations providing
coalition leadership to "keep things going." The responses indicate
that in the two states with diverse membership—that is, Tennessee
and Colorado—education groups were widely perceived as exercising
coalition leadership. But the data also show that such leadership did
not exist across states in any constant pattern. In California, there
appeared to be conflicting perceptions as to who was leading. The

chairwoman of the PTA was least mentioned, while teacher associations, administrator, and school board groups, along with the CSSO, were frequently mentioned, thus permitting California's Educational Congress to "enjoy" group leadership. In Massachusetts, legislators had difficulty recognizing the Educational Conference Board unless it was referred to as Charlotte Ryan's (PTA) group. In Michigan, Minnesota, and Texas, group leaders failed to see much leadership at all; rather, they viewed the coalition as a "hot air" group or "coffee klatch." New York's Educational Conference Board was looked upon as having passed its prime and, while still led by teacher and school board groups, as declining in influence and in its ability to hold groups together, particularly in view of the TA-TF merger.

The perceptions offered by the group leaders provide the basis for an assessment of coalition effectiveness. Table V-13 presents an

TABLE V-13 An Assessment of the Effectiveness of State
              Educational Coalitions

States with:			
Highly effective coalitions	Moderately effective coalitions	Generally ineffective coalitions	No coalitions
Colorado	California	Michigan	Florida
Tennessee	Georgia	Minnesota	Nebraska
	Massachusetts	Texas	Wisconsin
	New York		

evaluation in light of observations in the literature about the importance of educational coalitions in determining state-level policy, notably in the school finance area. Fully half the states studied had no coalition at all, or else a generally ineffective one, leaderless and meeting infrequently, if at all. The Massachusetts and New York Educational Conference Boards were found to be less viable than the literature has suggested. It seems that the generally nonurban states of Colorado and Tennessee had put together the most effective educational coalitions.

Review of Findings

In most states both EIG leaders and legislative respondents saw the "education lobby" as being fragmented and unable to agree on most legislative issues. It is revealing to summarize these findings in light of Iannaccone's typology of four basic descriptors of state educational policy systems: "locally-based disparate," characterized by localism in structures; "state-wide monolithic," characterized by state-level points of tangency among government agencies and interest groups; "state-wide fragmented," characterized by fragmentation, disunity, and often conflict rather than consensus; and, finally, "state-wide syndical" for those states with a government-sanctioned coalition or special commission.[6] No state studied fell into the syndical category; hence, that category is not shown below. The findings of the Educational Governance Project suggest that the twelve states studied may be described in Iannaccone's categories as follows:

"locally-based disparate"	*"state-wide monolithic"*	*"state-wide fragmented"*
	Tennessee	California
	Texas	Massachusetts
		Michigan
		Minnesota
		Nebraska
		New York
		Wisconsin
Florida		Florida
Georgia	Georgia	
	Colorado	Colorado

These data are interesting in that they show fragmentation evident in the northern or more industrialized states of California, Massachusetts, Michigan, Minnesota, Nebraska, New York, and Wisconsin. The southern states of Tennessee and Texas were largely monolithic, primarily due to the clear dominance of the teacher association in each state, which lacked competition from a teacher federation and which retained the bulk of school administrators under its umbrella. Florida was somewhat unique and could be considered largely state-wide fragmented. Because of the disarray of the teacher association, however, some elements of a locally-based disparate model also existed.

Similarly, Georgia showed some traits of the locally-based disparate, with relatively weak state interest groups overall. But attempts at unity in Georgia suggest that it might also be considered monolithic. Colorado, on the other hand, would be clearly fragmented were it not for the balance of power among the groups channeled through a highly credible coalition.

Speaking of educational coalitions, nine of the twelve states included in this study reported the existence of an educational coalition, with seven of them being formal organizations. Typically, the interest groups saw the coalitions as mechanisms for reducing the potentially divided positions the groups might otherwise take on the matter of school finance. The coalitions were intended to be a channel for amelioration of conflict to the end that legislators and others would perceive a greater degree of unity among the "education lobby." In this regard, at least two coalitions—in Tennessee and Colorado—included a broad range of noneducation groups that served to identify business and community interests with school finance problems.

In general, however, there were serious questions as to the value the interest groups placed on the coalitions. Florida, Nebraska, and Wisconsin reported no coalitions. Michigan, Minnesota, and Texas may as well have declared the coalition dead. In other words, in half the states a coalition could not have had any effect on education legislation. In four states—California, Georgia, Massachusetts, and New York—coalitions have had some effect. The latter two states, typical of the northeast, had long-standing Educational Conference Boards. But these were widely perceived as declining in effect on the policy system. In California, a newly formed coalition had limited experience; in Georgia, the coalition probably constituted an amalgamation of rather weak groups in the first place. In short, only in Tennessee and Colorado were the coalitions seen as being highly effective. In Colorado, particularly, the coalition included many noneducational groups and spoke authoritatively on school finance issues.

LEGISLATIVE INFLUENCE

Without discounting the importance of CSSO's, state boards, or governors, it can be safely assumed that state legislatures play the most vital role in the determination of educational policy. Decisions of major import, especially financial ones, are the substance of legislative activity and thereby attract interest group attention. To assess the pattern of relationships and influence between interest groups and legislatures, it is desirable to attempt to discover not only which groups are most influential, but also why they appear to be so.

Influence of the "Education Lobby"

Before considering which EIG's were perceived to be most influential in the legislature, it is appropriate, first, to look at an overall evaluation of the "education lobby." In other words, when major state-level education groups were viewed as a whole, how were they considered to "stack up" when compared with other lobbying groups? To ascertain the strength of the education lobby, as well as to compare interest group leader responses with those of legislators, both group leaders and legislative leaders were asked the same question: "How do the major education organizations stack up compared to other interest groups in the state? Would you say that, taken together, these organizations are: the top group, among the top groups, among the less important groups, or not at all influential?"

The responses of interest group leaders to this question provide the basis for Table V-14. This table indicates that most of these leaders believed the education lobby was at least "among the top

TABLE V-14 Frequency Distribution of Educational Interest Group Leader Assessments of the Influence of the "Education Lobby"

State	Top groups	Among top groups	Among less important groups	Not at all influential	Respondents
California	0	7	0	0	7
Colorado	0	6	0	0	6
Florida	1	1	2	0	4
Georgia	1	4	0	0	5
Massachusetts	0	4	0	0	4
Michigan	1	7	0	0	8
Minnesota	1	2	1	0	4
Nebraska	1	0	2	0	3
New York	2	1	1	0	4
Tennessee	4	2	0	0	6
Texas	5	1	0	0	6
Wisconsin	0	6	0	0	6

groups." The weakest ratings appeared in Nebraska and Florida; the strongest ratings were offered in Texas and Tennessee. Other than these two lowest and two highest states, the remaining eight were rather uniformly described as having an education lobby "among the top groups" in their respective states.

The responses of legislators to the question of education lobby influence constitute the data in Table V-15. The legislators tended to

TABLE V-15 Frequency Distribution of Legislator Assessments of the Influence of the "Education Lobby"

State	Top groups	Among top groups	Among less important groups	Not at all influential	Respondents
California	4	10	3	0	17
Colorado	3	9	4	0	16
Florida	2	1	2	1	6
Georgia	5	6	1	1	13
Massachusetts	0	4	1	0	5
Michigan	7	5	3	0	15
Minnesota	6	6	3	0	15
Nebraska	1	4	2	0	7
New York	1	5	3	0	9
Tennessee	5	6	0	0	11
Texas	4	5	0	0	9
Wisconsin	2	10	3	0	15

agree with interest group leaders that the education lobby was particularly weak in Nebraska and Florida. Surprisingly, however, New York legislators rated the education lobby as significantly less important than had New York interest group leaders. Also, Tennessee and Texas legislators did not find the education lobby quite as influential as the interest group leaders had. On the other hand, in Michigan and Minnesota the legislators rated the education lobby as more important than it was in the eyes of the interest group leaders. Yet it should be noted that these differences in perceptions of legislators and interest group leaders were small, given the breadth of the total rating scale. As a generalization, therefore, it can be said that the interest group leaders had a rather accurate sense of reality if one assumes that legislators were in the best position to assess the total lobbying picture.

Legislative Influence of the Individual Groups

While interest group leader responses were largely consistent with those of legislator interviewees on the previous question, the matter of which particular group had the most legislative influence was also tested with both classes of respondents. The EIG leaders were asked: "Among just the educational organizations, which ones are usually the most influential when public school policy is being decided by the legislature?" The replies are contained in Table V-16. These data show that the interest group leaders differed somewhat in the rankings they provided.

Teacher leaders ranked the teacher association as most influential in nine of the twelve states. In Colorado, the strong educational coalition (COED) was ranked first by teachers. Florida Association leaders were unsure of their response, and New York teacher respondents listed both administrator and school board groups first (in light of other data, one has to assume false modesty here).

Administrator group leaders agreed in seven cases that the teacher association was most influential. Agreement with the association respondent was also evident in Colorado (ranking the coalition first) and in Florida (where the administrator respondent did not provide any more conclusive data than did the association respondent). The school board groups seemed more reluctant to credit the teachers and much more disposed to rank themselves first. Because of inconclusive data, data not available, and the like, it was not possible to identify a trend in teacher federation responses. Overall, then, the teacher associations ranked first, followed by either the administrator or school board groups, with federation groups ranking fourth.

To determine legislator perceptions of the most influential groups, legislative leaders were asked: "Among just the educational groups, which ones are usually the most influential when education and school finance matters are being dealt with by the legislature?" Their responses (see Table V-17) are extremely interesting both when taken by themselves and when compared to interest group leader perceptions in Table V-16. The legislators, without exception, rated the teacher associations as most influential in the twelve states. To be sure, they believed the school board groups were equally effective in

TABLE V-16 Educational Interest Group Leader Perceptions of Most Influential Education Organizations When School Policy Was Being Decided by the Legislature

State	Responses of each group listed in order of perceived importance:			
	TA	AA	SBA	TF
California	TA,AA,SBA	AA,SBA,TA,TF	TA,SBA,AA,TF	TA,SBA,AA
Colorado	CO[a],TA,SBA,AA	CO,AA,SBA,TA	SBA,TA	SBA,TA,TF
Florida	INC	INC	INC	DNA
Georgia	TA,SBA	TA,SBA	SBA,AA,TA	NSO
Massachusetts	TA	TA,SBA,AA	SBA,TA	INC
Michigan	TA,TF,AA,SBA	TA,SBA,AA	TA,AA,SBA,TF	INC
Minnesota	TA,SBA,TF	TA,SBA	SBA,TA,TF	TA,TF,AA,SBA
Nebraska	TA	AA,TA,SBA	SBA	NSO
New York	AA,SBA	CO[b]	AA	M
Tennessee	TA,SBA	TA	TA,SBA	DNA
Texas	TA,SBA	TA,SBA	TA,SBA	NSO
Wisconsin	TA,SBA	TA,SBA	TA,SBA	DNA

Key:

INC = Inconclusive or evasive response

DNA = Data not available

NSO = No state organization

M = TF merged with TA; separate TF data not available

[a]Indicates Colorado's education coalition—COED.

[b]Indicates New York's education coalition—New York Educational Conference Board.

TABLE V-17 Legislator Perceptions of Most Influential Education
Organizations When School Policy Was Being Decided
by the Legislature

State	Rank order of influence for each group:			
	TA	AA	SBA	TF
California	1	3	2	4
Colorado	1	3	1	_a
Florida	_b	—	—	—
Georgia	1	3	2	NSO
Massachusetts	1	NM	2	NM
Michigan	1	2	3	4
Minnesota	1	NM	2	3
Nebraska	1	3	1	NSO
New York	1	3	2	M
Tennessee	1	NM	2	NM
Texas	1	NM	2	NSO
Wisconsin	1	3	1	4

Key:
  NSO = No state organization
  NM = Not mentioned by legislators
  M   = TF merged with TA; separate TF data not available

[a]Coalition really should be ranked 4; see text explanation.
[b]No ranking in Florida, because of insufficient information.

three of the states: Colorado, Nebraska, and Wisconsin. Yet, in general, the school board groups tended to be ranked second. The administrator groups made a much poorer showing than might have been expected. In only one state, Michigan, were they ranked as high as second by the legislators; in four other states they were not even mentioned as being among the more effective groups. The teacher federations were rated as high as third in Minnesota and fourth in the rest of the states where they were mentioned. It is also interesting to note that in Colorado the educational coalition was ranked fourth, ahead of the federation, which was not mentioned.

In comparing Tables V-16 and V-17, a number of similarities, as well as discrepancies, are quickly apparent. First, the interest group leaders who most closely approximated legislators in their answers were the teacher association leaders. However immodest, their ranking of themselves as most influential was verified by legislators. Teacher association leaders, like legislators, tended to rank school board associations as the second most influential interest groups. The responses of the administrator groups were similar to those of legislators, at least to the extent that administrator respondents ranked teacher association groups first in seven states. The administrator groups also tended to rank school board groups second in influence. The school board respondents ranked themselves ahead of the teacher groups in five states, thereby departing from the legislator assessments.

In both Tables V-16 and V-17 there are insufficient data in the teacher federation categories to make adequate comparisons between federation leader and legislator rankings. The fact that inconclusive or evasive answers were given in two states, and there was a refusal to rate in one state, might indicate that the teacher federations realized their unfavorable position and preferred not to comment on it.

Reasons for Group Influence

While it was important to determine which EIG's were perceived as most influential, it was also of concern to ask legislators and interest group leaders to give reasons why they ranked the interest groups as they did. As might have been expected, a number of legislator respondents were unable or unwilling to cite specific reasons for what appeared to be intuitive judgments. Other respondents gave such generalized answers as to preclude analysis. Still there were many legislator respondents who were able to give fairly specific reasons for their rankings. The analyses that follow are based upon these specifics.

Since teacher associations were ranked as being most influential, it is not surprising that several reasons can be enumerated. In at least seven states (except Florida, Georgia, Nebraska, Tennessee, and Texas), legislators emphasized what they perceived to be "well-heeled" teacher association operations. This perception appeared strongest in California and New York. One California legislator made the somewhat typical comment that "they (CTA) spend money all over the place," whereas a New York legislator fell back on the cliché of "spending money like a drunken sailor."

Paralleling the issue of large amounts of campaign money, the legislators similarly identified what they called "power," "clout," and "votes." These terms were mentioned frequently enough by legislators to convey clearly a sensitivity to the political action orientation of the teacher associations. Perhaps also falling in this context was the frequent mention of sheer "numbers" as a reason for teacher influence. Other reasons mentioned—information, expertise, status of members—were cited less frequently and largely confined to the less industrialized states such as Tennessee, Georgia, and Nebraska.

With respect to the school board associations, perceived to rival the teacher association groups in a few states, an entirely different set of reasons was advanced. The most commonly mentioned had to do with "status of members." Legislators tended to view school board groups as representing "locally elected officials" and as having status in their communities. This perception is consistent with, and reinforced by, the school board groups which claim that only they among the education groups truly represent an unselfish interest—the people.

Another very interesting explanation for school board legislative effectiveness had to do with group lobbyist or executive secretaries. In three states—Colorado, Nebraska, and Wisconsin—legislators made particular reference to the fact that the school boards had a "respected lobbyist" or "executive secretary of long experience." To be sure, in a number of other states, legislators offered the generalization that the school boards association was "credible" and "respected." But it was in those three states where legislators made frequent and specific mention of a person. This would indicate that where school board groups were most effective, such success was attributable as much to an individual as to the group, and perhaps more so.

The fact that administrator groups were ranked third in influence by legislators in some states and not at all in some other states produces a somewhat vague picture of the sources of administrator association strength. It appears that the legislators were emphasizing some of the same kinds of reasons given for school boards. Recognition was given to the "credibility" and "respect" which administrators—predominantly superintendents—enjoy as a result of their positions. Other legislators apparently were describing closely related reasons when they included "status" on the list. No mention was made of money, political power, numbers, and votes, as had been the case with teacher associations. And it was by far the exception that a legislator would note "effective lobbying." Unlike the school board groups, the administrator groups were not mentioned because of particular persons on their staffs.

Review of Findings

With respect to state legislatures, the "education lobby" was perceived, both by legislators and interest group leaders, as generally being among the top interest groups in the respective states. In fact, legislators in a few cases tended to rank the education lobby as being stronger than interest group leaders did. Teacher associations, administrator groups, and legislators were inclined to rank the teacher associations as being most influential in the legislature. School board groups often ranked themselves first, contrary to legislator perceptions. The school board groups did in fact rank second in influence in most states, and they were even ranked as "too close to call" with teacher associations in Colorado, Nebraska, and Wisconsin. Administrator groups generally were ranked a distant third and, in fact, were not even mentioned in four states as being influential in the eyes of legislators. The teacher federations in New York, particularly, but also to some extent in Minnesota and Michigan, were considered influential.

SOME CORRELATES OF EDUCATION LOBBY INFLUENCE

The preceding section sets forth the various reasons that legislators gave for the influence of the different state-level educational organizations. The perceptions that organization leaders had of their sources of power were also discussed earlier (see Table V-8). Beyond making comparisons among the four educational groups, it is important to explain why organized educators, taken together, were rated as having, when compared with other state-level interest groups, more legislative influence in some states than in others. Again, as in several prior chapters, rank-order correlations (rho) would be appropriate—given the crudeness of the measures and the small sample—and helpful in trying to identify possible explanatory variables.[7]

To begin this correlational analysis, legislator assessments (see Table V-15) can be used to construct a measure of the influence of the "education lobby" in state legislatures. If one gives legislator responses in each state scores of 3 for "the top group," 2 for "among the top groups," and 1 for "the less important group," then summing and averaging these scores produces a score for each state and permits ranking. Using the same scoring procedures, a measure of education lobby influence based on group leader (see Table V-14) rather than legislator perceptions can be constructed, and the states can be ranked on this variable. The two rank orders are shown in Table V-18. As can be seen, the two rank orders, with the notable excep-

TABLE V-18 Rank Orders of the Education Lobby on Perceived Legislative Influence When Compared with Other Interest Groups

Legislator perceptions		Group leader perceptions	
State	Rank	State	Rank
Tennessee	1	Texas	1
Texas	2	Tennessee	2
Michigan	3	New York	3
Minnesota	4	Georgia	4
Georgia	5	Michigan	5
California	6	Minnesota	6 (tie)
Colorado	7	California	6 (tie)
Wisconsin	8	Colorado	6 (tie)
Nebraska	9	Wisconsin	6 (tie)
Massachusetts	10	Massachusetts	6 (tie)
New York	11	Florida	11
Florida	12	Nebraska	12

tion of New York's placement, are rather similar. (The correlation coefficient between the two is .63.) The one based on legislator perceptions was used for this analysis.

In Table V-19 are reported the rho coefficients between an array of socioeconomic-political variables and education lobby influence.[8] An inspection of these coefficients indicates that the relatively powerful lobbies tend to be found in the less urbanized, less industrialized, and less affluent states. Three of the four southern states in our sample, it might be pointed out, are ranked in the top five: Tennessee (1st), Texas (2nd), and Georgia (5th). The political background variables have only small correlations with our influence variable, the

TABLE V-19 Relationships for Education Lobbies between Their
           Perceived Legislative Influence (Compared with Other
           State-Level Interest Groups) and Selected Socio-
           economic and Political Background Variables

Socioeconomic-political variables	Rho coefficients
Personal income per capita (1972 census data)	−.45
Population size (1970 census data)	−.06
Urban population (1970 census data)	−.50
Industrialization index (1960 census data)	−.31
Voter turnout, House of Representatives, 1972	−.13
Interparty competition (adapted Ranney Index), 1956-1970	−.03
Political culture (Elazar-Sharkansky Index), 1969	.02
Governor's formal power (Schlesinger Index), 1971	−.02
Legislature's "technical effectiveness" (Citizens Conference Rating), 1971	−.42

one exception (rho of −.42) involving the "technical effectiveness"
of the state legislature. Put simply, the less effective the legislature,
as rated in 1971 by the Citizens Conference, the more likely legislative leader respondents were to rate the education lobby as influential.

We developed two measures of the cohesion of the education
lobby, using data presented in Tables V-9 and V-10: (1) legislator
perceptions of unity among EIG's when confronted by a legislative
issue; (2) group leader, and other actor, perceptions of unity among
EIG's when confronted by a legislative issue. The first of these correlates .62 with the legislative influence of the education lobby; the
second has a rank order correlation of .42. Whether cohesion has any
independent effect on educator influence is difficult to determine,
particularly since the cohesion variables used, like those of influence,
were associated statistically with the socioeconomic background conditions of the states. For example, the census data figure for urbanization has a negative correlation of −.66 with legislator perceptions
of education interest group unity, and the latter also correlates −.66
with per capita personal income of the states.

As for the other resource and power variables, the rho coefficients
involving these and education lobby influence are shown in Table
V-20. These miniscule coefficients indicate that a state's ranking on

TABLE V-20 Relationships for Education Lobbies between Their
Perceived Legislative Influence (Compared with Other
State-Level Interest Groups) and Selected
Resource-Power Variables

Resource-power variables	Rho coefficients
Membership (summed for each state from Table V-1)[a]	.17
Money (summed for each state from Table V-3)[a]	−.03
Professional staff (summed for each state from Table V-4)[a]	−.07
Lobbying staff (summed: full-time, 1 point; part-time, 1/3 point; from Table V-5)[a]	.36

[a]Estimates were made for missing teacher federation data.

the influence variable cannot be predicted from its standing in rank orders based on "hard" measures of educational group membership, money, and professional staff. This is not to say, of course, that these resources are unimportant; only that they do not override contextual factors to the extent that they determine a state's relative standing. Lobbying staff, it might be noted, does have a modest correlation (.36) with the legislative influence of educational interest groups.

*   *   *

This examination of the resources, power, unity, and legislative influence of the major state-level educational organizations has led to some observations about the findings:

1. *The teacher associations are generally most effective.* As a generalization, teachers are viewed as being most influential in the legislative arena. Yet school board groups in Colorado, Nebraska, and Wisconsin were near equals at least, and in Colorado may have eclipsed the teacher association. It would be difficult to exaggerate the tremendous resource advantage that the teacher associations have over competing groups. In terms of sheer numbers, dollars, staff, political action, and the like, these associations are giants by comparison. One might conclude, that, after all, these groups should be most effective. Or, one might conclude that it is tantamount to failure for a teacher association to be equaled in influence by another educational interest group. The fact remains, however, that the teacher associations are very powerful indeed.

2. *Administrator and school board groups are generally most efficient.* One has to conclude that the cost per unit of influence escalates geometrically. If this is true, as we are concluding that it is, the administrator and school board groups operate more efficiently, albeit less effectively, in the state policy system. These organizations have done a good job of making dollars stretch, realizing full well that they are unable to compete with teacher association expenditures. Hence, the administrator and school board groups have turned more toward emphasizing the status of their members as "educational leaders" and "locally elected officials," respectively, and toward emphasizing the "common good" rather than a vested interest.

3. *The teacher federations are inconsistent.* It may have been akin to an Achilles' heel for the teacher federations to have decided long ago that a strong state unit was not needed or desirable. Such lack of emphasis at this level results in an inconsistent performance in state legislatures. In the EGP sample, only in New York (and perhaps in Minnesota and Michigan) did the federation show real strength, largely springing from urbanized, Democratic, labor affiliations. In California and Massachusetts (perhaps also in Wisconsin and Florida), the federation showed some evidence of potential. But in the remaining states virtually no organizational strength existed at the state level.

4. *Labor-management issues dominate interest group relationships.* Labor-management issues in the twelve states studied dominated the relationships between interest groups and other actors in the policy system, as well as among the interest groups themselves. The press of teacher groups for more financial support for schools was, and continues to be, motivated at least in part by teacher welfare objectives. The interest groups tend to pair—teacher groups versus administrator and school board groups—and divide sharply on questions of collective bargaining legislation, tenure, accountability, certification, professional practices boards, severance pay, unlimited sick leave, and a host of other labor-management issues. As teacher activism is sustained or increased, the roles and relationships in education policy making will also become increasingly enmeshed in labor and management orientations.

5. *Coalitions are crippled by labor-management splits.* It is notable that the most effective coalitions existed in Colorado and Tennessee

—two nonurban states with relatively little history of labor-management strife. On the basis of all the data in the EGP study, one must conclude that labor-management divisions among interest groups have hindered, if not crippled, most state coalitions. Further, it appears increasingly difficult for the interest groups to coalesce, even on the heretofore common ground of school finance, when less and less agreement can be found on a wide range of other issues.

6. *Teacher organizations emphasize political pressure for political decisions.* It is highly significant that teacher organizations have recognized and are prepared to exert political pressure for political decision making on educational issues. In fact, depending on uncertain future events, such as the state-level effect of Watergate, this is probably the most significant conclusion of this chapter.

It is extremely important to understand that so long as the major state-level interest groups compete on educational grounds, the school board and administrator groups can effectively use their "status of members" resource and educational logic to counter the dominance of the teacher associations. On the other hand, if the teacher associations are successful in shifting the "rules of the game" to political criteria, their dominance may become more and more unilateral. It is clear that school board and administrator groups, because of their constituencies, are unable to mount political campaigns, even if they have the money to do so.

It is possible, of course, that teacher activism may produce a strong counteraction working in favor of the "management" groups. The Florida Education Association, for example, is still trying to recover from its disastrous 1968 state-wide strike. The Colorado Education Association, as another example, at least temporarily fell from executive favor by censuring Governor John Love. But these may be isolated cases. The political nature of education policy making seems certain to increase, and with that development the continued growth of "teacher power" is likely.

NOTES—CHAPTER V

1. Major studies dealing with state education policy making are cited in Chapter I, n. 10. A recent review of the literature dealing with education politics generally is Paul E. Peterson, "The Politics of American Education," in Fred N. Kerlinger and John B. Carroll (eds.), *Review of Research in Education* (Itaska, Ill.: Peacock, 1974), pp. 348-389.

2. The relationships between educational interest groups and state boards, CSSO's, and governors are treated in JAlan Aufderheide, "The Place of Educational Interest Groups in State Education Policy Systems," unpublished dissertation, Ohio State University, 1973. This is a more comprehensive work, and it is the basis for this chapter.

3. See, for example, James B. Conant, *Shaping Educational Policy* (New York: McGraw-Hill, 1964), p. 37.

4. Michael D. Usdan, David W. Minar, and Emanuel Hurwitz, Jr., *Education and State Politics* (New York: Teachers College, Columbia University, 1969), pp. 168-175.

5. Michael D. Usdan, "The Role and Future of State Educational Coalitions," *Educational Administration Quarterly*, 5 (Spring 1969), pp. 26-42.

6. Laurence Iannaccone, *Politics in Education* (New York: Center for Applied Research in Education, 1967), chs. 3, 4.

7. Sidney Siegel, *Nonparametric Statistics for the Behavioral Sciences* (New York: McGraw-Hill, 1956), pp. 202-213.

8. See Appendix B.

VI — The Politics of School Finance Reform

— Peggy M. Siegel

Money may not grow on trees, but it is still the mother's milk of politics. Somewhere between these two worn clichés lies the topic of this chapter: "The Politics of School Finance Reform." Schools continue to thirst for fiscal nourishment at a time when local taxpayers demand that they be weaned, shifting more of the burden to state government. At this level, requests for education dollars enter the political process only to compete with an ever-expanding public sector. As a result, decisions are normally based on political expediency (that is, what can pass) rather than on "the best" educational arguments.

This chapter, concerned with the politics of school finance reform, specifically asks: What demands bring pressure to bear? How are pressures translated into public policy? Who does what to whom? How are decisions made? Who makes a difference in the outcome? In answering these questions, this chapter analyzes the process of getting from one school aid program to another without discussing the content, intricacies, or merits of either point.

Of the four states selected for comparison, three (Minnesota, Michigan, and Wisconsin) were studied extensively as part of the Educational Governance Project during 1972-73. The fourth was my employer in 1971-72, when I worked as a staff person in the Ohio General Assembly. All four states represent the same region of the country. Presumably, they share a somewhat common experience. All four states successfully enacted major school finance legislation between 1971 and 1973. Undoubtedly, the actual contents of each law reflect the particular blend of circumstances characteristic of each state.

The meaning of school finance reform has intentionally been left general here in order to encompass the nature of the legislation enacted in all four states. Accordingly, school finance reform can be thought of as attempts by state governments to restructure their school aid formula in order to provide greater equity in the distribution of educational revenues and in their tax structures. These efforts resulted in a sizable increase in state assistance to local school districts, property tax relief, and a reduction in the combined state-local wealth differentials between rich and poor school districts. The end results, however, varied in both scope and effectiveness. It is the *process* of passing school finance reform, irrespective of each state's distinct characteristics and laws, that reveals a surprising degree of similarity, and this is the topic of concern. The first section of this chapter offers an outline describing events leading to new legislation in each of the four states.[1] The second provides an interstate comparison on the ingredients, strategies, and individuals involved in adopting school finance reform, and then there are some concluding observations on the general process of enacting school finance reform legislation.

INDIVIDUAL STATE REFORMS

Ohio[2]

In 1971, the Ohio General Assembly survived what has been called "the most hectic, confused and indecipherable session in legislative history"[3] to succeed in enacting a state income tax. This feat was accomplished under a newly elected Democratic governor, John Gilligan, who had campaigned on the dual issues of more state aid to the schools and tax reform. Once elected, Gilligan turned to an appointed citizens' task force for recommendations on the tax issues and a more informal, in-house group of experts for advice on school finance. The governor then incorporated their proposals into the state's biennial budget, which he presented to a Republican-controlled legislature. The GOP held a 54 to 45 margin in the House and a 20 to 13 margin in the Senate. Amid school closings and public pressure for property tax relief, the House passed the income tax and school aid program, but substantially reduced original expenditure levels. Gilligan's greatest hurdle emerged in the Senate when organized labor refused to support the income tax without heavier business taxes and held half of the Democratic caucus to that position. Without a winning coalition for the income tax, Senate Republicans were able to engineer passage of a smaller budget based on a sales tax. Both versions of the budget then went to a joint conference committee for final resolution, with the House's income tax and the Senate's smaller expenditure levels emerging from the compromise.

Impatience to pass a budget was perhaps best captured by the House chaplain who opened the crucial floor session with the prayer: "Dear Lord, now that nine months have passed since we started expecting, may we be pregnant enough to be delivered. Amen."[4] After enduring nine months of grueling debate, eight interim budgets, and four conference committees, the General Assembly delivered the budget to a relieved governor, who signed it on December 20.

Elation was to be relatively short lived, however. Although the budget battle had ended, the tax war was hardly over. Opponents of the income tax placed it before the voters who, somewhat surprisingly, upheld the tax by better than a two-to-one margin state-wide, passing it in all eighty-eight counties. The final result represented the most significant reform of Ohio's tax structure in almost forty years.

While the fundamental issue in 1971 was taxes, the need for additional school funds became an important strategy in passing and retaining the state income tax. By working together, all of the educational interest groups managed to achieve their major objectives— additional state funds for education and a state income tax. The increased dollars, in turn, enabled all of the groups to obtain some specific program priorities. The availability of increased revenues for all state services, including education, also permitted a revision of the foundation formula. Because the major controversy was over taxes, however, the problems inherent in the existing formula were not resolved, nor was the General Assembly completely satisfied with the revisions. In 1973 the legislators added numerous guarantees and no-loss provisions, making Ohio's school aid program one of the most complex in the nation. In the 1974-75 school year, none of the districts were even on the regular formula, but on one or more of several existing guarantees. As a result, Ohio lawmakers were still searching, by 1975, for the means to implement major school finance reform.

Minnesota[5]

Lawmakers in Minnesota, like those in Ohio, were also busy enacting major school finance-tax reform legislation in 1971. The "Minnesota miracle,"[6] as it has been called, altered the old school foundation formula and received considerable national attention for revising the state's tax structure.

Against the backdrop of some disenchantment with the existing school aid formula and extreme unhappiness over rising property taxes during the late 1960's, the combined issues of school finance reform and tax relief took shape during the campaign for governor in 1970. Both candidates sought to embrace a politically attractive tax posture. School finance reform did not surface publicly as a concomitant issue until well into the race, and even then it was the result of public attention being focused by an influential citizens' lobby (the Citizens League). Asked his position on increased state aid to education, Wendell Anderson, the Democratic-Farmer-Labor (DFL) party candidate, indicated a preference for the state to assume the full cost of education. Anderson also suggested that a state-wide property tax—replacing, in full or in part, local millage—be used to fund his plan to more than double state school aid. The Republicans, assuming that Anderson's position was politically vulnerable, claimed that this would increase millage rates across the state and destroy local control. Public interest then focused on education as well as taxes. And, out of well-publicized exchanges between the two gubernatorial candidates, the school finance issue took shape. Still, throughout the ensuing barrage of partisan charges and countercharges, taxes remained the fundamental issue. This fact, perhaps more than any other, determined the outcome of the 1971 legislative session and resulted in the Omnibus Tax Act.[7]

Wendell Anderson won the election in a convincing fashion with 54 percent of the vote. The governor-elect then assembled a handful of trusted advisers to provide him with education and tax proposals.

In January 1971 Anderson offered the results in his "Fair School Finance Plan" as part of the state's biennial budget. The budget had to compete with at least five other bills dealing with the tax-school aid issue, many of them offered by Conservative (Republican) legislators as less extensive alternatives to the plan supported by the governor. One measure passed the House; another, the Senate.

The Conservatives held a margin of one vote in the Senate (34 to 33) and five votes (70-65) in the House, although several key Conservative senators shared Anderson's reformist philosophy. Spearheading the opposition to the governor was the Conservative caucus in the House, and the struggle had both a partisan and a philosophical orientation. Agreement could not be reached within the legislature, where the issue even pitted Conservative members of one house against colleagues from their own party in the other. The legislators then went into special session, eventually passing a Conservative-sponsored House bill in late July. Governor Anderson, who vehemently opposed the measure because it failed to grant tax relief or to remedy gross inequities, vetoed it, and the Conservatives could not override the veto. As public pressure for a settlement mounted, Anderson called another special session of the legislature. A ten-member tax conference committee appointed at his request by the legislative leadership of both houses met in private, marathon sessions. The conferees hammered out an agreement in mid-October that had sufficient DFL and Conservative backing to win approval from the full legislature. The package contained multiple special programs, raised state taxes, provided property tax relief and uniform district levy limitations, and substantially increased state aid to the schools. It was then signed into law by Governor Anderson, who termed it a satisfactory compromise.

The major thrust in Minnesota, as in Ohio, was to provide tax reform and property tax relief rather than to reduce expenditure disparities among local school districts. In 1973, therefore, the question of school finance reform again confronted Minnesota legislators, but there was little of the acrimony witnessed in 1971. The DFL was firmly in control of both the House and the Senate. The school aid bill was not treated, as it had been in the preceding biennium, as part of a larger tax-fiscal package. Major changes enacted by the legislature in 1973, with Anderson's support, extended the reforms accomplished two years earlier, but with greater emphasis on the equalization of state-local district expenditures and on a greater responsiveness to educational need. In 1973 Minnesota legislators, fulfilling the governor's campaign proposals, appropriated for education an amount more than double the state support figure for the 1969-1971 biennium.[8]

Michigan[9]

The Michigan legislature enacted a major school finance reform bill in 1973. To imply that this was an isolated event occurring during one year would, however, be misleading. The Bursley Act, named for Senate Education Committee Chairman Gilbert E. Bursley, was more correctly the product of a process of trial and error spanning a number of years. The push for school finance reform began with a serious study of education during the late 1960's. It gained impetus from mounting fiscal shortcomings and tax inequities at the local level. There were also inherent problems in the old school foundation formula, the rising cost of education, a court case, the frequency with which Michigan voters were willing to defeat property tax levies, and the near closing of the Detroit school system.

A rallying point for reform emerged with a new chief executive, when liberal Republican William Milliken moved up from his position as lieutenant governor to become governor in 1969. As a former state senator and chairman of the Senate Education Committee, Milliken had displayed an interest and some expertise in educational issues. Assuming control of the executive office when his predecessor went to Washington, he publicly aligned himself on the side of school finance reform, making it a major goal of his administration.[10] Since he was not yet equipped with specific education proposals, the governor appointed a small commission of noneducators, with himself as chairman, to develop legislative recommendations. During the next five years, the major task became devising both a program and a strategy that would result in passage of a new school aid formula.

In October 1969 Governor Milliken called a special session of the Michigan legislature in order to submit his commission's proposals. One source called them "the most radical restructuring of school financing ever officially backed on the U.S. mainland."[11] Faced with broad-based recommendations for change, which included full state funding of education with a state-wide property tax and the elimination of the elected State Board of Education, the Michigan legislature decided in 1969 to continue under the existing state foundation formula, albeit at increased expenditure levels. In 1970, school finance reform became intertwined with aid to parochial schools, which sidetracked the outcome. Despite a narrow electoral victory in November 1970, despite the growing disaffection of conservative members from the governor's own party over his liberal and pro-urban stances, and despite the worsening economic conditions in the state, Milliken continued to push for school finance reform during 1971. Modifying some of his earlier recommendations, he requested the legislators to reject the existing state aid program and to approve a constitutional amendment calling for repeal of the local property tax for the schools and a local enrichment tax to be equalized by the state. Because of the legislature's reluctance to support the constitutional amendment, the governor switched tactics and took his case to the public in 1972. Milliken combined forces with the Michigan Education Association, which collected enough signatures to get the issue of property tax relief (and a provision to lift the prohibition against a graduated income tax) on the November ballot. For a number of economic, political, and racial reasons, both measures were convincingly trounced by the voters.

Governor Milliken did not give up; he merely shifted tactics again. This time the governor advocated school finance reform and property tax relief that could be enacted by the legislature without voter approval, overcome traditional cleavages surrounding questions of property wealth and taxation, and satisfy a court challenge to the existing foundation formula. The November 1972 elections had increased Democratic control of the Michigan House (60 to 50). None of the 38 Senators had been up for reelection, which sustained the 19 to 19 split with Republicans in leadership positions by virtue of a Republican lieutenant governor. Milliken had to come up with a proposal that would satisfy bipartisan scrutiny without becoming submerged in the broader tax controversy.

Directed by their bosses, school finance advisers to the governor, the Senate Education Committee, and the Michigan Department of Education pooled their ideas to design a workable state aid program that could survive legislative and political differences. The product of this collaboration was a modified power equalization measure, known in Michigan as an "Equal Yield" formula, which the Senate education chairman, Bursley, introduced for the 1973 legislative session. The bill, which enjoyed relatively easy passage in the Senate, encountered its greatest challenge in the House, where the Democratic leadership offered several alternative, more costly proposals and where the debate became so intense that the Speaker even considered resigning his post.[12] The House passed a greatly modified Bursley bill so the measure went to a six-member joint conference committee to resolve differences between the two versions. The conferees eventually reached a consensus more in line with the House-passed bill, on which both houses concurred. Governor Milliken signed the new school finance measure into law on August 14. Earlier, but during the same session, the Michigan legislature had also provided, in separate bills, emergency special assistance for Detroit's school system and property tax relief for all of Michigan's needy residents. In addition, the legislators had enacted two measures that provided the first state tax reduction in memory.[13] All of these programs were made possible without increasing state taxes because of a substantial surplus in state revenues.

Developments in Michigan represented a case study in longitudinal politics. After nearly five years of proposals and political debate, Governor Milliken's determination paid off. He was finally able to achieve one of the major objectives of his administration—the enactment of school finance reform and property tax relief.

Wisconsin[14]

In 1973, the Wisconsin legislature approved a major change in the state's general school aid formula for the first time since it had been enacted twenty-four years earlier. Unlike the three other states, the most outstanding characteristic of Wisconsin's new revised formula was that it provided for the gradual recapture of school monies from the wealthiest districts.

When Democrat Patrick J. Lucey first became governor in 1971, the state's economic conditions delayed a serious redress of school finance reform. Looking ahead to the next biennium, however, Lucey appointed a broad-based citizens' task force to reexamine the entire method of funding elementary and secondary education in Wisconsin and to recommend ways to relieve the fiscal burden on the property tax by shifting to other means of public support. After one year, the task force recommended retaining the existing method of distributing state aid (a guaranteed valuation equalization formula), but suggested several significant revisions. As one educational source commented: "What was decided on was rhetoric around the candy bar—different wrapping but the same chocolate and nuts."[15] Still, the recommendations, particularly the power equalization-recapture provisions, generated intense opposition and became one of the key provisions in the governor's budget in 1973.

Governor Lucey incorporated most of the task force recommendations in the state budget, which he intended to use as "the vehicle for implementing major policy changes."[16] By 1973 economic and political conditions called for increased state aid to education and property tax relief. An anticipated state surplus, bolstered by federal revenue-sharing funds and projected growth from existing taxes, provided a comfortable cushion for school finance reform and property tax relief without raising state taxes. Both issues were popular among the general public and the two political parties. The basic partisan difference developed over the way to achieve these ends. Emboldened by the pending *Rodriguez* decision, Governor Lucey and the Democrats who controlled the Assembly (62 to 37) favored property tax relief through the school aid program, the largest part of the general purpose revenues in the state budget. The Republicans who controlled the Senate (18 to 15) wanted property tax relief in the form of direct payments or credits to the taxpayer. The governor also felt personally committed to the concept of power equalization and bargained extensively for its enactment. Although the scope and impact of the negative aid payments were compromised, power equalization became an important point in the budget process and was eventually retained.

Given the partisan margins in the Wisconsin legislature, it was predictable at the outset that Lucey's budget would encounter its greatest hurdle in the Republican Senate, with final compromises to be resolved in a joint conference committee. The governor introduced his budget on February 1, 1973. The entire package then went to the Joint Finance Committee, where the Democrats enjoyed an 8 to 6 majority. After almost three months of public hearings and committee deliberations, the committee accepted many of the governor's recommendations, but not before hearing a great deal of conflicting testimony and making significant revisions. It was during this time that the U.S. Supreme Court also handed down its *Rodriguez* decision. This reversal of a lower court decision declaring the Texas school aid program unconstitutional prompted increased and intense opposition to Lucey's power equalization proposal. While the Finance Committee retained the negative aid payment provision, it extended the phase-in period.

After less than a week of floor debate and with several Democratic amendments, the executive budget bill passed the Assembly by a vote of 54 to 42. The Senate Republicans were in a less favorable position. Conservative Republican leaders generally opposed the budget, but could not deliver the votes to pass an alternative. Less than a week after it received the budget, the Senate, following a ten-hour Democratic filibuster, voted not to concur with the Assembly version. This sent the budget to a six-member joint conference committee composed of three Assembly Democrats and three Senate Republicans, where the political potential inherent in a comprehensive budget bill came into play. The governor successfully bargained over noneducational items to assure passage of his school finance reforms. When the conferees appeared deadlocked, this strategy also included going to some of the major Republican business interests in the state with offers of favorable tax proposals. They, in turn, pressured the Republican conferees to compromise on power equalization. The Republicans finally accepted negative aid payments, but pushed implementation back to 1976.

On July 10 the conference committee recommended the budget for passage and sent it back to the Senate. Again, the scope of a program policy budget enabled the governor to bargain with individual legislators to obtain a voting majority in the Senate. Legislators were also aware that refusal to pass the budget endangered many of the programs within, programs that had little chance of enactment on their own. Three weeks of deliberations finally resulted in a 16 to 13 vote for the budget. Two days later, the Assembly easily concurred by a vote of 58 to 38. Perhaps the most powerful inducement for approving the budget was summed up by one Wisconsin Representative who stated: "any legislator can run on this budget and win."[17]

A satisfied governor signed the budget bill on August 2, 1973. In doing so, Lucey had achieved his major objective for the legislative session—providing substantial property tax relief through reform of the school aid formula, as well as placing power equalization in the statutes. He also received an added bonus, credit for tax reductions favorable to business, which placed the governor in a particularly good light for the 1974 elections. The school finance issue may not be completely settled, however. Since power equalization does not become effective until 1976, major battles may still remain.

THE FOUR-STATE COMPARISON

Any analytical construct superimposed on reality is, by nature, arbitrary. Things are never quite that simple. Yet comparative analysis dictates that some order be extended to real phenomena. In discussing the issue of school finance reform, slight modifications of the policy analysis framework set forth in Chapter 1 were felt to be useful. Accordingly, the process of enacting school finance reform in Ohio, Minnesota, Michigan, and Wisconsin is organized into four broad conceptual categories, different stages along a time continuum. These categories are interrelated and frequently overlap, but they make comparative analysis possible. The four stages are, briefly:

1. *Pressures for change*—those demands, factors, and events culminating in a recognition that the existing school aid programs are no longer adequate.
2. *Policy initiation and formulation*—the point at which pressures for change are translated into actual policy proposals.
3. *Legislative response*—the bargaining process during which alternatives are posed, political strategies are employed, and support or opposition is mobilized.
4. *Final resolution*—the last stage at which compromises are reached, and existing school aid programs are altered.

The following comparisons are based on a four-state sample. Analysis is, therefore, qualitative rather than quantitative, and, while conclusions are drawn, they do not necessarily extend to all states at all times and under all conditions.

Pressures for Change

Several conditions that existed in each of the four states in this sample made school finance reform possible, if not inevitable. In general, pressures for change materialized outside of the political system, but focused directly on the executive office and the legislature as the ultimate arbitrators. These pressures transcended normal partisan differences, thereby increasing the base of support for reform.

Economic factors. The problems originated with the way schools were funded. By the mid-1960's, educational costs in most states were rising at a faster pace than real estate valuations. Heavy reliance on the local property tax to pay for education meant that school boards and voters were constantly increasing their tax liability to qualify for state aid or simply to keep up with spiraling costs. Property taxes for the schools in Minnesota, for example, escalated by 83 percent between 1968 and 1971.[18]

As local property taxes skyrocketed, state dollars for education were also multiplying. Even so, allocations from state treasuries constituted proportionately less of the total, magnifying the local property tax burden. In Ohio, the state's educational effort between 1968 and 1971 was greater than the total increases appropriated for the previous twelve years. Yet, by 1970-71 the state's share of school costs had reached a low of 27.9 percent, down from its 50 percent contribution in the mid-1940's.[19] The local share was at a corresponding high of 65.8 percent.[20] State legislatures were also hard pressed to allocate more money for the schools while they were assuming fiscal responsibility for new and expanded public services, all competing for dollars from the same till.

State funds provided under the school aid formula were supposed to equalize wealth disparities among rich and poor districts. Frequently, however, the existing programs also institutionalized the discrepancies. The per pupil dollar amounts set by legislatures were often inadequate, and flat aids were extended to all districts, regardless of wealth. Rich school districts were, therefore, able to raise more money for their students, provide a smaller teacher-pupil ratio, and offer additional educational services—all with less tax effort.

These interrelated conditions—reliance on the regressive, relatively inelastic property tax; continued escalation of educational costs; competition for state dollars; and structural inequities in school aid programs—were built into the system of funding education. Together, they forged a demand that the method of financing be altered.

Concrete evidence of this pressure materialized in the frequency of taxpayer revolts and rumblings. Michigan voters defeated 42 percent of the operating levies and 62 percent of the bond issues from 1970 to March 1971.[21] Over a thousand irate citizens showed up at one school board meeting in Minnesota to insist that school expenditures be cut.[22] Local taxes for education were withheld in Wisconsin.[23] And some schools in Ohio were actually forced to close down because of a lack of operating funds. Disgruntled taxpayer demands for financing education from other revenue sources thus emanated primarily from strident cries for property tax relief. The result was that, from the beginning, the push for school finance reform was closely linked to the demand for property tax reform.

Judicial impact. Fiscal shortcomings of the present system were identified through another channel, the courts. Suits filed in numerous states challenged the constitutionality of financially discriminatory school aid systems. The most celebrated examples were the premier *Serrano* case in California and the *Rodriguez* case in Texas, which was appealed to the U.S. Supreme Court.*

In all four states the courts played a role in publicizing the fiscal problem, if not in prompting immediate action. Plans for reform in Ohio and Minnesota were well under way when *Serrano* was decided in August 1971. Even so, Governor Gilligan was apparently aware of the California Court's ruling. Following passage of the state budget, he admitted that a similar case filed by the Ohio Education Association might conceivably force a further restructuring of Ohio's school finance system and more taxes.[24] Minnesota had its own federal court suit challenging the school finance program in 1971. The court ruled against the state by refusing to dismiss the case, and it upheld the *Serrano* principle of "fiscal neutrality." Yet *Van Dusartz* v. *Hatfield* came very late in the process and did not constitute a ruling on the facts, but rather a confirmation that rich districts may and do enjoy both lower tax rates and higher spending. While the judge's opinion may have served as an inducement to support Governor Anderson's omnibus school-tax bill, reform did not come from a

---

Serrano v. Priest (96 Cal. Rp tr 601, 487 P. 2d 1241, 5 Cal. 3d 584) in which the California Supreme Court reversed a judgment of the lower federal district court on August 30, 1971. The Court ruled, 5 to 1, that the existing school finance system violated both the state and federal Constitutions by denying the plaintiffs equal protection of the law because it based the quality of a child's education upon the resources of his school district and ultimately upon the pocketbooks of his parents. Because most states had school aid systems resembling California's, based primarily on the local property tax, this case received widespread attention. A similar case out of Texas, *San Antonio Independent School District v. Rodriguez* (No. 71-1332) was appealed to the U.S. Supreme Court. On March 21, 1973, the Justices ruled, 5 to 4, that the existing school finance system in Texas did not violate the Equal Protection Clause of the federal Constitution (411 U.S. 1), in effect turning the responsibility for equalizing school expenditures back to the states.

direct judicial order, but rather from the operation of the political process.

The courts figured more prominently in Michigan and Wisconsin because of the time lapse between 1971 and 1973. By early 1973, similar suits had been filed in more states and the *Rodriguez* case had successfully made its way to the U.S. Supreme Court. On December 29, 1972, the Michigan Supreme Court, in a 4 to 3 decision, declared the existing method of funding the public schools unconstitutional. Governor Milliken had filed the case, hoping to use it to persuade the Michigan legislature to enact a new school aid formula. The Supreme Court's reversal of the *Rodriguez* decision came in the middle of the legislative debate. Observers in Michigan anticipated that their own State Supreme Court would reverse its original decision, with several newly elected conservative justices holding the balance of power. This did occur, but only after passage of the new school aid bill.

In Wisconsin, both the governor's task force and Governor Lucey had been counting on the pending *Rodriguez* decision to increase the support for power equalization. This hope dissipated with the Supreme Court ruling. Opposition forces, which had previously assumed a tentative wait-and-see attitude, coalesced and became activated. And, while power equalization was eventually enacted, one of the major compromises occurred shortly after the *Rodriguez* decision.

Thus, the actions of the court in school finance cases were of varying relevance in the four states. In Ohio and Minnesota, legislation had been passed before the wave of school finance suits were filed. But such court decisions represented a potential impetus for future revisions. Individuals in Michigan and Wisconsin were emboldened to push for reform in the face of the Michigan ruling or the pending *Rodriguez* decision. In both states, however, an "unfavorable" Supreme Court ruling did not squelch the push for reform. Consequently, it can be concluded that judicial input, when combined with the more immediate impetus of taxpayer revolts and school closings, added to the growing demand for change. Yet, in and of themselves, the courts did not provide the most compelling reason for reform.*

---

*The above conclusion is less true in other states, such as California and New Jersey, where school finance suits have been upheld on state (although different) grounds and where the courts have ordered the legislatures to come up with acceptable plans.

Research and study. Various studies of each state's school finance and tax systems constituted another pressure for reform. The products differed widely in scope, sponsorship, and authorship. National studies and the policies of other states provided an external source of information. The reports were funded by governmental or private sources and conducted by academicians, tax experts, professional consultants, or public officials and staff. Although such studies were generally not as salient nor as effective as tax revolts in galvanizing public support for reform, they had their primary effect on the policy makers themselves. The products offered evidence and a rationale for legislators intent on developing arguments in favor of reform.

In Michigan, a study sponsored by the State Department of Education in 1968 outlined the strengths and weaknesses of four general school aid plans, which then set parameters for future legislative consideration.[25] Two task forces reporting in the 1960's in Ohio pointed to the need for enactment of a state income tax. The influential Citizens League in Minnesota produced several tax-revenue studies during 1969-70. The results enabled the league to extend a forum for the two gubernatorial candidates, strongly encouraging them to take public positions on school finance. In Wisconsin, several governor-appointed task forces during the 1960's issued recommendations that were never enacted. Their failure helped to define the more successful positions adopted by Governor Lucey's task force in 1972.

At this stage, numerous individuals and groups were working independently to develop reform proposals and thus define the issue for eventual legislative enactment. Informal communications were often established among experts in the field, at universities, and in state government. They helped to set the boundaries of the issue and ease the transition from pressures for reform to actual policy proposals. It is perhaps during this early stage that the outside "experts" (that is, individuals with access to the policy makers by virtue of their professional credibility but without real political power) have their greatest impact.

Thus, economic, judicial, and analytical factors all demanded that the question of school finance reform be seriously considered. Such pressures were speeded to fruition by the broad-based nature of the issue itself. Financing schools and tax reform affect everyone. While wealthy districts are obviously better able to afford good schools than poor districts, the citizens of all communities notice and respond to great and lasting increases in their taxes—be they rich, poor, urban, rural, suburban, Democratic, or Republican. And, while each group may articulate different remedies, the general movement for change is broad and convincing. Pressures for reform also invariably link the school aid issue with the tax issue, not only in increasing state revenues for equalization and additional programs, but also in providing relief from the property tax. And these pressures, once vocalized by such a broad segment of the population, can hardly be ignored by those in or seeking office.

Policy Initiation and Formulation

In all four states, the governors served as the rallying point for initiating school finance reform legislation. Where state departments of education, school finance experts, or educational interest groups may have been promoting change for years, the executive office contributed the political resources to accomplish this end. Governors, therefore, became the major factor in translating pressures for change into actual pieces of legislation.

Education as a campaign issue. In varying degrees, the governors of Ohio, Minnesota, Michigan, and Wisconsin all capitalized on the need for educational reform in their election races. Both Gilligan and Anderson campaigned strongly on the school finance issue and, after their election, immediately set forth to enact such reforms during their first year in office. In Ohio and Minnesota, the nominees also firmly coupled their education proposals with programs to increase state taxes and offer property tax relief. Education thus became the most popular and broad-based defense for raising taxes. In contrast, Governor Lucey of Wisconsin waited until his second biennium in office, when economic conditions were more amenable, to propose school finance reforms. Here again, school aid programs became the major method of providing property tax relief, reportedly Lucey's foremost concern. Circumstances in Michigan created a slightly different situation. Because Milliken assumed office in 1969 upon the resignation of the former governor, he did not have to campaign for election until 1970. Before and during the race, however, Michigan's chief executive seized upon school finance reform as a major objective of his administration. And the education issue, in and of itself, appeared to be Milliken's fundamental concern.

Thus, allowing for different motives and situations, educational reform played a prominent role in all four gubernatorial elections.

Acknowledging the mounting pressures for change, the candidates (with the possible exception of Lucey) adopted school finance reform as a major campaign theme. In so doing, they further identified the problem, giving it publicity on a state-wide basis. This stance, in turn, enabled the nominees to attract the support of some influential allies, not only during the campaign but later.

Task forces and advisers. Once elected, the chief executives proceeded to translate their campaign pledges into specific policies. One tactic was to appoint a task force. Such groups had the potential to accomplish several objectives. Aside from developing recommendations for legislation, a task force helped to broadcast the issue through public hearings, lending it a "citizen's" legitimacy. A task force could bring together a wide range of special interests, serve as a forum for conflicting views, and increase chances for early compromise. The ensuing discussion could also identify likely points of contention, enabling reform proponents to plan a counterstrategy. And, by involving major state interests in deliberations, a task force could mobilize support for proposals once they reached the legislature.

The utilization of task forces, given their potential, differed in the four states. Governor Gilligan appointed a broad-based task force comprised of representatives from the major interests in Ohio. Charged with formulating proposals based on need (that is, how to raise revenues, but not how to spend them), the task force was then given independent rein. Gilligan turned to a less formal, in-house group of key advisers and several university people to develop a school aid program. Governor Lucey allowed his citizens' task force a whole year to come up with both tax and school aid proposals. Membership included not only important state-wide interests, but also several legislators and members of his own administration, the latter providing strong direction to the task force. In both Ohio and Wisconsin, the governors incorporated many of the task force recommendations into their budget proposals.

When he inherited the governor's office in 1969, Milliken appointed a small commission of noneducators, with himself as chairman, to study a wide range of educational concerns. After six months, the commission reported back, and Milliken called a special session of the legislature to introduce a comprehensive package of bills. Most of these proposals were not enacted in 1969. By 1973, the governor turned to key educational specialists from his office, the legislature, and the state department of education. These three individuals collaborated to write a new school aid program which the Senate's education chairman introduced and Milliken supported. Like Gilligan and Milliken, Governor Anderson also relied upon a handful of selected advisers to formulate the school aid program that he later offered as part of Minnesota's biennial budget. He did not appoint a task force, perhaps because the Citizens League had already filled such a role. In none of the four states were the chief executives equipped with ready-made legislative proposals when they assumed office. Instead, they turned to other sources for aid in formulating their school finance programs, emphasizing the issues, and mobilizing extensive support.

Executive proposals. The format in which school finance proposals are presented has a significant impact on the bargaining process and the eventual outcome. In Ohio, Minnesota, and Wisconsin, the governors introduced their school aid revisions as part of the state biennial budget, which included other appropriations and the taxes to fund them. School finance reform legislation is usually comprehensive and controversial. It requires enlarging the state's share of educational costs. Consequently, its inclusion in the budget enhances its chances of passage by enlarging the negotiating arena. School issues can be traded off against nonschool issues, especially along dollar levels. "Extraneous" or politically sensitive issues can be expended or used as bargaining leverage to gain support for key items. Since each legislator has only one vote on the entire package, numerous considerations enter in, enabling the governor and his supporters to negotiate and compromise for individual votes. Governor Gilligan, for example, was committed to a per pupil distribution formula; Governor Lucey, to power equalization. A comprehensive policy budget enabled both chief executives to bargain effectively over funding levels and other proposals in order to ensure passage of their priorities. Thus, the budget can be used as a skillful instrument in enacting school finance reform, particularly since education is such a large chunk of most state appropriations.

Parallel issues. Because school finance reform involves a major change in the state-local funding of education, the question of taxes is invariably involved. More state aid to education enabled legislators to provide substantial relief from the local property tax in all four states. The governors of Ohio and Minnesota also incorporated new state taxes. A more favorable economic situation in Michigan and

Wisconsin, based on surpluses from existing taxes and on federal revenue-sharing funds, enabled the chief executives to propose school finance-property tax reform without raising taxes. In addition, emphasis on the local property tax often precipitated an improvement of assessment procedures or an equalizing of the burden among different classes of real property. The impetus came from the courts, as in Ohio, or from the governor's budget, as in Wisconsin.

Other more tangential policies were caught up in the attempt to build a winning coalition. These smaller interests, such as the large urban school districts, vocational education, special education, or school building assistance proponents, vied for inclusion of their programs in the educational package in return for their overall support. School finance legislation can be defined as much by which programs were excluded as by which were retained. Aid to parochial schools represents an interesting case in point. Governors Gilligan and Milliken labored to provide state assistance to nonpublic schools as part of the larger educational package. Wisconsin, which has a strong tradition against parochiaid, successfully deflected the issue away from the larger concern of school finance reform. Legislation enacted in Ohio allocated some assistance to nonpublic schools, but it was subsequently ruled unconstitutional. The issue has been in and out of the courts ever since. Parochiaid remains salient at the state level, and it is periodically stirred up by certain vocal segments of the population, particularly when additional school aid is being considered.

The issue of accountability has recently sprung to the foreground of state educational politics, frequently in conjunction with school finance reform. The pressure for "better" education comes from at least two sources—taxpayers and legislators. Both want to ensure an efficient and an effective use of tax dollars, particularly the lawmaker who climbs out on a political limb to increase taxes for education. The end product is often some type of assessment legislation intended to prove that the additional expenditures constitute a wise investment. In Ohio, an accountability provision was inserted in the budget during the last conference committee. This was done at the insistence of several Republican House members, much to the chagrin and exasperation of state-wide educational interests. In contrast, the assessment program in Michigan was initiated by the State Department of Education.

An additional push for accountability emanated from within the executive branch as a fundamental challenge to the existing structure of educational decision making. The general trend was apparent in all four states; governors want more direct control over policy making in education. On the one hand, all four chief executives built up their own research capabilities and expertise by hiring personal staff responsible for education. The governors were then able to seize the initiative for policy formulation from departments of education, especially regarding school finance legislation. On the other hand, governors were also searching for more direct control over the state educational apparatus. The governor of Wisconsin, where there is no state board of education, wanted to appoint one. The governor of Michigan, where there is an elected state board, wished to appoint it if he could not abolish it altogether. The governor of Ohio, who claimed that no one bothered to listen to the elected board of education, rhetorically asked: "What need of thee have we?"[26] And the governor of Minnesota, who already appoints the board members, strongly suggested that agency officials coordinate their legislative proposals through his office. Each illustration indicates that governors who are willing to risk the political consequences of providing more state aid to education also want more direct control over the outcomes.

Formulating school finance proposals is by no means a simple task. Other issues, like taxes, parochiaid, and accountability, become crucial in the bargaining process and are capable of shaping the final product.

Legislative Response

Given the diverse and heterogeneous nature of legislative bodies and the interests they represent, the response stage is where interstate comparisons become most strained. So much depends upon individual personalities, inclinations, and idiosyncrasies that qualitative analysis is essential in trying to explain outcomes. For this reason, more space will be devoted to actual occurrences on a state-by-state basis.

"The governor proposes and the legislature disposes" is a commonly heard phrase in government, particularly within executive offices. The first part of the sentence is true, at least for school finance reform, as demonstrated in Michigan, Minnesota, Ohio, and Wisconsin. The second part is a value judgment, where one's reply depends on one's politics. In any case, as reactors, the legislatures of these four states determined the fate of the school aid measures. While it would be impossible to capture all of the political nuances once school finance reform entered the legislative domain, some comparable features across the states can be highlighted.

A house divided. The process of adopting school finance reform confirms that major legislation can be enacted by a governor of one political persuasion and a legislature of another. In all four states, no single party controlled both the executive and the legislative branches. In Ohio and Minnesota, Democratic governors played politics with Republican-led legislatures in 1971. Each political party controlled one house in Michigan and Wisconsin in 1973. The following tabulation presents the Republican-Democratic margins in all four states during the year in which school finance reform was passed:

State	Political affiliation		
	Governor	House or Assembly	Senate
Ohio	D	R: 54-45	R: 20-13
Minnesota	D (DFL)	R: 70-65 (Conservative)	R: 34-33
Michigan	R	D: 60-50	R: 19-19
Wisconsin	D	D: 62-37	R: 18-15

The chief executives had much in common. Anderson, Gilligan, and Lucey were Democrats. Milliken was a Republican, although he frequently relied upon House Democrats to enact his programs. The four governors had liberal-reformist leanings in the context of their particular states. All were freshman governors, if one includes Governor Milliken who was in his first elected term. Yet none of the governors were political novices. Collectively, they brought with them a wide range of political experiences that came in handy since each was the head of a highly competitive two-party state. All the governors sympathized with the needs of urban areas, and all were prone to support educational reform without necessarily having been professional educators themselves. (Gilligan once taught literature on the college level.) What is most important, all four governors had to formulate school finance proposals that would survive the legislative scrutiny of the opposing party.

Actually, in all four states the governors' strategy needed to encompass more than the financing of education. Lucey, Anderson, and Gilligan introduced their school aid provisions as part of the biennial budget, which also contained other state appropriations and property tax relief. In Minnesota and Ohio, education was coupled with comprehensive tax revisions and increases. Although Michigan's school finance bill was passed as separate legislation, the legislators concurrently enacted property tax relief, a variety of tax reductions, and enabling legislation to bail out the Detroit school system. In drumming up support for all of these programs, whatever their latitude, key legislative decisions proved crucial.

The impact of legislative structure. Given the partisan divisions in the legislatures, it was predictable at the outset that school aid measures would eventually wind up in a joint conference committee for final resolution. The political strategies were also predictable. Each party hoped to gain maximum political mileage for itself while embarrassing the opposition. Yet the nature of the tactics differed, molded by particular legislative structures.

In Ohio, the Republican House leadership decided to divide the governor's budget proposals into three separate bills. The school aid package was assigned to the education committee while the other appropriations and the tax sections went to other committees. The fiscal committee's deliberations over dollar levels certainly affected what the education committee could do. But the key policy decisions on the school aid package were made by the educational interests, administrative representatives, and the members of the education committee. They did not have to go to the fiscal committee for review. The education-appropriations sections of the budget were even passed separately from the tax proposals in the House. Deliberations over the school finance measures in the Senate were also made within the education committee, apart from the rest of the budget, although all three portions of the budget were eventually combined for a floor vote and for the ensuing votes. Leadership decisions superimposed on structure in Ohio, therefore, enhanced the roles of key legislators serving on the education committees and the state's major educational interests, with the real battles being fought over tax proposals.

Governor Anderson also introduced his education proposals as part of the budget in Minnesota. Yet the school aid measure was never assigned to education committees. Instead, it was deliberately

combined with other state appropriations and sent to fiscal committees. The Senate Majority Leader, a Conservative (Republican), was a
close personal friend of the governor and a proponent of his reform
measures. He was influential in engineering the circumvention of the
education committee when it seemed likely to bottle up Anderson's
proposals. As a result, the House Education Committee, which had
traditionally made revisions in the school finance formula in conjunction with the State Department of Education and educational interest groups (especially the Minnesota School Boards Association), was
effectively bypassed. The short-circuiting of this committee reduced
the influence of the Conservative education chairman, the dominant
school finance influence in previous sessions. It also lessened the
input of the education lobby which had enjoyed direct access to the
education committee. Other educational concerns, such as collective
bargaining and professional standards bills, also consumed the attention of the education groups, effectively competing for their effort
on the school finance issue. Because the education proposals went to
the same committee as the other appropriations, moreover, the bargaining arena was widened. The members of the more prestigious and
powerful fiscal committees were directly involved in education decisions. Since the main issue was taxes, the Minnesota Farmers Union
and the state AFL-CIO, the traditional mainstays of the DFL and of
Anderson, were also crucial in the negotiations.

The budget process was even more centralized in Wisconsin. The
legislature has a Joint Finance Committee, which is the only committee to examine the budget before it is voted on in either house. The
scope of the bargaining is, therefore, expanded to include all of the
programs in the budget. While members of the Joint Finance Committee specialized in various areas where their input certainly held
added weight, the committee's overall impact was magnified with the
same legislators making the initial decisions on all the proposals. The
structure also meant that key compromises were made promptly in
the Joint Finance Committee, in the hope of solidifying the support
of the Democrats and minimizing the need for major revisions at the
hands of the Republicans during future legislative action.

Prior efforts to combine the school aid and tax revision issues had
failed in Michigan, both in the legislature and at the polls. Governor
Milliken and the Senate Education Committee chairman therefore
collaborated on a school aid bill that was introduced as separate

legislation. The education and fiscal committees in both houses were involved in the bargaining process.

Once school finance bills were introduced, the committees to which they were sent deeply affected deliberations. In Ohio, the two education committees made the crucial school finance decisions. This function was performed by the two fiscal committees in Minnesota and by a joint committee in Wisconsin. Finally, the education and finance committees shared the responsibility in Michigan. Committee assignments could, therefore, determine the scope and context of the bargaining, the nature of the compromises, and the identity of important decision makers.

The impact of internal alliances and conflicts. One assumes that partisan politics, being what it is, enables governors to count on their own party for support and on the loyal opposition for the headaches. This proved valid in Wisconsin, where Governor Lucey relied heavily on a Democratic-controlled Assembly and experienced major altercations with the Republican-led Senate. School finance reform in Minnesota, Michigan, and Ohio did not, however, proceed according to these rules.

Some governors received support from unexpected corners. Governor Milliken's liberal prourban positions frequently attracted the backing of the Democrats who controlled the Michigan House. Enthusiasm over having elected Anderson governor of Minnesota, the involvement of key DFL legislators in the formulation of the budget, and close party margins in both houses—all helped to mold party solidarity in the governor's favor during protracted legislative struggles. Yet, Anderson also gained the support of many Conservative caucus members in the Senate who shared his reformist leanings. The Senate Majority Leader in particular was crucial in guiding the governor's (and his own) priorities through the legislature. For this he was vilified by members of his own party, capping off an intraparty squabble between House and Senate Conservatives. Opposition to Anderson's proposals was based on partisan, philosophical, and fiscal grounds and centered around the House Conservative caucus. And, for a time, the Conservatives were effectively able to thwart the DFL and the governor from passing their tax-school finance reforms.

Having the governor and the legislators from the same party does not always guarantee unity or even great affection, however. Conservative Republican legislators in Michigan were beside themselves over some of Governor Milliken's proposals. The Senate minority caucus was divided between Democrats loyal to the Ohio AFL-CIO and those loyal to Governor Gilligan, which temporarily impeded passage of the entire budget, including the school finance proposals. At the same time, Gilligan could take advantage of the situation in the House, where the moderate Republican leadership favored some form of an income tax. Amid the pressure of school closings, the GOP leaders finally capitulated and supported Gilligan's tax proposals, thereby providing the number of votes needed. This action also brought down the wrath of conservative House Republicans who saved their special condemnation for the House Speaker. Unlike Minnesota, however, GOP cooperation was not induced by any great love for the governor and his programs, but rather by economic and political necessity.

Thus, the unique dynamics of any legislature can place its personal stamp on state policies. Aside from normal partisan differences, factors that can affect the outcome of school finance reform include: rivalries among members of the same party, competition between two legislative houses, executive versus legislative prerogative, and long-standing traditions and interpersonal relationships.

A legislator's vote on school finance measures is also conditioned by the response of the people back home. Most lawmakers are primarily concerned about the effects of school aid bills on their own districts. Will their schools win or lose money? What do they hear from local educators and taxpayers? Interest groups that are developing political action arms are also starting to figure heavily in legislative decisions. All of these circumstances may mean that legislative leadership will no longer be able to demand party allegiance where school finance bills are involved. One must be cautious in generalizing about school aid votes, however, particularly when such votes are combined with larger tax-appropriation measures.

The posing of alternatives. One strategy used to challenge the governor's prerogative in initiating policies is to offer counterproposals. The opposition can seek to amend the governor's proposals, obstruct their progress, or substitute alternatives of its own. The choice, often determined by the powers at the opposition's disposal, is illuminated through the nature of its responses.

In Wisconsin, the Republican leadership in the Senate wanted to submit its own tax-school aid alternatives, but it did not have the votes. Instead, Republican leaders chose not to concur with the Assembly-passed budget, immediately sending it to a conference committee. Because the conferees were evenly divided along party lines, Senate Republicans hoped to elicit enough compromises to make Governor Lucey's package more palatable.

In Michigan and Ohio, one house managed to pass its own version of the governor's proposals. In Michigan, the House Democrats limited the school aid bill from three years to one year, hoping to enact a different formula later on. They also increased the price tag. In Ohio, and aided by the split in the Democratic caucus, Senate Republicans substituted a less expensive sales tax package with a teacher unit school aid formula for the House-passed income tax and per pupil formula. The result was the same in both states. The two versions were sent to a joint conference committee to iron out the differences.

The opposition in Minnesota had more success in obstructing the governor's proposals, at least in the short run. Faced with numerous school aid and tax alternatives in both houses, legislators were unable to reach a consensus during their regular session. While Anderson's "Fair School Financing Plan" languished, a Conservative-sponsored bill that had the Governor's approval passed the Senate during the first special session. The House passed a different bill. A conference committee then endorsed the House version, which was wearily accepted by the legislature. This measure was, however, unacceptable to Governor Anderson, who vetoed the school aid and tax sections. He then called the legislators back into special session.

Thus, the passage of major school finance-tax reform necessitated compromises in all four states. The tactics may have differed, depending on various conditions operative in each state. Yet the conference committee becomes an almost inevitable tool in reconciling the differences.

Final Resolution

Once the school aid bills reached a joint conference committee, the final bargaining stages involved relatively few individuals. Actual decisions were usually made in closed session. Even so, the governors could bring pressure to bear by focusing on the issues and by working through sympathetic members of the conference committee. They could also focus public opinion on the legislature in order to prompt speedy and favorable resolution. For example, following Governor Anderson's veto of the school aid-tax package in Minnesota, a conference committee convened in the governor's mansion sequestered from public view. Meeting in nonstop marathon sessions, the conferees and the governor's chief aides proceeded to hammer out a compromise. Given the close partisan margins in both legislative houses, the option of overriding Anderson's veto was never seriously considered. Anderson also played to the press by castigating the Conservative-passed tax bill for failing to grant tax relief or to remedy gross inequities. Public opinion polls indicated that the veto had popular support. A Minnesota court opinion, subscribing to *Serrano*-type principles, also weakened the Conservative position. Finally, the State Auditor, a Republican, warned that the state would soon run out of money.

Similarly, Governor Gilligan's bargaining position was enhanced by a fiscal crisis facing Ohio schools and by the need to cut back on existing state expenditures. In both states, moreover, key Republican leaders played a crucial role in the conference committee deliberations. As a conferee, the Senate Majority Leader in Minnesota assumed the function of mediator during final negotiations. His role was particularly crucial when tempers became frayed and compromises seemed impossible. In Ohio, House Republican leaders had already gone on record in favor of an income tax. They grudgingly coalesced with the Democrats to ensure retention of the income tax in the fourth and final conference committee report.

Michigan conferees had to resolve twenty-three different points of contention. The conference committee eventually retained the original form of the school aid package as it had passed the Senate, but it also granted substantial aid to the urban areas in order to gain the support of many Democrats from the cities.

Governor Lucey added a creative touch to conference committee deliberations in Wisconsin. Unable to agree with Republican Senate conferees, the governor surreptitiously offered property tax relief to some of the major business interests in the state, which, in turn, pressured the Republicans to reach a speedy compromise over the budget.

Unique situations had their effect in all four states. The scope of the legislation was, however, wide enough to allow for flexibility and bargaining. Each governor had to attract votes from the opposite party, yet retain the united support of his own party. This required compromise. In the final stages—where a deadlock could easily emerge and where the two sides were most evenly matched—saving face became an important factor. The strategy became one of maximizing gains and minimizing losses for all parties involved so that everyone who wished could take credit for the final package. It was even more important that the final package be capable of attracting enough votes for passage in both houses since the conference committee report was not amendable. Thus, the process of trade-offs had to encompass the entire legislature with the governor and his allies keeping a running tally of their votes. After waiting out this arduous process, the legislatures in all the states responded, and four relieved but battle-scarred governors emerged victorious.

*   *   *

Policy Makers. Legislatures have the ultimate responsibility for providing state aid to the schools. This situation dictates that lawmakers at the state level be active in educational decision making. More recently, it also seems to signify that *governors,* at least in the four states examined here, assert their own prerogatives in formulating and advocating school finance reform.

Assuming their willingness to take a stand, the four governors had numerous resources at their disposal with which to initiate such reforms. They could publicize the issues through election campaigns, while also attracting important political allies. They could appoint a citizens' task force to help define the issues, simultaneously giving them more attention and enlarging the pool of potential proponents. And they had ready access to the news media or to traveling around their states, thereby highlighting the issues and orchestrating indirect pressure on legislators for action.

The chief executives also had extensive information and research capabilities within their departments and easy access to outside expertise, frequently overwhelming legislators in this capacity. The governors could define the issues by utilizing their resources to determine which programs to embrace and which to omit. They could therefore construct workable coalitions, organizing and maximizing support and neutralizing or isolating the opposition. And the use of a policy budget enhanced such bargaining strengths.

Once their proposals entered the legislature, the governors seemed to step back, delegating the actual legwork to key administrative staff members and advisers. The latter were transformed from education or finance experts to political mediators and tacticians. When it appeared that legislators needed prodding, the governors assumed a more public posture, appealing for citizen pressure to be directed at the lawmakers. Going directly to the public can have problematic results, however. When opponents of the income tax placed it on the ballot in Ohio, citizens overwhelmingly upheld the tax. Yet Michigan voters defeated a similar referendum.

The ultimate power in the governor's arsenal is, of course, the veto. But this was used sparingly because it had the potential to arouse public wrath and turn the legislature against the chief executive. In Governor Anderson's case, the use of the veto was a wise gamble. It turned out to be publicly popular, and it gave the governor a second chance to achieve his tax and school finance reforms.

One qualifying comment needs to be made in interpreting the role of governors, however. The chief executives studied in this chapter ranked first (Wisconsin), second (Minnesota), and third (Michigan) in their involvement in educational policy making among the twelve governors included in the Educational Governance Project (Ohio was not part of the comparative research). This study of school finance reform is, therefore, biased in favor of educationally active governors. At the same time, it is no coincidence that the top three governors presided over states where major school finance or tax reform was enacted. This helps to account for their high involvement rankings.

These same four governors could also be considered liberal and reformist. This political bent may have led them to initiate new school finance-tax policies rather than to patch up existing programs. They set the pace, which cast the legislators in a reactive role.

What all of this comes down to is the centralizing powers potentially inherent in the executive branch. These powers appear especially potent when matched against a heterogeneous, decentralized legislative body which, by its nature, represents multitudinous interests.

At the same time, *legislatures* are developing countervailing capacities by building up their own independent resources in the form of increased professional staffing and research capabilities. These resources serve as a buffer against the executive branch and various interest groups and permit independent evaluation of proposals. Perhaps this independence will enable more legislatures to initiate school finance reforms, as occurred in Michigan and has more recently occurred in Ohio.

Whoever initiates changes, it is important that governors and legislators be willing to join together to enact something as comprehensive and costly as school finance-tax reform. Bills which provide more state aid to education, equalization of funds, revision or replacement of school aid programs, property tax relief, or new state taxes require the concerted efforts of both legislators and governors, plus all the powers they can bring to bear.

The process of passing school finance reform is as instructive concerning who is not involved as who is. It also pinpoints the types of functions performed. In all four states studied here, the fact that the governors assumed a more direct role in formulating policies for school finance had important consequences for other actors in the policy system. State departments of education and interest groups may have been advocating school aid reform for years, but the executive office provided the political clout necessary to provoke serious legislative consideration. In the process, the governors challenged the traditional role of education departments, which, except for providing raw data, may be omitted from the crucial formulation stages.

State boards of education in these four states appeared to play a minimal role in the actual passing of school finance reform. In an earlier stage they could attract attention to the issue by sponsoring studies and by supporting legislative resolutions calling for change. In Ohio, Michigan, and Minnesota (Wisconsin has no state board) they did not, however, have substantial input into the governors' or legislators' offices. This was especially true when a governor intentionally chose to work with a few close advisers, many of whom were not from the educational community.

Similarly, *state superintendents* (or commissioners) and *state departments of education* performed a secondary function in the actual passage of legislation concerned with school finance reform. Their strength came from being able to provide raw data showing the effects of each legislative proposal on local school districts. Yet such data sometimes had to be reinterpreted by staff members in the legislature in order to be utilized. And this input can be challenged by other, competing sources of information. The Ohio Education Association, for example, had its own computer capability, which it readily utilized during budget skirmishes. Departments of education may have exerted influence through their legislative liaisons who provide information and simultaneously promote the department's priorities. But such input was often based on personal relationships between legislators, governors, and department representatives. The political style and credibility of the state superintendent and the reputation of the department were also important. In any case, the policy-making influence allowed the state education agency is becoming more dependent on the lawmakers, themselves. Governors in these four states were moving to gain more direct control over the state educational apparatus. They were independently initiating and formulating their own education policies. With no direct constituency and no political clout, the state education agency appears susceptible to being locked out of important legislative decisions as well. If school finance reform is indicative of a future trend in educational policy making, then the state education agency may be becoming structurally removed from important fiscal deliberations.

Some *educational interest groups* faced a similar fate vis-à-vis the governor. Organizations like the NEA affiliates in Wisconsin and Ohio, which supported a governor during his campaign were in a better position to forestall this trend. For different reasons, both governors and teachers have a stake in altering the present system. Teachers advocate change that would maximize their own power relationships with educational management. Consequently, they aligned with governors also concerned with change, which tended to place administrator and school board groups on the defensive in an attempt to uphold the status quo. In some cases teacher associations, because they had a ready-made entrée into the governor's office, helped to shape educational policies. They could also circumvent formal bureaucratic channels in a way that other less politically active groups could not.

Once the school finance proposals were introduced into the legislatures, the role of education interest groups was less clear. Activity in Ohio, Wisconsin, Michigan, and Minnesota ranged from working together for similar goals, to relative inactivity, to working against each other. In 1971, the state education interest groups in Ohio were still talking to each other and could coalesce to promote increased state aid to education and the income tax. Their united effort was enhanced politically by the absence of organized opposition to education. The real fight came over taxes and expenditure levels. The organizations could also afford to work together because the additional money for education enabled all of them to achieve at least minor program objectives. The overall school aid package did not specifically pit rich districts against poor ones since practically all districts stood to benefit from the increased state assistance. Once the education package was locked in, however, only the Ohio Education Association joined a short-term coalition of major noneducational interests in Ohio to push for the income tax.

In Minnesota, the impact of the education groups in the bargaining process appeared to be minimal. Many of the state-wide groups had aligned with Governor Anderson, but some expressed reservations over his school finance proposals. In addition, the educational interests were concurrently devoting their political resources to other issues, such as collective bargaining and a professional standards board. Because the school aid issue was combined with taxes, the organizations contributing the most political weight to the governor's side were not the educational groups, but the traditional DFL power bases: the Minnesota AFL-CIO and the Farmers' Union. During final negotiations, however, the Minneapolis school district's legislative liaison was able to interject relevant figures into the bargaining process that bolstered the governor's case for providing more school aid to the cities. This, in turn, prompted another revision in favor of the agricultural areas.

In Wisconsin, the two major state-wide education groups were on opposite sides of many school issues. The Wisconsin Education Association worked closely with Governor Lucey and the Democrats in favor of power equalization. The Wisconsin Association of School Boards aligned with Senate Republicans in opposition to the local negative aid payments to the state.

The nature of the Michigan education proposals carefully avoided the traditional rich-poor alignments, mobilizing the local districts according to their school tax effort. This break from tradition also caught many educational interest groups off guard and unable to mount an effective opposition.

As long as rich school districts are granted no-loss guarantees and almost all districts receive more state aid, the education groups should be able to take positions reflecting their respective memberships. Or, as in Michigan, some school aid proposals may force a realignment of traditional education coalitions. Proposals that would

help poor districts at the expense of rich ones, however, may im-
mobilize the state-wide education groups whose constituencies contain all types of districts. As a result, unless firmly committed to the
realities of equalizing wealth disparities, the state groups may be
forced to work on more narrow, self-interested issues, leaving the
school finance issue to local educators.

An additional factor affecting the interest group role is the developing schism among educators. In the past, the groups could get
together periodically with key legislators on the education and
appropriations committees to increase the existing state aid formula.
Yet the old alliances are breaking apart at the same time that governors have either included school finance reform as part of their budgets or initiated revisions on their own. This split is enhanced by the
education groups, themselves, for they are not the slightest bit shy
about airing their labor-management squabbles in public and before
the legislators. In these four states, the more active groups in the
school finance issue were those that worked with the governors from
the beginning and were involved in political campaigns, contributing
endorsements, volunteers, and money to friendly candidates.

Policy Issues. Because *school finance proposals* must run the
gamut of the political system, a program that minimizes the losses to
local school districts has the most chance of gaining widespread support and, therefore, of success. If true equalization of funds is to be
provided, politics dictates that the total pot be substantially fortified
by a massive dose of more state aid. The use of the state budget
seems to be a good strategy in accomplishing major changes because
it can provide additional funds and because it enlarges bargaining
potential.

The nature of the *school finance-tax reform* package also appears
to be important. If events in Ohio and Minnesota are indicative, true
equalization of educational funds may be preempted by the need to
get a tax package enacted.* The fundamental issue in the two states
became securing additional state revenues. And this larger battle

---

*Interestingly, comprehensive tax revision did not turn out to be a political liability for
either Anderson or Gilligan, at least not initially. The DFL took control of both legislative
houses in 1972, and the Democrats in Ohio assumed control of the House and came within
one vote of taking over the Senate. The governor of Minnesota was then able to fulfill his
initial objectives of school finance reform during the 1973 session. Ohio had to wait until
1975, with a Democratic legislature and despite Gilligan's reelection defeat in 1974.

deferred significant equalization of state educational funds between rich and poor districts. In contrast, the most promising set of circumstances emerged when surplus funds already existed, as in the case of Wisconsin and Michigan, where policy makers could, therefore, concentrate on the actual redistribution of those revenues.

Despite the socioeconomic, cultural, political, and structural distinctions of each state, the *similarities in passing school finance reform* were abundant. Perhaps this is due to the nature of the education finance issue itself. Like other political issues, school aid reform touches upon many other programs. Scarce resources dictate intense competition among those who set the priorities, and there are both winners and losers. Yet school finance is not necessarily partisan. It transcends Democratic-Republican splits because educational finance affects every community. All legislators either have children or constituents with children in school. Education is also one of the most costly public services so that governors and legislators have to pay attention. School finance reform is therefore broad based, and the pressures for reform are general. Yet, paradoxically, school finance legislation is highly technical. Information and expertise constitute power, and they usually belong to a select group. Relatively few individuals actually hammer out the mechanics of a school aid bill. The majority of legislators are less concerned with the whole school finance picture than with how their districts will fare or what the people back home will say (and vote). Thus, while financing education is among the most salient of public concerns, it is also so specialized that a few individuals make the key decisions. Advocates of change must, therefore, be prepared with convincing arguments on both levels.

Inasmuch as school finance reform is accompanied by other "noneducational" issues, the bargaining process expands to take in *noneducational arguments.* So-called school people's reasons for advocating reform must therefore compete with economic realities and political strategies. The quantitative substance of school and tax proposals is also conditioned by the qualitative nature of decision making. Consequently, whether or not school finance reform emerges as a gubernatorial priority, it faces an even more complex set of interrelationships within the legislative halls. The final test depends, simply, on who has the votes. The decision-making process for school finance legislation appears to have undergone a fundamental change. Not long ago, a few key legislators and representatives from the state department of education and state-wide educational interest groups could periodically sit down and agree upon incremental changes in the school aid formula. The fruits of their endeavors would then be accepted by the full legislature. More recently, however, mounting pressures for a greater state role in funding education have made incremental change insufficient. As a big-ticket budget item, education encourages the involvement of not only the traditional educational representatives but also of governors and other legislators. And the breakup of educational interests within the school lobby has magnified the influence of some groups, while diminishing the impact of others. In any event, the combined effects of inflation, unanticipated costs, additional school programs, and voter resistance to more property taxes dictate that a broader range of state actors will become more involved in school finance reform decisions than ever before.

In discussing the process of enacting school aid proposals, I have purposely shied away from discussing the nature, merits, and shortcomings of specific reform programs; the contents and eventual impact of court cases; and the implementation of various educational statutes. Such issues, of course, need to be addressed. But, before they can be effectively answered, it is necessary to study the process that such changes must survive in order to become reality. Certainly no single answer applies at all times or in all places. Yet perhaps this chapter will alert readers interested in actualizing school finance reform to some of the things they might encounter.

NOTES–CHAPTER VI

1. The school finance reform statutes referred to in this chapter are known in each state as follows:

Ohio–Amended Substitute House Bill 475, 1971, the 109th General Assembly, Chapter 3317 of the Ohio Revised Code (the 1973 revisions are contained in Amended Substitute House Bill 86, 1973, the 110th General Assembly).

Minnesota–Laws of 1971, extra session, Chapter 31–H.F. No. 262 (the 1973 revisions are found in Laws of 1973, Chapter 683, S.F. No. 1626).

Michigan–Enrolled Senate Bill No. 110, (The "Bursley Act"), Act No. 101, P.A. of 1973.

Wisconsin–1973 Assembly Bill 300; Chapter 90; Laws of 1973.

2. A more complete version of this section is found in Peggy M. Siegel, "The Politics of School Finance Reform in Four Midwestern States, 1971-73," unpublished dissertation, Ohio State University, 1974. For further details on the taxation issue, the reader is also directed to Frederick D. Stocker, "The Rough Road to Tax Reform: The Ohio Experience," prepared for the Advisory Commission on Intergovernmental Relations in December 1971.

3. Ohio Education Association, *Ohio Schools*, September 24, 1971, p. 9.

4. Gongwer News Service, Inc., *Ohio Report*, December 10, 1971, p. 2.

5. This section is based entirely on the school finance issue written by Tim L. Mazzoni, Jr., in *State Policy Making for the Public Schools of Minnesota* (Columbus: Ohio State University, Educational Governance Project, April 1974), pp. 43-76.

6. Advisory Commission on Intergovernmental Relations, as reprinted in the Minnesota State Department of Education's *Update*, March 1972, p. 5.

7. Anthony Morley, "Minnesota," in *A Legislator's Guide to School Finance* (Denver, Colo.: Education Commission of the States, August 1972), p. 37.

8. Speech by Gerald W. Christenson, Minnesota State Planning Director, to a state-wide conference on "Education–Changing Perspectives," held by the League of Women Voters, Seattle, Washington, on December 8, 1973, unpublished manuscript, p. 5.

9. An expanded version of this section can be found in Edgar R. Hines *et al.*, *State Policy Making for the Public Schools of Michigan* (Columbus: Ohio State University, Educational Governance Project, 1974. See also Gene Caesar, Robert N. McKerr, and James Phelps, *"New Equity in Michigan School Finance: The Story of the Bursley Act,"* rev. ed. (Lansing, Mich.: Senate Committee on Education, June 1, 1974).

10. Frank A. Pinner, John N. Collins, and William A. Sederburg, "Decision Making on the Reform of Educational Finances in Michigan," a report to the Urban Institute, Washington, D.C., November 1, 1971, pp. 12-13.

11. Neal R. Peirce, *The Megastates of America* (New York: W. W. Norton and Co., 1972), p. 426.

12. Gongwer News Service, Inc., *Michigan Report*, June 28, 1973, p. 2.

13. *Ibid.*, May 2, 1973, pp. 1-2.

14. An expanded version of this section is found in Siegel, "The Politics of School Finance Reform in Four Midwestern States."

15. Interview with Archie Buchmiller, then Deputy Superintendent of Public Instruction, Educational Governance Project, May 4, 1974.

16. Governor Patrick J. Lucey, "Governor's Budget Message," 1971-1973, Part 1, "The Fiscal Problem," pp. 1-2.

17. Gongwer News Service, Inc., *Wisconsin Report*, July 26, 1973, p. 2.

18. Gerald F. Weiszhaas, "The 1971 Omnibus Tax Act," part of "Staff Progress Report: A Collection of Staff Work Papers," unpublished report by the Minnesota Tax Study Commission, January 1973, p. 31.

19. The Ohio Legislative Service Commission, "Ohio School Foundation Program," Report No. 94, January 1969; Ohio Public Expenditure Council, *Information Bulletin*, Nos. 71-78, p. 6.

20. *Rankings of the States, 1972* (Washington, D. C.: National Education Association, Research Division, 1972), p. 51.

21. *Full State Funding of K-12 Education* (Lansing, Mich.: Michigan Department of Education, October 25, 1971), pp. 3-4.

22. Gerald W. Christenson, "Planning for Human Resource Development for Minnesota in the 1970's," in *Financing Special Education in Minnesota* (Minneapolis: University of Minnesota, Division of Educational Administration, Fall 1972), p. 83.

23. Correspondence, Archie Buchmiller, Assistant Superintendent, Wisconsin Department of Public Instruction, May 21, 1974.

24. Gongwer News Service, Inc., *Ohio Legislative Report*, December 14, 1971, p. 2.

25. J. Alan Thomas, *School Finance and Educational Opportunity* (Lansing, Mich.: State Department of Education, 1968), pp. 332-335.

26. Columbus *Dispatch*, October 26, 1972, p. 8A.

VII — State Education Policy Systems

— Raphael O. Nystrand

Unlike preceding chapters that have focused upon the policy-making role of a particular actor or agency across the various states, this chapter examines the ways in which actors in respective states interrelate to produce policy decisions. The emphasis is on patterns of interaction that may exist among persons and agencies in the states. Or, stated somewhat differently, the goal is to describe policy-making systems.

A general theory of political systems has guided the conceptualization and conduct of the Educational Governance Project (EGP). This theory, as explained in Chapter I, suggests that factors in the policy-making system include general environmental aspects, immediate environmental features, a governmental structure comprised of policy actors, and policy outputs. It is the interaction among elements within and across these categories that is of concern when addressing the question of state educational policy making in a systems context. No single model can explain how the system works because the situation is too complex and the variables are too numerous to allow such a simplified explanation. There are, however, some generalizations that at least suggest ways of viewing the educational policy process across the states.

THE IANNACCONE TYPOLOGY

A useful baseline for comparative statements about state educational policy making is the work of Laurence Iannaccone.* Writing in 1967, Iannaccone reviewed studies of educational policy-making processes in several states and developed a series of comparative propositions about these processes. It is important to note that this work was necessarily based on post-factum analysis, rather than data gathered in relation to any single framework, much less one of his own design. His work is, nevertheless, the most comprehensive and systematic analysis of state educational policy making to date, and his conclusions form a benchmark for this analysis.

The central proposition offered by Iannaccone was that the most critical point in any state education policy system is the link between organized state education interest groups and the state legislature. His principal concern was with the "organized profession as it actually goes about influencing legislation,"† although he acknowledged that other actors could be involved in decision making. Focusing upon this linkage, Iannaccone identified four structural types that he termed locally-based disparate, state-wide monolithic, state-wide fragmented, and state-wide syndical.

The *locally-based disparate* structure (Type I) was characterized by emphasis on local contacts and relationships in the legislature. The most important interaction regarding policy formation was between legislators and schoolmen from their respective districts. In contrast the *state-wide monolithic structure* (Type II) was characterized by unanimity or coalitions among state-wide interest groups (for example, teachers, administrators, and schools boards) that spoke with a single voice to the legislature. By resolving their differences within the coalition, the monolith could represent state-wide interests to the legislature. The *state-wide fragmented* type (Type III) was characterized by the presence of state-wide organizations to represent the interests of various education groups but the inability of these groups to agree among themselves about a legislative program. The *state-wide syndical* type (Type IV) was characterized by a state-wide organization under government sponsorship serving as a broker

*Laurence Iannaccone, *Politics in Education* (New York: Center for Applied Research in Education, 1967), chs. 3, 4.
†*Ibid.*, p. 39.

among educational interests and presenting them to the legislature. Only a single state, Illinois, with its School Problems Commission, fit this category.

Iannaccone suggested that policy processes and the success of education interests within them would vary among the four structural types. For example, he suggested that differences regarding educational legislation would probably be resolved inside the legislature in disparate and fragmented states, within the monolith in monolithic states, and within the syndical operations of states of this type. He also observed that the four types could be considered a developmental construct in that states would pass through each of them in stages. More specifically, he argued that states began as locally-based disparate (Type I) types, would become state-wide monolithic (Type II) as education interests came together for common purposes, would move to state-wide fragmented (Type III) as these interests diverged, and finally would become state-wide syndical (Type IV) as participants including legislators wearied of conflict over educational issues.

INTERPRETATION OF EGP FINDINGS

Any comparison of the foregoing propositions with findings from EGP requires that one identify differences in the methodology of the two efforts. EGP was designed as a twelve-state comparative case study with similar questions asked of comparable actors about comparable issues in the respective states. As noted above, Iannaccone depended upon post-factum analysis of work done by others. EGP was also guided by a systems framework that took into account a relatively broad range of potential actors in the policy system. Iannaccone, on the other hand, wrote primarily from the perspective of interest groups. And, in the several years that have elapsed since Iannaccone wrote (an even longer time has elapsed since the authors he relied upon collected their data), substantial changes could have occurred. At best, then, the position is one of being able to compare two snapshots of the same phenomenon (state education policy making) taken at different times, with somewhat different cameras, at slightly different angles.

Iannaccone omits state boards of education in his analysis of policy making, preferring to focus upon education interest group relationships with the legislature. There is a historical and traditional point of view that would suggest that this is a serious oversight. According to this perspective, education has long had considerable policy-making autonomy through the efforts of state boards. More recent evidence suggests, however, that state boards lack policy influence.* EGP findings provide some support for both positions, but more for the latter one.

While state boards appear to lack the influence many members and their advocates would like, they appear to be important in some states on some issues. The most notable examples are: New York, where the Regents have long been regarded as influential; Texas, where the state board assumed the initiative regarding school finance reform; and Minnesota, where the board took the lead in pressing for school desegregation. Constitutional provisions and legislative actions provide important parameters for state boards of education. In every state (except Wisconsin, where there is no board) these factors establish some jurisdiction for the boards. For example, every state board studied had authority to set policy regarding curriculum standards, as well as authority over teacher certification, although this was shared in two states (California and Minnesota). Surely decisions in such areas are sufficiently important to state education systems that they should be considered in any comprehensive attempt to explain policy-making processes. EGP data did not, however, provide much strong evidence that boards initiate many proposals or mobilize support in these or other areas.

Taking account of exceptions such as those previously mentioned, the general finding of EGP research was that state boards primarily gave legitimation to the proposals made by chief state school officers. Even this statement requires qualification. It may well be that chiefs were guided by the "rule of anticipated consequences"† in making proposals to their respective boards, thus tending to present only those proposals which they were confident would receive approval. The study did indicate that chiefs sometimes respond to board members' suggestions in sharpening policy proposals for the board. In most of the states, however, board members,

---

*For example, see Gerald R. Sroufe, "State School Board Members and the State Education Policy System," *Planning and Changing,* 2 (April 1971).

†The concept is discussed by Carl J. Friedrich, *Constitutional Government and Democracy* (Boston: Little, Brown, 1941), pp. 589-591.

chiefs, and experts agreed that such behavior occurred less frequently than "often" (Table III-15).

Another arena in which to weigh state board action was the degree of involvement in policy decisions enacted by state legislatures. Viewed in this context, Iannaccone's lack of attention to state boards is plausible in light of EGP data. There was little indication that state boards played a direct role in this arena. Again, however, a version of the "anticipated consequences" phenomenon may have been operative. Several chief state school officers (CSSO's) did participate in legislative decision making. There is a rationale and some data in the perception of state board members for arguing that the initiative of chiefs in this arena was influenced by what they understood to be the preferences of their respective boards. This argument can be developed more specifically using a finding reported in Chapter II: boards that appoint their chief state school officers are perceived to be more influential than those that do not. While there is little direct EGP evidence of state board involvement in legislative policy making, EGP findings indicate that state boards may have indirect impact through the participation of CSSO's.

The preceding paragraph foreshadows a major difference in the findings of EGP and Iannaccone. Whereas Iannaccone was virtually silent about the policy-making roles of individuals in state systems, EGP data revealed that both CSSO's and governors were often active. While this difference may be attributable to changes over time or variations in research focus, more recent findings emphasize the need to include at least these two actors in an up-to-date conceptualization of policy systems.

Chiefs, as has already been noted, are perceived as highly influential in state agency policy making by members of state boards of education. Observers of the board-chief relationship concurred with this judgment in most instances. Most chiefs perceived, moreover, that they themselves should be active participants in the policy-making process, not only with the state board but with the legislature and the governor as well. The data in Chapter III indicate that, when legislators, governors, and interest group leaders were asked about the success chiefs enjoyed in influencing legislative programs, their responses varied from state to state. The significant point in light of Iannaccone's work, however, is that virtually all chiefs were seen as having some influence in this arena and some were thought to be highly influential.

It is interesting that EGP data indicated no correspondence between the perceived influence of chiefs in legislative and state agency arenas. Elected CSSO's appeared to have slightly more influence in the legislative arena than their appointed counterparts, but, of the four chiefs rated most influential in this arena, two were elected and two were appointed. Other factors moderately related to the influence of the CSSO in the legislative arena were size of the SDE staff, a populous state, and formal power of office. Correlates of perceived influence of the CSSO in the state agency arena included having a large, well-qualified staff, residing in an industrialized state, and working with a state board perceived to have a relatively strong policy influence.

If chiefs have great influence in the agency arena and some influence in the legislative arena, it seems important to ask in whose behalf such influence is exercised. While EGP data are not definitive on this point, they do suggest some possible answers. Where the governor appoints the chief, he may advocate the governor's program. Where the chief is elected, he may espouse his own program and present it as a platform to the public. Where a chief is appointed by the state board, he may advocate board positions in the legislature. In the latter two cases, especially, his positions will probably reflect the contributions of his staff and their assessment of public interests. Where differences of opinion exist among education interests in a state, EGP case studies suggest that the chief's position will more likely reflect the interests of management (that is, administrators and school boards) than those of teachers. This may be partly because most chiefs and their top staff members have had experience as administrators and likely have come to appreciate this perspective. For this same reason chiefs sometimes serve as points of access to the policy system for administrator groups who lack the resources that teacher groups and, to some extent, school boards have employed successfully with legislators. Because of the power chiefs possess, this is an important point of access.

The activity of governors in education policy making has been discussed (see Chapter IV). Three-fourths of the governors studied included education as a campaign issue in 1970, and most actively supported some kind of education proposal with the legislature. While some advocated curriculum change (for example, state-wide kindergarten), most were actively involved with the fiscal aspects of education. Sometimes this meant advocating fiscal equalization and reform; in other instances it meant accountability or cost reduction programs. Governors experienced varying degrees of success with their proposals in the education arena, but their position as chief executives gave them powerful leverage in negotiating with legislatures over policy outcomes. Because they frequently employed their own staffs, with perspectives different than those of state agency staffs, this often ensured that differing views would be incorporated into education policy proposals.

The fact that education proposals were advanced by governors helped to ensure that such proposals would not enjoy the special and protected status sometimes ascribed to them. They were likely to be seen as part of a legislative package that legislators viewed through partisan lenses, which meant that decisions about education proposals were sometimes made using criteria that had only limited relevance for education. These policy proposals became part of legislative trade-offs involving such matters as tax reform and property tax relief. In addition, education questions themselves were sometimes multifaceted, involving such general values as race, religion, and labor-management relations. Governors and other elected officials may allow their views on such matters to influence their attitude toward particular education proposals.

The fact that the governor's office serves as a point of access for persons and groups concerned about education issues is also important from a systems perspective. For example, a close relationship appeared to exist between the governor and the teacher associations in Tennessee, Texas, and Wisconsin. In such states as Florida and New York, governors appointed citizen task forces on education to formulate program recommendations. Growing citizen interest in legislation affecting the process of education and the increasing tendency for the governor's office to be seen as a source of state program proposals augurs for a broader gubernatorial role in education in the future.

EGP data indicate that Iannaccone was essentially correct in arguing that states would shift from Type II to Type III. There was relatively little evidence of state-wide monolithic behavior. Although several states continue to have coalitions of interest groups associated with education, these coalitions appear to be most effective in Tennessee and Colorado. Special cases also exist in Texas and Georgia, where the state teachers' associations continue to envelop professional educator groups, although formal coalitions are less prominent. In other states, either such coalitions do not exist, or their effectiveness has been vitiated by conflict over labor-management issues. Fragmented or not, however, the data indicate that in most states the "education lobby" is perceived as being among the most influential in the state. In cases where fragmentation does exist, teacher associations are ranked as the most influential of the education groups (although tied with school boards in three instances), followed by school boards, administrator groups, and teacher federations (where they existed). This diminished stature of administrator groups contrasts markedly with the position of dominance ascribed to them by Iannaccone in the state-wide monolithic type. This may reflect a shift not only in power relationships but also in the kind of power that is most salient in gubernatorial and legislative arenas. The growing capacity of teacher associations to deliver votes and campaign support to friendly legislators gains importance when seen from this perspective.

While EGP data suggest Iannaccone was correct in perceiving the shift from Type II to Type III politics, they also suggest that these categories may oversimplify reality. As has already been shown, governors, CSSO's, and state boards of education influence policy as well as legislatures and interest groups. Resolution of important issues often requires compromise among the range of parties involved. Iannaccone's typology may even oversimplify legislature-group relationships. EGP data indicate that even when states have moved to what Iannaccone describes as Type II and Type III status, contacts between legislators and local constituents, including school boards and superintendents, continue to be influential with legislators. For example, much of the impetus for change in the Florida foundation formula could be attributed to the efforts of urban legislators who responded to their constituents, and the tradition of localism remains particularly strong in Massachusetts. Legislators in Minnesota were divided by big city-outstate issues when considering school tax reform. The EGP study suggests that the basis on which an education issue is resolved in the legislature may depend upon the nature of the issue.

Iannaccone's prediction that Type III states would move to a syndical structure has not come to pass. Indeed, Illinois, the only state of this type at the time he wrote, has since modified its syndical structure in favor of a more traditional state board of education. It did appear at one time that state officials might establish formal mechanisms similar to the Illinois School Problems Commission to avoid conflict generated by fragmented education interest groups. What appears to have happened, instead, is that educators and, more important, governors, legislators, and the general public have come to see that they can live with conflict about educational issues.

At one time it was widely believed that education was above or at least outside the realm of politics. Local as well as state boards of education were generally viewed as being apolitical as well as nonpartisan. Educators sought to encourage such attitudes in both government authorities and the general public in the hope that the special status of schools would command generous attention when public resources were allocated. An important corollary to this position was the emphasis educators placed upon a united profession and the avoidance of conflict about school issues.

In recent years several developments have shattered the apolitical, nonconflict illusions associated with education. Foremost among these has been the fragmentation of professional interests over labor-management issues. The increasing militance of teachers, the secession of administrator groups from the NEA umbrella, and the willingness of school boards, administrators, and teachers to confront one another at local bargaining tables and in the legislatures have encouraged others to become combative about educational issues. Almost simultaneously schools manifested shortcomings in meeting the expectations which many citizens, particularly those in urban areas, had for them. The resulting tide of public criticism placed education on the defensive and intensified conflict over education. More recently, questions have been raised about the accountability or cost-effectiveness of education with the same result. Such questions have been particularly visible in light of the spiraling costs of education, accompanying increases in other public service costs, and mounting tax burdens.

Remember also that differences of opinion over schooling are often associated with fundamental value questions in the broader society, questions involving economic mobility, racial equality, and equity in taxation. In such a context it probably became impossible for many public figures to avoid taking positions on educational questions. It is not surprising that a majority of the governors involved in the EGP study campaigned on educational issues or that such questions were often prominent among legislative concerns. Gubernatorial and legislative interest in such matters often reflected the concerns of constituents throughout their states, as did the attitudes of chiefs and other formal actors. In short, EGP data suggest that policy proposals and outcomes were influenced by the actors' perceptions of public opinion.

As conflict about education has increased and the interests of education groups have fragmented, governors and legislators have perhaps become less inclined to accept the advice and policy suggestions of educators at face value. EGP data indicate that many education interest groups lobby vigorously and are, in fact, ranked among the most influential lobbies in a state. Teacher associations, for example, have resources that enable them to assemble research and lobbying staffs and, in most instances, also to make local campaign contributions through a political action arm. The historical sources of power attributed to education interest groups have been grass roots ties with particular legislators and information about the desirability and consequences of various policy alternatives. These continue to be important, but money, participation in campaigns, and the voting power of the membership have also become prominent sources of lobbying strength. The development of such resources is further evidence that educators have entered the political arena in traditional ways. The EGP data contain little indication that either educators who have become political activists or legislators and other public officials find such participation and the conflict accompanying it intolerable or dysfunctional. In the absence of public outcry, it is unlikely that this relatively open system will be changed by adopting syndical structures in the respective states.

*   *   *

The general impact of the EGP data upon the Iannaccone typology is to suggest a more complex system of state educational policy making. The relationship between interest groups and the legislature is important, and the developmental aspects of the typology have led to important understandings. Any adequate portrayal of state policy systems at the present time must, however, take into account the fact that there are multiple authoritative policy arenas. EGP focused upon two of special importance to education, the legislature and the state board, and viewed others such as the courts only indirectly. For each arena there are also multiple actors and points of access. It would appear that the impact of fragmenting the education interests in the respective states has been to create a more open or pluralistic system. The process through which policies are proposed, considered, and authorized in such a system will vary according to the issue. When issues are of relatively narrow professional concern, such as changes in teacher certification patterns, they are likely to be re-solved in the interface between the profession and the state agency or the legislature. If the proposed change is such that professional interests disagree concerning it, as they did with certification in Texas, the issue will probably be considered in a broader arena. If the issue is sufficiently broad that the public disagrees about it, as they do about school finance reform, resolution will attract still more par-ticipants.

The most important finding of EGP with regard to policy-making systems for education is that these systems are considerably more open than previous researchers have suggested. While educational interest groups or chief state school officers continue to hold a pre-ponderance of power regarding some issues in some states, the more general finding was that parties interested in affecting educational policy making usually had multiple opportunities to do so. Grass roots contacts with governors, interest groups in and out of educa-tion, chiefs, legislators, and state boards—all represent viable points of access to the system on different issues.

VIII — Recommendations

The involvement and influence of the different actors who participate in making state policy for the public schools have been the main concerns of the preceding chapters. The roles of members of state boards of education, chief state school officers (CSSO's), governors and their staffs, participants in educational interest groups, and state legislators (at least in terms of school finance reform) have been examined. Now the concern is what to recommend to those involved with making state education policy. Discussion is restricted to the state education agency—the state board, CSSO, state department of education—and its relationship to other policy actors. There are three reasons for such a focus. The initial one is that there are limitations in the data. The inner workings of state legislatures could not, for example, receive much attention given available research resources. Second, there are already several major studies and a host of recommendations relevant to general governance institutions.[1] The final consideration is that these components of education policy systems appear to be most amenable to change.

The recommendations are presented first as general concerns reflecting values and then as specifics, under four headings: state boards of education, chief state school officers, state departments of education, and education agency relationships.

STATE BOARDS OF EDUCATION

Attributing influence to the participants in complex decision processes is always hazardous. The fact that actor influence in state education policy making varies significantly both by state and by issue area makes generalization all the more problematic. Still, the data clearly reveal that some actors, for example, governors and CSSO's, are influential in many policy systems, at least on issues relevant to them. The data also point to the unmistakable weakness of state boards of education as policy-making participants. The typical state board studied was widely assessed by legislative leaders, governors' offices, and educational interest group spokesmen, as well as by EGP researchers, as being only a minor participant in influencing education legislation. It was much more influential in making state agency policy, but even in that arena the dominant figure was the CSSO, with the board being cast largely in a legitimating role.

These findings with respect to the policy-making influence of state boards are not surprising. The bodies operate under some obvious constraints. State board members, like others who sit on lay governing boards, serve on a part-time basis, may lack expertise, and often have limited access to data sources. Nor does the board, unlike most local school boards, have independent access to tax revenues. It depends on legislative action to obtain funds for the state education agency and for the schools of state. The role the state board can play in education policy making is, finally, contingent to a large measure on the power and interest of another governmental institution—the state legislature. Even in light of these constraints, however, state boards of education emerged as weaker policy participants than had been expected.

Certainly a reading of the impressive legal powers delegated to state boards of education indicates that these bodies are intended by constitution or statute to undertake policy-making functions along with other governing responsibilities. As Commissioner Ewald B. Nyquist of New York has said, "the consideration of policy issues and the making of policy are the prime reasons for the existence of state boards of education."[2] If this is the case, the negative evidence on the actual policy-making influence of state boards is cause for concern.

A second consideration has to do with the representativeness of state boards. As was noted in Chapter II and is more fully described in Chapter X, the demographic composition of state boards does not come close to mirroring that of their constituencies. Board officials are predominantly male, white, and middle aged; they are also better educated, more affluent, and more management-professional in occupation than the average citizen. Nearly half of these "lay" officials, it should be noted, have had experience as professional educators.

Mere membership in a social class or group does not mean that a public official automatically advocates its values, but it is difficult to believe that such affiliations have no influence at all or that state board members are not more sympathetic and accessible to those with similar backgrounds than they are to those with vastly different life experiences. Sroufe's question remains a fair one: "How can the board hope to represent Mexican-Americans, immigrants, blacks, parochial schools, students, and urban systems when its membership includes few of these persons, and, more important, when the experiences of these persons are foreign to the background of the state board [officials] ?"[3]

If most state boards are neither very influential nor representative, as EGP research suggests, then what should be done? One alternative is to do away with these institutions and to integrate educational governance with general governance at the state level. This approach is attractive to proponents of a centralized executive model. They argue that such a structure, where the CSSO is appointed by and directly responsible to the governor, is more conducive to achieving such goals as effective political accountability, efficiency in planning and decision making, and articulation among related state services. There are, however, other considerations that support the existence of lay governing boards. Four of the most basic ones have been stated by Cook and his colleagues:

In the first place, they have continuity that gives a perpetual life to a governing organization, a continuity that exists before and after the terms of office of secretaries or executive officers, the attendance of any student, or the tenure of any employee . . .

Second, they have the vital although negative function of insulating education from day-to-day politics and politically motivated interference. This is a deterrent force, essential even if never used.

Third, a lay board provides many useful links to the broader public community and provides a means for involving many competent people who possess skills that would otherwise be unavailable. The board can interweave the educational establishment with the rest of society. If it is a good board, it is not solely the servant of its staff, of students, of taxpayers, or of any group; it is an arena where all interests can be weighed and valued.

Fourth, a board can mobilize support, lead public opinion, protect education from bureaucratic in-fighting and lend intangible prestige to the institutions governed. . . .[4]

The problem is not with the value of the institution, itself. Rather, it is with the failure of the institution, as presently constituted, to fill its role adequately, especially where the third and fourth points are concerned. State boards of education must be more than a kind of institutional ornament, which means that, if they are to be preserved, they must be deliberately strengthened in terms of both power and representation.

Strengthening state boards might well require changes in the kinds of members that are recruited, in the resources (for example, legal authority, time, information, and expertise) that are available to members, and in the willingness to employ available resources to exert policy leadership with lawmakers and CSSO's. The following recommendations have been made with these considerations in mind:

1. In establishing electoral districts for board members or in appointing persons to serve on the state board, particular attention should be given to making this body broadly representative of the different interests and backgrounds of the state's citizens.

2. Besides the customary reimbursement for expenses, board members should be compensated for their part-time service at a level sufficient to allow persons with modest incomes to serve on state boards.

3. Provisions should be made for preservice and in-service training of state board members, especially regarding their policy-making relationships with legislators, governors, CSSO's, and interest groups. This training could involve organizations like the National Association of State Boards of Education (NASBE) and the Education Commission of the States (ECS), as well as state departments of education.

4. State boards should be established constitutionally, granted broad discretionary powers for education policy making (including control over teacher preparation and certification), and given the power to appoint and remove the CSSO. To encourage systematic evaluation of the chief's performance, as well as time for this official to develop and implement programs, the CSSO should serve on a

four-year (renewable) contract. The implementation of this recommendation will require constitutional and statutory changes in a number of states, a course of action we find desirable.

5. The policy role expectations that state board members hold for themselves, and for CSSO's, should be carefully examined by these officials with the intent being to establish an appropriate balance between public control and professional expertise in education policy making.

6. Along with using institutional mechanisms and department administrators, state board members should develop channels of personal access to state lawmakers and be willing to use these channels actively in seeking to influence education legislation in accord with board policy.

7. State board members should be provided with staff assistance for help in problem identification and data analysis. In some states persons from the office of the CSSO might have sufficient independence to serve this function. In at least a few states, we recommend that staff assistants independent of the office of the CSSO be employed so that experience with this kind of arrangement may be acquired. In no case should these assistants assume any administrative functions for the state agency.

8. Board officials and the CSSO should seek to enhance public awareness of the state board and its governing functions. This has clear implications for the time, location, physical setting, and media coverage of board meetings. But public awareness is most likely to be fostered if the state board focuses its energies on important policy issues and actively as well as openly seeks to deal with them.

CHIEF STATE SCHOOL OFFICERS

The office of the CSSO and the behavior of incumbents in that office, particularly as these are perceived by the other actors in the various state education policy systems, are most crucial. No single person in the state, unless it be the governor, appears to have more effect on the status and well-being of public education. This discovery came as something of a surprise since, until recently, many persons in and out of education would not have accorded so much influence to the CSSO. State boards of education see the CSSO as most important to their understanding of state policy issues.

Governors and legislators, while not as dependent on the CSSO as state board members, attach considerable importance to the office. Interest group leaders have some penchant to work directly with legislative leaders, but that relationship is often established through the efforts of the CSSO.

Despite the overall importance of the office, it varies considerably from state to state. In some states the chief is selected by the state board of education; in others, by the governor; in still others, by popular vote. There are indications that selection should be made by the state board. Almost always the chief is male, frequently he has a rural background, and often he is an in-state product—constraints that should not be imposed upon a person selected to fill this office. Only in some states is the chief free to set up his own team, a condition that should prevail in all states. Some states provide the office with great formal powers such as constitutional status, the official designation of the chief being executive officer of the state board, and require that the chief report to the governor and the legislature. In other states there is no mention of these responsibilities in either the constitution or the statutes. The salary for the CSSO varies widely among the states, and it is often too low to attract outstanding persons. In short, some states make provision for the office in accord with its importance; other states do not.

Any consideration of the influence of CSSO's must deal with two concerns. In some states, the influence of the chief overshadows that of the state board. EGP data offer support for the belief that both chiefs and boards can and should be strong. In other states the chief appears to have too little influence, particularly with the governor and the legislature. A CSSO should clearly influence, but not dominate, both the state agency and the legislative arenas. The following explicit recommendations could strengthen the office of the chief state school officer in many states:

1. The formal powers of the office of the chief state school officer should be enhanced through constitutional or statutory provision. At the very least, this would mean that the chief be designated the executive officer of the state board of education and that the chief or the board or both be required to report to the governor and the legislature at least annually on the state of the public schools and ways by which these institutions can be improved.

2. In selecting a CSSO, the state board should seek a person with demonstrated political, organizational, and technical skills. Political skills seem essential if the chief is to influence the governor and the legislature. Organizational skills are required as the chief determines the structure for, and the operation of, the department of education. Technical understanding of education seems necessary if the chief is to make wise decisions relative to the purposes and processes of education. In the states where CSSO's are still elected, these criteria should be used by political actors as they seek to influence the nomination of candidates for the office.

3. Recruitment to the office of CSSO should be open and, wherever possible, nation-wide in scope. "Open" means not constrained by requirements of residence, experience, or specific patterns of training; it does not mean the absence of criteria. Actually, as recommended above, persons with demonstrated political, organizational, and technical skills should be considered. Unless prohibited by the law, the search should be nation-wide in scope, and candidates both in and out of professional education should be considered.

4. The salaries of CSSO's should be comparable to those paid other top educational leaders in the state. The salaries paid superintendents of the larger school districts in the state and those paid presidents of state universities would serve for purposes of comparison.

5. Each CSSO should have the freedom to establish his own administrative team. At least at the levels of deputy, associate, and assistant superintendent the CSSO should be able to select his staff. These nominations might be subject to confirmation by the state board of education, but none of these assistants should be named by board action alone. In some states this would require a revision of civil service requirements so that top assistants would be exempt. Only when the CSSO can choose his own team can he be held responsible for his administration.

6. The CSSO and the state board of education should find ways of enhancing their partnership. The initiating role of the chief would not be diminished if he were to begin the development of his proposals from the expressed concerns of board members more frequently, if board members were to offer constructive criticism to the chief on his proposals more frequently, or if board members were to

participate in relationships with the governor and the legislature by way of state agency advocacy more frequently.

7. CSSO's should encourage the organization of their state boards to permit consideration of policy questions. This may require, at least with large boards, some kind of committee structure, an adequate allocation of time for board meetings, an agenda that focuses largely on policy questions and less on implementation minutia, and the provision of pertinent background data.

STATE DEPARTMENTS OF EDUCATION

The state department of education is the technical and managerial arm of the state education agency. To facilitate policy making, the state board and the CSSO must depend on the department for information and for the development of proposed courses of action. In recent years the staffs of state departments have doubled or tripled in numbers, but the characteristics of department personnel—rural background, teaching or administrative experience in rural or small-town schools, in-state residency—look much the same as they did some thirty years ago. Seldom are staff members sought from business, law, universities, or other agencies of government. Moreover, staff members are predominantly male and white, a condition that should be modified. In short, the department staff seems to be too homogeneous to represent many of the viewpoints and technical skills now needed in an education agency.

These conditions cause concern over recruitment practices followed in selecting personnel for state departments of education. There is also concern that, in the procurement of personnel, budget provisions involve extensive assistance from the U.S. Office of Education. Federal aid to state departments is not the problem. The uneasiness stems from the fact that such aid, often half of the state department budget, makes such agencies too dependent upon a federal agency and sometimes too willing to accept a federal program even when it does not meet the needs of the state. Because federal budget decisions are often made late in the fiscal year and support of certain programs is uncertain from one year to the next, not only can state departments of education be too dependent on federal action, but such support may be erratic in terms of amount, or it may not be forthcoming at all.

A conviction that state education agencies will have a more critical role in the future than they have had in the past increases this concern. Pluralistic decision making is upon us; no single agency or actor can dominate the scene as may have been possible in a simpler time. The state education agency, through its lay board (even though many former educators serve on such boards) and its professional staff, will have an enlarged role to play if education is to be appropriately represented to governors, legislators, interest group leaders, and other major actors. Areas that demand increased attention include planning, research, development, and evaluation, and each of these areas will require an expertise not often found in state departments in the past. With a focus on ways the department might help in policy making, not on management concerns, the recommendations are:

1. A wide range of expertise should be sought in staffing state departments of education. In addition to seeking competent personnel for the staffing of the long-standing regulatory functions such as allocating state aid, certifying professional personnel, and checking on instructional standards, persons with expertise in planning, research, development, and evaluation should also be sought. Such an organization should encourage assessment of what is being done and look ahead to what ought to be done, as well as maintaining day-by-day operations.

2. State departments should pursue an affirmative action employment policy with respect to sex and race. This is not to suggest precise quotas for women or members of minority groups, but competent women and minority persons should be encouraged to apply, and they should be seriously considered when positions are being filled. This matter needs particular attention over the next few years.

3. The recruitment program for departmental staff should be augmented by way of selection techniques and made more extensive in terms of sources of personnel. While informal recruitment by means of personal contact should be continued, more formal measures of advertising positions and screening candidates should also be established. In addition to looking toward teachers and administrators in the smaller schools of the state as a source of candidates, other sources such as urban schools, business, law, other agencies of government, and universities should be included. These latter sources, both in and out of state, are important when seeking expertise for some of the new functions such as planning and evaluation.

4. State departments should strive to increase state support and become less dependent upon federal support for their functions. Further, policy makers at the state level should exert influence at the federal level toward allocating federal funds into two categories: those for sustaining programs and those for experimental programs. Such a division would permit state departments to integrate federal money with state money more realistically than is now possible.

EDUCATION AGENCY RELATIONSHIPS

The milieu in which the typical state education agency functions, as described in Chapter VII, has become increasingly politicized and pluralistic. Broader participation, more intense group conflict, and growing public controversy—all are manifestations of the politicization of state education policy systems. True, "politics" in a basic sense has always been present. But the emergence of systems that encourage participation, allow for conflict, and are more visible makes their political nature unmistakable. Politicians, such as governors and legislators, have taken more assertive roles and some educational issues, such as school finance, have divided parties. Teacher associations have abandoned their traditional apolitical stance, using members, money, and grass roots support in an attempt to exercise political "clout."

Despite centralizing tendencies arising from the mounting costs and contentiousness of education, pluralism is a characteristic of education policy systems. Indeed, in most such systems that characteristic, as was pointed out earlier, has become dominant. The education lobby has long since split into warring factions in many states. More fundamentally, each issue area—for example, school finance, racial desegregation, teacher certification, and educational program improvement—tends to attract its own distinctive cluster of policy actors especially interested in the decisions enacted in that area.[5] While these issue clusters do overlap, particularly in states like Georgia and Texas, influential participants in one do not necessarily hold key positions in others. This pluralistic pattern, or "fragmentation" as some call it, is equally, if not more, evident in the lack of coordination between education and other state services.

The politicization of state school policy making may be distressing to those who hold that education decisions should rest on the "neutral" competence of professionals instead of on the influence-based accommodations of contending groups.[6] From the standpoint of comprehensive planning and rational decision making, a pluralistic system has some obvious drawbacks. Yet there are positive aspects to this development, including the increased visibility of decision making, the expansion of participation and debate, the formulation of new alternatives, and the opportunity afforded each cluster of policy participants to push ahead on problems deemed important. Indeed, the opening up of the relatively closed, consensual systems that once marked much state-level education policy making is viewed, on balance, as a healthy change. There are, however, serious problems of communication and coordination that have implications for the state education agencies as well as for other actors.

The various educational organizations are so divided in some states that areas of common interest are not even sought, much less found. Educators and politicians often talk past each other, a condition that has contributed to widespread mistrust of motive and performance on both sides. And state administrators in the different agencies, this probably being nowhere more true than in education, operate in a semiautonomous fashion as if the social problems of a state had little or no relation to one another. Recognition of these concerns gives rise to a number of recommended linkage devices:

1. State education agencies should actively encourage the various educational organizations to identify their common interests, interests that could serve as the basis for issue-oriented coalitions among those groups pursuing improved education. Such activity on the part of agency officials is likely to be successful only if undertaken in an evenhanded fashion, that is, where the state agency is looked upon as being fair and receptive to all groups, not just to those with a management orientation. Efforts should be made to broaden the base of these working arrangements or ad hoc coalitions by including non-educator groups.

2. A forum should be created. It might be called the governor's advisory council on education, and the governor, legislative leaders, the state board president, the CSSO, and higher education spokesmen could meet on a continuing basis to consider state education needs and priorities.

3. Arrangements should be established for regular interaction between the CSSO and other state department heads and for liaison

between the state education agency and other departments of government, particularly the state planning agency.

*   *   *

These, then, are our recommendations. There has been a deliberate attempt to refrain from drawing upon these recommendations to propose an "ideal" structure for state educational governance. We know of no such model that is suitable for all times and all states, for states vary too much in their educational and political needs and stages of development for any single structural prescription to be appropriate. Even the recommendations that have been presented should be selected and adapted in the light of state-specific conditions. Persons who are thoroughly familiar with conditions and who have to work with them are in the best position to make these choices. Chapters IX to XII do, however, give explicit attention to the values, structures, and evidence pertaining to a number of alternative governance models. Citizens interested in improving their state-level arrangements for governing the public schools might find these chapters, along with the analysis and recommendations presented in earlier chapters, helpful as a point of departure in their deliberations.

NOTES—CHAPTER VIII

1. See, for example, Citizens Conference on State Legislatures, *The Sometime Governments: A Critical Study of the 50 American Legislatures*, 2nd ed. (Kansas City, Mo.: the Conference, 1972).

2. Ewald B. Nyquist, "A State Board Gets the Agenda It Deserves," unpublished remarks made at Northeast Area Conference, National Association of State Boards of Education, May 15, 1972, p. 2.

3. Gerald R. Sroufe, "State School Board Members and the State Education Policy System," *Planning and Changing*, 2 (April 1971), p. 21.

4. P. Cook *et al.* "The Job of the Secretary for Educational Affairs," a report prepared for the Massachusetts Educational Conference Board, September 1970, VII-3.

5. A penetrating discussion of the strengths and weaknesses of pluralism is in Wallace S. Sayre and Herbert Kaufman, *Governing New York City* (New York: Russell Sage Foundation, 1960), ch. 19.

6. On the growing politicization of education policy making, generally, see Frederick M. Wirt and Michael W. Kirst, *Political and Social Foundations of Education* (Berkeley, Calif.: McCutchan, 1975), pp. 241-248.

PART TWO

MODELS

IX — Current State Arrangements for Educational Governance

A primary purpose of the Educational Governance Project (EGP), as noted in Chapter I, was the development and appraisal of alternative models for the state governance of public schools. Additional insights provided by the research reported in the first part of this book are the basis for considering the models, formal structures for the governance of education, in the remaining chapters.

Since policy making for education is a product of both general government and special government for education, this inquiry could be far-ranging and deal with the behavior of many government officials as well as with a host of interest group leaders. Instead, the scope is limited, quite specifically, to formal governmental arrangements within which the actors work and which presumably affect the policy-making process for education. Attention is focused on the state education agency, meaning the state board of education (SBE), the chief state school officer (CSSO), and the state department of education (SDE), with some consideration of the relationships between the state education agency and other formal actors in the system—namely, governors and legislators.

To sharpen this focus, this chapter traces the development of the state education agency, explains briefly the organizational arrangements in all fifty states and provides some additional detail for the twelve states included in the EGP study, points out some recent structural changes made in state education agencies, and, finally, sets forth what appear to be some of the major issues having to do with the formal structure of the state education agency and with relationships between the agency and other major actors.

DEVELOPMENT OF THE STATE EDUCATION AGENCY

Several colonial legislatures provided for the setting up of such agencies, but the concern, here, is limited to the period after the U.S. Constitution was ratified. The Constitution made no mention of education, leaving that function, in the language of that document, to the states or to the people. The federal plan, whereby some governmental functions were divided between nation and state, helps to explain the omission of education from the Constitution. The fact that many people considered schooling to be more a private than a public function was probably another factor.

Even though schooling was often left to individual or to church discretion, nearly every state made some effort to establish or encourage education. Six of the original thirteen states had constitutional provisions bearing on education, and eleven of the thirteen states had statutory provisions on the same subject. Only Rhode Island, at the time the Union was established, had neither a constitutional nor a statutory provision for education.[1] Most of the states admitted to the Union at later times had both constitutional and statutory language bearing on education.

In the early history of this country, the governance of education was a part of general governance, and little was done at the state level. One exception had to do with school lands. Many states, when they were admitted to the Union, received land that was to be used for school purposes, or the income derived from such land was to be used for school purposes. Often the state treasurer was charged with allocating funds derived from these lands. Although many schools were private, most states also provided that common schools, at first interpreted as elementary schools, were to be established in each town or district. Most of the support for such schools, however, was to come from local taxes, a practice that led to the strong tradition of local control of schools. This ideology, or at least the rhetoric, is still with us. As concern for the public schools increased, there was a move to create a special structure for their governance. At the local level this led, in Massachusetts, for example, to the separation of the school committee from the town selectmen in 1826. At the state level it led to the creation of the state education agency.

Early Forms

The first indication of a special structure for educational governance at the state level appeared when the Board of Regents of the University of the State of New York was established in 1784.[2] Initially, however, the Regents had jurisdiction only over academies and colleges. Not until 1904 was supervision of the public schools placed under their direction. In 1825 North Carolina set up an ex officio state board known as the President and Directors of the Literary Fund, and in 1837 this board was made appointive and given supervision over the public schools. The most significant move toward establishing a state board of education for the public schools was the creation of the Massachusetts State Board of Education in 1837. The governor, the lieutenant-governor, and eight citizens appointed by the governor for eight-year staggered terms comprised the board, which was itself empowered to employ a secretary as executive officer. The success of the Massachusetts Board of Education can largely be ascribed to the efforts of Horace Mann, who became the board's first secretary and held that position for twelve years.[3] By 1900 thirty-four states had established state boards of education,[4] many of which were composed completely or in part of ex officio members, that is, persons elected to other state posts such as the governor, the secretary of state, or the secretary of the treasury. Most states eventually removed all or most such members.

Almost concurrent with, and in some cases preceding, the establishment of state boards of education was the creation of the office of chief state school officer. Again, New York was the first state to establish such a post. In 1812 the legislature provided that a superintendent of common schools should be appointed by the council of appointment. The office was displaced in 1821, however, and it was not reestablished until 1854. In the interim the Secretary of State acted as ex officio superintendent.[5] Maryland, similarly, established the office in 1826, abolished it in 1828, and reestablished it in 1868. A superintendent of common schools, provided by Michigan law in 1829, became the superintendent of public instruction in 1836, the first such state office to continue to the present time.[6] Between 1830 and 1850 most states established the office of chief state school officer. By 1900 there were forty-eight chief state school officers, even though a few of the territories had not yet been admitted to the Union. By that time thirty-three of the states had authorized the office by constitutional provision, but four of these states later rescinded the constitutional arrangement and established the office by statute only.[7]

The CSSO has been known by a number of titles. The most common is superintendent of public instruction, next is commissioner of education, and there are still other variations in a few states. The method by which the chief is selected has also varied among the states. In 1896 CSSO's in thirty-one states were elected by the people; in nine, appointed by the governor; in three, appointed by the general assembly; in three more, by the state board of education; and, in two, there was as yet no such office.[8]

Over much of U.S. history, the SBE and the CSSO have had relatively small professional staffs. Beach has suggested that, until 1900, state departments of education were engaged chiefly in collecting statistics,[9] and, under those circumstances, only a few good clerks seemed to be required. As late as 1900, Beach reports, there were 177 professionals, including CSSO's, in all state departments combined, an average of fewer than four persons per state.

Since 1900

During this century there have been many developments in the state education agency: Forty-nine of the fifty states have established state boards of education with jurisdiction over elementary and secondary schools; all states have chief state school officers; the numbers of professional personnel in departments of education have increased enormously. These changes seem to represent a response to the expectations held for the agency. Beach points out that, from about 1900 to 1930, state departments were primarily engaged in inspection or the enforcement of standards. It is interesting that this was also the period of the scientific management movement, promoted by Taylor, who published his first book on the subject in 1911.[10] In any case, inspection of practices in local school districts did require more state department personnel than the collection of a few simple statistics from those districts. About 1930, Beach contends, state departments entered a leadership stage[11] that may have been influenced by the Hawthorne experiments in industry and the advent of so-called democratic administration in education.[12]

To what extent state education agencies have provided leadership in education over the past several decades may be a question, but there is no denying the fact that the agencies have taken on additional functions, greatly augmenting the professional staff in the process. Table IX-1 shows the increase of professional staff from

TABLE IX-1 Number of Professional Staff Members in Selected State Departments of Education, 1962 and 1972

State	1962	1972	Percent increase
California	249	375	151
Colorado	52	94	181
Florida	90	401	335
Georgia	160	345	216
Massachusetts	91	303	333
Michigan	65	242	372
Minnesota	100	213	213
Nebraska	45	125	278
New York	271	972	359
Tennessee	55	278	505
Texas	175	466	266
Wisconsin	71	204	287
TOTAL	1,824	4,018	220

Sources: Robert F. Will, *State Education—Structure and Organization,* Department of Health, Education, and Welfare (Washington, D. C.: U.S. Government Printing Office, 1964), p. 33; Sam P. Harris, *State Departments of Education, State Boards of Education, and Chief State School Officers,* Department of Health, Education, and Welfare Publication (Office of Education) 73-074000 (Washington, D. C.: U.S. Government Printing Office, 1973), pp. 42-43.

1962 to 1972 in the twelve states included in the EGP study. The percentage of increase over this decade ranges from 151 in California to 505 in Tennessee. For the twelve states the average percentage of increase is 220. In terms of numbers, the average number of professionals in the twelve states was about 150 in 1962 and 330 in 1972.

Some of the impetus for staff increases may have come from the state agencies themselves, but most of it probably came from external sources. In many states demands for school finance reform and for accountability increased. The push for accountability frequently meant a need for more information and better analyses, particularly in relating costs to outcomes. Even greater pressure came from the federal level. With the passage of vocational education provisions in 1917, the federal government began to extend federal aid to states for categorical programs. Such programs continued and came to full flower in the 1960's, particularly with the passage of the Elementary and Secondary Education Act.[13] Title V of that act was designed to improve state departments of education, and substantial funds were made available to state departments for this purpose. From 1966 to 1973, $175 million was allocated to improve state departments. Murphy[14] examined the impact of Title V funds on state departments of education and made detailed studies of three states. In two of the states the funds were used rather broadly through the departments to enhance many activities already underway. In the third state, where the department was less well developed, some Title V money was used to set up new programs, particularly in the planning and research areas.

Even though Title V money and other federal funds appear to have reinforced and augmented customary state department activities more than they have spurred reform, many departments seem to be doing more in the way of planning, research, and evaluation than they once did. At this point it should be noted that many state departments now receive at least half of their annual operating budget from federal sources. Federal money, which is subject to congressional and presidential decisions often made late in the fiscal year, makes the funding of state agencies uncertain. At times it even makes them more sensitive to federal demands than to state needs. Welcome as federal money has generally been, it would appear that state agencies must rely chiefly on state funds if they are to perform effectively for the people of the state.

PRESENT STATE AGENCY ARRANGEMENTS

Present arrangements for the state governance of education must also be viewed from the perspective of the state education agency, as it was defined at the beginning of this chapter. The agency serves two major functions. In one sense, it is an administrative arm of state government, responsible for implementing those programs stipulated by the constitution or enacted into law by statute. In another sense, it is a policy-making body, a role that is exercised through relationships with the governor and the legislature and through the actual formulation of policy in those areas entrusted to it by the constitution or delegated to it by the legislature. The state board of education and the chief state school officer appear to have major parts to play in policy making. The state department, as the professional arm of the board and the chief, appears to have a major part in the implementation of policy.

State Boards of Education

Forty-nine of the fifty states have state boards of education for elementary and secondary education. Only Wisconsin has no such board. Table IX-2 shows selected structural arrangements pertaining to these boards. In fifteen of the forty-nine states the members of the state boards are elected: in eight cases by partisan elections, in four cases by nonpartisan elections, in two cases by the legislature or legislative delegation, and in one case by local school directors (boards). In thirty-two states the governor appoints the state board of education members. In two states, Florida and Mississippi, the board is composed entirely of ex officio members.

The number of members on the board varies from three in Mississippi to twenty-four in Texas. Most boards range from seven to eleven members in size. Terms of office range from three years in Delaware to fifteen years in New York (recently modified to seven years). The length of term is usually from four to six years. In thirty-two states a per diem allowance and expenses are paid for board members while attending meetings; in seventeen states only expenses are paid. Per diem payments are usually modest, from ten dollars to fifty dollars for each day spent in board meetings.

In addition to the general supervision of elementary and secondary education, a mandate common to all state boards, the jurisdiction of state boards is frequently extended to other areas. Forty-four of the forty-nine boards exercise supervision over vocational education. In twenty-nine cases the state board of education is responsible for vocational rehabilitation, and in four cases—Idaho, New York, Penn-

TABLE IX-2 Structural Features of State Boards of Education, 1972

State	Selection			Member- ship	Term of office (years)	Compensation		Augmented jurisdiction		
	Elected	Governor appointed	Ex officio			Per diem	Expenses	Voca- tional educa- tion	Voca- tional rehabili- tation	Higher educa- tion
Alabama	p[a]	—	—	8 + 2X	4	X	X	yes	yes	no
Alaska	—	X	—	7	5	X	X	yes	yes	no
Arizona	—	X	—	8 + 1X	4	—	X	yes	yes	no
Arkansas	—	X	—	9 + 1X	9	X	X	yes	no	no
California	—	X	—	10	4	—	X	yes	yes	no
Colorado	p	—	—	5	6	—	X	no	no	no
Connecticut	—	X	—	9 + 1X	6	—	X	yes	yes	no
Delaware	—	X	—	6 + 2X	3	X	X	yes	no	no
Florida	—	—	X	7X	4	—	X	yes	no[f]	no
Georgia	—	X	—	10	7	X	X	yes	yes[f]	no
Hawaii	p	—	—	11	4	X	X	no	no	no
Idaho	—	X	—	7 + 1X	5	X	X	yes	yes	yes
Illinois	—	X	—	17	6	X	X	yes	no	no
Indiana	—	X	—	18 + 1X	4	X	X	no	no	no
Iowa	—	X	—	9	6	X	X	yes	yes	no
Kansas	p	—	—	10	4	X	X	yes	no	no
Kentucky	—	X	—	7 + 1X	4	X	X	yes	yes	no
Louisiana	p	—	—	11 + 1X	6,8[b]	X	X	yes	yes	no

State										
Maine	—	X	—	9	5	X	X	yes	no	no
Maryland	—	X	—	7	5	—	X	yes	yes	no
Massachusetts	—	X	—	11 + 3X	5	—	X	yes	no	no
Michigan	p	—	—	8 + 2X	8	X	X	yes	yes	no
Minnesota	—	X	—	9	6	—	X	yes	yes	no
Mississippi	—	—	X	3X	4	X	X	yes	yes	no
Missouri	—	X	—	8	8	X	X	yes	yes	no
Montana	—	X	—	8 + 3X	8	—	X	yes	yes	no
Nebraska	np	—	—	8	4	—	X	yes	yes	no
Nevada	np	—	—	9	4	—	X	yes	no	no
New Hampshire	—	X	—	7	5	—	X	yes	yes	no
New Jersey	—	X	—	12 + 2X	6	—	X	yes	no	no
New Mexico	p	—	—	10	6	X	X	yes	yes	no
New York	Leg.[c]	—	—	15	15	—	X	yes	yes	yes
North Carolina	—	X	—	11 + 2X	8	X	X	yes	no	no
North Dakota	—	X	—	7 + 1X	6	X	X	yes	yes	no
Ohio	np	—	—	23	6	X	X	no	yes	no
Oklahoma	—	X	—	6 + 1X	6	X	X	yes	no	no
Oregon	—	X	—	7	7	X	X	yes	no	no
Pennsylvania	—	X	—	17	6	—	X	yes	no	yes
Rhode Island	—	X	—	9	4	—	X	yes	no	yes
South Carolina	Leg.[d]	—	—	16	4	X	X	yes	no	no
South Dakota	—	X	—	7	5	X	X	yes	yes	no
Tennessee	—	X	—	12 + 3X	9	X	X	yes	yes	no
Texas	p	—	—	24	6	—	X	yes	yes	no
Utah	np	—	—	11	4	X	X	yes	yes	no

TABLE IX-2 (continued)

State	Selection				Term of office (years)	Compensation		Augmented jurisdiction		
	Elected	Governor appointed	Ex officio	Membership		Per diem	Expenses	Vocational education	Vocational rehabilitation	Higher education
Vermont	—	X	—	7	6	X	X	yes	yes	no
Virginia	—	X	—	9	4	X	X	yes	no	no
Washington	Local boards	—	—	14 + 1X	6	—	X	no	no	no
West Virginia	—	X	—	9 + 2X	9	X	X	yes	yes	no
Wisconsin[e]	—	—	—	—	—	—	—	—	—	—
Wyoming	—	X	—	9 + 1X	6	X	X	yes	no	no

[a] p = partisan election; np = nonpartisan election
[b] Some six and some eight year terms
[c] Elected by legislature
[d] Elected by legislative delegation
[e] No state board for elementary and secondary education
[f] Vocational rehabilitation was recently removed from the board

Sources: Most of these data are from Harris, *State Departments of Education*. For Illinois, recent constitutional and statutory changes were examined.

sylvania, and Rhode Island—the state board of education, often called the board of regents, is also responsible for higher education.

For ten of the twelve states included in the EGP study, there are considerable data on the demographic characteristics of members of the state boards of education. There is no state board of education in Wisconsin, and, because all state board members are ex officio in Florida, they are not included. In the ten states there were 112 voting members (some ex officio members were not voting members), and 64 of these members (59 percent of the total) completed the EGP questionnaire. The responses are summarized in Table IX-3. This is not an accurate picture for individual states since the percentage of return varied from state to state. Nor are all state board members accurately portrayed by the data in Table IX-3. The responses of 64 board members in ten states do, however, reveal the characteristics shown.

These data suggest that state board members are largely male, almost always white, and usually over forty years of age. Half of them have annual incomes of $30,000 or more, and nearly all have graduated from college. Generally they live in urban and suburban communities, and they divide about evenly between Democrats and Republicans in their political affiliation. Almost half of them have had some professional experience in education—the only factor that causes any surprise. Much of the literature on state boards indicates that board members are made up of laymen, not educators, a proposition that may be only half true.

The Chief State School Officer

Table IX-4 shows a number of structural features pertaining to the CSSO. In thirty-five states the office was established by constitutional provision, while in fifteen states the statutes alone provided the legal basis. In terms of selection, nineteen are elected: thirteen in partisan elections and six in nonpartisan elections. Twenty-six are appointed by the state board of education, and five are appointed by the governor. Appointment in eighteen cases is at the pleasure of the state board or the governor. In seven cases appointment by the state board is for a specified term ranging from one year in Delaware to not more than five years in Alaska. Most terms are for four years. In New Jersey appointment is by the governor, for a five-year term. For other terms of office shown in Table IX-4, the CSSO is elected. In

TABLE IX-3 Demographic Characteristics of State Board of Education Respondents in Ten States, by Percentages

State	Number responding	Male	White	Age 41 or over	Income 30,000 or more	College degree	Urban and sub- urban	Rural	Demo- crat	Repub- lican	Professional educational experience
California	5	60	100	60	50	100	100	0	20	80	60
Colorado	4	75	100	100	33	100	75	25	0	100	50
Georgia	5	80	100	60	75	40	80	20	60	0	20
Massachusetts	6	50	100	83	40	83	100	0	50	33	17
Michigan	8	75	88	50	17	100	88	13	50	38	100
Minnesota	6	67	83	100	40	67	83	17	83	17	33
Nebraska	5	100	100	100	25	80	60	40	40	60	40
New York	7	86	100	100	86	100	100	0	43	43	29
Tennessee	8	88	75	88	38	100	100	0	0	75	75
Texas	10	70	100	100	78	100	80	20	80	0	30
TOTAL	64	75	94	84	51	92	88	12	45	41	47

Source: Educational Governance Project.

TABLE IX-4 Structural Features Pertaining to CSSO's, 1972

| State | Legal basis | | Method of selection | | | | Relationship to board | |
	Constitu-tional	Statu-tory	Elected	Appointed by SBE	Appointed by governor	Term	Ex officio member	Capacity
Alabama	X		—	X	—	Pleasure of SBE	Yes	Secretary and executive officer
Alaska		X	—	X	—	Not to exceed 5 years	No	
Arizona	X		p	—	—	4 years	Yes	Executive officer
Arkansas		X	—	X	—	Pleasure of governor	Yes	Ex officio secretary
California	X		np	—	—	4 years	No	Secretary and executive officer
Colorado	X		—	X	—	Pleasure of SBE	No	Secretary
Connecticut		X	—	X	—	Pleasure of SBE	No	Secretary
Delaware		X	—	X	—	1 year	No	Executive secretary
Florida	X		p	—	—	4 years	Yes	Secretary and executive officer
Georgia	X		p	—	—	4 years	No	Executive officer
Hawaii	X		—	X	—	Pleasure of SBE	No	Secretary
Idaho	X		p	—	—	4 years	Yes	Administrative officer
Illinois	X		—	X	—	3 years	No	Executive officer
Indiana	X		p	—	—	2 years	Yes	Chairman of Board commissions
Iowa		X	—	X	—	4 years	No	Executive officer

TABLE IX-4 (continued)

State	Legal basis		Method of selection			Term	Relationship to board	
	Constitutional	Statutory	Elected	Appointed by SBE	Appointed by governor		Ex officio member	Capacity
Kansas	X		—	X	—	Pleasure of SBE	No	Executive officer
Kentucky	X		p	—	—	4 years	Yes	Executive officer
Louisiana	X		p	—	—	4 years	Yes	Secretary and executive officer
Maine		X	—	—	X	Coterminous with governor	No	Secretary
Maryland		X	—	X	—	4 years	No	Chief executive, secretary, and treasurer
Massachusetts		X	—	X	—	Pleasure of SBE	No	Chief executive officer and secretary
Michigan	X		—	X	—	Pleasure of SBE	Yes	Chairman
Minnesota		X	—	X	—	4 years	No	Executive officer and secretary
Mississippi	X		p	—	—	4 years	Yes	Chairman
Missouri	X		—	X	—	Pleasure of SBE	No	Chief administrative officer
Montana	X		p	—	—	4 years	Yes	Secretary
Nebraska	X		—	X	—	Pleasure of SBE	No	Executive officer and secretary
Nevada	X		—	X	—	Pleasure of SBE	No	Secretary

State							
New Hampshire	X	—	X	—	Pleasure of SBE	No	Chief executive officer and secretary
New Jersey	X	—	—	X	5 years	No	Official agent and secretary
New Mexico	X	—	X	—	Pleasure of SBE	No	Chief administrative officer
New York	X	—	X	—	Pleasure of regents	No	Chief administrative officer
North Carolina	X	p	—	—	4 years	No	Secretary and administrative officer
North Dakota	X	np	—	—	4 years	Yes	Executive director and secretary
Ohio	X	—	X	—	Pleasure of SBE	No	Secretary, executive and administrative officer
Oklahoma	X	p	—	—	4 years	Yes	President and executive officer
Oregon	X	np	—	—	4 years	No	Legislative liaison and executive officer
Pennsylvania	X	—	—	X	Pleasure of governor	No	Chief executive officer
Rhode Island	X	—	X	—	Pleasure of regents	No	Executive officer
South Carolina	X	p	—	—	4 years	No	Secretary and administrative officer
South Dakota	X	np	—	—	2 years	No	Secretary and executive officer
Tennessee	X	—	—	X	Pleasure of governor	Yes	Chairman

TABLE IX-4 (continued)

| State | Legal basis | | Method of selection | | | Term | Relationship to board | |
	Constitu-tional	Statu-tory	Elected	Appointed by SBE	Appointed by governor		Ex officio member	Capacity
Texas		X	—	X	—	4 years	No	Executive secretary
Utah	X		—	X	—	Pleasure of SBE	No	Executive officer
Vermont		X	—	X	—	Pleasure of SBE	No	Chief executive officer and secretary
Virginia	X		—	—	X	Coterminous with governor	No	Secretary
Washington	X		np	—	—	4 years	Yes	President; administrative officer
West Virginia	X		—	X	—	Pleasure of SBE	Yes	Chief executive officer
Wisconsin	X		np	—	—	4 years	No SBE	No SBE
Wyoming	X		p	—	—	4 years	Yes	Assists board
TOTALS	35	15	19	26	5			

Sources: Harris, State Departments of Education, and recent constitutional and statutory changes in Illinois.

seventeen states the CSSO is an ex officio member of the state board of education; in thirty-three states the chief does not have that status. In Table IX-4 an attempt has been made to characterize briefly the formal relationship of the chief to the state board. In many instances the chief is simply called the secretary, and in other cases the designation is executive officer or chief administrative officer of the board. In five states the CSSO is not only a member of the state board but also the official chairman of that body. While the formal relationship of the CSSO to the SBE varies among the states, in practice nearly all chiefs serve as executive officers of their respective state boards of education and as important professional advisers to the boards.

For the twelve states involved in the EGP, there is some demographic information on the CSSO's, and those data are summarized in Table IX-5. It will be noted that all twelve chiefs were male, that ten were white and two were black, that the average age was about fifty-seven, that the average salary was about $32,000, that seven of the twelve had their K-12 schooling in the same state where they were serving as CSSO, that half of the chiefs had received their K-12 schooling in rural communities, that three-fourths of the chiefs had served as public school teachers, that two-thirds of them had served as public school superintendents, and that, in seven of the twelve cases, chiefs had served in state departments of education prior to their selection.

It is readily admitted that these twelve CSSO's do not constitute a statistical sample of the fifty in the country. For instance, three women are currently serving as CSSO's, but males predominate. We also know that the two blacks in the states included in EGP are the only two blacks among the fifty; hence, the group is more predominantly white than the figures from that study suggest. In terms of other demographic characteristics, however, the twelve CSSO's in EGP are probably representative of the larger group.

The State Department of Education

The state department, as noted earlier, is composed largely of professionals in education and related areas. These persons are expected to implement policy decisions in education whether they are formalized by the legislature or the state board of education. Table IX-6 shows the numbers of full-time professionals employed in each of the

TABLE IX-5 Demographic Characteristics of CSSO's in Twelve States, 1973

State	Sex	Race	Age	Salary	K-12 schooling in same state	K-12 schooling urban or rural	Experience as public school teacher	Experience as public school superintendent	Prior experience in state department
California	M	B	55	$35,000	No	U	Yes	No	Yes
Colorado	M	W	54	35,000	No	U	Yes	Yes	No
Florida	M	W	57	36,000	Yes	R	No	Yes	No
Georgia	M	W	51	28,000	Yes	R	Yes	Yes	Yes
Massachusetts	M	W	61	30,000	Yes	U	Yes	Yes	Yes
Michigan	M	B	41	39,550	No	U	Yes	No	Yes
Minnesota	M	W	46	29,400	Yes	R	Yes	Yes	No
Nebraska	M	W	63	21,900	Yes	U	No	No	Yes
New York	M	W	58	51,275	No	U	No	No	Yes
Tennessee	M	W	64	25,000	No	R	Yes	Yes	No
Texas	M	W	68	31,500	Yes	R	Yes	Yes	No
Wisconsin	M	W	64	27,500	Yes	R	Yes	Yes	Yes
AVERAGE			56.8	31,927					

Source: Educational Governance Project.

TABLE IX-6 Full-Time Professional Employees of State
Departments of Education, 1972

State	Head-quarters staff	Regional office staff	Local and regional staffs in related programs
Alabama	124	3	213
Alaska	52	15	42
Arizona	161	16	106
Arkansas	155	307	165
California	375	106	45
Colorado	94	0	6
Connecticut	121	13	112
Delaware	68	0	0
Florida	401	42	0
Georgia	345	42	781
Hawaii	165	92	105
Idaho	49	0	0
Illinois	412	56	Not available
Indiana	110	40	0
Iowa	148	0	289
Kansas	124	0	0
Kentucky	203	1,209	294
Louisiana	129	87	2
Maine	101	0	27
Maryland	228	0	296
Massachusetts	303	26	0
Michigan	242	0	455
Minnesota	213	12	210
Mississippi	93	0	0
Missouri	135	183	331
Montana	91	0	0
Nebraska	125	0	96
Nevada	44	3	0
New Hampshire	74	312	63
New Jersey	300	135	64
New Mexico	110	3	142
New York	972	19	430
North Carolina	486	30	0
North Dakota	58	0	0
Ohio	320	30	0

TABLE IX-6 (continued)

State	Head-quarters staff	Regional office staff	Local and regional staffs in related programs
Oklahoma	159	0	0
Oregon	125	0	0
Pennsylvania	410	76	56
Rhode Island	86	208	0
South Carolina	280	0	0
South Dakota	47	10	48
Tennessee	278	135	332
Texas	466	58	0
Utah	86	0	105
Vermont	61	9	0
Virginia	210	43	0
Washington	142	0	0
West Virginia	83	34	392
Wisconsin	204	84	1
Wyoming	46	14	0
TOTAL	9,814	3,452	5,208

Source: Harris, State Departments of Education.

fifty departments. There are three categories: headquarters staff, field office staff, and related staff. The last two of the categories may require some explanation. Some states have found it desirable to regionalize their staffs, presumably to make them more accessible to local school districts and other clientele of state departments. Staffs in related programs serve in such areas as vocational rehabilitation, state museums, and state libraries.

Headquarters staffs range in size from 46 in Wyoming to 972 in New York, with the average being about 200. Regional staffs range in size from zero in many states to over 1,200 in Kentucky. We suspect that Kentucky includes many persons in that category that are not included by other states. There is also much variation among the states in terms of staffs in related programs. Much of this is accounted for by the presence or absence of such programs in the state department of education. As noted in Table IX-1, for instance, some state departments include vocational rehabilitation; others do not.

Ordinarily, personnel in a state department are divided into major areas such as instruction, administrative services, school finance, and planning and research. Frequently an associate or assistant state superintendent or commissioner will head each of the major divisions. Divisions, in turn, are often divided into bureaus or programs, and there may be programs for elementary education, for special education, for urban education, for experimental programs, and for computer services. Each bureau or program is usually headed by a director. The EGP study secured demographic data on state department directors that are summarized in Table IX-7. The population of directors shown in the table was derived in two ways. If directors in a state department numbered twenty or fewer, all such persons were included. If directors numbered more than twenty, a 30 percent random sample was drawn. The sampling procedure was necessary in four states—California, Georgia, New York, and Texas. Following these procedures, a total population of 145 was identified, and questionnaires were sent to all of these persons. Usable responses were received from 131, or 90 percent of the directors contacted.

The directors, as shown in Table IX-7, have an average age of forty-seven. They are 97 percent male and 94 percent white. In the group studied, 62 percent received their K-12 schooling in the same state as currently employed and 43 percent in rural communities; 61 percent completed college undergraduate programs and 64 percent had done graduate study in the same state as currently employed. One-third of the group had doctorates, and about three-fifths had at one time served as public school teachers.

In terms of the formal organization of departments, directors are at a third level of organization. The CSSO and the associate and assistant superintendents exceed them in terms of formal status. While directors are a part of the leadership cadre of a department of education, a study of them often demonstrates the staffing policy of a department more clearly than a similar study of the top administrators. If that is the case, it seems clear that in the twelve participating states, and perhaps in the others as well, that recruitment of staff personnel has focused on males and whites. While the prerequisite of teaching experience in the public schools may not be as common as was once the case in recruiting persons for state departments, a majority of directors have still traveled that route. The fact that one-third of the directors have earned a doctorate seems commendable,

TABLE IX-7 Demographic Characteristics of Program Directors in State Departments of Education in Twelve States, 1973

State	Respondents	Average age	Male	White	K-12 schooling in-state	K-12 schooling in rural community	Undergraduate college in-state	Graduate work in-state	Doctoral degree	Experience as public school teacher
California	15	49	15	12	3	7	7	10	7	12
Colorado	10	44	9	9	2	2	2	6	2	7
Florida	12	52	12	12	7	7	7	8	4	8
Georgia	9	43	9	9	5	3	5	3	3	5
Massachusetts	11	43	10	11	8	1	6	8	3	4
Michigan	9	48	9	9	4	2	4	5	5	7
Minnesota	8	41	7	6	8	7	6	5	2	5
Nebraska	12	50	11	11	11	8	10	9	2	9
New York	14	49	14	14	9	3	9	8	7	6
Tennessee	12	47	12	12	10	7	11	12	2	6
Texas	8	49	8	7	7	4	6	3	0	1
Wisconsin	11	45	11	11	7	5	11	7	5	6
TOTALS	131	47	127	123	81	56	80	84	42	76
PERCENTAGES	100	—	97	94	62	43	61	64	32	58

Source: Educational Governance Project.

and it suggests that they bring considerable expertise to their positions. At the same time, the fact that two-thirds of the graduate programs were completed at in-state institutions suggests some inbreeding.[15]

Relationships to Other Actors

These, then, are the formal arrangements for the state governance of education, particularly as reflected in the state education agency. But the agency does not have an independent life of its own. Its very existence depends on constitutional mandate and statutory provision, and, in most states, the agency can determine policy only in those areas where there is specific delegation. Certification requirements for teachers and administrators is usually one such area. To affect policy in other areas, such as school finance, the agency must influence the governor and the legislature. For the most part, few formal mechanisms have been established for the exercise of such influence. While the relationships between the agency and other actors in the policy system tend to be informal, many of them are rather well established. Most state agencies are called upon by governors and legislators for information about schools, about students, about student achievement, about allocation of money, and about a host of other things. In some cases governors seek input from the agency in terms of recommended legislation and budget proposals. In many cases governors and legislators call upon agency representatives, particularly the CSSO, for advice on proposed or pending legislation. In some cases the agency takes the initiative in recommending legislation to the governor and the legislature.

Governors, legislators, and agency officials are official actors in the policy system, but it is well known that there are many unofficial actors or interest group representatives in such a system. The most common education interest groups represent the teachers, the school administrators, and the local school boards. Noneducation interest groups, such as those representing business, labor, or agriculture, also take positions on educational policy questions, particularly those involving money and thus the tax structure of the state. Both kinds of groups are mentioned here only to suggest that the relationships of the state education agency involve both official and unofficial actors in the policy system. The concern is that the formal structure of the agency be such that necessary relationships with other policy actors be facilitated and not constrained.

RECENT REORGANIZATIONS OF STATE AGENCIES

The structure of state education agencies is not static. Over the entire history of these agencies, states have with some frequency reorganized them. The increase of state responsibility for education over the past decade or so may have accelerated the dynamic for change in the state structure for the governance of education. An examination of reorganizations in three states—Maine, Kansas, and Illinois—illustrates what has been going on in many states over the country.

Maine

Early in 1970 Governor Kenneth M. Curtis issued an executive order announcing that the Legislative Research Committee had joined with the Executive Department in preparing proposals for state governmental reform and reorganization to be submitted to the next legislative session. These proposals, completed late in 1970, were designed to strengthen gubernatorial responsibility, consolidate related state functions, increase the capability of the legislature to formulate state policy, and reduce duplication of programs.[16] Reorganization bills passed by the legislature in 1971 and 1972 culminated in a cabinet structure of government composed of twelve major departments. Education, one of the twelve, was placed in the Department of Educational and Cultural Services.

The new department, headed by a commissioner appointed by the governor, was to have jurisdiction over eleven existing agencies, including the State Board of Education, the Advisory Council of Vocational Education, the Commission for the Higher Education Facilities Act of 1965, the Commission on the Arts and Humanities, the Museum Commission, and the State Library. Members of the State Board of Education were also to be appointed by the governor. Of particular interest is the provision that the State Board of Education was to serve in an advisory capacity to the commissioner "except in certain specified areas chief of which is the operation of the vocational technical institutes where the Board has full authority."

Even such a brief review of reorganization in Maine is revealing. The reorganization in education was part of a reorganization in all of state government. The power and responsibility of the governor was enhanced. The governor's appointee, the commissioner, was also given extensive power and responsibility, including great discretion in areas of budget and personnel. The new structure was undoubtedly designed to consolidate many semiautonomous agencies and to provide far more coordination among governmental agencies. Much of this coordination was apparently to be achieved by means of the governor's cabinet or executive council, upon which each of the commissioners, including the Commissioner of Educational and Cultural Services, was seated. The place of higher education in the reorganization appeared somewhat ambiguous. It seemed that the administration of any federal aid for facilities in higher education would be under the direction of the commissioner, but the place of the Board of Trustees for the University of Maine was not mentioned; hence, it will probably continue on a somewhat autonomous basis. It should be noted, however, that the trustees were to be appointed by the governor and confirmed by the executive council.

Kansas

As early as 1960 Domian and Keller,[17] in their study of education in Kansas, noted the weakness of the state-level organization and recommended a board-appointed state superintendent. In 1965 the Legislative Council established and funded an Educational Interim Committee composed of eleven prominent Kansas citizens under the chairmanship of John H. Colburn. This committee submitted a report that focused on amending Article 6 of the state constitution to provide a state board of education, a state board of regents, and a commissioner of education to be appointed by the state board of education.[18] In 1966 the legislature adopted a resolution that placed the constitutional amendment before the voters of Kansas, where it was approved. This action cleared the way in 1968 for the legislature to enact the necessary statutes to implement the changes.

The principal provisions governing the new state education agency were as follows:

1. Members of the state board of education were to be elected on a nonpartisan ballot for four-year terms.
2. The elective office of state superintendent was abolished, and the new state board of education was empowered to appoint a commissioner of education as their executive officer.
3. The state board of education was given broad powers which in-

cluded the language, "the general supervision of the public schools."

The new State Board of Education was seated in January 1969, and by September of that year the board had selected the new commissioner of education.[19]

The reorganization of the state education agency in Kansas had certain distinguishing characteristics. The time required for reorganization seemed to be longer than in some states: it began with a study of the situation in 1960 and culminated with the new organization in place in 1969. The initiative for the change seems to have come largely from the legislature and not from the governor as it had in Maine. Again, by way of contrast with Maine, the Kansas reorganization dealt specifically with education and not with the general structure of state government. Even so, two other constitutional amendments, one providing for annual sessions of the legislature and the other a revision of the tax code, were submitted to the voters at the same time as the proposed change in education. Also, the Kansas legislators included under education a concern for both the schools and the colleges and created a new state board for each. The reorganization did clarify and relocate formal power and responsibility by lodging formal power with the board and not with the commissioner. The grant of power to the board actually led to a court case in which the state supreme court declared that, "the people of this state had no intention of giving up all control of their local schools to the state board of education when they approved the new constitutional article on education. An intention is clearly expressed in the constitution to have the legislators provide the guidelines for general supervision of the schools."[20] This decision reaffirmed the position that plenary power resides in the legislature and that state boards enjoy only power given to them by the constitution or delegated by statute.

Illinois

Not until 1973 did the legislature of Illinois formally establish a state board of education for the general supervision of the elementary and secondary schools of that state. In the meantime, a number of special purpose boards and agencies, each with limited jurisdiction, came into existence and operated over the years. These bodies included the following: the State Teacher Certification Board, the School Building Commission, the Board of Education for the Blind and Deaf, the Board of Examiners of the Chicago Public Schools, and the School Problems Commission.

The process of reorganization in Illinois was long and difficult. The special purpose boards and the elected superintendent of public instruction performed most of the functions that more unified state education agencies performed in other states. For many, the School Problems Commission, made up of legislators from the House and Senate and appointees of the governor, seemed to be a particularly adequate and a unique way of dealing with many educational problems at the state level. Even so, there have been several efforts over the past two or three decades to establish a state board of education and to give that board power to select the state superintendent. Changes of this nature require a constitutional amendment, and the voters of the state have not been inclined to permit such a modification.

A more comprehensive look at education in Illinois was authorized in the mid-1960s. After much encouragement from many groups in the state, the governor, the state superintendent of public instruction, and the School Problems Commission became joint sponsors of the Task Force on Education and appointed some fifty persons, including representatives from education, government, business, labor, agriculture, and civic groups, as members of the task force. William P. McLure, Director of the Bureau of Educational Research at the University of Illinois, was made chairman of the task force and director of the staff employed by it. The task force was divided into work groups, one of which was concerned with reorganization of the educational structure at the state level. The work groups and the task force, as a single body, held a number of meetings at which data collected by the staff were considered. In addition, the task force sponsored hearings over the state and encouraged citizens to make their input into the process. A report was made in 1966.[21] One part of the report recommended that a state board of education be established and that the board be given authority to appoint the state superintendent. This report and the activities that went into its preparation, particularly the participation of over fifty members and the hearings involving thousands of persons, appear to have been an influence in bringing the problem of state structure to the attention of the people of the state.

After living with the old (1870) constitution for a hundred years, legislators in Illinois decided to revise it and submit the new version to the people for their approval. The legislature took the steps necessary to set up the constitutional convention, or con-con as it came to be known, which met for six months in 1970. One part of the new constitution, Article X, Section 2, read:

Section 2. State Board of Education—Chief State Educational Officer

(a) There is created a State Board of Education to be elected or selected on a regional basis. The number of members, their qualifications, terms of office, and manner of election or selection shall be provided by law. The Board, except as limited by law, may establish goals, determine policies, provide for planning and evaluating educational programs and recommend financing. The Board shall have such other duties and powers as provided by law.

(b) The State Board of Education shall appoint a chief state educational officer.

In December 1970, by special election, the new constitution, including the article shown above, was approved by the people of Illinois.[22] A major obstacle to restructuring education at the state level had been removed. The next move was up to the General Assembly. The bill creating a state board of education and a superintendent of education was approved in June and signed by the governor in August of 1973. The governor appointed the board members in April 1974 and, after some delay, confirmation was obtained in the Senate. The board assumed full powers in January 1975 and a new chief state education officer took on his duties at the same time.

The new state board of education is composed of seventeen members appointed by the governor: sixteen from the five judicial districts, and one at large. Initially, board members drew lots for two-year, four-year, and six-year terms, after which all terms were to be for six years. Persons employed by schools or colleges or serving on boards for schools or colleges were not eligible for membership on the board. This provision was contested by the Illinois Education Association and the Illinois Federation of Teachers, but it was upheld by the Supreme Court of Illinois on the grounds that the law was designed "to prevent any potential conflict of interests...."[23] The court noted that persons previously connected with schools and colleges were not barred from membership on the board.

In setting up the powers of the new board of education the statutes specifically provided that "... the duties of the State Board of Education shall encompass all duties currently delegated to the Office of the Superintendent of Public Instruction and such other duties as the General Assembly shall designate" (Illinois School Code 122, 1A-4). As to scope, the new board is to be responsible for "educational policies and guidelines for public and private schools, preschool through grade 12 and vocational education." A further provision of the law states that: "The Board shall determine the qualifications of and appoint a chief education officer to be known as the State Superintendent of Education who shall serve at the pleasure of the Board except that no contract issued for the employment of the State Superintendent ... shall be for a term longer than 3 years. ... The Board shall set the compensation of the chief school officer and establish his duties, powers, and responsibilities."

Most of the characteristics of the Illinois reorganization have already been noted. It seems well, however, to emphasize that the process of reorganization was spread over a long period of time, twenty to thirty years, and materialized at least eight years after the work of the task force. Moreover, a great number of actors were involved. While the impetus in Maine seemed to come chiefly from the governor, and in Kansas largely from legislative leaders, the move for reorganization in Illinois can be ascribed to many persons, professionals in education and interested citizen groups such as the League of Women Voters. These people finally convinced the formal agencies that a task force should be established, and many of the same people participated directly in the constitutional convention.

The reorganization in Illinois is sensitive to the political realities of the state. Board members are appointed by the governor and not elected, a decision that obviously gives the incumbent governor considerable influence in determining the nature of the first board. But the governor is not given complete freedom. Board members are to be named from judicial districts, eight from the First Judicial District, which includes Chicago. Persons named to the board are subject to Senate approval and that approval, for initial board members, is apparently considered very carefully by the opposition party. As a further indication of party interest in the new board, no more than nine of the seventeen members can be of one political party.

Finally, there is specific mention in the statutes of the duties of the Illinois board. While in Kansas it required a State Supreme Court decision to make it clear that the legislature had plenary power and the state board only delegated power in educational matters, in Illinois the law refers specifically to transferring the duties *delegated* to the office of the State Superintendent "and such other duties as the General Assembly shall *delegate.*"

*   *   *

Reorganization of the state education agencies in the three states described above has been somewhat unique to each state. As for initiation, the governor seemed to provide the chief impetus in Maine, legislative leaders moved the idea forward in Kansas, and a wide variety of actors sponsored the change in Illinois. Most of the work in Maine seems to have been done in three years. In Kansas it required nine years, and in Illinois it took decades. Apparently Maine achieved reorganization through statutory changes. In both Kansas and Illinois, a constitutional provision had to be changed by vote of the people before the legislature could effect the necessary statutory changes. In Maine, once again, reorganization of the state education agency was part of a complete revamping of the structure for all of state government. In Kansas, there was some general reorganization of the legislature, as well as changes in the structure for education. In Illinois, constitutional authorization for changing the education structure led to the adoption of a new state constitution, which also affected other governmental arrangements. Thus, in all three states reorganization in education was, in some sense, part of a larger process of governmental reorganization.

While the process of reorganizing the structure for education varied somewhat among these three states, many common issues emerged. *The first issue had to do with the nature of the state board of education.* How large should the board be? What should be the length of term for board members? Should educators be prohibited from service on the board? Should there be an attempt to balance the party membership of board members? Should board members be selected at large or from divisions of the state? Should board members be paid or reimbursed for expenses only? Perhaps the biggest question was: Should board members be elected or appointed by the governor? Each of the three states answered all of these questions in somewhat different ways.

A second issue is related to the scope of the state board's jurisdiction and the nature of its power. For instance, should the board have jurisdiction over both higher and lower education? In Kansas and Illinois it was made clear that jurisdiction pertained chiefly to elementary and secondary schools, while in Maine there was some ambiguity on this point. Another question of scope has to do with vocational education: Is this function to be under the state board of education, or should a special purpose board be created for that function only? All three of the states moved toward a common agency for vocational and general education. Still another question of scope concerns whether the state education agency should have jurisdiction over cultural affairs such as museums, libraries, and other institutions having to do with the arts and humanities or whether jurisdiction should be limited to formal schools. Maine favored the more comprehensive view, while Kansas and Illinois tended to accept the more traditional position.

Fully as important as the scope of the board's jurisdiction is the nature of that jurisdiction or the formal power delegated to the board. In Maine, the board, with some exceptions, was explicitly cast in an advisory role to the commissioner of education, who was an appointee of the governor. In both Kansas and Illinois the sovereignty of the state reposed in the board, and the chief state school officer served as the board's executive but not as its superior. In these two states, the boards obviously had more independence than the state board did in Maine. The Kansas board, where members were elected, appeared to have even more autonomy than the Illinois board, where members were appointed by the governor.

The third issue has to do with the chief state school officer. Is he to be elected by the people or appointed and, if appointed, by whom—the governor or the state board of education? Both Kansas and Illinois rejected election as a method of selecting the chief state school officer and made appointment by the state board of education mandatory. Maine moved from board selection to gubernatorial appointment as a way of selecting the CSSO.

Another aspect of this situation was alluded to above: Is the CSSO to be superordinate or subordinate to the state board of education? In terms of formal power, Maine made the chief superordinate to the board, while Kansas and Illinois made him subordinate to the board. In none of the three states does the chief have the independence that popular election, still a practice in many states, would have provided him.

The power of the governor in education emerges as a fourth issue. Most governors have become more active in the education arena, but the concern here is with the formal structure that places more power with the governor. In Maine the reorganization of state government into a cabinet structure was designed to give the governor more power and, correspondingly, more responsibility in all areas, including education. A logical extension of that position is appointment of the CSSO by the governor. In Kansas, on the other hand, there was a deliberate attempt to place power in a state board of education and not in the governor's office. In Illinois the formal arrangements are midway between Maine and Kansas. The Illinois board is given considerable power, but members of the board are appointed by the governor with the approval of the Senate. In a sense, we forecast, in these three states, the models that are set forth in Chapter X.

NOTES—CHAPTER IX

1. Ellwood P. Cubberley and Edward C. Elliott, *State and County School Administration* (New York: Macmillan, 1915), pp. 12-15.

2. Ellwood P. Cubberley, *State School Administration* (Boston: Houghton Mifflin, 1927), p. 282.

3. *Ibid.*, p. 283.

4. Ward W. Keesecker, *State Boards of Education and Chief State School Officers*, Bulletin No. 12, Federal Security Agency (Washington, D. C.: U.S. Government Printing Office, 1950), p. 12.

5. Cubberley, *State School Administration*, p. 271.

6. *Ibid.*

7. Keesecker, *State Boards of Education and Chief State School Officers*, p. 27.

8. *Ibid.*, p. 34.

9. Fred F. Beach and Andrew H. Gibbs, *Personnel of State Departments of Education* (Washington, D. C.: U.S. Government Printing Office, 1952).

10. See Frederick W. Taylor, *Shop Management* (New York: Harper and Bros., 1911).

11. Beach and Gibbs, *Personnel of State Departments of Education*.

12. See Roald F. Campbell *et al.*, *Introduction to Educational Administration* (Boston: Allyn and Bacon, 1971), ch. 4.

13. Stephen K. Bailey and Edith K. Mosher, *ESEA: The Office of Education Administers a Law* (Syracuse, N.Y.: Syracuse University Press, 1968).

14. Jerome T. Murphy, "Grease the Squeaky Wheel," Center for Education Policy Research, Graduate School of Education, Harvard University, 1973.

15. For a more complete treatment of state department personnel, see Gary V. Branson, "The Characteristics of Upper Level Administrators in State Departments of Education and the Relationships of these Characteristics to Other State Variables," unpublished dissertation, Ohio State University, 1974.

16. *State of Maine, Governmental Reorganization* (Augusta, Me.: State Planning Office, 1973), p. 7.

17. Otto E. Domian and Robert J. Keller, *Comprehensive Educational Survey of Kansas* (Topeka: Kansas Legislative Council, 1960).

18. Report to the Education Committee, Kansas Legislative Council, October 21, 1965.

19. Dewey Wahl, *Problems of Transition: Changing a State Department of Education from a Partisan to a Nonpartisan Political Structure* (Madison, Wisc.: Department of Public Instruction, 1973), ch. 2.

20. *State ex. rel. v. Board of Education*, 212 Kansas 482 (1973), p. 499.

21. William P. McLure and Paul J. Misner, Education for the Future of Illinois (Springfield, Ill.: Task Force on Education, 1966).

22. See Janet Cornelius, *Constitution Making in Illinois, 1818-1970* (Urbana: University of Illinois Press, 1972), ch. 7.

23. *Hoskins et al.* v. *Daniel J. Walker*, 57 Ill. 2nd 503 (1974).

X — Alternative Arrangements for State School Governance

This chapter sets forth alternative structures for state governance of elementary and secondary education. Each of the three sections in the chapter deals with a different class of models—centralized executive, separate agency, and a combined version of the two—for establishing school governance arrangements at the state level. For each class there is, first, a discussion of competing values, followed by brief descriptions and diagrammatic representations of alternative models. Finally, evidence and insights gained through the Educational Governance Project (EGP) research are presented.

FOCUS AND LIMITATIONS

There are, admittedly, emphases and limitations in the approach used here. The term "model," as it is used, refers to a simplified representation of formal governmental arrangements. As for "governance," it means the function of making policy decisions, as distinguished from the administering of such decisions.

Most of the models do conform, at least in broad outline, to "what is," but a few represent only "what might be." All are, of course, someone's version of "what should be." The focus in each model is on the policy-making components of the state education agency (SEA)—that is, the state board of education (SBE) and the chief state school officer (CSSO)—and on the formal linkages between this agency and the governor's office and the legislature. Other aspects of the state structure are treated as "givens," as are relationships between SEA's and both federal and local agencies involved with school policy making. Recognition of this delimitation, which was necessitated by the available data, suggests that implementation of any model would require careful examination of other structural aspects.

The models were also deliberately chosen so that they could be characterized in terms of a few selected variables. (A number of structural options relevant to all the models are considered in Chapter XI.) To have developed models that were both detailed and valid would have meant an in-depth investigation of state constitutional and statutory provisions, which would have exceeded available resources and yielded products with narrowly limited applicability. Participants in EGP-sponsored regional conferences* had advised that a more general approach be employed and particularly recommended that "the models be presented as were the early Ford Mustangs . . . one can select a basic model and then add on a considerable number of features to meet the needs or concerns of a particular state system."[1] Since such an approach is consistent with the conviction that no one model is appropriate for all states at all times, it was heeded. States vary enormously in their political, as well as their educational, needs and stages of development; no model, therefore, should be adopted without thorough analysis of state-specific conditions.

In order to decide upon the variables used to characterize the models, it was assumed that the basic structural dimensions involved the separation of the SEA from general government and, related to this, control of the SEA. The two central questions thus become:

1. How much and what kind of formal separation should there be between the SEA and the general governance structure? For example, should this agency be simply another executive department or should it have considerable autonomy?

2. Who should have governing authority with regard to the SEA?

*Conferences were held in late 1973 in Denver, Chicago, New York, and Atlanta. More than 250 educational and political leaders attended.

For example, should the formal control structure emphasize the governor, a lay state board, or the CSSO?

The variables most directly relevant to answering these questions, it appears, are the breadth of education policy-making authority assigned by law to the SEA, and the different formal procedures employed by states to select the state board and the CSSO. For this reason, policy-making authority and selection procedure variables constitute the basis for models used in this volume; other variables are included only when it becomes necessary in order to elucidate a particular model.

When assessing a governmental arrangement, it is essential to think about not only what the structure is but also what its consequences are and for whom it works. Structures, intentionally or not, are never neutral. Each makes it easier for some values to be realized rather than others, and for some persons to influence policy decisions rather than others. Assessments of such consequences, especially as voiced by the regional conference participants, are presented for each class of models, along with some evidence and considered judgments concerning the consequences of the different governance arrangements found in the states studied by EGP.

Two final points need to be made about the treatment of model consequences in this chapter. First, these consequences should be thought of as tendencies or probabilities that can be attributed to a particular model and not as necessary concomitants of its adoption. Factors like the socioeconomic development and political culture of a state, or the abilities and intentions of its public officials, condition, perhaps decisively, the impact of a governance structure. Second, the model consequences discussed are process, rather than output, characteristics. No statements are made about the relationship between a given model and changes in such areas as teacher performance or student achievement. Though structure can affect policy outcomes of this sort, the many intervening variables and the limitations of available data preclude any but the most speculative comment.

SECTION I: CENTRALIZED EXECUTIVE MODELS

COMPETING VALUES

The doctrine of public administration that Kaufman terms "executive leadership" has long been favored by political scientists and governmental reformers. Since the mid-1960's, it has received impetus from several sources, including an infusion of federal funds from officials anxious to have strong governors with whom federal agencies could deal. Those who espouse this doctrine have sought, through its implementation, to make state government

more orderly, rational, and visible. Their strategy was to try to reduce the autonomy of government agencies by consolidating them into great functional departments, each to be headed by an appointee of, and both legally and politically responsible to, the chief executive. . . . Constitutional and statutory sources of agency independence were to be eliminated, or at least curtailed as far as possible. The executive branch was to be turned into an administrative pyramid, with the governor at the top—and in charge.[2]

Executive leadership, as applied specifically to the organization of school governance at the state level, calls for ending the autonomy of the SEA and for expanding gubernatorial authority in its control structure through the power of appointment and removal of agency officials. The objectives that supporters of a centralized state structure for education hope to achieve are many, but the most important can be set forth in relation to four general goals: accountability and responsiveness, comprehensive planning and decision making, administrative efficiency, and access to gubernatorial influence.

Accountability in a large democratic polity typically depends on two kinds of relationships: the relationship of elected officials to constituents and the relationship of public bureaucracies to elected officials. According to the doctrine of executive leadership, these relationships are only likely to be effective in terms of accountability when responsibility to the electorate is through a highly visible, well-known political leader such as the governor and when this leader is granted sufficient authority to hold accountable the various agencies for which his office is responsible. Such accountability linkages, so advocates claim, are essential to the responsiveness of state government, for, if public officials and agency administrators cannot be held accountable, they will not respond to public needs and desires. "The point," Pitkin writes, "of holding [the representative] to account after he acts is to make him act in a certain way—look after his constituents, or do what they want."[3]

The "fragmentation" of state governmental structure is seen by centralization supporters not only as undermining accountability and responsiveness, but also as preventing policy makers from taking an overall view of social problems, developing a broad-based plan to confront them, or utilizing state resources efficiently. It is often observed, in this connection, that there seems to be little coordination among state educational programs, notably between those in higher and in K-12 education, and that there is even less communication with noneducational but related state services. Indeed, some people support centralized governance primarily because they think educational concerns should be dealt with "realistically" in the context of total state needs and resources, rather than in the isolated fashion fostered by a semiautonomous SEA. A centralized executive, it is argued, facilitates comparison of the claims of education with those of other public services, as well as those of taxpayers, in comprehensively planning and formulating state policy, and a coordinated structure employing principles of hierarchical management permits economies and promotes cost-benefit efficiency in the expenditure of state resources.

A final argument for integrating SEA's into the executive branch of state government has more to do with an analysis of the current political status of education than with values of the sort mentioned above. As one knowledgeable observer predicts: "Education simply costs too much and is too volatile and visible to stay insulated and out of the political mainstream for much longer in most states . . . the major question for the future is not whether but how education is to be linked with the general governmental and political system."[4] A centralized model is attractive to some persons who believe that education has become a "gut-level issue" in the body politic and who are apprehensive about how well the schools will succeed in competition for dollars with other public services and with the demands of taxpayers. If adequate resources for education increasingly depend on political influence and if such influence is most likely to be attained through effective access to the governor's office, then a state structure that binds the SEA and the governor to each other has logic, even if the goal is simply the economic welfare of education.

While an integrated structure with the governor as the center of state government has many adherents among political scientists and students of public administration, it has generally been condemned by educators, including those most involved with policy-making institutions and the governmental relationships of SEA's. Many such persons attended the EGP regional conferences, and their reactions to a centralized model were predictably critical. To begin with, most conference participants rejected the contention that the governor is the appropriate focus of an education accountability system. Some saw "lay control" as being best realized through an elected state board of education, and a few emphasized an elected chief state school officer. Even those who opted for a governor-appointed state board tended to hedge this power with restrictions—lengthy tenure and overlapping terms for board members as well as prohibiting gubernatorial appointment of the CSSO—designed to curtail the influence of the chief executive.

Other weaknesses of a centralized executive model, according to detractors, are its lack of concern for "education as such" and its inability to guarantee effective state-level advocacy for educational programs. The contention here is that the end of a semiautonomous status for SEA's, through education becoming "simply another undistinguishable function of state government," will discourage giving adequate attention to school needs and prevent the kind of leadership necessary to "provide any real forward thrust to educational thinking."[5] More disturbing to school supporters is the specter that some governors will decline to act as "a public voice for education" or that they will be disinterested or hostile to its development.

A third objection voiced frequently by conference participants stemmed from the fear that schools would become too much enmeshed in "politics." In their words, a structure that closely links the SEA to the governor is vulnerable to "excessive partisanship," "patronage rather than professionalism," and "political indoctrination." One participant echoed the sentiments of most when he asked, rhetorically, "Does anyone really trust politicians?" Along with the desire that education be shielded by structural barriers from political manipulation, there was the belief, expressed by many conference participants, that policy making in this area would experience a lack of continuity and, perhaps, "chronic instability" if change in state education leadership accompanied every new governor.

Two other values often cited by conference critics of centralization involved the preservation of a system of checks and balances and the encouragement of professional competence. That the institutions of state government are, in Sharkansky's words, "more divided and beset with internal checks than the national government" was evidently considered by most conference participants to be, on the whole, a good thing.[6] Constraints on gubernatorial power, especially with regard to education, were supported in order to prevent "too much authority [being] concentrated in the hands of too few people" and to maintain widespread access to the policy-making machinery. While the primacy of "lay control" was repeatedly stressed by conference participants, many contended that the state governance structure had to be especially responsive to the information and proposals of professionals. "Schools will suffer if educators are not heeded" was the ominous prediction. Along with being opposed to "political interference" in what they perceived to be the domain of professional competence, conference participants indicated that the enhancement of SEA professionalism should have a higher priority as a reform measure than the integration of executive branch departments.

STRUCTURAL VARIATIONS AND EXAMPLES

Basic Model

In what might be called its basic form, the centralized executive model gives the SEA the status of an executive department, just like any other, with its head appointed by and serving at the pleasure of the governor. This CSSO has no constitutional authority. Acting as the governor's cabinet officer, the CSSO is responsible for the implementation of K-12 education policy. A state board of education is not an integral feature of this model. If such a body is established, consistency with a centralized executive approach suggests that the SBE be confined to an advisory role or to the exercise of a narrow range of delegated powers compared with those lodged with most existing state boards. A diagram of key authority relationships is shown in Figure X-1.

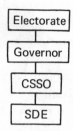

FIGURE X-1

Basic Centralized Executive Model

Modified Version

In spite of the enthusiasm with which many political scientists and governmental reformers have embraced a centralized structure, not a single state employs a model exactly like that in Figure X-1 to govern its schools. There are, however, a few states where the chief executive does appoint both the state board and the CSSO and gubernatorial authority clearly is stressed in the structural arrangements for education. One state, Tennessee, which was studied by the EGP, currently uses such a modified version of the centralized executive model (see Figure X-2).[7]

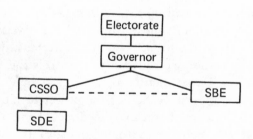

FIGURE X-2

Modified Centralized Executive Model (Tennessee)

In Tennessee the twelve members of the State Board of Education are appointed by the governor.* Gubernatorial power in this respect

---

*In addition to these twelve members there are three ex officio representatives on the Tennessee State Board of Education.

is constrained by the lengthy terms of board officials (nine years), and by the legal stipulation that each of the three geographic-political divisions of the state ("grand divisions") be represented by four members and that each of the two leading political parties have at least three board appointees. Moreover, while Tennessee's state board has no constitutional foundation, it does possess statutory authority to undertake policy making and regulatory action for K-12 education (these same officials also constitute the State Board for Vocational Education).[8]

Statutory authority, coupled with restrictions on gubernatorial appointments, does give Tennessee's state board more independence than that envisioned in the centralized executive model, but not much more. The governor, along with making appointments to the board, serves on that body as an ex officio member. More important, it is the governor and not the state board who appoints and holds responsible the commissioner of education. And the governor's appointee, the commissioner, is, by law, not only a voting member of the state board, but also its chairman.

While the commissioner does have the statutory authority to carry out a wide variety of administrative duties, the central role of the governor is evident even in these statutes. For example, the commissioner is empowered to appoint most heads and subordinates in the State Department of Education, but these appointments are "subject to the governor's approval." The commissioner can, in certain circumstances, request that appropriate authorities "protect, recover, or force collection" of school funds, "provided the governor shall first give his approval to such action."[9] As such statutes indicate, in Tennessee it is the governor who ultimately controls the State Department of Education. Department programs must be consistent with the governor's priorities since he has the power to modify the programs or replace the administrators who direct them. Thus, it seems fair to say that the State Department of Education in Tennessee "works for" the governor's office, not "in cooperation with" as is the case in most states.

A modified version of the centralized executive model, then, operates in Tennessee. It is difficult to say what the consequences of such a governance structure are, for countless other factors are also at work. The case study data do permit at least three observations. The first and most obvious is that a centralized approach offers an effective mechanism—hierarchical authority—by which governor-CSSO conflict can be resolved and by which the values presumed to exist in a cooperative relationship between these two officials can be maintained. During the EGP study in Tennessee, an angry controversy erupted between Governor Winfield Dunn and Commissioner E. C. Stimbert, a controversy that led directly to Stimbert's resignation. Despite the fact that the commissioner took his case to the press and the people, the dispute remained settled, for that official in the end served "at the pleasure of the Governor."[10] In a centralized structure it is difficult, although not impossible, as Stimbert's immediate predecessor demonstrated, for a CSSO to acquire an independent base of power to sustain his position. When he is at odds with the governor's priorities, the CSSO has little choice publicly but to agree with them or to resign.

A second observation based on educational governance in Tennessee has to do with the political nature of the State Department of Education. In 1971 Murphy[11] described the department as having a "prebureaucratic, political and personal orientation," an orientation he attributed, in part, to the extensive use of patronage in staffing. "Governors in the past," he wrote, "apparently exercised their discretion by appointing political friends to SEA jobs."[12] Many of the case study respondents also believed that the state department had been the object of Democratic Party patronage over the years and that, when Republicans took control of the governor's office in 1971 (the first time in fifty years), they were no more prepared than their rivals to discount entirely party affiliation in approving SDE appointments. Traditional expectations were well captured by a former Democratic leader when he remarked: "If my party had the governorship, I would not expect my governor to keep commissioners or weedcutters—that I didn't think were loyal to my administration."[13]

The dispute alluded to earlier between Governor Dunn and Commissioner Stimbert had as a principal cause the issue of patronage. Without getting into the barrage of charges and countercharges that surrounded the commissioner's leaving office, it would appear that the governor's view was that political direction had to continue to be a factor in the operation of the SDE. This practice was both customary and compatible with the state's governance structure. On the other hand, the commissioner evidently saw the SDE from a professional's standpoint, one that had little room for political considerations. The difference in values—one that reflects a basic conflict between proponents and opponents of a centralized executive—contributed to Stimbert's forced resignation. It should be added, however, that the new commissioner, Benjamin Carmichael, was, according to some close observers, encouraged by Governor Dunn to continue upgrading the SDE and was given a "free hand" in filling department positions.

A final observation is that Tennessee's State Board of Education is widely perceived as being a very marginal actor in state school policy making. No doubt there are many reasons for this weakness, not the least of which are deficiencies that afflict virtually all lay boards—lack of time, information, and expertise. Yet it is hard to believe that the centralized structure is not among the causal conditions. As one long-time legislator reasoned, the Tennessee "system is a strong executive-type organization dominated from the top and this relegates the Board to a relatively minor role."[14] There were signs in the early 1970's of the state board's seeking an enlarged policy-making role, but it remains doubtful whether a governmental arrangement like that in Tennessee permits, much less facilitates, the emergence of a strong state board of education.

Secretary of Education Approach

Another variant of the centralized executive approach has just recently emerged in which all levels of public education are the responsibility of one gubernatorial appointee, the secretary of education. Four states—Pennsylvania, Massachusetts, Virginia, and South Dakota—were using the secretary model in early 1974, and it is being given serious consideration in several others. Because this appears to mark the beginning of a broader trend, given the politicizing forces at work in education, Massachusetts appears among the case study states. EGP also obtained documents for the other three states, and informal interviews were conducted in Pennsylvania and Virginia.[15]

The secretary of education approach, as it was implemented in Pennsylvania, Massachusetts, and Virginia, does exhibit some similar characteristics. The secretary of education (in Massachusetts the title is Secretary of Educational Affairs) is always a member of the governor's cabinet; he is appointed and serves at the pleasure of the chief executive. His responsibilities, in each state, embrace the full spectrum of public education—institutions of higher learning, elementary-secondary schools, and diverse other agencies having a direct relationship to public education. Certain general functions also appear to be common to gubernatorial expectations for this position, including: reporting and recommending needed changes to the governor; providing state-wide advocacy for education; serving as a two-way communication channel between the governor and education agencies; winning legislative support for gubernatorial proposals in education; articulating education with other state services represented on the governor's cabinet; coordinating the activities of various education agencies; conducting studies, developing information systems, and disseminating findings; reviewing agency budgets; and promoting efficiency and economy in education agency programs. These functions, it should be added, are performed in a governmental structure where education policy is enacted by a state board of education, a legislature, and a governor's office. There is a governor-appointed state board in each of the states that has a secretary of education, and that body has formal powers comparable to those of most other state boards. (In Pennsylvania, a single board has had responsibility for all publicly supported education since 1963.)

Though there are some common elements, there also are many differences in the way that states have implemented the secretary of education model, differences that are found chiefly in the authority and staffing of the office. The Secretary of Education in Pennsylvania, clearly the strongest office, has, since 1969, been the cabinet officer for education. He exercises all of the prerogatives of the CSSO position and is, therefore, empowered to act as the chief executive officer of the State Board of Education (see Figure X-3). Like

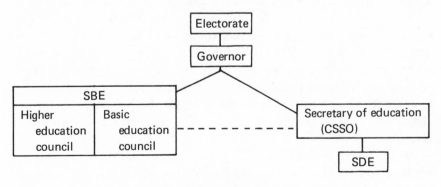

FIGURE X-3
Secretary of Education Model (Pennsylvania)

other CSSO's, he has had the opportunity to play a central role in policy deliberations of the board and to exert line authority over the resources of a large state agency. As long as he retains the confidence of the governor, the secretary commands an unusually powerful position in Pennsylvania. In this connection, Pennsylvania's current Secretary of Education, John C. Pittenger, has stated:

In Pennsylvania's system, if the governor and the secretary of education are on good terms—and the system makes it likely that they will be—the secretary has access to the governor's political power. He can get the governor's support for legislative and budgetary initiatives. He can, when necessary, enlist the governor's assistance in persuading other cabinet officers to do what has to be done. And he can exercise some influence over the governor's policies in fields relating to education, to see to it that they are not inconsistent with his own.[16]

In marked contrast, the Secretary of Education in Virginia, a post created in 1972 as one of six cabinet posts to improve management efficiency in the executive branch, seems to be in a rather tenuous position. Though called upon in a guideline to undertake, among other duties, "close scrutiny of the manner and effectiveness" of the operation of all agencies under the office's jurisdiction,[17] Virginia's secretary is not involved in their administrative direction. ("No effort shall be made to operate the agencies assigned to the Office of Education," reads another part of this guideline for the position.)[18] Nor does the secretary have a CSSO's standing with the State Board of Education, for that status is accorded the State Superintendent of Public Instruction. The secretary in Virginia, when compared with the same official in Pennsylvania, has less access to the information and expertise in the Department of Education and other education agencies. Yet the first secretary in Virginia had little choice but to rely heavily on those sources, for he had virtually no staff resources of his own. Coordination, rather than control or even supervision, appears to be the main objective of the cabinet-level post in Virginia, and marginal status is further suggested by the reluctance of Governor Mills Godwin to fill the position and by the absence of concern other education policy actors display toward this delay.[19]

In its structural outline the secretary's office in Massachusetts resembles that found in Virginia (see Figure X-4), but the position appears to be significantly stronger in Massachusetts, where the secretary has specific statutory authority to perform several major duties

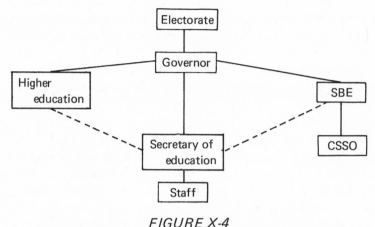

FIGURE X-4

Secretary of Education Model (Massachusetts)

including the power to "conduct comprehensive planning with respect to the functions of said office and coordinate the activities and programs of the state agencies therein," to "conduct studies of the operations of said agencies," to "recommend to the Governor such changes as he shall deem desirable in the laws relating to the organization, structure, efficiency or administrative functions, services, procedures, and practices of any such agency," and to "review and act upon budgetary and other financial matters concerning said agencies."[20] This last power gives the Secretary of Educational Affairs, like other cabinet secretaries, the authority to examine, add, delete, or modify budget requests coming from the agencies within the jurisdiction of the office. This power of budget control was formerly lodged in Massachusetts' Office of Administration and Finance, which still exercises general budget review functions.

To bolster his statutory authority, the first Massachusetts secretary was also provided with staff support. The first secretary was appointed in January 1972 (the act establishing a governor's cabinet had actually been passed in 1969), and within a year a staff of some twenty persons was involved in carrying out the tasks of the office.[21] Central among these, in accord with Governor Francis Sargent's broader thrust toward instituting executive branch reorganization, was the formulation of a plan to restructure the governance of education in the state.[22]

A plan for educational reorganization in Massachusetts in 1973, which proposed sweeping changes at both the state and the regional levels of educational governance, recommended that the secretary's position (to be renamed Secretary of Educational and Cultural Affairs) have substantially enlarged authority.[23] Besides a greater capacity to act on agency budgets and on management and coordination matters, the secretary would play a major role in recruiting state board and regional council members, would sit as a member of the two proposed state policy boards (one for K-12 and one for higher education), and would approve, as the governor's representative, board appointments to the two top administrative positions (Commissioner of Elementary and Secondary Education and Chancellor of Post-Secondary Education). Along with these new responsibilities, the secretary would be empowered to call for the investigation of educational problems at all levels and to design systems to improve citizen participation in education decision making at all levels.

Using an analogy made by Governor Sargent, the secretary would occupy a "middle position" in the proposed reorganization plan, somewhere between a "kind of mild-mannered manager . . . a Clark Kent" and one who "sets staffing ratios for all local school districts . . . a Superman-figure." The plan, in the governor's words, "tries to keep the policy-control in lay boards" and "the supervision and coordination of all the levels of education in the hands of a Cabinet Secretary." In the same vein the governor declared that, unlike all his other reorganized cabinet posts, the Secretary of Educational and Cultural Affairs would have "supervision" but not "control" over education; that "control is a key function left to the governing boards, and to an extent by regional councils."[24]

Despite substantial variation in the way that the secretary of education model has been put into practice, there can be no doubt that the values of centralization are being sought in this approach. In each of the three states there is concern for comprehensive planning and decision making, for coordination among educational programs and between these programs and other public services, for efficiency and economies in program administration, and for effective working relationships between the education agencies and the governor's office. Yet it must be pointed out that all of these states have also continued the governance structure that preceded the creation of a cabinet secretary for education, including a policy-making state board of education.

Retention of the old decentralized state structure probably reflects, perhaps to a large degree, the estimate made by centralized executive supporters of political realities. Even so, the "blend" between new and old, between secretary of education and lay governing boards, can be justified in terms of benefits to be achieved through such a hybrid structure. According to this rationale, best articulated in Massachusetts, the values of a centralized structure are augmented, or made more acceptable, by those associated with lay boards—namely, continuity, representativeness, checks and balances, and insulation against "politics." A strong cabinet secretary, it is argued, does not preclude, but rather contributes to, a strong state board and a strong chief state school officer. The secretary's role is primarily to assist in forging an effective and efficient state partnership in areas like planning, setting priorities, evaluating, and securing resources. Governmental power, the advocates maintain, is not a zero-sum game in which one party gains only if the others lose, and they predict that a mutual strengthening of the different state-level governance components will be one outcome of a secretary of education model.[25]

Opponents of the secretary approach forecast a much different set of consequences. They contend that executive branch centralization is the obvious dynamic in this approach, that its long-run effect will be to diminish the authority of lay boards and their professional administrators. "Centralized authority and governance," writes Ginger, "even in education, will, once permitted, make gradual and inevitable encroachments on the representative decision-making process."[26] Critics also point to the high risks of "political tampering," of enervating conflict between secretary and SBE or CSSO, and of destroying an "independent" power base for education.

That the secretary of education model embodies a centralizing thrust is clear. In fact, the primary initiative in each state for its adoption came from the governor's office. It is because of this emphasis that the model is most appropriately classified under the centralized executive heading. Nevertheless, it is far from certain that instituting a cabinet secretary leads "inevitably" to the demise of the state board and the unchecked concentration of power. It may well be, as Cook suggests, that a secretary of education can help overcome the inherent weaknesses of state boards by assuming functions that the boards do poorly—for instance, monitoring the effectiveness of agency management—while freeing those bodies to engage actively in a policy-making role.[27] In any event, since the model is relatively new and not completely implemented in even the few states where it has been established, persuasive evidence on consequences is not yet available. There is no research-based reason to accept Ginger's negative judgment that "the secretary systems now existing have not brought to those states the changes and improvements it was hoped they would bring."[28] Yet neither can a secretary's recital of his accomplishments be taken as a balanced assessment of effects.[29]

SUMMARY

The rationale behind using centralized executive models for state educational governance rests with the claim that they promote such general decision-making values as accountability, responsiveness, comprehensiveness, and efficiency, as well as with the more pragmatic contention that the best point of access for education, if it is to secure necessary resources, lies in a close relationship with the governor's office. Opponents of such an approach deny that it is consonant with "lay control," that it makes adequate provision for the state-level advocacy of educational programs, or that it maintains stability in education policy making. Critics also claim that a centralized structure opens the door to "politics," restricts accessibility to the decision-making process, and retards the professionalism of the SEA.

Not a single state employs a fully centralized model to govern its schools. In several, however, the chief executive does appoint the CSSO as well as state board members. One such state, Tennessee, was studied by the EGP, and impressions of state educational governance in Tennessee, based on this case study, are: that the governor has greater control over the state education agency there than in other states investigated; that there is a mechanism—hierarchical authority —to prevent prolonged governor-CSSO conflict; that the SEA has historically been a politicized agency, a source of party patronage; that the SBE occupies an unusually weak position.

Another variant of the centralized executive approach has recently emerged—a model in which all public education is under one gubernatorial appointee, the secretary of education. Where this office has been instituted there are some commonalities: the secretary is a member of the governor's cabinet; the responsibilities of the position embrace higher as well as K-12 education; and there are gubernatorial expectations for such functions as reviewing, coordinating, and advocating with respect to state educational programs. Along with these commonalities, there are significant differences in the way that states have established the model, especially concerning the authority and staffing of the office. In Pennsylvania, the secretary is also the CSSO, and top state department personnel are directly responsible to the secretary. In Virginia, by way of contrast, the secretary does not hold the position of CSSO; nor has the office been provided with staff support. Coordination, not control, is the function emphasized in Virginia. In Massachusetts, though he does not exercise the prerogatives of a CSSO, the secretary does have a more powerful position, and he will be even stronger if a proposed plan for the reorganization of educational governance in Massachusetts is adopted. Since the secretary model has only recently been established and exists in just four states, evidence on the consequences of such an approach is not available, or at least it was not at the time of this study.

SECTION II: SEPARATE AGENCY MODELS

COMPETING VALUES

The values that advocates maintain are realized in a semiautonomous status for SEA's have already been set forth as part of the discussion of centralized models. These values, once again, include "lay control," educational program emphasis, insulation from partisan politics, policy-making continuity, and professional competence. Even among those who wish to separate education from the general government structure, however, there are fundamental disagreements, particularly over who should control the SEA. The control question, as typically framed, is twofold: Who should be represented on state boards? What authority should state boards have over the CSSO?

The prevailing ideology of state board representation, obvious from both the normative literature and the comments of educational leaders, is based on two core beliefs. The first is that the duty of a representative is to attend to the general interest, not those of a parochial nature.[30] This Burkean philosophy translates into repeated injunctions that state boards renounce "special interest" representation and act instead as spokesmen for the "people of the state."[31] Related to this is the second belief, namely, that state board officials should be "better" in some ways than those whom they represent, rather than simply mirroring their constituents. It is a constant theme in the prescriptive writings and one that was repeatedly voiced by conference participants that any state board selection procedure is acceptable provided it brings to office the "right sort of people," that is, "people with outstanding ability," "distinguished citizens," "highly competent and dedicated members," "the public spirited," and other worthy candidates. Such people, so the argument goes, are best qualified, with the aid of professionals, to understand the "real" educational needs of the state and to deal constructively with them.

While such beliefs appear to have been widely shared by conference participants, some took issue with the "philosopher king" ideal they saw embodied in them. And a few participants vocally condemned them as being "antidemocratic." These critics interpreted the underrepresentation of various social groups on state boards as being proof of the elitism of the boards and of the fraudulence of the claim that they were "representative bodies." As Sroufe has put it: "How can the boards hope to represent Mexican-Americans, immigrants, blacks, parochial schools, students, and urban systems when its membership includes few of these persons, and more important, when the experiences of these persons are foreign to the backgrounds of the state board men?"[32]

Rejecting the position that a select group of board officials—their competence or virtue notwithstanding—can adequately "represent" the different educational interests in a state, some conference participants urged that these bodies incorporate a diversity of perspectives and a broad base of representation. These participants were particularly concerned about whether disadvantaged and "nonmainstream" persons were effectively represented, for their doctrine of representation holds that a social group will have its interests protected and advanced in the governance process only to the extent that there is "actual representation" (as opposed to "virtual representation") among the decision makers.

Those who wanted the state board to be a forum for the articulation of the education needs of diverse groups were also disturbed by what they perceived to be a lack of accessibility to the electorate. Lengthy terms for board members, along with a narrowly constricted and nearly invisible recruitment process, were looked upon by some conference participants as major obstacles to being responsive to constituents. Other participants, however, declared that there were important values to be realized in having these bodies insulated from the electorate. Continuity in policy making was cited in this regard as was the likelihood that a protected board would be willing to take innovative and forward-looking positions on unpopular issues. Indeed, just as two theories of representation were pitted against each other by conference participants, their remarks also pointed to a conflict between a board's being responsive to its public and a board's taking innovative positions in sensitive areas.

The question of who gives direction to SEA's is partially answered by the approach to the representativeness of state boards that is adopted. But it depends, too, on the relationship between these bodies and CSSO's. For a majority of our conference participants, "lay control" had as its key structural manifestation a state board of education. And, in their view, a board could exercise this responsibility to the people only if it had the power to appoint and remove the CSSO. Any other relationship, it was argued, would result in divided authority and the prospect of state board-CSSO conflict, a disunity that would undermine the effectiveness of the education agency with other policy actors. Many conference participants also expressed dismay over the "politics" they attributed to an independently elected CSSO. In the words of one participant, "election causes the CSSO to be a full-time politician who would have to worry about the political ramifications of each of his actions."

Giving the CSSO an independent base of power to act as "spokesman for education" was championed by a few EGP conference participants. Strengthening the office, they contended, would fix accountability on a "highly visible figure," not on unknown board officials. Additionally, it would guarantee, as much as any structure could, that education would have an effective advocate "to ensure that the state's responsibility for education is fulfilled." Denying the assertion that a popularly elected CSSO, because of political sensitivities, is incapable of offering leadership, proponents claimed that an elected official has the political "clout" required to advance state educational programs. These participants evidently shared the assessment made by California's Wilson Riles, an elected CSSO, at a seminar on educational governance: "Being elected gives a man a constituency. When I talk to the governor, it's as a peer. I got 54% of the vote, just as he did—and he understands that. We don't have to belabor that point. And when I'm talking to legislators or appearing before legislative committees, they understand where I'm coming from."[33] Unlike the critics, the advocates of an independent CSSO saw responsiveness to the electorate as providing both a "mandate for change" and an essential influence resource ("a constituency"), and not as a leadership-inhibiting relationship.

STRUCTURAL VARIATIONS AND EXAMPLES

Whatever the state structure, an SEA does not have the autonomy of a local school district and its governing board. All SEA's must depend on general governance institutions for laws and budgets. Even so, pressure to set education apart structurally from other public services has been strongly felt at the state level. Based on their twelve-state survey in the late 1960's, Usdan and his colleagues concluded that, while there were "various basic structures" of state governance, "they seem to represent different ways of seeking some common objectives, especially the isolation of education from the broader arena of politics, the relief of legislatures and executives from educational responsibility, and the reinforcement and preservation of the influence of the profession in control of the educational system."[34] Three separate agency models—independent regents, the elected state board, and the elected CSSO—will be discussed here. Though distinct in some important ways, these models are alike in that the key education officials, whether state board members or the CSSO, have a base of authority independent of the governor.

Independent Regents Model

Education as a "fourth branch of government" is most closely approximated structurally at the state level by the New York Board of Regents. Both the regents and their chief administrative officer, the Commissioner of Education, are constitutionally established and, by statute, have extensive policy-making, administrative, and judicial authority with respect to all educational services, preschool through senior citizen. The State Education Department (SED), which these officials direct, exists as an "independent body separate and apart" from the governor, the attorney general, and the comptroller, the only other constitutional officers. Party connection does play a part in the "election" of regents by the legislature. As one regent described it, "you become a Regent like a judge, because you know a politician." But the overriding criterion in recruitment has been that the nominated persons have distinguished themselves in public service, that they be "citizens with honor."[35] Once elected, regents are protected from political and public pressures by fifteen-year terms (reduced to seven in 1974) of office, as well as by an apolitical tradition and informal board norms that encourage independence of action. The New York structure is outlined in Figure X-5.

It is evident from the case study that the regents, together with the commissioner, continue to play a central role in state education policy making in New York, though recently there have been "cracks in their pedestal."[36] Further, both friend and foe alike attribute the independence and power of these officials, at least in part, to structural characteristics: the recruitment process for regents, long terms

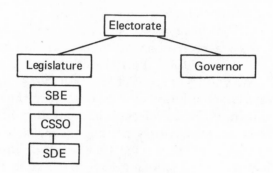

FIGURE X-5
Independent Regents Model (New York)

of office, and the vast legal authority lodged with regents and com-missioner.

Speaking very generally, it appears that the most basic effect of the New York structure, operating in conjunction with a long-estab-lished tradition of being "above politics," has been the insulation of much state education policy making from external pressure. The regents, the commissioner, and the education department have typi-cally enjoyed great freedom in their exercise of authority, including the freedom to take controversial and sometimes unpopular positions on sensitive social-educational issues like school funding and racial desegregation. Such positions in the broader context of a rapid politicization of education have fueled the demand coming from many state legislators, as well as from the governor's office, that the autonomy of the regents and the department be restricted. Among the regents, themselves, there has been discussion of possible struc-tural modifications such as shorter terms of office.[37]

Defenders of the regents maintain that an independent agency, one that is shielded from both partisan politics and transitory shifts in public opinion, is in the best position to identify and articulate state education needs, and to act on those needs in a courageous and forward-looking manner. To prove this contention, supporters often point to the innovative record of education policy making in New York. While many factors may have contributed to this pacesetter status, the state's governance arrangements appear to have fostered independent, comprehensive, and effective advocacy of education, along with a disposition to address policy questions in educational and moral, rather than political, terms. It seems that some insulation of the sort afforded the Board of Regents is a necessary condition for public officials to confront volatile issues and to undertake unpopular courses of action. This has been most apparent in New York in the determined efforts made by the commissioner, strongly backed by the regents, to advance the cause of school desegregation, efforts that at times have aroused intense public controversy.

What to advocates is hailed as the structural capacity for detached, deliberative, and innovative policy making is perceived by critics as promoting an irresponsible "elitism," one that lacks responsiveness to the education public, adaptability to changing needs, and cooperative relationships with other governmental institutions. It is certainly true that regents and the commissioner are not directly accountable to constituents as are elected officials and that lengthy board terms do work against these officials holding the education agency accountable for its policy actions. Moreover, the regents have historically relied upon a closed style of policy making—deliberation in private sessions, with decisions announced in public meetings—that has narrowly constricted visibility and tended to limit access to infrequent formal presentations and the use of established SED channels.[38]

Despite various attempts by the education department and even by the regents to improve their relationships with elected state officeholders, relations are strained, a condition that reflects more basic causes than just communication difficulties, though the latter do exist. Judging from case study data, state legislators have been antagonized not only by the prodesegregation stance of regents and commissioner, but also by recommendations for increased state funding put forward by education officials.[39] From the perspective of tax-conscious lawmakers, the programs proposed by the regents are excessively costly and create "unrealistic" expectations on the part of the education public. And many legislators clearly resent being prodded on the school finance issue by the well-publicized "pronouncements" of the regents. These same concerns, it would seem, have also motivated the governor to seek to extend his influence over educational expenditures. While Governor Rockefeller was forced to abandon his proposal that there be an inspector general for elementary-secondary education, a State Office of Education Performance Review was established in 1973.[40]

As long as elected leaders in New York saw little political currency in extensive involvement with education and had little technical capability to deal with the school issues that confronted them, the autonomy and power of the regents and education department were viewed with widespread approval, not condemnation. But this situation has undergone dramatic, and perhaps fundamental, change in the last decade. Education has become politicized, and politicians have acquired staff support. Though it can be argued that the advantages of an insulated policy-making body are now even more necessary to offset the interest-calculating, short-run perspectives endemic to a highly political milieu, pressure for a more responsive and accountable structure of state educational governance in New York is mounting. Some reduction of regental independence has already occurred as legislators have begun to scrutinize closely the political ideology of candidates, especially on the busing issue, and have restricted by law (1974) the term of new appointees to seven years. And further erosion as a consequence of further politicization of education is to be anticipated.[41]

Elected State Board Model

An independent regents model for the governance of elementary-secondary education exists only in New York and even in that state it is obvious that the model is under increasing attack. A much more prevalent version of the separate agency approach is one in which considerable policy-making authority is delegated to the SEA, the authority being exercised by a popularly elected state board and a chief state school officer selected by the board. This model, which parallels the structural arrangement of most local school districts, is depicted in Figure X-6.

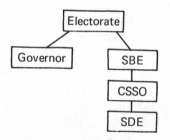

FIGURE X-6
Elected State Board Model

Since World War II there has been a marked trend toward using popular election as the device for board member recruitment and giving those officials power to appoint and remove the CSSO. Surprisingly enough, in 1948 not one state was following this pattern; by 1972 it had become established in eleven states.[42] Giving support to this movement was the policy position adopted by the Council of Chief State School Officers in 1944, a position maintained until 1965 when that organization reverted to being neutral on the subject. The council's position during the twenty-year period that it supported this movement called for a state educational governance structure where:

there should be a nonpartisan lay state board of education of seven to twelve able citizens, broadly representative of the general public and unselfishly interested in public education, elected by the people . . . for long overlapping terms without pay. It is desirable that the boards select the chief state school officer . . . and determine his compensation and his term of office.[43]

While nonpartisan election was proposed by the council, in most states where this model is currently employed members of the state board are chosen on a partisan ballot.

In assessing the elected state board model, it is instructive to examine comparative data, rather than relying on observations and judgments confined to single state examples. There is evidence relevant to the question of formal selection—popular election versus gubernatorial appointment—and whether it affects board member behavior. Most commentators who have provided normative answers to this question have assumed that selection method does make a difference. Yet research, including EGP research, casts doubt upon this assumption.

EGP data permit comparisons between elected state boards and appointed state boards on an array of variables. In the sample there are four boards where members are popularly elected, five boards where officials are appointed by the governor, and one board where the legislature selects the members. (Information on the number of board officials from each state who responded to interview schedules is contained in Table I-3.) The greatest concern here is with elected-appointed state board comparisons with respect to representativeness, decision style, and policy-making influence. Analysis with respect to the last of these is fully presented in Chapter II (see particularly Figures II-1 and 2 and Table II-12). The conclusion was

that, while elected boards were generally perceived as having somewhat more influence than appointed boards, this perception can
probably be attributed to the fact that all four of the elected boards
appoint their CSSO, a power that three of the five appointed state
boards lack.

There is a contention, often suggested in the literature, that an
elected state board is more insulated from political interference than
one with members appointed by the governor. Neither an investigation of specific decision processes nor questioning of board members
bore this out. Board members interviewed were asked whether
"political figures ever became involved in school issues in which the
state board had the authority to make the decision." Some 58 percent of the elected board respondents answered "yes," but so did a
nearly identical percentage (57) of appointed officials. When asked
to identify the political figures who became so involved, 58 percent
of the elected members, as against 52 percent of the appointed members, named state legislators. The data indicate, then, that board
member perceptions of political interference do not vary by selection
method. Instead, they seem to depend primarily on whether a state
has a legislature that has become, for whatever reason, active in
school policy making. In states like Colorado, Michigan, Massachusetts, and California, the common complaint of board officials is that
"the legislature is always threatening to pass bills, or actually passing
them, in areas of legitimate board action." For these board members
the legislature as the "big school board" is an ever-present reality.

Representativeness of state boards. In analyzing the concept of
representation, Pitkin defines a representative body as one "acting in
the interests of the represented, in a manner responsive to them."[44]
As for "acting in the interests of the represented," the social background of state board officials, regardless of the selection method, is
so homogeneous and upper-middle class that their capacity to represent different segments of the public is suspect. Data on selected
demographic characteristics of state board members are reported in
Table X-1. They show the typical board official among our respondents to be white (94 percent), male (75 percent), and middle aged
(84 percent are forty-one years of age or older). His occupation is to
be found in business or the professions (70 percent). He is affluent
(51 percent earn over $30,000 annually) and is almost certain to be
well educated (92 percent are college graduates; 58 percent hold an

TABLE X-1 Selected Demographic Characteristics of State Board
Respondents (in percentages)

	SBE respondents		
Characteristics	Total (N = 64)[a]	Appointed (N = 30)	Elected (N = 27)
Personal			
Male	75	70	78
White	94	90	96
Age 41 or above	84	80	85
Income			
15,000 or more	91	92	86
30,000 or more	51	46	45
Education			
College degree	92	87	96
Graduate degree	58	57	59
Occupation			
Business owners, officials, and managers	28	29	23
Professionals	42	39	45
Professional education experience			
Yes	47	43	55
No	53	57	45

[a]Includes seven respondents from the New York Board of Regents.

advanced degree). Elected board members do not differ appreciably
on any of these attributes from appointed board members.

That SBE's should be composed of lay persons is a point accepted
without dispute by those who have written about these bodies. But,
as is shown in Table X-1, such a prescription is at odds with the background of nearly half (47 percent) of the board members in the EGP
sample, for these officials indicated that classroom teaching, school
administration, or some other professional educator experience had
been part of their career pattern. This is somewhat truer of elected
board members (55 percent) than of appointed board members (43
percent).

Whatever else may be said about the representative nature of state
boards, it is obvious that the demographic characteristics of board
members do not come close to mirroring the characteristics of their

publics. Of course, there is no reason to believe that they would. Studies have long since invalidated the "log cabin" theory of political recruitment.[45] Still, state board members do seem to be more disproportionately drawn from the upper strata of American society than, say, local school board members.[46] While the mere categorical representation of a group by a public official should not be taken to mean that he or she will automatically advocate its values, it is hard to believe that such affiliations do not count at all or that state boards are not more accessible and responsive to those with similar socioeconomic backgrounds than they are to those with vastly different life experiences.[47]

Turning now to "acting . . . in a manner responsive to them [that is, to constituents]," the research that has been done on *local* school boards indicates that these bodies do not represent the public so much as they legitimate administrator policies. Local board members, Zeigler concludes from a survey of a national sample of school districts, "lacking a meaningful relationship to an external political constituency, fall easy prey to the superintendent's claim for 'expertise.' "[48] This deference, Zeigler argues, is augmented by the fact that local board officials are recruited largely from civic and business worlds where efficiency and conflict avoidance are central values.

To examine state board members' conceptions of their representational role, three Likert-type items were included in the questionnaire that interviewees were asked to complete. The three items, the replies indicating an external constituency orientation, and the percentage of board members who gave these replies—all are shown in Table X-2.

As can be seen from Table X-2, approximately half (49 percent) of all board respondents agreed that a public official should work for what his constituents want, even if this should conflict with the official's own views. The other board members (51 percent) signified by their disagreement that a representative's personal convictions ought to have priority. On whether the advice of experts should be followed in making policy, the board member respondents were much more in accord. Only one out of five (21 percent) reacted negatively to this statement. A brokerage role for state boards—that is, seeking compromises among competing interests—again divided our respondents, 51 percent seeing this as their "central task" and 49 percent rejecting this role prescription. The brokerage role statement did

TABLE X-2 State Board Respondents' Representational Role
              Orientation (in percentages)

| Statement | Constituency oriented response | SBE respondents | | |
		Total (N = 64)[a]	Appointed (N = 30)	Elected (N = 27)
"A public official's first duty is to work for what most of his constituents want even though this may not agree with his personal views."	Agree	49	53	48
"The central task of a policy maker is to seek compromises among conflicting interests."	Agree	51	33	67
"Whenever possible, a policy maker should follow the advice of acknowledged experts in the making of important decisions."	Disagree	21	17	19

[a] Includes seven respondents from the New York Board of Regents.

produce a substantial difference in responses between elected board members and appointed board members. Some two-thirds (67 percent) of the first group agreed with the statement compared with only one-third (33 percent) of the appointed officials. This differential response is what one would predict from democratic theory in which elections are assumed to be related to responsiveness. The other two statements, it should be noted, did not elicit such a division.

Does the decision-making behavior of state boards of education reflect interest representation—that is, a responsiveness to the particularistic demands of geographic sections, social classes, or organized groups? Or, does this behavior reflect conformity, at least outwardly, to the norm that a state's officials should attempt to represent equally all the people in that jurisdiction? The board members interviewed were questioned as to whether any person on their board acted as "the spokesman" for geographic sections or racial-ethnic groups. Board member responses to this question (see Table X-3)

TABLE X-3 State Board Respondents' Perceptions of Interest Representation (in percentages)

| | SBE respondents | | |
Question and response categories	Total (N = 72)[a]	Appointed (N = 38)	Elected (N = 26)
"Are there members of the state board who feel that they should be the spokesman on the board for particular geographic sections or racial-ethnic groups in the state?"			
"No" (none)	53	55	54
"Just a few"	26	29	19
"Most"	8	3	12
"Nearly all"	13	13	15

[a]Includes eight respondents from the New York Board of Regents.

indicate that more than half (53 percent) believed that none of their colleagues engaged in this form of representational behavior, 26 percent said that "just a few" did so, and only 21 percent saw this kind of representation being acted upon by "most" (8 percent) or "nearly all" (13 percent) of the members of their boards. Although elected boards and appointed boards were almost identical in the large percentage of officials who denied the occurrence of interest representation, and in the small percentage who replied that it involved nearly all board members, there were minor differences in the other categories of response, with the elected boards being slightly higher than the appointed boards.

It is usually assumed that the method of selection for a public office is linked to the representational behavior of its incumbent. Specifically, it is assumed that elections "are crucial processes for insuring the political leaders will be somewhat responsive to the preferences of some ordinary citizens."[49] Yet our data on attitudes toward external constituencies, as well as on perceptions of actual interest representation, suggest that elected board members are not much more responsive than appointed board members, though the former did embrace in substantially larger numbers (by 34 percentage points) the importance of the brokerage role in policy making. One important reason, perhaps, why elected state boards do not differ greatly from appointed state boards in their representational role is to be found in the process by which the elected officials are actually recruited to office. There is considerable evidence to the effect that school board elections, whether state or local, are bland, noncompetitive affairs in which policy issues are avoided, public involvement is slight, and candidate exertions are minimal.[50] If this is the case, then the election mechanism is not likely to have the results predicted by democratic theory, including that of board members' being attentive to external constituencies.

Decision style of state boards. Previous research on state boards has revealed only a few behavioral differences between members who are elected and those who are appointed. Indeed, there has been only one rather constant finding—elected state boards experience more conflict in decision making than appointed state boards. Sroufe, in the late 1960's, conducted a national survey of state board members (67 percent responded to his mailed questionnaire), focusing on the self-role expectations of these officials. In his data, "the only statistically significant differences between elected and appointed board members were that elected board men assumed greater responsibility for establishing maximum standards as opposed to minimum standards, and elected members anticipate less unanimity regarding board decisions than appointed members."[51] Cox did a study in 1971 that compared an elected state board (New Mexico) with an appointed one (Arizona) with respect to the number of decisions by function enacted by these bodies over a six-year period. He found that the percentage distributions of decisions over the functional categories were about the same for both boards, causing him to conclude that "method of selection . . . apparently had little or no effect on the functioning of these boards." Yet Cox also discovered, consistent with one of Sroufe's findings, that the decision process of the two boards differed markedly. "It appears," he observed, "that a board selected by the people is much more prone to have split decisions. . . ."[52]

To pursue further the relationship between election as the means of state board selection and the presence of conflict in state board decision making, board member interviewees were asked about the extent of agreement on their state board when it confronted a major policy issue. Our question, the five response categories, and the distribution of board member replies are presented in Table X-4. These

TABLE X-4 State Board Respondents' Assessment of the Extent of Agreement on Their State Board (in percentages)

	SBE respondents		
Question and response categories	Total $(N = 73)^a$	Appointed $(N = 38)$	Elected $(N = 26)$
"Which one of these statements comes closest to describing the agreement on your board when it decides a major policy issue?"			
Board is harmonious, little serious disagreement.	7	8	7
Board is usually in agreement, but there are board members who sometimes dissent.	53	61	35
Board often is divided but the lines of division depend on the issue that is confronting the board.	33	21	50
Board tends to divide into rival factions of nearly equal strength.	5	11	0
Board tends to divide into rival factions, but there's a clear working majority on the board.	3	0	8

[a] Includes nine respondents from the New York Board of Regents.

data disclose some contrasts between elected and appointed board members. Some 69 percent of the appointed members, as against 42 percent of those who were elected, checked one of the first two alternatives, indicating that their boards employed a basically consensual approach to policy issues. Conversely, exactly one-half of the elected officials said issue-by-issue disagreements prevailed on their boards. Such a pluralistic pattern of issue cleavages was pointed to by less than one-quarter (21 percent) of the appointed board members. The two groups were quite similar in their perceptions of factional alignments; only 8 percent of the elected respondents, compared with 11 percent of the appointed respondents, saw such a division on their board.

If appointed state boards experience more agreement and less conflict than elected state boards in dealing with policy issues, as EGP data along with Sroufe's and Cox's suggest, then what implications does this have for the decision-making process? A consensual style does enable a state board to move expeditiously through crowded agendas in a manner that reduces controversy and vulnerability to external groups. It also permits a state board to act in a unified manner in advancing a policy proposal in the legislature. The three state boards in the EGP sample—Nebraska, California, and Michigan—that were most divided were perceived by numerous lawmakers in those states as being hampered by their disunity in effectively advocating a board position on education legislation. But while clearly an influence resource in some ways, a stress on internal cohesion and on a consensual decision-making style does have its shortcomings in others. Because it seeks to avoid or suppress conflict, such a style does not encourage the generation or searching examination of policy options, at least at the state board level. Consequently, it is not a style, by its nature, that is conducive to board member control, as opposed to bureaucratic control, of policy making.[53]

To summarize the findings on elected versus appointed boards, there are positive relationships in the data between the election method of selection and the constituency orientation, interest representation, and conflictual decision making of state boards. None of these relationships, though, is very strong. And the finding that the four elected boards were widely viewed as being more influential in their policy systems than the five appointed boards is probably accounted for by the fact that three of the latter lack control over their CSSO. In all, the differences that might reasonably be ascribed to selection method seem small, almost inconsequential, when compared to the similarities between most elected and most appointed state boards, especially in terms of social class composition and perceived lack of influence as education policy makers.

Elected Chief Model

One additional model should be included under the separate agency classification, even though it normally has a governor-

appointed state board as a component, and that is the state governance structure where the key education official is a constitutionally
established and popularly elected chief state school officer. In the
early 1900's this was the most popular approach (in 1920, thirty-
four states had elected CSSO's); by 1972 the number of states employing the model had dropped to nineteen. In its most prevalent
form, a policy-making state board of education, appointed by the
governor, is a part of this arrangement (see Figure X-7). But in five

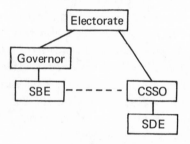

FIGURE X-7
Elected Chief Model

states board members are chosen by other means, and in one state
there is no state board. In all cases, however, constitutional status
and popular election give the CSSO an independent base of policy-
making influence.

In the EGP sample four states have an elected chief: California,
Florida, Georgia, and Wisconsin. Of these, California and Georgia
have governor-appointed state boards. In Florida this body is comprised of ex officio members, and there is no state board in Wisconsin. The CSSO is an appointed official in eight states: Colorado,
Massachusetts, Michigan, Minnesota, Nebraska, New York, Tennessee, and Texas. In seven of these, the state board selects the chief,
but in Tennessee the CSSO is appointed by and is responsible to the
governor. The chief state school officer in each of the twelve states
was interviewed, and other respondents were questioned about the
CSSO, respondents such as legislative leaders, governors' staffs, state
board members, and educational interest group representatives (see
again Table I-3). Unlike the situation with state boards, there is no

previous empirical research on which to base a discussion of CSSO's. From EGP analyses, however, a number of comparisons involving elected versus appointed chiefs can be made. Two of the comparisons, one focusing on selected characteristics of CSSO's and a second having to do with their policy-making influence, received detailed attention in Chapter III. Some of the findings pertinent to the consideration of an elected chief model will be reviewed here.

Personal and professional characteristics. All twelve incumbents at the time of the EGP study were male, ten white and two black (the only blacks, it should be noted, among all fifty CSSO's). The average age was 46.8 years. There was no appreciable difference in terms of sex, ethnicity, and age between elected and appointed officials considered as groups. This was not the case when it came to the in-state and rural identification of CSSO's (see Table III-2). The elected officials consistently indicated somewhat greater in-state identification (an overall percentage of 71 as against 54) and rural identification (an overall percentage of 75 as against 44) than did their appointed counterparts.

There were also data on the recruitment routes to the position of chief state school officer (see Table III-2). Nine of the twelve CSSO's had been public school teachers; seven had been public school principals; four had served as subordinate administrators in a district central office; eight had been public school superintendents; four had held positions in higher education. The most marked difference between elected and appointed CSSO's was that none of the former had served either as a central office administrator (other than superintendent) or in higher education, compared with 50 percent of the appointed officials for each of these positions. In analyzing the data further, it was found that only two of the twelve CSSO's had ever held nonpublic school positions as part of their career pattern, and both of these had also been teachers and principals at one time. Recent attempts to recruit administrative talent from such fields as business, law, and public administration to top education posts were not reflected in the recruitment routes of the twelve CSSO's, regardless of selection method. Besides obtaining some general information on the careers of the twelve CSSO's, attention was directed to the position each held immediately prior to his selection as chief. In seven states the CSSO had been recruited from within the state department of education. In three of the other five cases the state board had sought persons outside the department who were or had been district superintendents. In the last two cases governors had become involved, one reportedly encouraging a CSSO candidate to run for that office and the other, who had the power of appointment, selecting a district superintendent. Thus, it would appear that the main career routes to becoming a CSSO are: state department service, a public school superintendency, or some combination of the two. Moreover, in only one state was the new CSSO recruited from beyond state boundaries. Seven at the time of their selection were true insiders, recruited from the state department staff, and the remaining four were insiders in the sense of holding a superintendency in the same state. While appointment as the CSSO selection method may permit, as its sponsors claim, a nation-wide search for the best-qualified person, this search in the eight states using this method nearly always culminated in the choice of someone close to home.

Policy-making influence. One important finding having to do with CSSO selection method and policy-making influence has already been discussed: state boards that do not appoint the chief are all near the bottom with respect to influence. This does not mean that weak boards automatically make for strong CSSO's or vice versa. The statistical association between state board influence and CSSO influence, to the extent one appears to exist, is not an inverse one.

Of central interest was whether elected CSSO's were more influential in education policy making, especially with elected officials like legislators and governors, than appointed CSSO's. The argument for an elected chief, it will be recalled, banks heavily on the contention that a CSSO selected in this manner, because he speaks for a voting constituency, is likely to be a more effective advocate for education than one who is appointed. To assess the influence of chiefs in their respective legislative arenas, the judgments of the other major actors in these arenas—legislative leaders, governors and their staffs, and educational interest group spokesmen—were sought. The replies that were used to develop legislative influence scores for the CSSO's are reported in Table III-12, along with average rankings on the legislative influence index used. Reviewing these discloses that elected CSSO's were seen by other actors in their legislative arenas as being more influential than appointed CSSO's. (Elected officials have a higher average ranking, 4.25 as against 7.00, than those appointed.)

But the differences were not great. And of the four CSSO's ranked at the top in overall legislative influence, two had been appointed by the state board (Texas and Michigan) and two had been popularly elected (Georgia and California). All chiefs holding the bottom four positions in this rank order had, however, been selected through appointment.

Along with the CSSOs' influence on educational legislation, their influence on policies enacted by the state education agency was also examined. Unlike the legislative arena, where some chiefs are perceived to be powerful actors but others are seen as having only marginal impact, the CSSO is nearly always the dominant figure in the agency arena. State board members expect the chief to provide leadership on policy questions. The chief sets the agenda and controls the information going to the board. Board members seldom oppose the CSSO on major issues. Indeed, the typical board gives the chief little direction, and the direction that is given appears to be gentle and infrequent. In short, while formal authority to determine education policy is usually lodged with the state board and the CSSO is largely dependent on that body for authority, the actual flow of dependence and influence in policy making tends to be just the reverse of that posited in law.

Based on the perceptions of state board members, CSSO's, and educational interest group leaders, plus the case study data, an index of the policy-making influence of chiefs in the state education agency arena was constructed to rank CSSO's (see Table III-17). When completed, it showed only a slight correlation between CSSO selection method and agency influence, a correlation that favored the appointment method. (The average ranking for appointed chiefs is 5.5; for elected officials, 7.3.) It is somewhat surprising that there is no statistical relationship (rho = $-.02$) between CSSO legislative influence and influence in the education agency. That is, a chief may have great influence in both arenas, in neither arena, some influence in both, or great influence in one but little in the other. The data simply show no association between the two types of influence.

The three state boards in the EGP sample that lacked the authority to appoint the CSSO were particularly weak in their perceived policy-making influence, but this does not mean that such boards are always associated with powerful chiefs. On the contrary, there is a positive correlation of moderate size (rho = $.45$) between the rank order of states based on board policy-making influence and the rank order based on CSSO influence in the agency arena. This suggests that both boards and chiefs can have influence; it does not sustain the notion that a strong board will have a weak chief or that a strong chief will have a weak board. To be sure, there appear to be examples of both in the data. Still, these do not reflect the typical relationship. Influence in the state education arena does not exist in some fixed amount so that one actor gains only at the expense of another; many actors may exert influence in this arena. Finally, it can be argued from other data that one way to help the board, as well as the chief, become an important policy actor is to let the board select its own chief. Appointive chiefs, for example, more frequently solicit ideas from board members. They also have more freedom to select and discharge their own staff members, a condition essential to an effective organization. Evidently state boards are more disposed to allow a chief the freedom to form his or her own team when that official is a person of their selection.

SUMMARY

This section began with an observation that, even among those who contend that the state education agency should be separated structurally from other executive departments, there is disagreement about who shall control education at the state level. In the prevailing view of state board representation, this body is seen as a deliberative one where the "most competent people" act for all segments of the public. Consistent with this view is the belief that the state board should be insulated not only from general governance institutions but also from the electorate. The counter philosophy is that the diverse education interests of a state should be "actually" represented on state boards and that these bodies should be forums where competing interests can be articulated and accommodated in the policy-making process. The responsiveness of board officials to constituent sentiments, as opposed to their own or a professional's definition of educational need, is an integral part of this philosophy. A second aspect of agency control involves the authority relationship between the state board and the CSSO. Most conference participants, like most commentators in the literature, wanted the board to be able to appoint and remove the chief, this power to be exercised in the name of lay control, organizational efficiency, education leadership, and removing the SEA from politics. Yet an independent CSSO had proponents who argued that an elected status creates both appropriate agency responsiveness to the public and the political "clout" necessary to wield effective influence in decision-making arenas like the legislature and governor's office.

The first separate agency model described was the independent regents approach, as exemplified by the state structure in New York. This structure, headed by a powerful Board of Regents and Commissioner of Education, has over the years shielded education policy making from constituent and political pressures, and it has encouraged an independent, comprehensive, apolitical response to educational issues. But the rapid politicization of education in New York has been accompanied by mounting criticism of the regents by elected state officials, who contend with some reason that this structure discourages accountability and responsiveness, limits accessibility to the public, and retards adaptability to changing conditions. Regental "pronouncements" on school finance and vigorous enforcement actions by the commissioner, backed by regents, on school desegregation have particularly roused the ire of elected officials. The legislature has begun to give close scrutiny to the political viewpoints of nominees to the Board of Regents and, in 1974, it reduced the term of newly elected members from fifteen to seven years. In the meantime, the governor established an Office of Education Performance Review to provide an outside assessment of state expenditures and performance in education. Clearly, there is increased conflict in the state structure for educational governance in New York and the independent regents model is under attack.

The next separate agency model presented had as its essential feature an elected state board. Comparative data were drawn upon to provide evidence on the consequences of this model. In particular, elected versus appointed board comparisons were made with respect to representativeness, decision style, and policy-making influence. In terms of representativeness, appointment and election procedures had almost identical results in producing board members with the following personal characteristics: white, middle-aged or older, business or professional occupation, high income, and extensive formal education. Stated differently, neither selection method led to state boards that, in terms of demographic composition, represented more than a narrow spectrum of the public. Both did, though, recruit to these "lay" bodies a substantial number of persons with professional educator experience: 55 percent of EGP's elected board respondents and 43 percent of the appointed ones had such experience. Neither the biographical data nor state board behavior indicate that able persons are more likely to be obtained through one selection method rather than the other. Both methods seemed to have the same effect in terms of the kind of people recruited to state board offices.

There were some differences between elected and appointed boards in their perceived responsiveness to external constituents. Elected officials were slightly more likely to be perceived as speaking for particular geographic or racial-ethnic groups, but most board members interviewed, regardless of mode of selection, denied that this sort of interest representation characterized their board. Twice as many elected board member respondents as appointed board member respondents (67 percent to 33 percent) agreed with the role description that their central task was to seek accommodations among conflicting interests. Such findings hardly constitute strong evidence. Yet, taken together, they point to the conclusion that elected state boards are somewhat more responsive to external constituencies than their appointed counterparts are. This difference is, however, far smaller than would be predicted from democratic theory, a condition that might be explained in part by the lack of competitiveness in state board election campaigns.

In a consideration of state board decision style, EGP data were consistent with the earlier findings of Sroufe and Cox. Elected boards were rated by their members as having a lower level of agreement than the comparable rating provided by appointed board members, though a consensual style tended to prevail on both kinds of boards. Elected boards, if the respondents are to be believed, experience somewhat more issue-by-issue conflict in the enactment of policy than do appointed boards. Such conflict, while reducing a board's capacity to move efficiently through agenda items and increasing its vulnerability to external groups, probably does give board members a greater voice in the policy-making process than does a consensual style of decision making.

As for the policy-making influence of the ten state boards studied, these bodies, whether elected or appointed, were typically minor participants in such a process. The boards, perceived as having little influence in the legislative arena, were overshadowed by the CSSO when it came to agency policy making. The elected boards, as a group, were given higher influence ratings by other actors in their policy systems than the appointed boards, but perhaps this was because three of the five appointed state boards lacked the authority to appoint their chief, rather than because of any difference in influence between elected and appointed boards directly attributable to selection method.

The final model considered under the separate agency classification features a constitutionally established and popularly elected chief state school officer. Again, the election and appointment methods of selection were compared, this time in relation to selected biographical data about the CSSO's and their policy-making influence in both the legislative and the state education agency arenas. The first thing to stress in reviewing the biographical differences between elected and appointed CSSO's is that there were some. Notably, elected chiefs indicated more in-state and rural identification than appointed chiefs. Such differences do not, however, loom large in comparison with the similarities in personal and professional characteristics between the two groups of officials in the EGP sample.

As for policy-making influence, different findings about elected versus appointed chiefs indicate that election does give a CSSO a modest means of influence in the legislative arena—a voting constituency—that cannot be claimed by an appointed official. Such a resource does not in itself ensure influence. Much depends on the energy and the skill of the chief. Not all of the elected CSSO's in the sample had substantial influence in legislative policy making for the public schools, but some clearly did. On the other hand, so did a few appointed chiefs, indicating that an elected status is not the only important resource. Formal authority, information-generating capacity, and the ability to inspire trust are other important ones. As for CSSO influence in the state education agency arena, an influence quite distinct from that commanded in the legislative arena, it bore little relationship to selection method. Where CSSO's are selected independent of state board control, either by gubernatorial appointment or by popular election, these bodies are weakened in their policy-making influence. Yet a powerful chief does not necessarily mean an impotent board. Quite the contrary, EGP data show a positive relationship between the influence of the board and the chief, suggesting that both can play an important role in the education policy system.

SECTION III: COMBINATION MODEL

COMPETING VALUES

The values attributed to a centralized executive, as well as those attributed to an SEA having a semiautonomous status, were discussed earlier. A combination model that many regional conference participants saw as a "good compromise" among competing values is one in which the governor's appointive power extends to state board members, but not to the CSSO, who is responsible only to the board.

In the estimation of proponents, such a combination of features ensures the governor a "voice" in the school policies determined by agency officials. And the appointment link between the state board and the governor's office is seen as contributing to the attainment of objectives associated with centralization, objectives such as comprehensive planning, coordination among state services, and access to gubernatorial resources. Progress is to be made toward these objectives, so the argument goes, without the SEA coming "under the governor's thumb." Rather, the intent of the combination model is to bring education "close to the governor but not too close." Supporters believe that enough separation can be built into this governance structure—for example, by constitutional as well as statutory provision for the state board, by lengthy and overlapping terms for board members, and by formal control over the CSSO—to establish the SEA as its own policy-making arena, one shielded to a substantial degree from both politician and constituency pressure. Such insulation, according to several conference participants, enables the state board and its chief to make "courageous decisions" on controversial policy questions. Moreover, the presence of an authoritative state board in this structure was pointed to by these participants as promoting continuity of membership, "lay" involvement in decision making, and a check on excessive executive influence.

In addition to a best-of-both-worlds kind of argument, supporters of the combination model maintained that "governors tend to pick higher-quality people for appointments, and these officials are usually better qualified than those we elect." The belief that appointment, as opposed to election, yields able and disinterested board members was frequently voiced during EGP regional conferences. Correspondingly, much political negativism was directed toward the electoral process as the device for state board selection. "Good" candidates, it was said, could not be induced to run for this office. Instead, "special pleaders" and "defenders of particular interests" would be recruited to the state board, with the "welfare of the state as a whole" being neglected.

Sharp criticism of this combination approach was expressed by both separate agency and centralized executive advocates. From the viewpoint of the former, the inclusion of gubernatorial appointive power in the model renders it vulnerable to political intrusions. Governors, it was asserted, often choose "party hacks" and political campaigners for top posts; a few participants went so far as to claim that gubernatorial appointment must result "ultimately" in gubernatorial control of state board policy. Participants who espoused the election of board members attacked the combination model primarily because it does not have, in their judgment, any "direct line of accountability" between the SEA and the public, and, hence, is unlikely to be responsive to public concerns. "When accountability becomes diffuse, it is lost," remarked one critic.

On the other hand, several central executive advocates contended that merely to grant governors appointive power in state board selection is far from sufficient to cope with the problems of policy-making fragmentation, duplication of effort, and absence of political accountability. One prominent state education official detailed his objections to a "sanitized" combination model as follows:

duplication of planning effort (also of computers, printing units, etc.);

possible resistance to efforts of the governor's office to link education with health and other human resources agencies;

legislative program may be competitive with governor's;

may resist reform efforts of either governor or legislature.[54]

From the perspective of this official, the secretary of education model, not the combination model, represents the true compromise between the competing values of a centralized executive and lay governing boards.

STRUCTURAL EXAMPLE

In two models described earlier in this chapter, a combination of structural features is readily apparent. One of these, the secretary of education model, appears to have a centralized executive emphasis, while the second, the elected chief model, qualifies for a separate agency classification. For these reasons only one combination model is discussed.

Governor-Appointed Authoritative Board Model

As of 1972, the most commonly used (in fourteen states) structure for state education governance that reflected a combination approach might have been called the "governor-appointed authoritative board model."[55] It featured a governor-appointed state board of education that had substantial policy-making authority and the power to select and remove the CSSO (see Figure X-8). It should be added that the governor's authority to make board appointments was

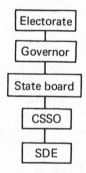

FIGURE X-8
Governor-Appointed Authoritative Board Model

usually subject to restrictions. Board members served fixed terms, terms that in practice were always staggered and often exceeded the governor's in length. Confirmation of state board appointments by one or both houses of the legislature was a frequent requirement. Furthermore, stipulations in law usually called for geographic representation and sometimes for party balance. The thrust of this model, judging from these features, was not only to link the governor's office structurally with the SEA, but also to design this linkage in a way that would curtail gubernatorial influence in agency policy making.

Appointed versus elected board comparisons, described and summarized earlier in this chapter, will not be restated here. Two additional points do warrant some discussion. The first has to do with the responsiveness and innovative capacity of appointed state boards, and the second deals with the influence that such boards have with governors.

Responsiveness and innovation. Insight into the relationship between responsiveness and selection method is afforded by the case study data on the desegregation issue. These data suggest that board officials whose security of tenure is protected either by very lengthy terms or by appointed status are the most willing to take unpopular actions. This willingness to undertake what supporters proclaim to be "morally right" positions is evident in the way that school desegregation has been confronted in the states studied. The four state boards —New York, Massachusetts, Minnesota, and California (until the last reversed its policy in 1970)—that have taken definite steps over the years to establish or at least to support a state-level desegregation policy are all insulated to some degree from the electorate. The protected status of the New York Board of Regents has already been described, and the other three boards are all appointed bodies. Insulation does not ensure innovative policy in controversial areas, but a structure that shields board members from external pressures does, if the desegregation issue is a valid test, increase the probability of such policy. It is, however, the board and the chief who must ultimately decide what is to be done.

Zeigler, after examining efforts to reform local school governance arrangements, observed that "for those who want responsiveness, it is taken on faith that a school which is responsive to client demands will, at the same time, be experimental and innovative, thus leading to an improvement in the quality of education." Reacting to the optimism of these reformers, Zeigler raised the specter that "the demand of innovation and responsiveness may be in conflict."[56] EGP data suggest that a dilemma of this sort confronts those who seek to design state structures for educational governance.

Influence with governor. In the findings on state board influence there is one big surprise, this being that governor-appointed boards were seen as having less influence with the chief executive than popularly elected ones. Because this finding contradicts one of the principal arguments for an appointed board, some explanation is in order.

Perceptions of board members toward state board-governor relationships are contained in Table X-5. Only about half (51 percent) of

TABLE X-5 State Board-Governor Relationships as Perceived by
Board Member Respondents and Persons in the
Governor's Office (in percentages)

Relationship measure	All state boards[a] (N = 10)	Elected state boards (N = 4)	Appointed state boards (N = 5)
Board members (N = 72) responding that their board had a "direct working relationship" with the governor or his staff	51	58	37
Board members (N = 71) who believed they had a "means of influence" with the governor	38	41	24
Governors' personal staff (N = 29)[b] rating the state board as an "important source of ideas and advice" for the governor's office	38	46	36

[a]Includes New York in addition to the four elected and five appointed boards.

[b]Includes the governor in six states.

all board member respondents looked upon their state board as having any sort of "direct working relationship with the governor or his staff." Contrary to the conventional wisdom on this subject, 58 percent of the elected board officials, compared with 37 percent of those who were gubernatorial appointees, indicated such a relationship. Just 38 percent of the board members interviewed believed that they had "any means" to influence the governor. Again, the percentage is higher for elected officials than for appointed ones (41 percent as against 24 percent).

Governor's office respondents also were questioned about their assessment of the state board. They were asked to compare board members with other persons as a "source of ideas and advice for the governor's office." Their replies, also reported in Table X-5, show that less than 40 percent considered the state board to be an "important source." And, as with the other perceptions, elected boards were evaluated somewhat more positively than appointed boards, 46 percent of the interviewees rating the former as important versus 36 percent for the boards that the governors had appointed. Clearly, gubernatorial appointment of state board members does not guarantee a close association between this body and the governor's office; in the states studied, the opposite was more often the case.

That appointment by the governor and access to that official were not related for the state boards examined was an unexpected finding. Persons on the governor's staff were widely perceived by both board members and outside observers to be the key influentials in recommending nominees to the chief executive for board appointment. Once the appointment had been made, however, the governor traditionally adopted a "hands off" policy toward the state board, a reflection undoubtedly of either lack of saliency to him or the risks involved in challenging the societal norm that the schools should be kept free from "politics." Just as the governor did not seek to exert much influence in state board affairs, so members of that body had little access to his office. As one board member put it, "we go our separate ways after the appointment." And, as for the boards, their isolation from the governor and from other political leaders was reflected in their lack of influence.

Just as fieldwork for EGP was reaching its conclusion (early 1973), there were signs of expanded governor-state board contacts in several states, one with an elected board (Colorado) and two with appointed boards (Georgia and Minnesota). The politicization of educational issues had encouraged, or pushed, the governors into taking a more active interest in school policy making, and this, in turn, apparently enhanced the saliency of the state board for the chief executives. Further, in each of these states a majority on the state board shared the governor's party affiliation. This facilitated a mutuality of views that promoted further contact. Such trends and conditions, if they should become general, will increase the amount of interaction between governors and state boards. This will be especially true in states where there is political party congruence, a condition more readily met where there is gubernatorial appointment of the board.

SUMMARY

A number of EGP conference participants saw a structure in which the governor appointed the state board and the state board appointed the CSSO as being a workable compromise between the competing values of a centralized executive and a separate agency. Such a model, in the judgment of participants, brings education "close to the governor but not too close." Many conference participants also asserted that appointment results in better board members than election. Some critics of this combination model denounced it for being too political. Others argued that it lacks accountability to the electorate. Still others, reflecting the centralized executive perspective, denied that it adequately addresses the many problems of a fragmented governance structure.

Two findings derived from comparing elected versus appointed state boards received additional emphasis. (Most of these findings were reported in the second section of this chapter.) There was some evidence, based on the investigation of school desegregation policy making, that appointed boards were more likely than elected boards to act on volatile issues and to adopt unpopular positions. This finding suggests that architects of state governance structures may face a real dilemma in trying to foster both responsiveness and innovativeness. A second finding indicated, surprisingly, that elected boards at the time of the EGP inquiry were perceived as having greater influence with governors than appointed boards, albeit neither kind of board was generally seen as having much influence. In several states governor-state board contacts are expanding, however, and this is encouraged by political party congruence between the governor and the board majority. It appears that gubernatorial appointment of board members is likely, in time, to result in the form of governor-state board interaction predicted for it.

*   *   *

This has been a discussion of the values that opinion leaders, notably, in this case, regional conference participants, expect to attain by structuring state-level school governance in different ways. Seven alternative governance models, classified under three headings, have been set forth, and relevant research findings have been applied. Since relevant research findings have already been summarized, it seems best to conclude the chapter with two brief comments on the kinds of choices that confront persons interested in changing state structures for educational governance.

These choices depend on *the values that the governance structure should attempt to realize* and, conversely, on *the values that must be given up, or at least deemphasized, by the adoption of a particular structure.* Is the structure to stress coordination and efficiency, or is it to strive for representativeness and multiple points of public access? Is the structure to promote state-level advocacy for education, or is the articulation of education with other human services a more important goal? Is priority to be given to the structure's capacity to be responsive to constituents, or is the structure to insulate policy making from external pressures? These and many other questions indicate possible value conflicts. And the choices of values that face those who design educational governance structures will be difficult ones.

After the values are chosen and compromises are worked out, then decisions must be made about the structural means most likely to achieve desired goals. The models should suggest a useful range of alternatives and anticipate some of their consequences, but the evidence is quite limited, even at the general level of analysis. Anticipation of state-specific consequences of a model's adoption would require a thorough understanding of the particular situation, including political traditions, organizational norms and interests, and the personalities involved. A systematic investigation of these factors would appear to be imperative to any restructuring effort.[57] To undertake any major structural change in state educational governance without such study is to invite disappointment and failure.

NOTES—CHAPTER X

1. Written communication from EGP conference participant, December 10, 1973.

2. Herbert Kaufman, *Politics and Policies in State and Local Government* (Englewood Cliffs, N. J.: Prentice-Hall, 1963), p. 41.

3. Hanna F. Pitkin, *The Concept of Representation* (Berkeley: University of California Press, 1967), p. 57.

4. Written communication from EGP conference participant, November 20, 1973.

5. Written communication from EGP conference participant, March 26, 1973.

6. Ira Sharkansky, *Public Administration*, 2nd ed. (Chicago: Markham, 1970), p. 86.

7. Gary V. Branson and Donald J. Steele, Jr., *State Policy Making for the Public Schools of Tennessee* (Columbus: Ohio State University, Educational Governance Project, February 1974).

8. *Ibid.*, p. 25.

9. *Tennessee Code Annotated*, Sec. 49-103; 49-105.

10. Branson and Steele, *State Policy Making for the Public Schools of Tennessee*, pp. 62-63.

11. Jerome T. Murphy, "Grease the Squeaky Wheel," report for the Center for Educational Policy Research, Graduate School of Education, Harvard University, February 1973, p. 362.

12. *Ibid.*, p. 361.

13. Branson and Steele, *State Policy Making for the Public Schools of Tennessee*, p. 64.

14. *Ibid.*, pp. 80, 96-98.

15. Interviews with four respondents in Pennsylvania and three respondents in Virginia were conducted on March 7-9, 1974.

16. John C. Pittenger, "Should the States Have Secretaries of Education?—'Yes,' " *Compact*, Education Commission of the States, 8 (January-February 1974), p. 15.

17. "Mission of the Office of Education (Virginia)," unpublished draft memorandum, n.d., p. 4 (mimeo).

18. *Ibid.*, pp. 4-5.

19. This was the case as of our staff interviews with Virginia respondents, March 8, 1974.

20. General Laws, Chapter 6A, Section 4, of the Commonwealth of Massachusetts.

21. Peggy M. Siegel, *State Policy Making for the Public Schools of Massachusetts* (Columbus: Ohio State University, Educational Governance Project, February 1974), p. 76.

22. *Ibid.*, pp. 67-86.

23. "Summary of the Educational and Cultural Affairs Reorganization Act (Massachusetts)," unpublished document, June 1973, 1-1H of Section 15 (mimeo).

24. "Testimony of Governor Francis W. Sargent on the Reorganization of Educational Affairs," June 21, 1973, pp. 4, 6 (mimeo).

25. The most reasoned statement of this philosophy is in Paul W. Cook *et al.*, "The Job of the Secretary for Educational Affairs," report prepared for the Massachusetts Educational Conference Board, September 1970 (mimeo). For other arguments in favor of the secretary model, see particularly Pittenger, "Should the States Have Secretaries of Education?" pp. 15-16.

26. Lyman V. Ginger, "Should the States Have Secretaries of Education? —'No,' " *Compact*, Education Commission of the States (January-February 1974), p. 17.

27. Cook *et al.*, "Job of the Secretary for Educational Affairs," VII-4.

28. Ginger, "Should the States Have Secretaries of Education?" p. 18.

29. See, for example, the list of "accomplishments of the Executive Office of Educational Affairs" in Massachusetts as reported in Joseph M. Cronin, "Plan for Reorganization," report by the Executive Office of Educational Affairs, January 1973, pp. 59-61 (mimeo). A much less impressive recital of accomplishments is contained in "Secretary of Education Calls Job 'Exciting, Challenging, Rewarding,' " *Public Education in Virginia*, Virginia State Department of Education (Winter 1973), pp. 2-4.

30. The classic statement that the "general good," and not "local purposes," ought to guide the representative was made by Edmund Burke in reference to the British Parliament. See his "Speech to the Electors of Bristol" (1774), *Works* (New York: Somerset Publications, reprint of 1899 edition), II, p. 12.

31. According to Will and his colleagues, the usual recommendation of students of state educational administration is that: "The Board truly represents the people of the state. . . . This is intended to preclude any special interest representation on the Board." Robert F. Will *et al.*, *State Education Structure and Organization* (Washington, D. C.: U.S. Government Printing Office, 1964), pp. 8-9.

32. Gerald R. Sroufe, "State School Board Members and the State Education Policy System," *Planning and Changing*, 2 (April 1971), p. 21.

33. Remarks made by Wilson Riles at educational governance seminar.

34. Michael D. Usdan, David W. Minar, and Emanuel Hurwitz, Jr., *Education and State Politics* (New York: Teachers College, Columbia University, 1969), p. 170.

35. Edward R. Hines, *State Policy Making for the Public Schools of New York* (Columbus: Ohio State University, Educational Governance Project, February 1974), p. 90.

36. *Ibid.*, pp. 89-103.

37. *Ibid.*, p. 103.

38. *Ibid.*, p. 91.

39. *Ibid.*, p. 99.

40. *Ibid.*, pp. 144-145.

41. For a penetrating assessment of these events, see Michael Usdan, "Elementary and Secondary Education," in Robert H. Connery and Gerald Benjamin (eds.), *Governing New York State: The Rockefeller Years* (New York: Academy of Political Science, 1974), pp. 230-238.

42. Sam P. Harris, *State Departments of Education, State Boards of Education, and Chief State School Officers*, Department of Health, Education, and Welfare Publication (Office of Education) 73-074000 (Washington, D. C.: U.S. Government Printing Office, 1973), pp. 60-71, 76-77.

43. Quoted in Lerue W. Winget *et al.*, "State Departments of Education within State Governments," in Edgar Fuller and Jim B. Pearson (eds.), *Education in the States* (Washington, D. C.: National Education Association, 1969), II, p. 79.

44. Pitkin, *Concept of Representation*, p. 209.

45. See, for example, the discussion of the social characteristics of state legislators in Thomas R. Dye, "State Legislative Politics," in Herbert Jacob and Kenneth N. Vines (eds.), *Politics in the American States: A Comparative Analysis*, 2nd ed. (Boston: Little, Brown, 1971), pp. 176-180.

46. M. Kent Jennings and Harmon Zeigler, "Interest Representation in School Governance," *Urban Affairs Annual Review* (1972).

47. On the importance of social status to gaining access, see L. Harmon Zeigler and Hendrik Van Dalen, "Interest Groups in the States," in Jacob and Vines, *Politics in the American States*, pp. 150-153.

48. Harmon Zeigler, "Creating Responsive Schools," *Urban Review*, 6 (No. 4, 1973), p. 40.

49. Robert Dahl, *A Preface to Democratic Theory* (Chicago: University of Chicago Press, 1956), p. 31.

50. Zeigler, "Creating Responsive Schools," p. 40; Sroufe, "State School Board Members and the State Education Policy System," p. 20.

51. Gerald Sroufe, "An Examination of the Relationship between Methods of Selection and the Characteristics and Self-Role Expectations of State School Board Members," unpublished dissertation, University of Chicago, September 1970), p. 163.

52. Rodney Cox, Jr., and Waldo Anderson, "Shall State Boards of Education Be Elected or Appointed?" report by Bureau of Educational Research and Service, University of Arizona, May 1972, pp. 15-16 (mimeo).

53. See the argument in Herbert Simon *et al.*, "Dividing the Work: Specialization among Organization Units," in Edward V. Schneier, *Policy Making in American Government* (New York: Basic Books, Inc., 1969), pp. 218-221.

54. Written communication from conference participant, November 27, 1973.

55. Harris, *State Departments of Education*, pp. 60-71, 76-77.

56. Zeigler, "Creating Responsive Schools, p. 43.

57. A revealing analysis of the interaction of "formal structural factors" with "nonformal structural factors" is in Thomas R. Williams and David K. Wiles, "The Analysis of Two-Tiered Systems of Education Governance," *Planning and Changing*, 4 (Summer 1974), pp. 67-78.

XI — Structural Options

The presentation of models has been deliberately focused on a few variables—extent of policy-making authority delegated to the state education agency and selection methods for the state board and the chief state school officer (CSSO). While these variables seem most essential to the design of state governance arrangements for the public schools, other structural features must also be considered in elaborating on a basic model. This chapter sets forth the advantages and disadvantages of a number of these features, citing, when possible, research findings and indicating, in some cases, our preferences. (The preferences of the political and educational leaders who responded to the Educational Governance Project (EGP) survey questionnaire are described in Chapter XII.) The structural options discussed have to do with state board characteristics, CSSO characteristics, scope of state education agency (SEA) authority, and SEA-general governance linkages. One or more of these options might be applied to any of the models set forth in Chapter X.

STATE BOARD CHARACTERISTICS

Five characteristics of state boards of education merit attention: term of office, size, staffing, service and compensation, and partisan affiliation.

Term of Office

There are two considerations regarding term of office for state board members. The first is whether members' terms are to be concurrent or overlapping, and the second is the length of the term itself. Continuity seems to be promoted by overlapping terms, and nearly all state boards are chosen with this in mind. Length of term, on the other hand, varies among state boards from three years in Delaware to fifteen years (reduced to seven in 1974) in New York. Most board members have lengthy terms of office. As of 1972, thirty-two of forty-eight state boards had provisions for terms of five years or longer (in nine states it was eight years or longer).[1] Given the rate of societal change, terms in excess of three to five years seem questionable if state boards are to be responsive bodies.

It was interesting to see if, among the ten state boards studied by EGP, there were any strong relationships between terms of office and subjective measures of state board interest representation, external constituency orientation, conflictual decision style, and policy-making influence.* To do this, the states were ranked on each of these variables, and correlation coefficients (Spearman rho) were computed. These are reported in Table XI-1.

TABLE XI-1 Relationship for State Boards between Length of Term and Selected Measures of Board Performance

Selected performance measures	Rho coefficients
Interest representation	−.56
External constituency orientation	.32
Conflictual decision style	−.09
Policy-making influence	.38

As can be seen, only one of the statistical associations can be classified as being even of moderate size, this being the rho of −.56 between term of office and the degree to which board members are perceived as representing particular geographic or racial-ethnic interests. The longer the term, the less interest representation is seen as

---

*These variables are discussed in Section II of Chapter X.

occurring, a finding consistent with the belief that lengthy terms for public officials reduce their responsiveness to external groups. An alternative interpretation is that officials who serve long terms come to have a broader and less provincial view of policy questions than those whose tenure is shorter.

Board Size

As of 1972, the size of membership of state boards of education ranged from three in Mississippi to twenty-four in Texas. The most common sizes were seven members (ten boards) and nine members (ten boards).[2] Much has been written about the supposed virtues of governing boards, or councils, of different size. In this literature the smaller the board, the more likely that it will be unified and efficient; the larger the board, the more likely that it will have a wider representation and be more prone to conflictual decision making. The evidence relevant to these assertions is meager. Still, some inferences of a supporting nature can be derived, as Winter points out, from small-group research.[3]

While it appears that a board size of five or fewer is too small to be very representative and that one in excess of twenty is likely to encounter problems with procedural efficiency, there is little indication as to whether the variation between such extremes makes much difference in terms of state board performance. Again, rank-order correlations can be used to explore the relationships between board size and other variables (see Table XI-2). The coefficients reported in this table were unexpected in light of the literature. Although size has virtually no statistical association (rho = .14) with board influence, it is inversely related to measures of interest representation

TABLE XI-2 Relationship for State Boards between Size of Membership and Selected Measures of Board Performance

Selected performance measures	Rho coefficients
Interest representation	−.49
External constituency orientation	−.37
Conflictual decision style	−.12
Policy-making influence	.14

(−.49), external constituency orientation (−.37), and conflictual decision style (−.12). For the ten state boards, it is the smaller bodies, not the larger ones, that tend to be perceived as being more representative and as experiencing greater conflict. Such findings do not warrant, of course, positive assertions about cause and effect, yet they do challenge the usual presumption about the relationship between the size of the board and its performance.

Staffing

State boards of education, like their local counterparts, do not have their own staffs. Consequently, the state board, having no independent capacity to establish agendas, depends on the CSSO and other department personnel to perform this function. And it relies on these administrators for information on the agenda items. The EGP data showed that nearly half (47 percent) of the board member interviewees identified no external source of information on these items. Of those who did cite an external source, most named either one of the state-level education interest groups or local school officials.[4]

The fact that a lay governing board, state or local, is heavily dependent on information selected and interpreted by its chief administrative officer and his staff, organized with regard to agenda priorities usually established by them, is used by some commentators to support the contention that the board is unable to undertake a significant policy-making role. As one observer concluded, "complex decisions are made on the basis of educational realities as delineated by the very people whom the board is supposed to govern."[5] One recommendation that logically flows from such a conclusion is that lay boards should have their own staffs, staffs capable of assisting board members in obtaining data needed to deal with a policy issue and in analyzing data received from administrators.[6]

In the normative literature on state boards, it is rare to find a recommendation that independent staffs be provided for these bodies. There are, however, exceptions. For instance, a minority proposal included in the report made by the Citizens Commission on Basic Education in Pennsylvania called for the State Board of Education to have

its own staff with particular competence in long-range planning, interpretation of educational research, and evaluation of educational programs. This staff should be kept small and should have no responsibility for administering programs established to carry out Board policies. Its principal function should be to assist the Board in policy determination through providing or securing assessments of the effects of various proposed policies which the Board is considering and to do research regarding emerging issues which the Board may wish to consider.[7]

The discrepancy between what the law stipulates to be the state board's governing role and the reality of administrator influence in this process suggests that independent board staffs be considered. If the pendulum of policy-making power has indeed swung a long way toward the CSSO, then staffing for state boards might help redress the imbalance between professional expertise and public control.

Critics do raise many strenuous objections to staffing proposals like that put forward in the Pennsylvania report. Implementing such a proposal, they contend, will lead to increased operating costs, duplication of effort, communication "gaps" and mistrust between board and CSSO, unproductive conflict with department administrators, and staff offices becoming the "political tools" of board members. Those who oppose independent board staffs point out that most state boards are authorized now to insist that relevant, balanced, and accurate information be furnished by state departments (in twenty-six states the CSSO is appointed and can be removed by the board). In their judgment, therefore, the appropriate remedy for a board that remains dissatisfied with the agenda or the information provided by the state department is to replace the CSSO with a person responsive to board requests.

Board Member Service and Compensation

Service on state boards is done on a part-time basis (most board member respondents estimated they spent four to six days per month on board work), and these officials receive little compensation (expenses plus, in some states, a modest per diem allowance).[8] Part-time involvement is defended not only as being appropriate to the duties to be performed, but also as guarding against board members' "meddling" in administration. "A full-time board," argues one CSSO, "simply cannot stay with policy making; it inevitably gets its fingers into every aspect of the administrative operation."[9] As for the absence of substantial compensation, this is justified on the grounds that financial inducements would attract board aspirants who are more concerned with monetary gain than devotion to public service.

EGP data portray state board officials as an unusually successful group of Americans; most being affluent, well educated, and engaged in managerial or professional occupations. Many factors obviously contribute to the demographic composition of state boards; among them is the fact that board membership is largely uncompensated. This encourages persons who can pursue symbolic rewards like status and the satisfaction of service without paying much heed to financial costs and discourages capable low-income candidates from seeking state board office. While it can be argued that to attach attractive compensation to state board offices would invite the candidacy of persons interested primarily in money, it also holds promise for expanding the social class membership of these bodies. It is true that compensation for board members, especially if made available on a per meeting basis, would probably increase the amount of time members spend, thereby increasing the risk that they would interfere in matters perceived as being administrative in nature. This happened in Los Angeles, where the city school board, as of 1970, was the highest paid in the country ($75 per meeting and $750 per month maximum).[10] A case study of this board suggests, nonetheless, that a greater time commitment on the part of state board members may lead to greater public involvement in education policy making. Indeed, it may be necessary to risk some board interference in administration in order to gain more board involvement in policy making.

Political Party Recruitment

A constant theme in the writings on boards of education, widely voiced by participants in EGP regional conferences, is that schools and party affiliation do not mix. There is no Republican or Democratic way to educate children. Nonpartisan recruitment allows the best-qualified people to seek office, and party considerations should not be permitted to get in the way of a rational assessment of the personal attributes and issue positions of candidates. The rebuttal, often advanced by political scientists, is that partisan recruitment, primarily through the election mechanism, is the best available device to prescreen candidates, focus on the issues, represent a broader public than interest groups, and make officeholders less vulnerable to personal attack.[11]

Partisan affiliation affects state board member recruitment in most states. Where these officials are popularly elected, it more often than not is on a partisan ballot; where they are appointed, it is by a partisan leader, the governor. EGP data on the board recruitment process support two inferences: that political parties play a passive role in board elections and do not perform most of the functions usually ascribed to them in this process, even in states employing a partisan ballot; and that party leaders, as opposed to education interest group leaders, have more influence in board member recruitment where these public officials are appointed than where they are elected.

Three of the state boards studied—Colorado, Michigan, and Texas —are elected on a partisan ballot and party identification seems to be crucial in influencing voter choice in these states. Bridges, after investigating voter patterns for both the state board and the governor's office in the three states in 1970, observed that, "apparently, winning or losing the office of state school board is highly related to the performance of the candidate for governor from the same party; this phenomenon is consistent with a partisan explanation of voting behavior."[12] Several board members interviewed expressed the same sentiment. In Michigan, in particular, board members often commented that they were merely "the tail-end of a partisan ticket" and thus that state board election results "had nothing to do with who is running or their qualifications." A board official in Colorado echoed this assessment, saying in reference to his own election that it was a "coat-tail thing—I shouldn't have won."

Although political parties endorse state board candidates in Colorado, Michigan, and Texas, thereby providing the decisive cue for voters—they evidently do not do much else to influence the process by which board members reach office. When board member respondents in these states were queried about how they became interested in seeking that office, most (60 percent) replied that it was their own idea, which meant that they, in effect, were self-recruited. Others named various individuals and groups who had solicited their candidacy. The most frequently mentioned (by 35 percent) were local school people, that is, boards and superintendents. As for party involvement in campaigns, this was minimal according to state board respondents. Only two, both from Colorado, mentioned substantial financial support, and none said that the party had supplied workers for his or her campaign.

If state boards rank low among the priorities of political parties —other than providing endorsements they do little to recruit or to elect these education officials—then who does become actively involved in state board campaigns? In the four states studied where the boards were elected, the answer, for the most part, was "educators," particularly state-level teacher organizations and local school people. By way of contrast, political leaders were identified most frequently as being influential in the appointive process for board members.

Of the five states where boards were appointed—Massachusetts, Minnesota, California, Georgia, and Tennessee—only in Massachusetts was there a formal advisory committee that recommended state board nominees to the governor, the Massachusetts Advisory Council on Education (MACE). In the remaining four states the process of state board appointment was unstructured. Board members interviewed were asked to evaluate eight groups in terms of whether each was "very influential," "somewhat influential," or "not influential" in recommending board candidates to the governor. These assessments were then scored as follows: "very influential"—3 points; "somewhat influential"—1 point; "not influential"—0 points. The average score for each group is reported in Table XI-3.

TABLE XI-3 State Board Member Assessments of the Influence of Different Groups in Nominating State Board Candidates to the Governor

| | Assessment averages | | | | |
Groups	Massa-chusetts	Minne-sota	Cali-fornia	Georgia	Ten-nessee
Governor's staff	2.57	3.00	3.00	.71	2.50
Party leaders	.14	2.60	1.50	1.00	2.25
Legislators	.71	3.00	.10	1.29	.75
Chief state school officer	.83	.60	1.20	.86	1.38
Other SBE members	1.14	.40	1.50	.43	.25
State teachers association	.33	.20	.20	.29	.63
State administrators association	.33	.40	.40	.14	.13
Local school boards	.33	.40	.30	.43	.13

Using the data contained in the table and ranking the eight groups by their average influence score across the five states produced this ordering (average influence score in parenthesis):

Governor's staff	(2.36)
Political party leaders	(1.50)
(outside legislature)	
Members of the legislature	(1.17)
Chief state school officer	(.97)
Current SBE members	(.74)
State teachers association	(.33)
Local school boards	(.32)
State administrators association	(.28)

It is clear from this rank order that state board members saw politicians, such as governors, party leaders, and legislators, as being much more influential in the appointment process than the various educator groups. These groups, on the face of it, have considerably less access to the recruitment process where state board members are chosen by the governor than where board officials must bid for support in elections.

Before leaving the subject of state board characteristics, it should be emphasized that, whether board members are appointed or elected, partisan or nonpartisan, the role played in state board recruitment by such noneducator groups as those involved with labor, business, or civil rights is insignificant. And none of the selection procedures creates much opportunity or much stimulus for broad public involvement. Both Sroufe and Bridges, in explaining why the different selection methods produce similar results, stress the lack of saliency of the state board office for voters, political parties, governors, legislators, and even interest groups except for some groups comprised primarily of educators.[13]

There have been signs of change as the politicization of education has affected the apolitical character of state board recruitment. In some states, board elections are now more vigorously contested. In a few other states governors and their staffs have begun to scrutinize board member appointments more carefully. Even so, for state boards to be widely perceived as important institutions in education policy-making—hence, for selection mechanisms to be efficacious in producing well-qualified and representative board members—requires, it appears, that these bodies have more policy-making resources and be more willing to use these resources than they now do. Unless such a strengthening of both resources and intention takes place, state boards will continue to be marginal actors in the policy process in most states, whether a partisan or a nonpartisan recruitment option is employed.

CSSO CHARACTERISTICS

Three characteristics of the position of chief state school officer are now discussed: term of office, legal requirements, and salary.

Term of Office

In more than half the states, CSSO's serve fixed terms of office. In the remaining states chiefs hold their office at the pleasure of the governor or the state board of education. The usual term for a CSSO, where a fixed term exists, is four years.[14]

Two considerations appear to be involved in deciding the term of office for a CSSO. First, does it encourage periodic evaluation of the chief's performance by the appointing official or the electorate? Although the jobs of CSSO's who serve at the pleasure of a superior are, in a formal sense, in constant jeopardy, such a relationship may not be as likely to ensure systematic performance evaluation as a time-definite arrangement. And, second, is the CSSO given enough time to develop programs and to carry them out? A term appointment of at least four years may be needed to meet this criterion.

Requirements for Office

Most states have established legal requirements for the position of chief state school officer. Among the twelve CSSO's studied here, all the elected chiefs had to meet a residency requirement, whereas most of the appointed chiefs (63 percent) had to have certain kinds of educational experience. A majority of both elected CSSO's (75 percent) and appointed CSSO's (63 percent) had to have professional training in education. The presence of such legally stipulated requirements means that the chief state school officers often are recruited from within the states in which they serve and have a strong professional education background. Only one of the twelve chiefs was not an in-state choice. All but one had held a teaching or an administrative position, usually both, in the public schools, with the lone exception having had experience in higher education.

Although these requirements may seem reasonable, it should be recognized that any legal requirement for an office limits the pool of potential candidates. In the case of the CSSO, many of the statutory constraints do not seem highly relevant to the central tasks of that position, tasks that involve playing an important role in education policy making and managing a large public bureaucracy. While the policy-making role of the CSSO is the only role studied here, the data suggest that every effort should be made to find persons who can exert appropriate influence in both arenas where education policy is determined—the legislative arena as well as the education agency arena. For the state agency, professional expertise and some political skill are needed. But for legislators and governors, the necessary attributes must be posed in reverse order: political skill and professional expertise.[15] These criteria appear to be far more significant than place of residence or a prescribed pattern of experience.

Salary

Past studies of CSSO salaries found that they tended to be low when compared to other administrative positions in education with similar responsibilities.[16] Moreover, since in most states the salary of the chief sets the ceiling for the professional personnel in the education department, this situation has broad and probably negative ramifications for agency recruitment.

The average salary in 1972 for the twelve CSSO's in the EGP sample was $31,927, ranging from $51,275 in New York to $21,000 in Wisconsin. There is no way of knowing just how much CSSO's should be paid, but one useful comparison can be made. In 1969-70 Knezevich collected comprehensive data on the salary of local school district superintendents.[17] Since his data were obtained about two years earlier than the CSSO data, the salary figures for the district superintendent have been revised upward by 10 percent in order to compare them with CSSO salary figures. If the average salary for CSSO's ought to match that of district superintendents in the 112 largest districts of the country, then $33,000 (average salary in 1969-70 plus upward adjustment of 10 percent) seems a fair yardstick. If this measure is used, it appears that five of the twelve

CSSO's studied had salaries equal to or exceeding that amount. If applied to the fifty states, only fifteen CSSO's received a higher salary in 1972.[18] Most chiefs, it seems, are paid rather modest salaries relative to their duties and responsibilities.

SCOPE OF SEA AUTHORITY

Three issues involving the scope of SEA authority seem to be of major concern: the inclusion of higher education, the inclusion of vocational education, and the removal of teacher certification and preparation.

Inclusion of Higher Education

While the focus of the EGP was on elementary and secondary education, the question of the relationship of the state education agency to higher education continues to be raised. There are three possible positions regarding the scope of authority of the SEA. Research data bearing on these positions are quite limited, but the logic governing each of them can be set forth.

The first position related to the inclusion of higher education as part of the jurisdiction of the SEA is a negative one: leave higher education out. This is the practice in forty-six of the fifty states. In two out of three recent reorganizations described in Chapter IX, there was a deliberate attempt to separate the state governance of higher education from K-12 education. Kansas created a board for higher education at the same time that it created its present state board. Illinois, in forming its first state board, apparently felt that it should not disturb the board for higher education, an instrumentality brought into existence about a decade earlier.

Apart from the fact that it is the prevailing practice, there are two more arguments for keeping the governance of higher education out of the SEA. The first of these is the question of time. Many people believe that, if the state board of education is concerned with policy questions for both higher and K-12 education, lower education will be slighted. Since board members serve on a part-time basis, usually with little or no compensation, their agendas must be limited. Because most board members are thought to attach greater prestige to colleges than they do to schools, it is feared that any selection of agenda items concerning higher education would tend to be considered before those concerning K-12 education. This line of argument was used recently in Tennessee when jurisdiction for higher education was taken from the state board and a new board for higher education was created. Yet, in New York, where the Board of Regents has responsibility for both higher and lower education, there has been no move to divide its jurisdiction.

Another condition affects the time demands on board members. In New York the Board of Regents deals with major policy questions only and does not serve as the operating board for any of the colleges and universities in the state. In 1948 the Board of Trustees of the State University of New York was created to serve as the governing board for all of the state colleges.[19] This action apparently relieved the regents of the need to consider many operating questions and seemed to make their overall function more viable. The situation in Idaho is quite different. The Board of Regents of the University of Idaho actually serves as the operating board for four institutions of higher education as well as the state board for elementary and secondary education. Some persons in Idaho are convinced that the board allocates most of its time and energy to higher education.

A second argument for keeping the governance of higher and lower education separate is based on their distinctive traditions. In many respects the beliefs and practices applied to elementary and secondary schools vary significantly from those applied to colleges and universities. For instance, schools are subject to much state governance through a body of statutory law provided by the legislature and a body of administrative regulations authorized by the state board of education. In contrast, colleges, particularly major universities, in most states have been accorded great institutional autonomy. These differences also extend to the student bodies of the schools and colleges. Compulsory education laws apply to most of the students in the schools. Youngsters are made to attend, and, since they are not yet adults, their hours at school are well regulated. College students, on the other hand, attend by choice. Their daily schedules are flexible, and their personal lives are becoming less the concern of the institution. Even the financial support of K-12 and higher education differs appreciably. Schools are almost completely supported by local and state tax revenues, but colleges supplement their state appropriations with student fees, foundation and federal government grants, and private gifts. In short, the traditions surrounding schools and colleges do differ and may pose problems for any agency with a penchant for standardization. Recognition of such differences appears to have influenced the development of Wayne State University, which was once a teachers' college under the jurisdiction of the Detroit Board of Education, and the establishment of a separate Junior College District in Chicago, which was once under the jurisdiction of the Chicago Board of Education.

Although time limitations of board members and different traditions for higher and K-12 education argue for keeping higher education out of the SEA, these arguments did not prevail in New York and Idaho. Nor has separation of governance for higher and K-12 education been acceptable in Rhode Island or Pennsylvania, where the agency has recently been reorganized. In both instances the new agency has jurisdiction over higher and K-12 education. In Pennsylvania the consolidation was part of the reorganization that created the office of Secretary of Education, discussed in Chapter X. In Rhode Island the focus was on the creation of a Board of Regents with broad powers and with a statutory mandate to organize into three "subboards": one for elementary and secondary education, a second for postsecondary education, and a third for "special populations and types" such as the handicapped and the use of the electronic media.[20]

There appear to be educational, managerial, and political arguments for placing both higher education and K-12 education under the jurisdiction of a single state agency. The educational arguments suggest that there is no sharp break between lower and higher education; hence, the formal policy-making structure should not be divided. There is much to be said for this position. In terms of academic programs, the argument goes, there should be articulation between secondary and higher education. And, articulation arrangements should remain flexible so that such programs as advanced placement, which affect both schools and colleges, can be easily adjusted. In terms of vocational, adult, or continuing education, there should be ways of reducing unnecessary overlap between schools and colleges. The case for a single SEA is even more persuasive when it is recognized that education goes on in many settings in addition to traditional schools and colleges. The comprehensive state agency in New York has apparently been more successful than most such agencies in recognizing nontraditional ways of learning as exemplified in the high school equivalency diploma and the external college degree program. Policy for a total education program might well be more easily and appropriately coordinated by one agency than by multiple agencies.

The managerial argument stresses the efficiency of a single agency approach to all of education. This argument suggests that one agency can eliminate the costly and unnecessary duplication that often characterizes programs developed by two agencies. Again, much of this duplication may characterize programs in vocational and continuing education. For instance, some high schools and community colleges in the same community offer programs with little regard for possible overlap.

The political argument for a single agency seems to be an extension of the managerial argument, but it also grows out of the movement to rationalize state government, particularly to lodge more power and responsibility with the governor. At least partial application of this concept in Maine was described in Chapter IX. An attempt was made to place scores of state agencies in ten or twelve departments, each headed by a commissioner appointed by and responsible to the governor. In such an arrangement the governor, and presumably the legislature, would prefer to deal with broad categories of functions such as welfare, natural resources, and education. In the case of education a comprehensive definition that would include all kinds of programs and institutions under the direction of a single state agency was sought.

Discussion, until now, has been limited to the exclusion of higher education from, or the inclusion of higher education under, the jurisdiction of the SEA. A third possibility incorporates some features of both of the above plans into what has sometimes been called an education superboard.[21] Such a plan could be superimposed upon agencies already in existence for lower and higher education. Where separate state agencies for elementary and secondary and for higher education already exist (in at least 26 states),[22] both agencies might be required to report to the superboard. Such an arrangement would seem to remove some of the policy-making responsibilities from the state board of education and the state board for higher education and place those responsibilities with the superboard. The subordinate boards would be cast more in the role of operating or implementing agents. Though this arrangement might promote coordination of educational programs, it obviously raises the question of how many layers of government are needed.

As the concept is examined, it may be that political leaders will opt for a superoffice in place of a board. In a sense, the development of the office of secretary of education in four states, noted in Chapter X, is a move toward such an office without the encumbrance of a superboard. Since a superofficer or secretary of education is a creature of the governor, the whole question of how much power to place in the governor's office is also at issue.

The options that have been discussed are basically simple ones. Should there be one state education agency with jurisdiction over both lower and higher education? Or, should there be two state education agencies, one for lower education and one for higher education? Or, assuming two agencies, as is now the case in a majority of the states, should a superboard or superoffice for education be created? If a state chooses the first option, it does appear desirable to create some kind of link between the two agencies to give specific attention to coordination problems. For example, in the recent reorganization that took place in Illinois such a mechanism was created. The statutes require the establishment of a standing Joint Education Committee to be composed of three members appointed by the State Board of Education and three members appointed by the State Board for Higher Education. The committee, charged with developing policy on matters of mutual concern to both boards, meets at least quarterly and reports annually its findings and recommendations to the State Board of Education, the State Board for Higher Education, and the General Assembly.

Inclusion of Vocational Education

Another option having to do with the scope of authority of the SEA involves the question of where to place responsibility for vocational education. In forty-four states vocational education is under the direction of the general SEA, while in six states a special board and staff have been created for vocational education. Historically, a state board for vocational education originated at the behest of the federal government when the Smith-Hughes Act was passed by the Congress in 1917. At that time most states decided to make the state board of education also serve as the state board for vocational education. Some states had no state board of education, notably Illinois and Wisconsin, and other states apparently found their state boards unsuited for this new responsibility; hence, special boards were created, some of which persist to this day.

In 1917 there was another condition that provided some argument for a special board. Most high schools were still selective in terms of the academic ability of students and tended to stress preparation for college much more than preparation for work. Political leaders sometimes responded to the beliefs of persons in business, labor, and agriculture that school people, whether lay or professional, had little capacity to look at the nature of vocational training.

In the half century since that time there have been many changes. High schools now enroll nearly all youth. For many school people the high school must now concern itself with both preparation for work as well as preparation for living. Some students choose to emphasize the academic; others, the vocational. But most youths fourteen to eighteen years of age need to give some time to each. These developments have not satisfied those who see vocational education as being quite distinctive and often shortchanged by general educators. There is, however, little evidence to support the contention that the regular state agency has discriminated against the vocational education program.

Teacher Preparation and Certification

A critical policy-making area that for many years has been delegated to the state education agency is teacher preparation and certification. All eleven of the state boards studied by Schweickhard in the mid-1960's were empowered to set general requirements for elementary and secondary teachers and had the authority to issue, renew, and revoke certificates.[23] While state boards were authorized to determine policy in the area, nearly all states created advisory councils on teacher preparation and certification. Most were extralegal—that is, they were established by state boards using their implied power—or voluntary. Eleven, however, were created by statute. Generally speaking, these advisory councils included representatives from teacher and administrator organizations, along with representatives from teacher training units of colleges and universities.[24]

With the emergence of "teacher power" as a significant new reality in state education politics, traditional arrangements for policy making in the certification area have been vigorously challenged in several states. At the time of this study the issue was particularly salient in Minnesota.[25] (In California, a special commission to administer teacher certification was established in 1970.) As set up by the legislature, the Minnesota Teacher Standards and Certification Commission has fifteen members: four elementary teachers; four secondary teachers; three representatives of higher education; one school administrator; two representatives of the public; and one person having the responsibility of a counselor, vocational teacher, school nurse, remedial reading teacher, speech therapist, librarian, or psychologist. The commission members are appointed by the governor for four-year terms. Except for the college members and the public representatives, all persons on the commission have to be certificated and have five years teaching experience in Minnesota, including the two years immediately preceding their appointment.

The new law authorizes the commission to: "develop and create criteria, rules, and regulations for the certification of public school teachers and interns"; "from time to time . . . revise or supplement the criteria for certification of public school teachers"; and "establish criteria for the approval of teacher education programs." But the power to formulate policy is qualified by the phrase, "subject to approval by the State Board." If the state board vetoes a commission proposal, the board has to give "written notice of such disapproval within 120 days after the receipt of the proposal, including its reasons."

The commission—"subject to criteria, rules, and regulations approved by the State Board of Education"—is accorded the exclusive right to issue all teaching certificates and the corresponding right to revoke them for any one of five causes specified in the law. There is no provision for teachers to appeal a commission decision to the state board. Aside from the usual recourse to the courts, the commission is vested with authority to certify teachers. This power with regard to school superintendents and principals is retained by the state board.

Although the Teacher Standards and Certification Commission in Minnesota does possess considerably more legal power than the customary advisory council, having as it does the statutory authority to initiate and to formulate policy, final authorization remains a prerogative of the State Board of Education, a limitation apparently not found in Oregon.[26] In that state the legislature, in 1973, gave to an already established Teacher Standards and Practices Commission extensive legal control over the preparation and licensure of teachers.* Thus, it appears that there are three basic options open for state-level governance of the teaching profession: to continue delegating this governance to the SEA, this agency to be assisted by an advisory council representing different segments of the profession and the teacher-training institutions; to vest responsibility for certain policy-making or administrative functions in a special commission or board on which educators are heavily represented, but with the power of final approval being retained by the SEA; to create a fully independent commission by statute to exercise legal jurisdiction over the preparation and licensure of teachers. Even in the last, of course, ultimate authority rests with the state legislature, for it can modify or repeal the law establishing the commission.

Several reasons are advanced for removing, in part or in whole, control of the teaching profession from the SEA. First, there is the contention that teachers are "best equipped to make expert judgments" on entry into, continuation in, and exit from the profession and that they have the most interest, being professionals themselves, in developing high standards of preparation and practice. Second, it is argued that only if teachers control their profession can they legitimately be held accountable for performance by the public. As expressed by Oregon's Superintendent of Public Instruction: "If education is to become a profession, its members must assume responsibility for their actions and for the results they achieve. If we expect the profession to clean its own house, the profession must have the tools to do the job."[27] Finally, it is contended that having the teaching profession govern itself is not incompatible with public control of education. "There need not be a fear," to quote a leader of the Minnesota Education Association, "that delegation of such responsibility would cause the public to lose control. To delegate a right is not to relinquish it, but only to fix responsibilities. . . ."[28]

Critics of the movement to divest SEA's of their traditional authority for certification maintain that the establishment of independent governing commissions would only fragment further the

---

*But it should be noted that the Oregon Board of Education appoints the Commission members and can remove them "for cause" following a hearing. And the Oregon board can "request," after a review and a hearing, that a commission rule or standard be set aside or amended as not in the public interest.

state education policy system, a system presently beset by a lack of comprehensive planning, of articulation among state services, and of efficient allocation of resources. Of even greater concern is the prospect of educators extending their influence over state policy making for the public schools. Such influence, in the view of many observers, is already excessive compared with that of other groups. And the formation of educator-dominated teacher standards and certification commissions is seen as accelerating the erosion of public control of education. As for the contention that professionals should make the decisions regarding the membership and standards of their profession, opponents stress that teachers, unlike most doctors and lawyers, are public employees, and the militancy of organized teachers is interpreted, in the words of one critic, as performing basically a "self-serving guild function."

Whether delegating to educators authority to govern their profession can be made compatible with effective public control of the schools, as advocates claim but opponents deny, is a fundamental question that can be answered only by examining operating examples of the different options. Only a few states have established commissions, and they are relatively recent in origin. There is no evidence, therefore, by which to compare certification policy making as undertaken by an independent commission with that process when undertaken by a state education agency. What has been done here is to emphasize the growing importance of the issue for educational governance, to set forth what appear to be the major structural options, and to present some of the contending arguments.

SEA-GENERAL GOVERNANCE LINKAGES

In every state, education is under the jurisdiction of a special structure of governance that is independent to at least some degree of general state governance arrangements. Put differently, in no state at present is education treated as just another executive department. Events of the past decade have, however, challenged this status and have prompted a concern for links between education and general governance institutions. One such event has been the development of state planning agencies.

SEA-State Planning Agency Liaison

In 1960 there was no formal organization for state-wide planning in thirty-one of the states. By the end of the decade this number had been reduced to four.[29] Combining technical capability with, in most cases, ready access to the governor, the state planning agency is in a position to formulate comprehensive plans to use state resources, including education, to realize state goals. Jennings' argument for increased liaison between this agency and the one that engages in planning in education—the SEA—is persuasive:

Planners have a good deal in common and the sharing of ideas is beneficial to those who plan for education and those who plan in education. It would seem to be a logical kind of activity through which educators might expand their cooperative relationships. The advantages of working with the state planning agency are prior exploration of joint tasks to be performed, specifications of resources to be provided, and sanctioning of arrangements with an approved plan. . . . In addition, it is suggested that this liaison would provide an excellent conduit for the continual readjustment of planning to political considerations.[30]

Links with Governor and Legislative Leaders

While liaison for the purpose of improving planning had the approval of most EGP regional conference participants and state departments may have little choice but to move in this direction, proposals to create formal links between the SEA and elected state officeholders evoked much controversy. The option here is whether a new structure should be established to link the state board and CSSO with the governor and legislature. Watson, among others, has strongly argued for such a link as an appropriate response to the politicization of state education policy making. Indeed, he indicates that the state board might consist of "representatives of the legislative and executive branches, additional prominent citizens, and nominees of professional organizations."[31] This arrangement is seen as not only facilitating "communication flow across what have become internal boundaries," but also giving the state board both the status and political power to be an effective policy-making actor. A few conference participants also were attracted to this approach, proclaiming it to be the "reality model."

There are a number of objections to using the state board itself as the linkage mechanism: it would be extraordinarily cumbersome in composition and hard to implement; it would encourage "unproductive conflict for the reason that it is extremely difficult to pinpoint responsibility or accountability"; it is unlikely that elected political leaders would give adequate time to board work, thus leaving control on most issues with educator groups and agency administrators; and it is being abandoned by the only state (Illinois, with its School Problems Commission) that has tried the approach. These objections proved cogent enough to prevent the inclusion of a linkage state board structure among the basic models in this volume. Still, the problem of linkage with general governance institutions is a serious one for SEA's. This conviction is supported by data showing that most state boards and many CSSO's lacked forums for sustained and productive interaction with governors and legislative leaders.

One linkage option that seems worthy of consideration has been suggested by Sroufe. He proposes the establishment of a governor's council for education. Its membership would include the president of the state board, the CSSO, the chairmen of the House and Senate education committees, and the chairmen of the relevant appropriations committees. The Council would advise the governor, and its primary function would be to bring together the central actors to consider the education needs and resources of the state. It is Sroufe's hope that:

the Governor's Council would secure for education, in some measure, the benefits of a close working relationship with the governor. At least, the Council would provide a legitimate and appropriate forum for the education interests of the state, as represented by the board and the chief state school officer, to be presented to the governor and chief legislative leaders.[32]

Barring the adoption of a fully centralized model for state-level educational governance, it may be that Sroufe's proposed council, or some variation of it, is necessary as an effective link between education and politics in most states.

*   *   *

The questions underlying the various options that have been discussed in this chapter, and that we think should be of concern to those who seek to design state education governance structures, can be summarized as follows:

1. How long should the term of office be for a state board member? How many members should there be on a state board?

Should these bodies have their own independent staffs? Or, should they rely principally on state departments of education? How much time should state board members devote to their duties and what compensation should they receive? Should state board recruitment be partisan or nonpartisan?

2. Should CSSO's serve at the pleasure of an appointing official or should they serve fixed terms? If fixed, how long should the term be? Should there be any professional or residence requirements for the position of CSSO? What salary should be paid to the CSSO?

3. Should higher education be included under the jurisdiction of the SEA? Or, should it have its own governing board? Or, should there be a superboard over both higher and lower education? Should vocational education be included under the jurisdiction of the SEA or should it have its own governance structure? Should control over teacher preparation and certification remain a prerogative of the SEA or should it be vested, in whole or in part, in an independent commission?

4. Should liaison be established between the SEA and the state planning agency? Should a formal structure be established to link the state board and the CSSO with the governor and legislative leaders?

While these questions must be answered in creating a state structure for education, it bears repeating that they are not the crucial ones in deciding upon a basic governance model. The more fundamental considerations (see Chapter X) are the amount of discretionary authority to make education policy that is delegated to the SEA and the selection methods used to choose members of the state board and the CSSO. Chapter XIII draws upon all the different variables to explicate the three models that seem to constitute the most useful points of departure for citizens thinking about changes in their state education governance system.

NOTES—CHAPTER XI

1. Sam P. Harris, *State Departments of Education, State Boards of Education, and Chief State School Officers,* Department of Health, Education, and Welfare Publication (Office of Education) 73-074000 (Washington, D. C.: U.S. Government Printing Office, 1973), pp. 60-61, 76-77.

2. *Ibid.,* p. 70. Harris includes American Samoa, Guam, and the Virgin Islands in his summary, but excludes the ex officio boards in Florida and Mississippi; hence, his figures are somewhat different from ours.

3. William O. Winter, *The Urban Polity* (New York: Dodd, Mead, 1969), pp. 292-293.

4. For a fuller treatment of state board information, see Chapter II.

5. Bruce S. Cooper, "A Staff for School Boards," *Administrator's Notebook,* 21 (No. 3, 1972), p. 2.

6. *Ibid.*

7. Citizens Commission on Basic Education, Commonwealth of Pennsylvania, *Report* (November 1973), p. 175.

8. Harris, *State Departments of Education,* p. 70.

9. Written communication from EGP conference participant.

10. Tim L. Mazzoni, Jr., "Political Capability for Urban School Governance: An Analysis of the Los Angeles City School Board, 1967-1969," unpublished dissertation, Claremont Graduate School, 1971, ch. 9.

11. Michael D. McCaffrey, "Politics in the Schools: A Case for Partisan Board Elections," *Educational Administration Quarterly,* 7 (Autumn 1971), pp. 51-63. Also see Willis D. Hawley, *Nonpartisan Election and the Case for Party Politics* (New York: John Wiley, 1973).

12. Edwin M. Bridges, "Elected versus Appointed Boards: The Arguments and the Evidence," unpublished paper, 1972, p. 11 (mimeo).

13. *Ibid.,* pp. 20-21.

14. Harris, *State Departments of Education,* pp. 76-77.

15. See the discussion in Chapter III.

16. Lerue W. Winget *et al.,* "State Departments of Education within State Governments," in Edgar Fuller and Jim B. Pearson (eds.), *Education in the States* (Washington, D. C.: National Education Association, 1969), II, pp. 100-107.

17. Stephen J. Knezevich (ed.), *The American School Superintendency* (Arlington, Va.: American Association of School Administrators, 1971).

18. Harris, *State Department of Education,* pp. 92-93.

19. M. M. Chambers, *Higher Education in the Fifty States* (Danville, Ill.: Interstate Printers, 1970), p. 255.

20. M. M. Chambers, *Higher Education and State Government, 1970-75* (Danville, Ill.: Interstate Printers, 1974), pp. 222-223.

21. Wendell H. Pierce, "Time for the Educational Superboard?" unpublished paper, September 20, 1973 (mimeo).

22. *Ibid.*

23. Dean M. Schwieckhard, "The Role and Policy-Making Activities of State Boards of Education," report of a special study project of Title V, Section 505, of Public Law 89-10, September 1967, p. 53.

24. T. M. Stinnett, "Teacher Education, Certification, and Accreditation," in Fuller and Person, *Education in the States*, II, pp. 401-402.

25. Tim L. Mazzoni, Jr., *State Policy Making for the Public Schools of Minnesota* (Columbus: Ohio State University, Educational Governance Project, February 1974), pp. 105-120.

26. Features are briefly described in "1973 State Education Legislation and Activity: General Governance and Administration, A Survey of the States," II, No. 3, a research brief prepared by the Education Commission of the States, April 1974, p. 100.

27. *The Common* (June 1974), p. 9.

28. "MEA Legislative Objectives, 1971," prepared by the Minnesota Education Association, 1971, p. 2.

29. Robert Jennings, "Politics and Planning for Education: The Mix at the State Level," *Planning and Changing*, 3 (Fall 1972), p. 5.

30. *Ibid.*, pp. 9-10.

31. D. Gene Watson, "Alternatives for Educational Governance at State Level," in David T. Tronsgard (ed.), *Six Crucial Issues in Education* (Denver, Colo.: National Association of State Boards of Education, 1972), p. 53.

32. Written communication from Gerald Sroufe, March 16, 1973.

XII — Survey of Preferences for Alternative Models

— David W. O'Shea

As one of several approaches to the development of alternative models for the state governance of education, it seemed desirable to ascertain the preferences of informed persons regarding this matter. Thus, in 1973 a survey was conducted to determine the distribution of preferences regarding alternative ways in which the formal policy-making structure of state governance of education might be organized. Eight alternative structures, outlined in Figure XII-1, were presented to respondents who then indicated their preference. In addition, respondents were asked their opinion regarding individual components of educational governance structure, using the questions listed in Appendix E. Results of the survey, together with an analysis of factors associated with respondents' choices, are presented here.

The survey was conducted among persons attending selected meetings of national organizations concerned with educational governance and participants in a series of regional meetings organized by the Educational Governance Project (EGP) as follows:

Respondents

1. Staff meetings of the United States Office of Education, held in February 1973   15

Respondents

2. Annual meetings held in Summer 1973 of:
   Education Commission of the States   115
   State directors of school board associations   24
   National Conference of Professors of Educational
   Administration   66
3. Regional meetings organized by the EGP, Fall
   1973 in:
   Denver   47
   Chicago   66
   New York   51
   Atlanta   55
4. Participants in above meetings who returned ques-
   tionnaires by mail   26
   TOTAL   465

While limiting respondents to conferees at a highly selective series of meetings leaves problematic the generalizability of the findings, it is not unreasonable to assume that the meetings utilized drew together a representative cross section of opinion leaders in state educational affairs. Support for this assumption is provided by the fact that the distribution of responses from the 205 persons attending annual meetings of their organizations in the summer of 1973 paralleled rather closely the responses from the 219 who attended later regional meetings organized by EGP. Selected comparisons are presented in Appendix D. Stability of responses between these two sets of meetings points to the existence of established opinions on the topics raised, and also to the reliability of the survey instrument in ascertaining those opinions.

Three areas of concern shaped the content of the survey questionnaire. Of prime interest was the problem of determining the distribution of preferences among persons involved with state government with regard to alternative models for the formal policy-making structure of state educational agencies. Secondarily, preferences were sought regarding the characteristics of the state board of education and relationships between the board and other areas of state government. Similarly, preferences were sought also with regard to selected characteristics of the office of chief state school officer (CSSO) and relationships between this position and other divisions of state

MODEL 1

Chief state school officer is an appointed member of the governor's cabinet. CSSO is responsible to the governor for implementing educational policies, authority for which remains with the governor.

MODEL 2

As in Model 1, CSSO is appointed by the governor, in whose cabinet he serves. In addition, the governor appoints a state board of education. The board has limited policy-making power; for example, with regard to teacher certification.

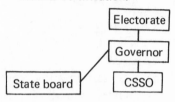

MODEL 5

- Appointment to the state board is determined by the governor or leaders of the legislature.
- Appointees are selected from among persons nominated by a blue ribbon committee and are expected to serve lengthy terms (eight years or more).
- Again, the state board appoints the CSSO and has considerable policy-making authority.

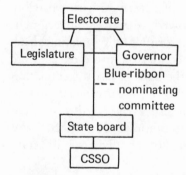

MODEL 6

Similar to Model 5 except that:

- (a) Nominations to the state board are made by a committee representing groups of professional educators.
- (b) Board membership is restricted to professional educators, such as teachers, administrators, and persons from colleges of education.

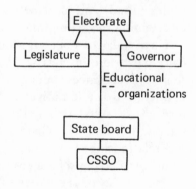

MODEL 3

Governor appoints the state board which, in turn, selects the CSSO who serves as the board's chief executive. The board has considerable policy-making authority.

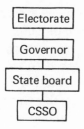

MODEL 4

As in Model 3, the governor appoints the state board, but the CSSO is elected, and as a constitutional officer shares authority for educational policy making with the board.

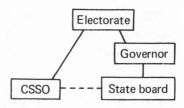

MODEL 7

This model parallels the typical local school board structure: a board with considerable policy-making authority whose members achieve office through nonpartisan elections and are not compensated for service. The board appoints its own CSSO.

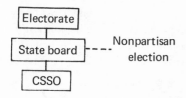

MODEL 8

Similar to Model 7, with the exception that members of the state board achieve office through regionally based partisan elections and receive attractive compensation for their services.

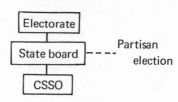

FIGURE XII-1
Alternative Models for the Formal Policy-Making
Structure of State Education Agencies

government. Finally, the questionnaire elicited responses regarding the extent to which the state education agency should be allowed policy-making authority over ten separate areas of educational activity, and higher education.

ALTERNATIVE MODELS

The eight alternative models presented to respondents are displayed in Figure XIII-1. Above each model is a brief description of its dominant characteristics. Respondents were asked to view these models and then, taking each in turn, to indicate whether they personally found it acceptable or not and whether they thought it acceptable politically in their own state. Having evaluated each of the models, respondents were then asked to choose from among all eight:

1. The model most closely approximating the existing structure of educational governance in their own state.
2. The one model preferred personally by the respondent.
3. The model most acceptable politically in the respondent's state.

The most important findings of the survey are reflected in the data presented in the third column of Table XII-1.

TABLE XII-1 Distribution of Responses to Questions Regarding Eight Alternative Models of the Policy-Making Structure of State Education Agencies (N = number of respondents)

Model number	Model which respondents judged to be closest to their state's structure	Model preferred by respondents (percent)	Model most likely to be politically acceptable
1	4.8	4.2	4.3
2	9.9	6.3	7.8
3	27.9	28.5	24.9
4	24.8	4.6	18.1
5	7.7	23.8	15.2
6	0.7	6.5	2.4
7	19.0	21.8	20.9
8	5.3	4.2	6.4
N	416	432	421

PREFERRED MODELS

The data in Table XII-1 show that, when respondents were asked to select the one model which they preferred personally, most choices were distributed among three alternatives: Models 3, 5, and 7. Further, as indicated by comparing data in the second and third columns of the table, though Model 4 approximates the existing structure in the home states of about one-fourth of the respondents, it attracted little support. This discrepancy between an existing and preferred structure points to dissatisfaction among educational leaders in some states with regard to educational governance, a topic pursued later in this chapter.

The pattern of preferences evident in Table XII-1 relates to specific characteristics of the alternative models. For example, the attractive feature of Model 3 is the fact that the board, appointed by the governor, has the prerogative of naming its own CSSO. Models 1 and 2 lack this possibility, each having a CSSO appointed by the governor, a feature found generally unacceptable. The option of an elected CSSO is also unacceptable, as indicated by the small proportion expressing preference for Model 4. Apparently most respondents feel that state boards should have unambiguous authority, whether elected or appointed, and that the structure of educational governance should not allow the state board's chief executive an independent base of power from which he might challenge board decisions, rather than implement them.

Model 5, the second to receive substantial support as being the personal preference of respondents, parallels Model 3 in having an appointed board which, in turn, appoints the CSSO. Differentiating this structure from Model 3, however, is the fact that input to the process of board selection is broadened to include both legislators and leading citizens. Clearly this broadening of participation in board selection is approved by many respondents.

Model 6, which attracted little support, is differentiated from Model 5 only by the composition of the nominating committee. In Model 6, committee membership would be restricted to representatives of educational organizations, allowing professional domination of the selection of state boards, an option that had little attraction for respondents. Response to Model 7 reflects the presence of strong, though minority, sentiment for state boards elected on a nonpartisan basis. Model 8 is differentiated from

Model 7 in allowing for partisan election of the state board, an option drawing little support.

In general, therefore, Models 3, 5, and 7, are the ones most favored. Among these three, and especially between Models 3 and 5 on the one hand and Model 7 on the other, however, there are major differentiating characteristics. Given these differences, the question arises as to whether each model may be drawing support from distinctive, and different, groups among the persons completing the questionnaires, a possibility explored next.

Differential Support for Alternative Models

The existence of distinctive patterns of support for alternative models receives confirmation from the pattern of intercorrelations among respondents' choices, shown in Table XII-2. While data in

TABLE XII-2 Intercorrelations among Respondents' Preferences for Each of Eight Alternative Models of the Structure of State Governance of Education[a]

Model	1	2	3	4	5	6	7	8
1		0.72	0.16	0.16	*	0.16	−0.17	*
2			0.16	*	*	*	−0.28	*
3				*	0.24	*	−0.20	*
4					*	0.14[b]	*	0.16
5						*	*	*
6							*	0.18
7								0.42
8								

[a]Correlations omitted did not reach 0.01 level. In fact, all but one of those shown were significant at the 0.001 level; the total number of respondents in all cases was greater than 400.
[b]Significant at 0.002 level.

Table XII-1 are derived from respondents' selection of one model from among all eight, correlations in Table XII-2 are generated by respondents' appraisal of models separately. Respondents were given the option of checking each as very acceptable, acceptable, unacceptable, or very unacceptable.

One fact that becomes apparent from the pattern of intercorrelations in the table is presence of division between persons favoring appointed, as compared with elected, state boards, reflected in the negative correlations between Model 7, incorporating nonpartisan election, and Models 1, 2, and 3, those most unambiguously appointive in terms of state boards.

The substantively interesting relationships, of course, are those between Models 3, 5, and 7, the only ones to receive a majority of favorable choices from respondents as shown in Part II of Appendix E. While Models 3 and 7 have one of the strongest negative associations in Table XII-2, reflecting a tendency for persons choosing the one to reject the other, Models 3 and 5 are linked positively, indicating that the same respondents were likely to opt for both.

Apart from the interrelationships among the three most favored models, two other correlations—those between Models 1 and 2, and between Models 7 and 8—are worth noting. The former correlation, 0.72, is by far the highest between any pair of models, though its importance is in doubt. As shown by data in Table XII-3, the correlation reflects the fact that a high *proportion* of persons finding Model 1 acceptable also opt for Model 2. However, the actual *number* of persons accepting either model is relatively small. The great majority of respondents rejected both.

TABLE XII-3 Distribution of Choices Regarding Acceptability of Models 1 and 2[a]

Model 1	Model 2		TOTAL
	Acceptable	Unacceptable	
Acceptable	67	46	113
Unacceptable	18	292	310
TOTAL	85	338	423

[a]Acceptable combines questionnaire items "very acceptable" and "acceptable"; unacceptable similarly combines "very unacceptable" and "unacceptable."

The next highest correlation, 0.42, is found between Models 7 and 8, both of which incorporate an elected state board. The actual distribution of responses to both models is displayed in Table XII-4.

TABLE XII-4 Distribution of Choices Regarding Acceptability of
Models 7 and 8[a]

Model 7	Model 8		TOTAL
	Acceptable	Unacceptable	
Acceptable	74	140	214
Unacceptable	18	190	208
TOTAL	92	330	422

[a]See note under Table XII-3.

Again, the importance of the association between Models 7 and 8 is
limited by the fact that relatively few respondents actually found the
latter acceptable, though, of those who did, most opted also for
Model 7, generating the positive correlation.

In summary, therefore, the pattern of responses displayed in Table
XII-2 confirms that respondents tend to separate into distinctive
groups with regard to preferences for alternative models of educational governance. The main distinction lies between those persons
opting for models characterized by appointed versus elected state
boards, with a majority opting for appointment, either exclusively by
the governor (Model 3) or by the governor with added input from
legislators and prominent citizens (Model 5). Further insight into
these differential sources of support is gained by exploring the background characteristics of respondents favoring the alternative models.

Background of Respondents

When responses were analyzed in relation to background characteristics of persons completing the questionnaire, most proved to be
unrelated to preferences. Among such background factors were occupation; state of residence; experience as a professional educator; and
type of area in which respondents resided, whether rural, suburban,
or urban. One characteristic, though, did emerge as influential:
current position in state or local government, a factor closely related
to whether respondents were politicians or not. The relevant data are
displayed in Table XII-5, showing the distribution of choices between the three most preferred models, 3, 5, and 7, by respondents'
current position in state and local government.

Data presented in Table XII-5 show that educational governance based upon appointed boards, exemplified by Models 3 and 5, attracts majority support from persons in each of the three current position categories. Among these categories, however, state-level politicians (row 1) expressed strongest support for the two appointive models and, conversely, gave relatively weak endorsement to Model 7, a structure characterized by an elected board.

TABLE XII-5 Distribution of Mutually Exclusive Choices between the Three Most Preferred Models by Respondents' Current Position in State or Local Government (N = number of respondents)

Current position in state or local government	Model number			Other models (percent)	N
	3	5 (percent)	7		
Governor's office, legislator, or legislative aide	32.9	26.0	8.2	32.9	73
CSSO, state board member, or state department employee	27.1	27.1	25.4	20.4	59
Other state employee, or local board of education member	34.9	20.9	24.4	19.8	86
None of the above and no response	24.8	23.4	24.3	27.5	214

These differential orientations to the recruitment of state board members are confirmed by data presented later, in Table XII-11, showing the pattern of response to the first question in the survey instrument. Instead of seeking preferences among alternative models, this question asked whether respondents preferred an elected or appointed state board, presenting three alternative modes of appointment and three types of election. Again, respondents holding political office in state government showed strongest approval of appointment, 82 percent opting for this procedure compared to 65 percent of respondents in the other two current position categories. Attractiveness of gubernatorial appointment among all respondents may be due to the fact that, whatever its defects, it has the advantage of maximizing the probability of a good working relationship between the state board and the chief executive. Among persons holding policy positions in state government, strong support for appointive boards reflects respondents' feelings that they should be in direct control of appointments to key positions in educational governance, a service for which ultimately they are responsible in any case. Respondents in the category of policy makers in state government included the four state governors who returned questionnaires, fourteen persons employed in governors' offices, and fifty-six members of state legislatures.

Influence of Existing Governance Structures

While respondents' current positions in state government and their attitudes regarding elected versus appointed state boards both influence their choice of preferred model, another potential source of influence upon choice is the existing structure of educational governance in respondents' states. People may prefer what they are used to. What the data actually reveal is that, while there is a positive association between existing and preferred models, it is not substantial. What is strong, by contrast, is the association between existing models and those judged to be politically possible in each state.

The correlation between respondents' choice of model as approximating the existing structure in their state and their preferred models is 0.29, as measured by Gamma.* While positive, this degree of association is not sufficient to give one much confidence in existing models as a basis for predicting those that are preferred.

By contrast, the association between respondents' designation of the model which approximates existing state structure and the model they judge most politically possible is 0.60.† Clearly, existing structures are a relatively good basis for predicting respondents' estimates of what is politically possible. These findings suggest that, while a majority of respondents assume that the structure of educational governance in their state is, in fact, the one most likely to be possible

---

*Cross-tabulation of choices for existing and preferred model generates a chi-square of 181 (d.f.), which is significant beyond the 0.001 level.

†Cross-tabulation of choices for existing model and politically possible model generates a chi-square of 735 (49 d.f.), which is significant beyond the 0.001 level.

politically, only a minority find their existing model to be the one they prefer, a conclusion that bears upon the question of levels of satisfaction with existing governmental arrangements, a topic discussed later.

To explore the actual pattern of relationships between existing and preferred models, data were examined in the form presented in Table XII-6.

TABLE XII-6 Proportion of Persons Selecting as Their One Preferred Model the Same Model They Cite as Approximating the Existing Structure in Their State, and Proportions Selecting Models 3, 5, and 7 (N = number of respondents)

Existing model	Preferred model								
	1	2	3	4	5	6	7	8	N
					(percent)				
1	20.0		25.0		15.0		20.0		20
2		20.5	30.8		23.1		17.9		39
3			49.1		21.9		10.5		114
4			23.8	9.9	17.8		27.7		101
5			6.6		61.3		9.7		31
6			0.0		66.7	33.3	0.0		3
7			7.9		21.1		46.1		76
8			45.5		13.6		4.5	13.6	22
Percent preferring each model	4.4	6.7	28.3	4.4	23.4	6.4	22.2	3.9	406

It is evident from the data in Table XII-6 that two factors result in the degree of association between existing and preferred models being relatively low. One is that, while the three most popular Models—3, 5, and 7—were strongly preferred by respondents from states in which these same models approximate existing structures, only in one case, that of Model 5, did more than 50 percent of the persons citing this as their existing structure proceed also to choose it as their single most preferred structure. Model 3 received 49 percent of the choices of those for whom it is the existing model; Model 7 received 46 percent.

The other factor reducing the degree of association between existing and preferred models is that respondents from states which do not use structures approximating Models 3, 5, and 7 distribute more than half their preference choices among these three models anyway, tending to reject their existing state structures.

As with Table XII-1, data in Table XII-6 again show Model 4, characterized by an elected CSSO, as the structure most obviously rejected. While cited by 101 respondents as the model approximating the existing structure in their state, only 9.9 percent checked Model 4 as their personally preferred structure. The great majority distributed their choices between Models 3, 5, and 7.

In contrast to the pattern of relationships between existing and preferred models, shown in Table XII-6, the more substantial association between existing and politically possible models is displayed in Table XII-7.

TABLE XII-7 Proportion of Persons Selecting as the Politically Possible Model for Their State the Same Model They Cite as Approximating the Existing Structure and Proportions Citing Models 3, 5, and 7 (N = number of respondents)

Existing model	Most politically possible model								
	1	2	3	4	5	6	7	8	N
				(percent)					
1	45.0		25.0		0.0		20.0		20
2		60.0	10.0		10.0		5.0		40
3			61.3		15.3		9.9		111
4			16.3	60.2	3.1		11.2		98
5			0.0		75.0		9.4		32
6			0.0		66.7	0.0	0.0		3
7			9.1		11.7		66.2		77
8			20.0		0.0		15.0	55.0	20
Percent of all citing each model	4.5	8.2	25.9	17.5	14.7	1.7	21.2	6.2	401

The most obvious finding presented in Table XII-7 is evident from the diagonal percentages showing the proportion of persons selecting as the model most politically possible in their state the same model cited as actually existing. In contrast to Table XII-6, all but two of the eight diagonal proportions in Table XII-7 exceed 50 percent. This is true even for Model 4. Despite being held in relatively low esteem in terms of preference, 60 percent of respondents in states characterized by Model 4 type governance structure judge this to be the most politically possible. This discrepancy between preferred and possible models raises the question of the degree of satisfaction among respondents with regard to existing models, an issue discussed next.

Correlates of Dissatisfaction

Respondents were asked, "In general, how do you feel about the present structure for educational governance in your state?" Of the 454 persons checking this question, 57.4 percent expressed satisfaction and 42.5 percent were dissatisfied. In seeking correlates of dissatisfaction, three factors appear important: the existing structure of educational governance in a state; the current position in state government held by respondents; and whether respondents are employed as teachers at either the elementary, secondary, or college levels.

The pattern of association between satisfaction of respondents and the characteristics of their existing structures of state educational governance is outlined in Table XII-8. From the table, a relatively

TABLE XII-8 Proportion of Respondents Expressing Satisfaction with the Model of Educational Governance They Cite as Existing in Their Own State

Satisfied respondents	Model approximating existing state structure								
	1	2	3	4	5	6	7	8	TOTAL[a]
					(percent)				
Percent	45.0	46.3	76.3	43.4	75.0	100.0	56.5	59.9	59.2
Number	20	41	114	99	32	3	76	22	407

[a]Based upon respondents who checked existing models, as well as replying to the satisfaction question.

clear pattern of satisfaction emerges, reinforcing findings presented in Tables XII-1 and XII-6. If one ignores Model 6, checked by only three respondents, Models 3 and 5 evoke the highest levels of satisfaction. The response to these two models emphasizes again the popularity of governance structures allowing for appointed state boards, which in turn appoint their chief state school officers. Model 4, by contrast, generates the least satisfaction, reflecting dislike among the respondents, all of whom are persons well informed about state school educational affairs, with the practice of electing chief state school officers. Also evoking relatively low satisfaction are Models 1 and 2, neither of which allows state boards to appoint their own chief executives, a problematic aspect of Model 4. In summary, therefore, data in Table XII-8 show that respondents are most content with Models 3 and 5, most discontent with Models 1, 2, and 4, and about equally divided between satisfied and dissatisfied with Models 7 and 8.

Looking at other correlates of dissatisfaction, while some existing models are much preferred over others, creating between-model variance in satisfaction, there is also variance in response to individual models, generating in-state differences in levels of satisfaction. Both types of variance become apparent when one analyzes satisfaction with existing structures in terms of respondents' current positions in state government, which, as shown in Table XII-5, is one individual background factor related to respondents' choice of preferred model. Specifically, as shown in Table XII-9, satisfaction with existing structures is highest among persons actually working within such structures; state board members, chief state school officers, and state department employees. This suggests that pressures for structural change are more likely to come from outside, rather than from within, existing state educational agencies.

Table XII-9 allows us to view the pattern of satisfaction with existing governance structures between persons in the various current position categories, while controlling for different models. To facilitate presentation of these data in a meaningful way, the models are separated into four groups on the basis of three criteria: their intercorrelations, shown in Table XII-2; the proportion of respondents expressing satisfaction with the model, shown in Table XII-8; and specific characteristics unique to each model. First of all, the two most popular models, 3 and 5, are placed together. These are posi-

TABLE XII-9 Proportion of Respondents Expressing Satisfaction with Existing Structure of Educational Governance by Current Positions in State or Local Government, and by Model of Existing State Structure of Educational Governance

| | Current position in state or local government | | | | | | | | All respondents | |
| | State board member, CSSO, state department employee | | Governor's office, legislator, legislative aide | | Department of Administration and/or Finance, local board of education, other | | No current position in state or local government | | | |
Existing models	Percent	Number	Percent	Number	Percent	Number	Percent	Number	Percent	Number
3, 5	90.0	22	75.0	28	71.0	31	67.4	43	76.0	146
7, 8	70.5	17	58.8	17	65.0	20	41.3	24	57.1	98
1, 2, 6	60.0	5	55.5	11	41.6	12	41.7	24	48.4	64
4	46.1	13	53.3	15	42.1	19	42.4	33	43.4	99
All models	73.3	60	59.0	78	58.2	91	48.2	139	57.4	454

tively correlated in terms of respondents' preferences, and both are characterized by appointed state boards.

Models 7 and 8 share the common characteristic of an elected state board, and are also highly correlated as preferred models. They were identified as approximating existing structures of educational governance by 24 percent of respondents, over half of these same respondents expressing satisfaction.

Models 1, 2, and 6 are also placed together. Models 1 and 2 have the highest intercorrelation of any pair, as preferred choices, and both evoke relatively low levels of satisfaction. Essentially, a lot of respondents disliked both these models. Model 6, though empirically trivial, having been named as an existing model by less than 1 percent of respondents, is included with Models 1 and 2 as it is positively correlated as a preferred model with the latter.

Finally, Model 4 is treated separately since it is unique in having an elected CSSO. While identified as an existing structure by 25 percent of respondents, only 43.4 percent of these same persons expressed satisfaction with Model 4.

Returning to Table XII-9, a comparison of the data in the last row, for all models, with that in the preceding four rows shows that, even when the models are grouped separately, persons working within state education agencies (column 1) still express the highest levels of satisfaction, except with regard to Model 4. This model evokes most satisfaction from politicians (column 3), though only a little more than half of these were favorable. In contrast to the sentiments of persons in state education agencies, among those without current positions in government (column 7) the proportion satisfied is low for each model except 3 and 5. Overall, therefore, the pattern of satisfaction with *existing structural arrangements* for educational governance at the state level parallels respondents' preferences among the eight *alternatives* with which they were presented.

Before leaving this table, it should be pointed out that the findings presented in the bottom row, showing a definite pattern of association between current position and existing governance structure, could be spurious. These data may reflect a disproportionate distribution of respondents in each current position category in relation to existing models. For example, if respondents in column 1 included a disproportionate number of persons who identified their existing state structure as approximating Models 3 and 5, which are highly favored, then all sixty respondents in that current position category would appear to have a higher-than-average level of satisfaction. While empirically this would be true, its meaning would be that the respondents who are working within state education agencies show a higher level of satisfaction than those in other current position categories because, relative to respondents in the other categories, a disproportionate number come from states where existing governance structures approximate Models 3 and 5. Of course, the fact that persons working within state education agencies continue to show up as the most satisfied with existing structures even when the models are separated out, with the one exception of Model 4, reduces the importance of the possibility of a spurious relationship when the data are aggregated. In any case, the distribution of respondents across models within each category of current position in Table XII-9 is quite close to the distribution of all respondents between existing models, the data on which are provided in Table XII-1. For example, in Table XII-1, Models 3 and 5 are identified as approximating existing state structures by 35.6 percent of all respondents. Therefore, if the sixty respondents directly involved in state educational governance (column 2, Table XII-9) were distributed between models in the same proportion as all respondents, there should be twenty-one who identified Models 3 and 5 as approximating their existing state structures, a figure quite close to the actual twenty-two. Similarly, for Models 7 and 8, the expected number of respondents is fifteen, compared to the actual seventeen; for Model 4, one of the least favored models, the expected figure is fifteen, while the actual is thirteen, again quite close. A larger departure from the expected figure occurs for respondents in column 2 who identified either Models 1, 2, or 6 as the structure in their home state. Here the expected number is nine, which is larger than the actual five, but would not substantially alter the aggregate proportion of satisfied respondents for all cases in column 2. The relatively close relationship between expected and actual numbers of cases holds for each of the other columns in Table XII-9.

In summary, therefore, persons participating most directly in educational governance are most satisfied with the existing structures; those least involved are also least satisfied. Respondents directly involved in areas of state or local government other than education generate a proportion satisfied that falls between the two extremes. Further, Models 3 and 5 attract most satisfaction; Model 4, least.

As noted earlier, the fact that persons least involved in state governance of education also are least satisfied suggests that pressures for change are most likely to emerge from outside, rather than from within, existing state educational agencies. One clue as to a possible source of pressure for change lies in the differential distribution of dissatisfaction among respondents according to their occupations. Among the more than twenty categories into which respondents' occupations were coded, in only three such categories did a majority of respondents record dissatisfaction with the existing pattern of educational governance in their state, and these categories were governor's staff, teachers (elementary and secondary), and college faculty. As shown in Table XII-10, the proportion dissatisfied in these

TABLE XII-10 Proportion of Respondents Expressing Dissatisfaction with Existing Structure of Educational Governance in Their State by Selected Occupations

Respondents' occupation	Respondents' satisfaction		Number of respondents
	Satisfied	Dissatisfied	
	(percent)		
Governor's staff	28.5	71.5	7
Teacher (elementary and secondary)	41.1	58.9	17
College faculty	47.2	52.8	91
Other occupations	61.4	38.6	311
All respondents	57.4	42.6	454

three occupations contrasts strongly with the 42.6 percent overall level of dissatisfaction, though only for college faculty is the number of respondents sufficiently large for one to have much confidence in the findings.

Of particular interest is the fact that teachers, whether at the elementary, the secondary, or the college levels, are relatively dissatisfied. Reasons for this are not ascertainable from the survey data, but one may hypothesize that the problem of economic resources is at issue. Teachers are increasingly dependent upon the state educational agency for access to resources, both for salaries and for services needed to facilitate instructional activities. Certainly there is growing militancy among teachers, and some of their dissatisfaction is evidently directed toward the state. Interestingly, persons working for the state educational agency are the most satisfied, as described earlier, a condition that predicts tension between state officials, on the one hand, and front-line personnel, the teaching staffs, on the other. Some insight into the changes in structure that might be sought in the future is derived from the earlier analysis of the distribution of preferences among alternative models. While Models 3, 5, and 7 are the most frequently chosen, Models 2 and 4 are those most commonly rejected. Further information on possible directions for future developments in state education agencies is provided by responses to a variety of specific questions included in the survey instrument regarding components of the policy-making structure of educational governance.

ALTERNATIVE COMPONENTS

As a second task, the survey sought preferences with respect to a number of specific components or characteristics of state structures for the governance of education. The relevant questions are reproduced in Appendix E. The first of these questions addressed the issue of board member selection, offering respondents six choices; three related to appointment by the governor, and three covering alternative modes of election. Results are displayed in Table XII-11.

Data in Table XII-11 show that, for all categories of respondents, a majority favor appointment of state board members. As might be expected, politicians most strongly favor appointment. Their responses in column 1 across the three types sum to 82.4 percent, compared to an average of 65.0 percent for each of the remaining columns. Further, politicians especially favor appointment by the governor subject to approval of the legislature. It is also of interest that persons in this same category, who are themselves elected to office, show least support for the election of board members. This finding parallels the data in Table XII-5, which show that Model 7, in which the board is elected on a nonpartisan ballot, receives least support from politicians relative to Models 3 and 5, both of which allow for appointed boards.

Among respondents favoring election, the great majority chose the

TABLE XII-11 Distribution of Preferences for Alternative Methods of Selecting State School Board Members (N = number of respondents)

Method of board selection	Current position in state or local government				
	Governor's office, legislator, legislative aide	State board member, CSSO, state department employee	Department of Administration and/or Finance, local board of education, other (percent)	No current position in state or local government	All respondents
Appointed by governor	27.9	16.6	16.5	11.4	17.0
Appointed by governor, subject to legislature	40.6	33.2	27.5	24.8	30.2
Appointed by governor, from citizen committee list	13.9	15.0	19.8	26.9	20.5
Nonpartisan election	12.7	25.0	25.2	29.0	24.0
Partisan election	3.7	3.3	2.2	4.4	3.5
Election by local school board members	1.2	6.6	8.8	3.5	4.6
N	79	60	91	141	455

nonpartisan approach, an orientation reflected in the preference among respondents for Model 7 as compared to Model 8. Respondents who do not hold positions in state or local government (column 4 of Table XII-11) give strong support to an elected board, though still providing a majority in favor of appointment.

As for the models, data in Table XII-11 suggest that the one structure which, in fact, would receive greatest support was not offered as an alternative. This would be a structure like Model 5, but omitting the citizens' committee, allowing only for legislators' approval of the governor's nominees. Overall, such a model is the most favored among the appointive options in Table XII-11, and it is especially attractive to politicians (column 1). Among persons holding no position in state government (column 4), the citizens committee is somewhat more attractive. Both procedures, the citizens committee and approval of the governor's appointments by the legislature, are combined in Model 5, one of the three most preferred structures.

Confirmation of the pattern of responses to the preference survey is provided by data from an earlier study that also sought respondents' opinions on governance structure.

Comparison with 1971 Survey

It is interesting to compare the findings in Table XII-11 with those from a 1971 survey conducted by Lindman.* In a questionnaire addressed to an audience similar to the one which received the preference survey for 1973, respondents were asked to check whether they favored the appointment of state boards, or their election. Comparability between responses to the two surveys is restricted by the fact that Lindman presented respondents with only one type of appointment, made by the governor acting alone. Lindman's respondents were, however, allowed to select between the same three modes of election used in the study done in 1973: nonpartisan, partisan, or by local school board members. Results are presented in Table XII-12.

Perhaps the most interesting finding presented in Table XII-12 is that, as with comparable data from the more recent study presented in Table XII-11, elected politicians (column 1) again gave priority to

*Erick L. Lindman. "Intergovernmental Relations and the Governance of Education," unpublished report to the President's Commission on School Finance, prepared by the Education Commission of the States, Denver, Colorado, 1971.

TABLE XII-12 Distribution of Preferences among Respondents to 1971 Education Commission of the States Survey Regarding Methods of Selecting State School Board Members[a] (N = number of respondents)

Methods of board selection	State governors and legislators	CSSO's and state board members	Presidents of state associations of school boards (percent)	Other[b] respon- dents	All respon- dents
Appointment by governor	66.3	43.0	57.1	40.0	51.2
Election on nonpartisan ballot	23.9	39.3	32.1	47.6	36.4
Election on partisan ballot	7.0	7.6	7.2	2.2	5.2
Election by local board members	2.8	10.1	3.6	9.6	7.2
N	113	79	28	130	350

[a]Data from Erick Lindman, "Intergovernmental Relations and the Governance of Education," report to President's Commission on School Finance, prepared by Education Commission of the States, Denver, Colorado, 1971.

[b]Other categories used were presidents of state associations of school administrators, PTA leaders, presidents of state teachers' associations and federal officials.

the appointment of state board members by the governor, while other categories of respondents were relatively more favorable toward elected boards. Comparisons between Tables XII-11 and XII-12 also show stronger support for elected boards among respondents to the survey made in 1971. This difference, however, is due to the nature of the options provided by the two surveys and indicates the importance of adding to the structure of educational governance elements that allow for broadened public participation. In contrast to Lindman's questionnaire, the more recent preference survey added two options to simple appointment by the governor: appointment subject to approval of the legislature, or appointment from among persons recommended by a citizens nominating committee. Of the three modes of appointment, that allowing for the governor's nominees to be subject to approval by the legislature proved to be especially attractive, as shown in Table XII-11. Inclusion of the legislature in the appointment process is presumably a major reason why respondents to the preference survey, in comparison to those replying to Lindman's questionnaire, were drawn away from the option of an elected board.

Other State Board Characteristics

When respondents to the questionnaire section of the preference survey were asked about length of service on the state board, 54.5 percent chose four years and gave overwhelming support for periods of service to overlap between members. In terms of size, 52.6 percent of respondents opted for eight to eleven members, 22.6 percent suggested five to seven, and 20.7 percent chose twelve to fifteen. These members should be compensated for attendance at board meetings in the view of 97.6 percent of respondents, though opinion varied as to amount. Of those respondents who favored compensation, 37.5 percent chose $25.00 to $50.00 per diem, plus expenses. A close second opinion, chosen by 34.5 percent, was that board members should receive only expenses.

A more complex aspect of the structure of state boards of education is the question as to legally required categories of membership. Of eight separate categories offered, only one, representation of different geographic regions, attracted more than 50 percent of affirmative responses. The other options for legally required memberships, all attracting considerably less than 50 percent support from respondents, were, in rank order:

	Percent
Minority group members	29.6
Local school board members	26.1
Teachers	24.0
School administrators	23.8
Representatives of major political parties	23.2

	Percent
Students	21.5
Representatives of non-public schools	20.5 (number of respondents was over 426)

A final structural component of state boards for which preferences were sought was whether the board, for its own staff services, should rely upon personnel from the state department, or have an independent staff, exempt from civil service. Sentiment ran close on this issue, with 54.8 percent of respondents approving board reliance upon state department personnel.

To assess the role of state boards in relation to the legislature and the governor, respondents were asked how important a role the state board should play. Results are presented in Table XII-13. The data

TABLE XII-13 Proportion of Respondents Selecting among Alternative Degrees to Which State Boards Should Be a Source of Advice to the Legislature and the Governor (N = number of respondents)

Source of advice to:	State board should be:				
	Not a source	Minor source	Major source	Most important source	N
			(percent)		
Legislature	0.4	6.1	71.8	21.7	461
Governor	0.7	5.0	71.2	23.1	459

presented in the table show that respondents consider the state boards as very important sources of advice to policy makers, over 20 percent proposing that they are the most important source.

The Chief State School Officer

A second set of questions in the survey instrument addressed the specifics of the role and function of the CSSO. The first of these questions sought to elicit preferences regarding the CSSO's role in policy making. Responses are distributed as follows:

Percent

The CSSO should—
   be solely an administrative
     officer   6.9
   be an administrative officer
     and help with the formula-
     tion of policy   57.6
   share formal policy-making
     authority with the state
     board of education   33.1
   exercise formal policy-
     making authority in his
     own right   2.4 (number of respondents
                                 was 463)

Evidently, therefore, the priority preference is the second, in which the CSSO would primarily focus upon administration and help with, rather than formulate, policy.

A related question asked how much direction the state board should give to the CSSO in connection with his administrative duties. Responses were:

	Percent
No direction	6.9
Some general direction	50.3
Much general direction	38.2
Specific and detailed instructions	4.5 (number of respondents was 463)

Most of the questions discussed elicited rather consistent responses across various categories of respondents when subjected to analysis. In response to the above question, however, those persons whose current position in state government was a party office again had a distinctive viewpoint. These respondents, working in the governor's office, the legislature, or as legislative aides, responded as follows:

	Percent
No direction	4.9
Some general direction	39.5
Much general direction	45.7
Specific and detailed instructions	9.9 (number of respondents was 81)

In contrast to other respondents, those involved directly in partisan politics opted more frequently for the state board playing a very directive role in relation to the CSSO.

Variation between groups holding different positions in state government was also apparent regarding the next question, soliciting preferences regarding ways in which the CSSO should be selected. the data generated are presented in Table XII-14.

From Table XII-14 it is apparent that, while a majority of respondents in all four groupings favor CSSO's being appointed by state boards, this procedure receives relatively less support from politicians, that is, persons in the governor's office, legislators, and legislative aides. Among persons in this category of current position, a

TABLE XII-14 Proportion of Respondents Opting for Different Modes of Selecting Chief State School Officers, by Current Position in State Government (N = number of respondents)

	Current position			
Selection of CSSO	Governor's office legislator, legislative aide	State board member, CSSO, state department employee	Department of Administration and/or Finance, local board of education, other	No position in state government, no reply
			(percent)	
Appointed by governor	16.0	0.0	4.4	3.0
Appointed by governor, subject to approval of legislature	17.3	6.7	9.9	12.1
Appointment by state board of education	53.1	80.0	81.3	70.6
Nonpartisan election	8.6	11.7	4.4	11.7
Partisan election	4.9	1.7	0.0	2.6
N	81	60	91	231

substantial minority, 33 percent, are attracted to the option of the CSSO being appointed by the governor. Overall, election to the office of CSSO draws relatively little support, confirming the earlier findings regarding the lack of support for Model 4.

On the question of whether or not there should be legal requirements for the position of CSSO, 75 percent of 417 respondents said yes. For the three requirements specified, responses were as follows:

	Percent	Number
Legal residence in the state	64.2	293
Professional educator	85.9	306
Experience as a school district superintendent	43.5	262

The final question relating to the role of the CSSO asked how important this officer should be as a source of advice to the legislature and the governor on educational matters. Findings replicated those for the same question regarding the role of the state board, with over 70 percent of respondents agreeing that the CSSO should be a major source of advice to both the governor and legislature, and close to 20 percent proposing that he should be the most important source.

Having covered alternative characteristics and functions of state boards, and possible variations in recruitment practices and job characteristics for CSSO's, the survey instrument sought preferences regarding the degree of policy-making authority that should be accorded the state education agency for selected tasks.

Policy Role of State Boards

Respondents were provided the following list of areas of activity and invited to indicate how much policy-making authority at the state level should be given by the legislature to the state education agency in relation to each area. Responses to the "All" and "Nearly all" options were aggregated and are presented here, ranked according to the proportion of affirmative responses.

	Percent	Number
Professional certification	81.6	458
Planning and research	76.4	457
Federal aid and federal assistance programs	68.8	458
Curriculum and course of study	67.1	459

	Percent	*Number*
Assessment of pupil performance	62.7	458
School district organization and reorganiza- tion	60.4	452
School desegregation	54.0	448
Buildings and sites	52.8	459
School finance, including the state foundation programs	49.7	455
Levying state-wide taxes for public school finances	24.0	454

The rank order of responses to the above list of activities exhibits an interesting distribution. At the one extreme very strong approval is granted to the proposal that state education agencies (SEA's) take over all, or nearly all, policy making authority in relation to the certification of professionals in education, a personnel function. As activities move closer to financial affairs, involving problems of re-source allocation within the state, respondents become increasingly reluctant to pass all authority to the education agency, evidently strongly disapproving the granting of taxing authority.

Finally, with regard to areas over which state education agencies should have authority, the survey questionnaire sought respondents' views as to whether SEA's should extend their responsibility beyond elementary and secondary levels to include higher education. A majority, 59.0 percent of 434 persons responding, favored the idea of SEA's taking responsibility for community colleges. Only 36.1 percent, however, favored SEA's extending their authority to cover four-year colleges and universities.

Analysis of these responses shows some variation between persons in different current positions in state government. Interestingly, the group most favorable toward SEA's overseeing community colleges was that which included state board members, CSSO's, and state department of education employees. Of the fifty-eight persons from this group who responded, 65.5 percent (6.5 percent above the average), favored community colleges coming under the state agency. At the other extreme, only 48.6 percent of seventy-four respondents in partisan political positions, that is, governor's office, legislators, and legislative aides, favored extending board responsibility to community colleges. These differing orientations within state government, between those directly involved in educational governance and those concerned with overall governmental problems, indicates a possible area of tension in some states.

*   *   *

Several conclusions emerge from the findings presented here. First of all, *among persons informed about educational governance at the state level, existing structures evoke varying levels of satisfaction.* Specifically, Models 3 and 5 stand out as eliciting most approval, while Models 1, 2, and 4 were evaluated as satisfactory by less than half of the respondents. Dissatisfaction with Model 4 has important policy implications as this type of structure, characterized by an elected CSSO, presently exists in nineteen states. As shown by data in Table XII-6, most respondents from these states would actually prefer Models 3, 5, and 7, which suggests the probable direction of future efforts at changing existing governance structures.

A second major conclusion relates to the question of preferred models. From the findings *it is evident that Models 3, 5, and 7 are preferred by respondents generally,* not only by those from states with elected CSSO's. Models 3 and 5 are characterized by appointed boards, which in turn appoint their chief executive officers. The two models differ in that Model 5 admits the legislature and a blue-ribbon nominating committee into the selection of board members. Model 7 contrasts to 3 and 5 in that it allows for nonpartisan election of board members, paralleling the typical structure of local school district governance.

Implicit in the reasons why Models 3, 5, and 7 attract the support of the respondents are the arguments against the other alternatives. Model 1 has no state board. Model 2 creates an ambiguous relationship between state board and CSSO, both being appointed by the governor. From the findings it is evident that respondents want the CSSO to be appointed by the board. Even when the CSSO is elected, as in Model 4, this procedure is largely unacceptable.

Model 6 found little support, presumably because it differs in a rather crucial respect from the strongly favored Model 5. In Model 6 the nominating committee for state board members is composed of representatives of educational organizations, throwing control to the professionals, a generally unwelcome option. Finally, Model 8 drew little support because of sentiment against partisan election of state board members.

Models 3 and 5, which represent variants of a structure in which the governor appoints state board members, together attracted the preference of 52.3 percent of respondents, compared to 21.8 percent opting for Model 7, with an elected state board. This result is surprising in view of the prevalence of Model 7-type structures at the local school district level. Apparently, *among persons informed about state governance of education, there is a relatively high level of consensus that, as the governor and the legislature have ultimate responsibility for education, they should also be allowed control over key positions in the structure of educational governance. In fact, of all feasible models, one that data in Table XII-11 suggest would attract support from the single largest proportion of all respondents would be a structure similar to Model 5, but without the blue-ribbon nominating committee.* Appointment to the state board would be made by the governor, subject to approval by the legislature.

A third set of conclusions relates to the background of respondents. Findings demonstrate that *expressed preferences were dependent on respondents' current position in state government and on whether or not respondents were teachers, especially at the college level.* For example, while no more than 25 percent of respondents in any category of current position in state government selected Model 7 as their most preferred choice, which allows for an elected state board, among politicians support for this model dropped to only 8.2 percent. Conversely, politicians showed relatively strong support for Model 3, in which the board is appointed by the governor.

In addition to being associated with variation in choice of preferred model, *the current governmental position of respondents was also related to satisfaction with the existing model in their own state.* In general, persons employed directly in educational governance were the most satisfied; those without any current governmental position were the most dissatisfied.

This finding indicates that *pressure for change in the structure of educational governance is most likely to come from external sources, rather than to emerge internally.* One specific source of demands for change is likely to be faculty members at colleges and universities. Among respondents, persons from this occupational group were especially dissatisfied with existing educational governance structures.

Finally, *preferences for specific components of the structure and functions of state boards and the role of chief state school officer were mostly nonproblematic, and elaborated upon the findings detailed with regard to alternative models.* Particularly interesting, of course, is the finding that an additional structure, similar to Model 5 but omitting the nominating committee, would have proved especially attractive to respondents. This has obvious policy implications, as do the findings regarding the distribution of opinion concerning the jurisdiction of state boards over higher education. *While a majority of respondents in all categories of current position in state government rejected state boards controlling four-year colleges and universities, only politicians produced a majority against state boards extending jurisdiction over community colleges.* Other groups of respondents favored this development, especially persons engaged directly within state educational agencies. It appears, therefore, that in some states tensions exist within the government itself regarding who should have jurisdiction over community colleges, a topic worth further investigation.

XIII — Making Use of the Models

Looking back over these chapters on models, one can see that Chapter IX depicts briefly the structural components of the state education agency as it now exists in each of the fifty states. Some attention is given to the historical development of the agency, as well as to recent changes in Maine, Kansas, and Illinois. Recurring issues that emerge when such changes are contemplated center around the nature of the state board of education and the scope of the board's jurisdiction; around the role ascribed to the position of CSSO and its relationship to the board and to other actors in the policy system; and, finally, around the power placed in the governor's office to influence policy making for education.

Chapter X sets forth three classes of structural arrangements or models for the governance of elementary and secondary education at the state level. The first class included three models designated centralized executive models; the second class included three models designated separate agency models; the last class was composed of one model only, and it was called simply the combination model. For each class and, indeed, for some of the individual models, competing values were elaborated. It seems, for example, that centralized executive models allocate more power to the governor, separate agency models allocate more power to the state education agency,

424

and the combination model attempts to balance power between the governor's office and the state education agency. Research bearing directly upon any of these models was weighed.

There was an attempt to keep the basic features of each model simple. In the centralized models the governor appoints both the CSSO and the state board, if there is one; in the separate agency models the board is elected either by the legislature or the public, and the CSSO is appointed by the board (or for one model, publicly elected); in the combination model the board is appointed by the governor with legislative approval and the board selects the chief. At the same time it was recognized that a number of options that might be made a part of one or more models should receive some attention, so these options formed the basis for Chapter XI.

Chapter XII represents still another approach to the problem by focusing on the preferences of informed persons with regard to the structural arrangements at the state level for the governance of public education. In all, 465 persons rather broadly representative of political and educational actors and of all fifty states expressed such preferences. Of the models described in Chapter X, the arrangements selected most frequently by the persons responding to the EGP preference survey were as follows: the governor-legislature-elected board that selects its own chief, the publicly elected board that selects its own chief, and the governor-appointed board that selects its own chief.

In this final chapter there are rather explicit suggestions of how any person or group of persons concerned with appraising the structural arrangements for the governance of public education in any state may start such a task. To aid in this process, three of the seven models described in Chapter X, one from each class, were selected for comparative analysis, along with certain options discussed in Chapter XI. These models, although none is specifically recommended, do emphasize a particular set of values, and those who would reform the state structure must decide which values they wish to maximize. This final chapter also points out some of the limitations that pertain when modifying structural arrangements.

THREE POINTS OF DEPARTURE

Perhaps the content of the previous chapters will assist citizens to examine their state structure for educational governance, and perhaps it will help those working to improve this structure. If so, it seems best to conclude this volume by setting forth additional structural description of three models, one drawn from each class. This would illustrate how models can be elaborated beyond the basic variables treated in Chapter X by including options discussed in Chapter XI. Such an approach would also place in sharp relief the many alternatives that require consideration. And, most important, it would stress models that appear to be particularly useful as points of departure for those thinking about changing their governance structure.

The first model has as its defining characteristic a governor-appointed secretary of education, an official who sits as a member of the governor's cabinet, and whose responsibilities embrace the full spectrum of a state's educational and cultural programs. Such a centralized approach has long been propounded by political scientists and governmental reformers. The growing costs, visibility, and politicization of education, phenomena that receive attention in Part I, particularly in Chapter IV, have created a press in many states to reduce the structural autonomy of the education agency and to extend executive control over its activities. Although this thrust has varied manifestations, the one that has attracted the most attention in the past few years is the secretary of education model. This model, as was observed in Chapter X, has been implemented quite differently in the four states currently employing it. And the "strong" version presented here is most closely approximated in Pennsylvania. Choices of structural options for this model were made primarily on the basis of consistency with the underlying philosophy of the secretary approach.

Despite, or perhaps because of, politicizing forces, opinion leaders who responded to the EGP preference survey indicated little enthusiasm for the centralized executive doctrine being extended to education. Only some 10 percent, as shown in Chapter XII, named either of the two models in which the governor appointed the CSSO as being the one they personally most preferred. And neither of these models was found to be acceptable by anywhere near a majority of these respondents (just 27.4 percent for Model 1 and 20.6 percent for Model 2) in the preference survey reported in Chapter XII. Correspondingly, both of the centralized models evoked a much higher than average level of dissatisfaction.

In marked contrast, the second model presented here, the combination approach called the "governor-appointed authoritative board model" in which the governor appoints the state board but that body appoints the CSSO, attracted the most support from survey respondents. Nearly two-thirds indicated that this model was acceptable to them and 28.5 percent checked it as the one they most preferred. Of those who saw this structure as existing in their state, 76.3 percent expressed satisfaction, the highest figure for any alternative. For these reasons, and because the governor-appointed board approach has been widely recommended by students of state school administration, this structural arrangement is included among the three models described in this section. Decisions about the options for this model were made by selecting, whenever possible, the ones most frequently named by our preference survey respondents.

The final model to be presented in some structural detail is characterized by an elected state board and a board-appointed CSSO. This structural pattern is not only supported by long tradition in local school governance, but it also represented the choice of many survey respondents. Nearly 22 percent opted for a nonpartisan elected board model as their most preferred alternative and an additional 4 percent checked the model based on a partisan election. While an independent regents model also attracted widespread approval (Model 5 in the EGP survey was personally most preferred by 23.8 percent), such a structure is found only in New York and, even in that state, criticism is mounting. The other model in the separate agency classification, which has an elected CSSO as its central feature, is found in many states. But that number has steadily declined in the twentieth century, and the model has evoked far more dissatisfaction from survey respondents than any other. Indeed, O'Shea found that, while the elected chief model, Model 4 in the survey reported in Chapter XII, was "cited by 101 respondents as the model approximating the existing structure in their state, only 9.9 percent checked Model 4 as their personally preferred structure."

The elected board structure, then, is the one described in this section. Recent criticisms of the policy-making performance of state boards are taken into account, and several options intended to make these bodies more broadly representative and more actively involved in the policy process are included. We also added the linkage option, establishing a Governor's Advisory Council on Education. These options appear to be at odds with established practice and, judging from EGP survey respondents, with prevailing sentiment. Still, research findings of the sort discussed in Chapters II and X concern

	Secretary of education model	Elected state board model	Governor-appointed authoritative board model

KEY AUTHORITY RELATIONSHIPS	The secretary of education is an appointed member of the governor's cabinet. The secretary exercises the prerogatives of the CSSO, and the responsibilities of this office embrace the full range of state educational and cultural programs, as well as K-12 schools. The secretary is also chief executive authority for a governor-appointed state board, a body that does have, by statute, some policy-making authority	The state education agency has a semiautonomous governmental status. It is governed by a state board whose members achieve office through election. The board appoints the CSSO to serve as its chief executive. The state board has both constitutional and statutory authority, and considerable policy-making authority for K-12 and vocational education but not for higher education	While the state education agency does have a special governmental status, there is direct linkage to the governor through his appointment, subject to legislative approval, of board members. They, in turn, select the CSSO who serves as the board's chief executive. The state board has both constitutional and statutory foundation, and has considerable policy-making authority for K-12 and vocational education but not for higher education
STATE BOARD CHARACTERISTICS			
Selection	Appointed by the governor	Elected from districts on either partisan or nonpartisan ballot	Appointed by the governor, subject to confirmation by the legislature
Term of office	4 years; overlapping	4 years; overlapping	4 years; overlapping
Size	Medium (7-11)	Large (12-15)	Medium (7-11)
Service-compensation	Part-time; compensation for expenses and small per diem allowance	Part-time but more board service (e.g., several meetings per month) than usual; expenses plus attractive per diem	Part-time; compensation for expenses and small per diem allowance
Staff information resources	Department for research, planning and evaluation in the governor's office, as well as such units in the state department of education	Small staff directly responsible to board in addition to staff resources provided by the state department of education	Staff resources made available by the state department of education

CSSO CHARACTERISTICS	Model 1	Model 2	Model 3
Authority	Statutory authority for cabinet-level responsibilities and CSSO administrative duties; directly responsible to governor	Statutory authority for administrative duties; directly responsible to the state board	Statutory authority for administrative duties; directly responsible to the state board
Selection	Appointed by the governor	Appointed by the state board	Appointed by the state board
Statutory qualifications	None	None	Professional educator
Term of office	Pleasure of the governor	4-year contract; renewable	4-year contract; renewable
Compensation	Comparable to those of other cabinet positions with similar responsibilities	Comparable to those paid local school superintendents in the largest districts	Comparable to those paid local school superintendents in the largest districts
SCOPE OF AUTHORITY			
Higher education	Included under the authority of the secretary and state board	Not included under state board jurisdiction; a separate board for higher education	Not included under state board jurisdiction; a separate board for higher education
Vocational education	Included under the authority of the secretary and state board	Included under the authority of the state board	Included under the authority of the state board
Teacher preparation-certification	Included under the authority of the secretary and state board	Included under the authority of the state board	Included under the authority of the state board
SEA-GENERAL GOVERNANCE LINKAGES			
SEA-state planning agency	To agency through cabinet structure, as well as informal liaison	Informal liaison only	Informal liaison only
Linkages to governor-legislature	To governor through cabinet structure	Through formally established governor's advisory council on education	Informal relationships and legal requirement for state board-CSSO report to governor-legislature

FIGURE XIII-1

Three Different Models for State Governance of the Public Schools

those who believe that governing boards should be influential public representatives and advocates in determining education policy.* Options directed toward this end warrant consideration, along with more customary recommendations.

A structural description of the three models begins, in Figure XIII-1, with a diagrammatic representation and brief statement of key authority relationships. This is followed by various options relating to state board and CSSO characteristics. Finally, there are some choices having to do with the scope of authority of the state education agency and linkages between this agency and general governance institutions.

To repeat an earlier statement, it is necessary, when considering a governance arrangement to think about not only what the structure is but also about what its consequences are and for whom it works. Any structure tends to encourage some values and not others, and makes it easier for some actors, rather than others, to exert influence. Assessment of such consequences is always speculative, and efforts to identify structural effects (see Chapter X) did not reveal many sizable correlations. Nonetheless, some tendencies can be associated with the adoption of each model.

Notwithstanding the presence of a policy-making state board, centralization is the dynamic of the secretary of education approach. Such values as decisional efficiency, coordination among state programs, comprehensive policy making, political accountability, and access to gubernatorial resources are stressed. The elected state board model, on the other hand, is intended to foster such values as educational program advocacy, insulation from partisan politics, policy-making continuity, "lay control," and the utilization of professional expertise. It is difficult to say to what degree these two different arrangements are successful in realizing their respective value emphases, especially in the absence of well-established secretary models. It appears that most of the values associated with each probably exist as tendencies, but EGP data cast doubt on some. One example is the extent to which "lay control" is promoted in the typical board structure.

As for the governor-appointed authoritative board model, there is some doubt that it really represents a balance between two sets of

---

*Gerald R. Sroufe, "State School Board Members and the State Education Policy System," *Planning and Changing*, 2 (April 1971), pp. 15-23.

competing values, as some proponents argue. In light of the EGP finding that governor-appointed boards are perceived as having even less contact and influence with the chief executive than elected boards, the typical appointed board structure may well have much the same value emphasis in operation as the elected board structure. Both tend to work more toward the values inherent in separation than toward those advanced by centralization. There are some indications in the data that appointed boards are less responsive to external constituents, less prone to conflictual decision making, and more likely to confront volatile issues. None of these findings, though, is compelling enough to persuade us that appointed boards differ much from elected counterparts in behavior, at least as they are now constituted.

Clearly, the secretary of education model works to strengthen the role of the governor, and those who have access to this office, in state education policy making. And, based on the EGP study of the Tennessee structure in which the governor appoints both the state board and the commissioner, the secretary model probably weakens the influence of state boards and state department administrators in this process. Conversely, the elected state board model enhances the role of agency officials and their educator clients at the expense of the chief executive. But whether, even in a separate agency approach, the state board is an influential policy actor depends on the resources —such things as legal authority, time, staffing, and expertise—available to this body and the board's willingness to utilize these resources to affect policy making. The elected board model described in this chapter deliberately augments the influence resources of the state board. Whether expectations for an active policy role emerge is, of course, another matter.

Again, the governor-appointed board structure seems to be more like the elected board structure in its impact on policy-making influence than it is like the secretary model. Governors in the EGP sample were as little involved with appointed boards as with elected boards; indeed, they were even less so. And neither kind of board had much influence with the chief executive or other political leaders. The option of a governor's advisory council on education, included in the elected board model, is one structural response to this situation.

*   *   *

We hope that a consideration of the models shown above, combined with reference to earlier sections of this book, will provide a place to begin for those who wish to consider the structure for the governance of public education in a particular state. If none of the three models explicated above seems to provide such a beginning, many other combinations of models and options are possible. We are convinced that state-specific conditions must be introduced by people who understand them and will be affected by any changes proposed.

Once again, the models, by their very nature, must deal with structural arrangements. But change in structural arrangements alone may not appreciably alter the process of policy making within a state. In other words, there are limitations in what may be expected from changes in state structure, limitations that seem to derive from a number of conditions. For instance, structure usually pertains to formal arrangements; it seldom deals with informal arrangements such as "kitchen cabinets" and other extralegal devices employed in policy making. Then, too, formal structure may or may not be adequately related to the context in which policy making goes forward, such as the political culture of a state. Perhaps, most important of all, people make a difference. In several of the case studies conducted by EGP, it became entirely clear that a new incumbent, particularly a new CSSO, could, within the same structure, alter both the process and the substantive content of policy making.* In short, in the governance of public education there are many variables, and formal structure is but one.

Despite these limitations, structure does seem to make some difference. For instance, as noted in the study of state boards of education in ten states (see Chapter II), the legal authority of the board to appoint its own CSSO was strongly related to the policy-making influence of the board. This relationship suggests that there is an association between active boards in the sense of policy influence and their power to exercise control over the appointment of their own executive. Also, a board that appoints its own executive officer tends to be more willing to give that executive a free hand in appointing subordinates than a board that has its chief executive

---

*For instance, see JAlan Aufderheide, *State Policy Making for the Public Schools of California* (Columbus: Ohio State University, Educational Governance Project, 1974).

thrust upon it. In the study of CSSO's in twelve states reported in Chapter III, there was a moderate relationship between composite measures of the formal power of the office of the CSSO and the policy-making influence of the CSSO with the governor and the legislature. Formal power of office seemed to contribute to greater policy-making influence in the legislative arena.

In conclusion, we reiterate our two major concerns: (1) *formal structure must be seen as one of many variables in any plan for the reorganization of state governance for education, but undue reliance cannot be placed on structure alone,* and (2) *at the same time there should be a recognition that structure can make some difference.* It is quite clear that how people choose to work within a structure makes a difference. It also seems that formal structure may permit, may actually encourage, certain kinds of behavior on the part of policy makers. Even if changing structure does not guarantee desirable changes in behavior, the fact that it might encourage such changes seems to be sufficient inducement to consider structural arrangements.

APPENDIXES

Appendix A
(for Chapter II)
Constructing the State Board Variables

POLICY-MAKING INFLUENCE

Our index of state board policy-making influence incorporates the general assessments of different groups of actors and supplements their assessments with case study data on specific decision processes. The scoring procedures for these various components, and the weights assigned to them in constructing the final index, are subjective; they represent our judgments as to the importance and validity of each response and each variable.

INFLUENCE IN THE LEGISLATIVE ARENA

The legislative influence index is based on the responses to three interview questions and on EGP findings on the school finance issue in each of the ten states.

Questions and scoring. Legislative leaders (N = 112) were asked, "How would you assess the importance of the State Board in actually formulating and working for education legislation?" Points were given to each respondent as follows:

	Points
Single most important participant	5
One of the most important participants	3
Participant of minor importance	1
Not important at all as a participant	0

Points for legislative leader respondents in each state were then summed and averaged. This gave each state board a raw score on the variable, ranging from 2.2 (Texas) to .33 (Nebraska). The raw scores for each state board, and the score assigned on a 1 to 5-point scale, are shown below:

State board	*Raw score*	*Scale score*
Texas	2.20	5
Georgia	1.92	4
Colorado	1.62	3
New York	1.55	3
Michigan	1.50	3

Tennessee	1.10	2
Massachusetts	1.00	2
Minnesota	.93	2
California	.93	2
Nebraska	.33	1

Educational interest group leaders (N = 36) were asked, "Does the State Board *ever* take the lead in promoting education legislation?" Here we assigned points directly to each state board as follows:

	Points
Three or more respondents said "yes"	5
Two respondents said "yes"	3
One respondent said "yes"	2
If one educational interest group respondent, other than	
main spokesman, said "yes"	1
No respondent said "yes"	0

The scores we assigned on a 1 to 5-point scale for each state board are shown below:

State board	Scale score
New York	5
Texas	3
Minnesota	3
Michigan	3
Colorado	2
Massachusetts	2
Georgia	1
Tennessee	1
California	0
Nebraska	0

Respondents in the governor's office (N = 29) were asked, "Compared to other individuals, how important are board members as a source of ideas and advice for the Governor's Office?" Points were given to each response as follows:

	Points
Single most important source	5
An important source	3
A minor source	1
Not at all important as a source	0

Points for the governor's office respondents in each state were then summed and averaged. This gave each state board a raw score on the variable, ranging from 3.0 (Minnesota) to .50 (New York). The raw score for each state board, and the score then assigned on a 1 to 5-point scale, are shown below:

State board	Raw score	Scale score
Minnesota	3.0	5
Texas	2.3	4
Tennessee	2.3	4
Colorado	2.3	4
Nebraska	1.3	3
Michigan	1.2	2
Massachusetts	1.2	2
California	1.0	2
Georgia	.7	1
New York	.5	1

After examining a school finance issue (1971 to 1973) in each state, we assigned points directly to state boards as follows:

	Points
Visible leadership attempts	5
Took policy position; tried to mobilize support	4
Took policy position on issue; did little else as a board	2
Discussion, no policy position	1
Did not take policy position or discussion	0

The score we assigned on a 1 to 5-point scale for each state board is shown below:

State board	Scale score
Texas	5
New York	4
Michigan	2
Colorado	2
Massachusetts	2
Minnesota	2
Georgia	2
Tennessee	2
California	2
Nebraska	1

Constructing the legislative index. In using the above scale scores to form the index of state board legislative influence, we weighted each variable as follows:

Variable	Weight
Legislative leader assessment	3
School finance findings	2
Educational interest group assessment	1
Governor's office assessment	1

The weighted variables were then combined as shown to create the legislative influence index.

| State board | Score on weighted variables | | | | Final adjusted score (total ÷7) | Ranking |
	Legis- lators	School finance issue	Educa- tional groups	Gover- nor's office		
Texas	15	10	3	4	4.6	1
New York	9	8	5	1	3.3	2
Colorado	9	4	2	4	2.7	3
Michigan	9	4	3	2	2.6	4 (tie)
Minnesota	6	4	3	5	2.6	4 (tie)
Georgia	12	4	1	1	2.6	4 (tie)
Tennessee	6	4	1	4	2.1	7
Massachusetts	6	4	2	2	2.0	8
California	6	4	0	2	1.7	9
Nebraska	3	2	0	3	1.1	10

Influence in the State Education Agency Arena

The state education agency index is based on the responses to two interview questions and on the EGP findings on the desegregation, certification, and educational program improvement issues in each of the ten states.

Questions and scoring. State board members (N = 68) were asked how frequently the CSSO's approach consisted of the following: "Takes ideas or suggestions from board members and develops these into a policy proposal?" Points were given to each response as follows:

	Points
Often	5
Sometimes	3
Rarely	1
Never	0

Points for state board respondents in each state were then summed and averaged. This gave each state board a raw score on the variable, ranging from 4.2 (Nebraska) to 2.0 (California). The raw score for each state board, and the score assigned on a 1 to 5-point scale, are shown below:

State board	*Raw score*	*Scale score*
Nebraska	4.2	5
Minnesota	4.0	4
Michigan	4.0	4
New York	3.9	4
Colorado	3.5	3
Tennessee	3.2	2
Massachusetts	3.2	2
Texas	3.0	2
Georgia	3.0	2
California	2.0	1

Educational interest group leaders (N = 36) were asked, "On matters where it is the final authority, does the State Board give real direction to the State Superintendent or does it just formalize his recommendations?" Here we assigned points directly to each state board as follows:

	Points
Three or more respondents said "real direction"	5
Two respondents said "real direction"	3
One respondent said "real direction"	2
One education interest group respondent, other than main spokesman, said "real direction"	1
No respondent said "real direction"	0

The scores we assigned on a 1 to 5-point scale for each state board are shown below:

State board	Scale score
Texas	5
Minnesota	3
New York	3
Nebraska	3
Colorado	2
Michigan	1
Tennessee	1
California	1
Georgia	0
Massachusetts	0

After examining the desegregation, certification, and educational program issues in each state, we assigned points directly to state boards as follows:

	Points
Much board leadership on one or more issues	5
Some board leadership on one or more issues	4
Some shared leadership with CSSO on one or more issues	3
Some shared leadership with CSSO on one issue	1

The score we assigned on a 1 to 5-point scale for each state board is shown below:

State board	Scale score
Minnesota	5
New York	4
California	4
Massachusetts	4
Nebraska	3
Michigan	3
Texas	3
California	3
Tennessee	3
Georgia	3

Constructing the agency index. In using the above scale scores to form the index of state board policy-making influence in the agency arena, we weighted each variable as follows:

Variable	Weight
Educational issues findings	2
Educational interest group assessment	2
State board member assessment	1

The weighted variables were then combined as shown to create the agency influence index:

State board	Scores on weighted variables			Final adjusted score (total ÷ 5)	Ranking
	Educational issues findings	Educational groups	Board members		
Minnesota	10	6	4	4.0	1
Texas	6	10	2	3.6	2 (tie)
New York	8	6	4	3.6	2 (tie)
Nebraska	6	6	5	3.4	4
Colorado	6	4	3	2.6	5
Michigan	6	2	4	2.4	6
California	8	2	1	2.2	7
Tennessee	6	2	2	2.0	8 (tie)
Massachusetts	8	0	2	2.0	8 (tie)
Georgia	6	0	2	1.8	10

Overall Policy-Making Index

Our composite measure of state board policy-making influence is constructed by combining the legislative index with the agency index as shown:

State board	Influence in the legislative arena (adjusted score)	Influence in the SEA arena (adjusted score)	Overall policy-making influence score
Texas	4.6	3.6	8.2
New York	3.3	3.6	6.9
Minnesota	2.6	4.0	6.6
Colorado	2.7	2.6	5.3
Michigan	2.6	2.4	5.0
Nebraska	1.1	3.4	4.5
Georgia	2.6	1.8	4.4
Tennessee	2.1	2.0	4.1
Massachusetts	2.0	2.0	4.0
California	1.7	2.2	3.9

POLICY-MAKING RESOURCES

Six policy-making resource variables were constructed: (1) legal authority, (2) time devoted, (3) policy emphasis, (4) information utility, (5) cohesion, and (6) prestige.

Legal Authority

The components and scoring procedures used in developing the legal authority index are outlined below:

Authority dimension and its components	Scoring procedure
Legal foundation of SBE	
Constitutional provision	+1.5
Statutory provision	+0.5
SBE—CSSO division of formal authority	
SBE authority over all major responsibilities*	+3.0
SBE authority over all but one major responsibility	+2.5
SBE in authority, but CSSO has some major responsibilities	+1.5
SBE control of the state department of education	
SBE appoints CSSO and all other top-level SDE administrators	+3.0
SBE appoints CSSO and some other top-level SDE administrators	+2.5
SBE does *not* appoint CSSO, but appoints most other top-level SDE administrators	+1.0
SBE does *not* appoint CSSO or most other top-level SDE administrators	+0.5
SBE scope of authority	
SBE is comprehensive board for all education	+3.0
SBE has authority over K-12 and vocational education, but not higher education	+1.5
SBE has authority over K-12, except certification and vocational education, but not higher education	+1.0
SBE has authority over K-12, not vocational or higher education	+1.0

Table A-1 shows the scores that the different state boards received on each authority dimension and on our composite measure.

---

*In the EGP survey these legal responsibilities were (1) determination of policy, (2) administration of K-12 schools, (3) distribution of state funds, (4) determination of courses of study, (5) textbook adoption, (6) teacher certification, (7) school-building plans.

TABLE A-1 Legal Authority of State Boards—Four Selected Dimensions and
           Overall Index

State board	Legal foun- dation	SBE/CSSO division of formal authority	SBE approval of SDE personnel	SBE scope of authority	Overall index of SBE legal authority
Elected by people					
Colorado	1.5	3.0	3.0	1.0	8.5
Michigan	1.5	2.5	3.0	1.5	8.5
Nebraska	1.5	3.0	3.0	1.5	9.0
Texas	1.5	3.0	2.5	1.5	8.5
Appointed by governor					
Massachusetts	.5	3.0	3.0	1.5	8.0
Minnesota	.5	3.0	3.0	1.0	7.5
California	1.5	1.5	1.0	1.0	5.0
Georgia	1.5	3.0	1.0	1.5	7.0
Tennessee	.5	2.5	.5	1.5	5.0
Elected by legislature					
New York	1.5	3.0	2.5	3.0	10.0

Time Devoted

This variable is based on board member responses to the question, "In general, how much time are you able to devote, formally and informally, to the work of being a board member?" Points were given to each response as follows:

	Points
Week or more per month	4
Four to six days per month	3
Two or three days per month	2
Day or so per month	1
Less than day per month	0

Points for board member respondents in each state were then summed and averaged. This gave each state board a score on the variable, ranging from 4.0 (Michigan) to 1.8 (Tennessee). These scores and the rank order on this variable are shown below:

Michigan	4.0
Georgia	3.6
New York	3.6
Colorado	3.5
California	3.4
Texas	3.2
Minnesota	3.0
Massachusetts	2.7
Nebraska	2.6
Tennesee	1.8

Policy Emphasis

This variable is based on board member responses to the question, "What portion of its meeting time does your board devote to what might be called the legal approval of routine items?" Points were given to each response as follows:

	Points
About three-quarters	4
About half	3
About one-quarter	2
Almost none	1

Points for board member respondents in each state were then summed and averaged. This gave each state board a score on the variable, ranging from 2.7 (California) to 1.2 (New York). These scores and the rank order (based on *lowest* scores) on the variable are shown below:

New York	1.2
Texas	2.1
Georgia	2.2
Minnesota	2.3
Michigan	2.3
Massachusetts	2.4
Colorado	2.5
Tennessee	2.5
Nebraska	2.6
California	2.7

Information Utility

This variable is based on board member responses to the question, "In terms of meeting your needs in deciding upon education policies how would you rate the information provided for the board by the state department?" Points were given to each response as follows:

	Points
Almost always meets needs	5
Usually meets needs	3
Sometimes meets needs	1
Almost never meets needs	0

Points for board member respondents in each state were then summed and averaged. This gave each state board a score on the variable, ranging from 4.11 (New York) to 2.20 (Nebraska). These scores and the rank order on the variables are shown below:

New York	4.11
Georgia	3.86
Colorado	3.67
Texas	3.36
Michigan	3.33

Minnesota	3.33
California	3.10
Massachusetts	2.71
Tennessee	2.50
Nebraska	2.20

Cohesion

This variable is based on board member responses to the question, "Which one of these statements comes closest to describing the agreement on your board when it must decide a major policy issue?" Points were given to each response as follows:

	Points
harmonious . . . little disagreement	1
usually in agreement . . . sometimes dissent	2
often divided . . . on the issue	3
rival factions . . . but clear majority	4
rival factions . . . equal strength	5

Points for board member respondents in each state were then summed and averaged. This gave each state board a score on the variable, ranging from 3.6 (Nebraska) to 1.6 (Massachusetts). These scores and the rank order (based on *lowest* score) on the variable are shown below:

Massachusetts	1.60
Minnesota	2.00
Colorado	2.00
Tennessee	2.25
Texas	2.27
Georgia	2.29
New York	2.30
Michigan	2.80
California	3.20
Nebraska	3.60

Prestige

This variable is based on the descriptive language used by different policy actors to characterize the state board in their state. Based on the language (see the text discussion in Chapter II), we ranked the ten state boards as follows:

Very high prestige	New York	1
High prestige	Texas, Georgia, Minnesota, and Massachusetts	2 (tie)
Mixed prestige	Michigan, California, Tennessee, Colorado	6 (tie)
Low prestige	Nebraska	10

POLICY-MAKING EXPECTATIONS

Three variables were constructed pertaining to policy-making expectations: (1) sense of policy-making efficacy, (2) state board self-role expectations, and (3) state board expectations for the CSSO's role.

Sense of Efficacy

The three questionnaire items and the replies indicating a sense of policy-making efficacy are all reported in Table II-8. The average percentage of agreement by board member respondents and the rank order on this variable are shown below.

	Percent
Colorado	92
Michigan	92
Tennessee	91
Minnesota	89
Massachusetts	83
New York	80
Nebraska	78
California	73
Texas	63
Georgia	27

Self-Role Expectations

The five questionnaire items and the replies indicating a board policy role are all reported in Table II-9. The average percentage agreement by board respondents with such a role and the rank order on this variable are shown below:

	Percent
Colorado	95
New York	91
Nebraska	88
Texas	88
California	84
Massachusetts	83
Minnesota	82
Tennessee	80
Michigan	78
Georgia	76

Expectations for the CSSO's Role

The eight questionnaire items and the replies indicating a CSSO policy role are all reported in Table II-10. The average percentage agreement by board respondents with such a role and the rank order on this variable are shown below:

	Percent
Tennessee	91
Michigan	83
Massachusetts	82
Nebraska	80
California	74
Minnesota	73
New York	73
Georgia	66
Colorado	63
Texas	54

CONCLUDING COMMENT

In this appendix we have tried to set forth both the data and the judgmental procedures used in constructing the state board variables and rank-orders. Obviously, other variables and different rank-orders can be derived from our study. And we hope that readers who are dissatisfied with these efforts can find enough data here, in the text, and in the related case studies to develop their own rankings.

Appendix B
(for Chapter II)
Variables and Data Sources

The nature of the variables and their data sources for the socioeconomic and political correlations (with state board policy-making influence) shown in Table II-13 are the following:

Socioeconomic measures

1. Population size, 1970

Data sources

Census data reported in U.S. Bureau of the Census, *Census of Population, 1970 General Social and Economic Characteristics*, Final Report, United States Summary (Washington, D.C.: U.S. Government Printing Office, 1972), p. 468

2. Rate of population growth, 1960-1970

Census data reported in National Education Association, *Rankings of the States, 1972*, Research Report 1972 R-1 (Washington, D.C.: National Education Association, 1972), p. 8

3. Per capita income, 1972

Census data reported in U.S. Bureau of Census, *Census of Population*, p. 541

4. Population has four or more years of high school, 1970

Census data reported, *ibid.*, p. 493

5. Urbanism—People in towns of 2,500 or less, 1970

Census data reported, *ibid.*, p. 420

Political measures

1. Party competition, 1956-1970. Index developed by Austin Ranney. The various Ranney scores (measures of Democratic Party strength) were subtracted from the midpoint (.50) of his scale to generate state scores on an interparty competition variable

Data sources

Austin Ranney, "Parties in State Politics," in Herbert Jacob and Kenneth Vines (eds.), *Politics in the American States* (Boston: Little, Brown, 1971), p. 87

2. Voter turnout, 1970 House elections

U.S. Bureau of Census, *Statistical Abstract of the United States* (Washington, D.C.: U.S. Government Printing Office, 1971), p. 366

3. Political culture, Elazar-Sharkansky Scale, 1969. The scale ranges from 1.0 (most traditionalist culture) to 9.0 (most moralistic); intermediate scores are given to individualist culture and various cultural syntheses

Ira Sharkansky, "The Utility of Elazar's Political Culture: A Research Note," *Polity*, 2 (January 1969)

4. Legislature "Effectiveness," 1971. Composite index developed by the Citizens Conference based on five dimensions: (1) functionality, (2) accountability, (3) informedness, (4) independence, and (5) representativeness

John Burns, *The Sometime Governments* (New York: Bantam, 1971), p. 52

5. Formal powers of the governor, 1970. Composite index developed by Joseph Schlesinger based on four dimensions: (1) tenure, (2) appointment, (3) budget, and (4) veto

Joseph Schlesinger, "The Politics of the Executive," Jacob and Vines, *Politics in the American States*, pp. 222-232

6. Localism, percentage of revenue to K-12 schools from local sources

National Education Association, *Rankings of the States, 1972*, p. 50

Appendix C
(for Chapter IV)
Constructing Gubernatorial Variables

INVOLVEMENT INDEX

The index of gubernatorial involvement in educational policy making was constructed by assigning points for the extent of governors' involvement in each of the four policy-making stages.

Scoring for governors' involvement in support mobilization was based on case study data according to the extent to which governors were involved with the SEA (primarily the CSSO), EIG leaders, and legislative leaders in major fiscal legislation affecting public schools. The scoring procedure was:

	Points
Mobilizing the SEA	1
Not mobilizing the SEA	0
Considerable involvement in mobilizing EIG leaders	2
Some involvement in mobilizing EIG leaders	1
No involvement in mobilizing EIG leaders	0
Great involvement in mobilizing legislative leaders	3
Considerable involvement in mobilizing legislative leaders	2
Some involvement in mobilizing legislative leaders	1

Assigned scores for governors' involvement in support mobilization are shown below:

State	Mobilized SEA	Mobilized EIG leaders	Mobilized legis-lative leaders	Total
California	1	0	3	4
Colorado	1	0	1	2
Florida	1	0	2	3
Georgia	0	0	1	1
Massachusetts	0	1	1	2
Michigan	1	1	2	4
Minnesota	0	1	3	4
Nebraska	0	1	1	2
New York	0	0	3	3
Tennessee	0	0	1	1
Texas	1	2	1	4
Wisconsin	0	2	3	5

Scoring for governors' involvement in issue definition was based on Table IV-2 and case study data. Scoring for governors' involvement in proposal formulation was based on case study data according to the extent of governors' involvement as key initiators of educational policy proposals. Scoring for governors' involvement in decision enactment was based on case study data according to the extent of governors' involvement in the final enactment of the legislative decision affecting school finance and tax reform. Points were assigned as follows:

	Points
Great involvement	5
Considerable involvement	4
Moderate involvement	3
Slight involvement	2
Virtually no involvement	1

ACCESS TO LEGISLATIVE PARTY RESOURCES

Governors' access to legislative party resources, as a resource variable, was based on data in Tables IV-7 and IV-8. Two assumptions were made: 1) that governors had greater access to legislative party resources in the more politically competitive two-party states than in one-party states, and 2) that governors had greater access to legislative party resources where they had political party majorities in legislatures, rather than those having a majority in only one house or minorities in both houses. The scale below indicates that the New York governor was ranked first in having the greatest access to legislative party resources. By using case study data as a tie-breaking mechanism, we derived an eleven-state ranking for governors. Nebraska was excluded because of its nonpartisan elections.

TABLE C-1 Governors' Access to Legislative Party Resources

State	Degree of political party competitiveness	Governors' political party lineup	Ranking
California	Competitive	Split[a]	6
Colorado	Competitive	Majority	2
Florida	Semicompetitive	Majority	8
Georgia	Noncompetitive	Majority	9
Massachusetts	Competitive	Minority	7
Michigan	Competitive	Split[a]	5
Minnesota	Competitive	Majority	3
New York	Competitive	Majority	1
Tennessee	Noncompetitive	Minority	11
Texas	Noncompetitive	Majority	10
Wisconsin	Competitive	Split[a]	4

[a]A split political party lineup is defined as governors having less than majorities in both houses but more than minorities in both houses. Thus, a majority in one house and a minority in one house would be considered as "split." Either a majority or a minority in one house and an evenly divided lineup in the other house would also be considered as "split."

Appendix D
(for Chapter XII)
Validity and Reliability of Survey Questionnaire

To check whether models used in the questionnaire elicited accurate responses, we present the distribution of respondents, by state, who selected Model 4 as approximating the existing structure in their state. Model 4 is characterized by an elected CSSO.

TABLE D-1 Distribution of Choices of Model 4 as Approximating the Existing State Educational Governance Structure by Respondents from States in Which CSSO Is Elected, and by States in Which CSSO Is Appointed[a]

| | Number of respondents choosing | | |
States	Model 4	Other models	TOTAL
Elected CSSO			
Arizona	5	0	5
California	12	2	14
Florida	4	1	5
Georgia	8	1	9
Idaho	6	1	7
Indiana	3	1	4
Kentucky	12	1	13
Louisiana	1	1	2
Mississippi	1	0	1
Montana	1	1	2
North Carolina	5	2	7
North Dakota	6	0	6
Oklahoma	2	0	2
Oregon	6	0	6
South Carolina	2	0	2
South Dakota	5	5	10
Washington	3	3	6
Wisconsin	4	3	7
Wyoming	5	3	8
TOTAL	91	25	116

TABLE D-1 (continued)

	Number of respondents choosing		
States	Model 4	Other models	TOTAL
Appointed CSSO			
Arkansas	1	7	8
Nebraska	1	12	13
New Jersey	1	6	7
Vermont	1	4	5
Other states	0	255	255
TOTAL	4	284	288

[a]Data on states with elected CSSO's obtained from Sam P. Harris, *State Departments of Education, State Boards of Education, and Chief State School Officers,* Department of Health, Education, and Welfare Publication (Office of Education) 73-074000 (Washington, D.C.: U.S. Government Printing Office, 1973), pp. 76-77.

The data in Table D-1 show that, of 116 respondents from states with elected CSSO's, 91, or 79 percent, chose Model 4 as approximating their existing governance structure. Of 288 respondents from states with appointed CSSO's, only 4 chose Model 4. These results demonstrate relatively high validity for the models.

An internal check on the validity of the models is provided by comparing responses to the models with replies to related questions. In all, 229 persons expressed a preference for either Model 3 or Model 5, both characterized by appointed boards, and also responded to Question 1, which asks how state board members should be chosen. Replying to the question, 92 percent of the 229 respondents opted for appointed boards. Conversely, of 94 persons who selected Model 7, with an elected board, as their preferred model, and also replied to Question 1, 93 percent opted for an elected board in their reply.

A check on the reliability of responses to the survey questionnaire is provided by comparing distribution of responses at different points in time. In the summer of 1973 questionnaires were completed by 205 respondents attending annual meetings of the Education Commission of the States, State Directors of School Board Associations, and the National Conference of Professors of Educational Administration. Responses from these groups, whose members represent a cross section of opinion leaders in the field of state governance of education, may be compared with the responses from 219 persons attending regional conferences in fall 1973, organized by the Educational Governance Project staff. These meetings, held in Denver, Chicago, New York, and Atlanta, were attended by invited participants. Invitees were, again, persons actively interested in educational governance at the state level, and included politicians, state board members, education department personnel, and other involved citizens.

As shown in Table D-2, the distribution of preferences among the eight alternative models of the structure of educational governance was quite similar for both groups of respondents, attesting to the reliability of the survey instrument.

TABLE D-2 Distribution of Preferences among Eight Alternative Models by Respondents at National Meetings and at Later Regional Conferences (N = number of respondents)

Models	Respondents attending	
	National meetings[a]	Regional conferences[b]
	(percent)	
1	5.0	4.2
2	8.8	5.2
3	27.6	30.2
4	6.6	3.3
5	24.3	24.1
6	5.5	7.5
7	19.3	20.8
8	2.8	4.2
N	181	212

[a]National meetings, held in summer of 1973, were those of the Education Commission of the States, State Directors of School Board Associations, and National Conference of Professors of Educational Administration.

[b]Regional conferences, organized by the Educational Governance Project, were held in Fall 1973 in Denver, Chicago, New York, and Atlanta.

Appendix E
(for Chapter XII)
Responses to Survey Questionnaire

PART I. ALTERNATIVE COMPONENTS OF THE FORMAL
POLICY-MAKING STRUCTURE OF STATE EDUCATION AGENCIES

1. Members of the state board of education should be: (Check one.)

	Percent of respondents
1. Appointed by the governor	15.9
2. Appointed by the governor, subject to approval by the legislature	30.7
3. Appointed by the governor, but from a short list of names prepared by a blue-ribbon committee	21.4
4. Elected on a nonpartisan ballot	24.0
5. Elected on a partisan ballot	3.5
6. Elected by local school board members	4.6 (number of respondents was 459)

2. Members of the state board of education should serve for a period of: (Check one.)

	Percent of respondents
Two years	2.6
Four years	54.5
Six years	35.8
Eight years	5.0
Ten years	2.2 (number of respondents was 464)

3. Terms of individual state board members should be: (Check one.)

	Percent of respondents
1. Overlapping	96.6
2. Concurrent with that of the governor	3.4 (number of respondents was 464)

4. Size of the membership of state boards should be: (Check one.)

	Percent of respondents
1. Five to seven members	22.6
2. Eight to eleven members	52.6
3. Twelve to fifteen members	20.7
4. Sixteen or more members	4.1 (number of respondents was 464)

5. Compensation for state board members should be: (Check one.)

	Percent of respondents
1. None	2.4
2. Expenses for attendance at board meetings	34.5
3. $25.00 to $50.00 per diem, plus expenses	37.5
4. $50.00 to $100.00 per diem, plus expenses	20.3
5. Regular salary, part or full time	5.4 (number of respondents was 464)

6. Should it be stipulated in law that membership of the state board must include: (Check yes or no for each item.)

	Percent of respondents Yes	No	Number of respondents
1. Local school board members	26.1	73.7	441
2. Students	21.5	78.5	428
3. Teachers	24.0	76.0	434
4. School administrators	23.8	76.2	428
5. Minority group members	29.6	70.4	429
6. Representation of different geographic sections	68.5	31.5	454
7. Representatives of the major political parties	23.2	76.8	426
8. Representatives of nonpublic schools	20.5	79.5	429

7. With regard to its own staff services, should the state board rely upon help from personnel assigned to it by the state department of education, or should the board have its own independent staff, members of which would be exempt from civil service?   (Check one.)

	Percent of respondents
1. Board should rely upon state department personnel	54.8
2. Board should also have its own independent staff	45.2 (number of respondents was 456)

8. In relation to the legislature and the governor, how important should be the state board of education as a source of advice on educational legislation, including school finance? (Circle one number for each item.)

1. As a source of advice to the legislature, state board should be:

	Percent of respondents
1. Not a source	0.4
2. A minor source	6.1
3. A major source	71.8
4. The most important source	21.7 (number of respondents was 461)

2. As a source of advice to the governor, state board should be:

	Percent of respondents
1. Not a source	0.7
2. A minor source	5.0
3. A major source	71.2
4. The most important source	23.1 (number of respondents was 459)

9. With regard to policy-making authority, the chief state school officer should:

	Percent of respondents
1. Be solely an administrative officer	6.9
2. Be an administrative officer and help with the formulation of policy	57.6
3. Share formal policy-making authority with the state board of education	33.1
4. Exercise formal policy-making authority in his own right	2.4 (number of respondents was 462)

10. In relation to the administrative duties of the chief state school officer, how much direction should be given by the state board of education?

	Percent of respondents
1. No direction	6.9
2. Some general direction	50.3
3. Much general direction	38.2
4. Specific and detailed instructions	4.5 (number of respondents was 463)

11. The selection of the chief state school officer should be achieved through: (Check one.)

	Percent of respondents
1. Appointment by the governor	5.2
2. Appointment by the governor, subject to approval by the legislature	11.9
3. Appointment by the state board of education	70.8
4. Nonpartisan election	9.7
5. Partisan election	2.4 (number of respondents was 463)

12. (a) Should there be specific legal requirements for the position of Chief State School Officer?   (Check one.)

	Percent of respondents
Yes	75.8
No	24.2 (number of respondents was 417)

(b) If Yes, legal requirements for the office should include: (Check yes or no for each item.)

	Percent of respondents		Number of respondents
	Yes	No	
1. Legal residence in the state	64.2	35.8	293
2. Professional educator	85.9	14.1	306
3. Experience as a school district superintendent	43.5	56.1	262
4. Other	54.9	42.3	71

13. In relation to the legislature and the governor, how important should the chief state school officer be as a source of advice on educational matters?

1. As a source of advice to the legislature, the chief state school officer should be:

	Percent of respondents
1. Not a source	0.7
2. A minor source	4.8
3. A major source	75.9
4. The most important source	18.6 (number of respondents was 419)

2. As a source of advice to the governor, the chief state school officer should be:

	Percent of respondents
1. Not a source	0.7
2. A minor source	3.9
3. A major source	70.8
4. The most important source	24.6 (number of respondents was 415)

14. In general, how do you feel about the present structure for educational governance in your state?   (Check one.)

	Percent of respondents
1. Very satisfied	5.9
2. Satisfied	51.5
3. Dissatisfied	35.9
4. Very dissatisfied	6.6 (number of respondents was 454)

15. How much policy-making authority at the state level should be given by the legislature to the state education agency (state board, CSSO, and department of education) in relation to each of the following areas?   (Circle one number for each item.)

	Percent of respondents				
	All	Nearly all	Some	None	Number of respondents
1. Curriculum and course of study	31.4	35.7	28.3	4.6	459
2. Professional certification	43.0	38.6	14.6	3.7	458
3. School district organization and reorganization	17.7	42.7	36.3	3.3	452
4. Federal aid and federal assistance programs	26.9	41.9	28.6	2.6	458
5. Buildings and sites	23.0	29.8	37.6	9.6	457
6. School finance, including the state foundation program	11.2	38.5	45.7	4.6	455
7. School desegregation	15.6	38.4	39.5	6.5	448
8. Assessment of pupil performance	34.3	28.4	27.9	9.4	458
9. Planning and research	29.1	47.3	21.9	1.8	457
10. Levying state-wide taxes for public school finances	8.1	15.9	29.7	46.3	454

PART II. ALTERNATIVE MODELS FOR THE FORMAL POLICY-MAKING STRUCTURE OF THE STATE EDUCATION AGENCIES

1. Distribution of responses to questions regarding acceptability of alternative models for the formal policy-making structure of state education agencies (see diagram of Models in Figure XII-1 of main text).

How acceptable would you *personally* find each model for your own state?

	Percent of respondents				
Model number	Very accept- able	Accept- able	Unaccept- able	Very unaccept- able	Number of respondents
1	7.4	20.0	36.3	36.3	430
2	6.1	14.5	44.3	35.1	427
3	29.6	35.3	25.5	9.6	439
4	4.4	17.4	44.2	34.0	432
5	17.6	40.6	32.9	8.9	438
6	5.6	12.9	42.8	38.6	425
7	18.1	33.1	32.6	16.2	426
8	4.7	17.0	45.8	32.5	424

How *politically* acceptable do you think each model would be in your state?

	Percent of respondents				
Model number	Very accept- able	Accept- able	Unaccept- able	Very unaccept- able	Number of respondents
1	4.0	28.5	42.7	24.8	424
2	4.0	24.5	48.9	22.6	421
3	16.6	47.6	27.7	8.2	429
4	8.7	33.3	39.4	18.6	424
5	7.0	43.7	40.4	8.9	428
6	1.4	11.9	45.6	41.1	421
7	11.9	46.3	29.9	11.9	421
8	3.4	26.9	48.6	21.2	416

2. Please consider all eight of the models (see Figure XII-1 in main text) and indicate:
   1. The model which in your view most closely *approximates* the existing structure of educational governance in your state.
   2. Of all eight models, the one which *personally* you would prefer most if educational governance was reorganized in your state.
   3. Of all eight models, the one which you think would be most acceptable *politically* in your state.

	Percent of respondents		
Model number	*Approximates existing state structure*	*Model personally preferred*	*Model most politically acceptable in state*
1	4.8	4.2	4.3
2	9.9	6.3	7.8
3	27.9	28.5	24.9
4	24.8	4.6	18.1
5	7.7	23.8	15.2
6	0.7	6.5	2.4
7	19.0	21.8	20.9
8	5.3	4.2	6.4
NUMBER OF RESPONDENTS	416	432	421

3. In addition to elementary and secondary education, should the state board have responsibility for: (Check yes or no for each item.)

	Percent of respondents		*Number of respondents*
	Yes	*No*	
(a) Two-year community colleges	59.0	41.0	434
(b) Four-year colleges and universities	36.1	63.9	429

If yes to (a) or (b):

If responsibility of the state board included some part of higher education:

1. Which model would you *personally* find most acceptable for your state?
2. Which model do you think would be most acceptable *politically* in your state?

	Percent of respondents	
Model number	*Personally acceptable for your state*	*Politically acceptable in your state*
1	3.6	2.9
2	4.3	10.3
3	26.2	18.7
4	5.0	13.9
5	28.0	20.1
6	7.2	3.3
7	22.2	23.8
8	3.2	7.0
NUMBER OF RESPONDENTS	279	273

PART III. RESPONDENTS' BACKGROUND CHARACTERISTICS

1. Distribution of respondents by occupation (N = number of respondents)
   Politicians (N = 52)

Governor	4
Governor's staff	7
Legislators	41

   Educators (N = 285)

Chief state school officer	9
Chief state school officer's staff	17
Chancellor for higher education	2
Professors of educational administration	29
Teacher (elementary or secondary)	18
College faculty	91
College president or administrator	14
Executive of state-wide educational organization	29
Federal government	2
Executive director, school board association	20
Staff, county office of education	1
School district superintendent	37
Assistant principal	2
U.S. Office of Education	12
Principal	2

   Business executives, professionals (other than educators), and others (N = 97)

Business executive	18
Lawyer	2
Lobbyist	4
Researcher	9
Housewife	13
Miscellaneous	24
Other profession	27
TOTAL RESPONSE	434

2. Distribution of respondents by state

	Number of respondents		*Number of respondents*
Alabama	3	Hawaii	1
Alaska	5	Idaho	7
Arizona	7	Illinois	27
Arkansas	10	Indiana	4
California	14	Iowa	10
Colorado	18	Kansas	10
Connecticut	7	Kentucky	14
Delaware	10	Louisiana	3
Florida	13	Maine	2
Georgia	9	Maryland	31

Massachusetts	9	Pennsylvania	4
Michigan	14	Rhode Island	1
Minnesota	12	South Carolina	3
Mississippi	1	South Dakota	11
Missouri	3	Tennessee	14
Montana	2	Texas	13
Nebraska	13	Utah	8
Nevada	4	Vermont	5
New Hampshire	2	Virginia	15
New Jersey	8	Washington	7
New Mexico	7	West Virginia	5
New York	25	Wisconsin	10
North Carolina	7	Wyoming	8
North Dakota	6	Virgin Islands	1
Ohio	12	Washington, D.C.	1
Oklahoma	3		
Oregon	6	VALID OBSERVATIONS	445

3. Your experience, if any, as a professional educator.   (Check all that apply.)

	Number of respondents
1. No experience as a professional educator	81
2. Taught school at one time	291
3. Presently teaching	82
4. A school principal	147
5. Local district superintendent	128
6. Employed by a state department of education	73
7. Employed by the U.S. Office of Education	31
8. Other professional experience	161

4. Your current position, if any, in state or local government.   (Check one.)

	Respondents	
	Percent	Number
1. Governor's office	4.8	18
2. Legislator	14.9	56
3. Legislative aide	1.9	7
4. Member of state board of education	7.5	28
5. Chief state school officer	2.9	11
6. State department of education	7.5	21
7. Department of administration or finance	1.6	6
8. Local board of education	4.3	16
9. Other	18.7	70
10. None	37.9	142
TOTAL NUMBER		375

5. Your past experience, if any, in state or local government.   (Check all
that apply.)

	Number of respondents
1. Governor's office	13
2. Legislator	38
3. Legislative aide	19
4. Member of state board of education	10
5. Chief state school officer	9
6. State department of education	48
7. Department of administration and/or finance	12
8. Local board of education	55
9. Other	60
10. None	158

6. Education-related organizations in which you currently hold membership.   (Check your primary affiliation.)

	Number of respondents
1. Administrator organization	231
2. Teachers' association	160
3. Teachers' union	8
4. School board association	81
5. Nonpublic school organization	44
6. Other	74
7. None	54

7. Your current position, if any, as an official spokesman for: (Check all
that apply.)

	Number of respondents
1. Administrator organization	44
2. Teachers' association	33
3. Teachers' union	5
4. School board association	50
5. Nonpublic school organization	16
6. Other	48
7. None	181

8. What is the approximate size of the town or city where you permanently reside?   (Check one.)

	Percent of respondents
1. Less than 2,500	6.0
2. 2,501 to 10,000	9.1
3. 10,001 to 50,000	31.9

4. 50,001 to 100,000   14.6
5. 100,001 to 250,000   12.4
6. 250,001 to 500,000   10.4
7. Over 500,000   15.7 (number of respondents
                                         was 452)

9. How would you characterize the area where you reside?   (Check one.)

                                    Percent of
                                    respondents
1. Rural   19.3
2. Suburban   41.0
3. Urban   39.5 (number of respondents
                                         was 451)